BY GUNNAR PEDERSEN

THE HIGHWAY ANGLER

Alaska Viking Press
P.O. Box 11-3231
Anchorage, Alaska 99511

Cover photograph courtesy of Einar Pedersen Illustrations by Patrick Morgan McEwen and Joe Nedland Fish mounts courtesy of Tom Elias of Hunter Fisher Taxidermy and Ken and Carol Guffey of Ken's Taxidermy.

ISBN 0-9621551-1-X

Printed in the USA on acid-free paper.

DEDICATION

In memory of a longtime friend and fishing companion, Miki, who patiently stood by my side with anticipation, awareness, strength, and endurance through twelve challenging and adventuresome years in the wilds of Alaska. May his gentle spirit that touched our hearts always be with us.

SPECIAL THANKS

I would like to extend my deep appreciation to Joe Nedland of Nedland Design & Illustration, Krys Holmes of Winterholm Press, and Mary and Bob Humphrey of Humphrey Computer Graphics for their guidance and hard work in making this book possible; and also to my family and friends for showing continual interest and support. —G.P.

The Highway Angler

TABLE OF CONTENTS:

Introduction

This book comes out of observations and experiences I have had while fishing along the road system in Alaska for more than twelve years. It also includes general information put forth by the Alaska Department of Fish & Game, and from numerous conversations I've had with anglers and sport fishing guides. I have tried also to cover some of the more important points that will help bring about a successful fishing trip. Basic they may be, but I believe they will prove to be of value to anyone who is somewhat unfamiliar with fishing in general, or with fishing along the road in Southcentral or Interior Alaska.

Many roadside waters in Alaska produce catches comparable to the remotest rivers and streams. Even along the busiest highways, you can find excellent action from all five species of salmon, trout, char, grayling, halibut and other sporting species. The major difference between roadside and remote locations is certainly not the lack of scenery, but rather the fact that one must almost always expect to share a stretch of water with other anglers. Remember, the great outdoors is the playground of a great many residents of our state. Also keep in mind that, though large crowds of anglers are often found at the more popular salmon fisheries, there are many lakes and streams that receive relatively little angling pressure. The main point is to treat everyone around you as you would like to be treated yourself.

One way to counter the presence of other anglers is to hike up- or downstream a few hundred yards. Often, just a little distance from the highway makes a big difference in the rewards you will reap — usually less company and more fish.

Alaskan waters, remote or roadside, are not always packed with fish just waiting to assault anglers' lures. As a matter of fact, it is just as easy to get skunked in Alaska as anywhere else in the world. The key is timing. Most species, particularly in flowing water, have very specific periods of the year when they congregate in numbers. Timing is especially crucial in salmon fishing, as just a week or two can mean the difference between a successful fishing trip and a disappointing one. And to complicate matters, various species and watersheds have their own unique timing.

This book focuses heavily on the issue of timing for different species and drainages. The more popular and productive fishing spots along the road are highlighted from the rest by easy-to-read tables showing when the various species are present throughout the year. In addition, quality of fishing to be expected, average and maximum size range, and proven effective lures are given for the more commonly taken species. Less popular waters only have brief descriptions on the most frequent kinds of fish, fishing quality, best time to try, and the average size range.

Many of the lakes along the highways in Alaska offer good fishing but may be somewhat hard to fish due to shallow, weedy shorelines. Such areas are best tackled by canoe or small raft. This is also true of certain sloughs and large rivers.

If you are serious about catching fish, it's a good idea to invest in some hip boots and a pair of Polaroid sunglasses. The boots will allow you to move more freely around the fishing area, through shallow channels or into deeper waters of a lake or river. The glasses are ideal when spot-casting to individual fish that are holding along the bottom in clearwater streams. They also protect your eyes from the intense glare from the sun's rays reflecting off the surface of the water. And they serve as effective shields from flying lures with sharp hooks.

Now for some words about our furry fishing pals, the bears. These large animals may be encountered anywhere in the state, but are especially numerous along shallow and clear salmon spawning streams in late summer and fall. The bears will forage on fish to fatten up for the long, cold winter ahead. Bears are, for the most part, very shy creatures and will avoid confrontation with humans as much as possible. But just because you're not able to spot any bears in the area doesn't mean that none is present. With a very keen sense of smell and hearing, a bear can pick up the scent or sound of a person approaching from a long distance away. At such time, the bears usually leave the stream area and hurry off into thick brush. But don't count on it.

The best precaution to employ when hiking along the trails away from the road is to make a lot of noise. Clap hands, sing, shout, talk loudly, blow a horn, shake a can with rocks, or play music. Also, keep all food away from the tent and sleeping area to prevent a potentially dangerous situation.

Last, please keep Alaska clean and pure. Pack in what you pack out, and practice conservation. Kill and keep only what you need, releasing everything else alive. It makes good sense. But perhaps most of all, wear a big smile and enjoy yourself.

Good luck, and good fishing.

Gunnar Pedersen
Anchorage, Alaska
April 1992

CHAPTER 1

Pacific Salmon

The Southcentral and Interior regions of Alaska enjoy an abundance of five species of Pacific salmon—king, red, pink, chum, and silver salmon. A sixth species, the Cherry or Masu salmon, does not frequent Alaskan waters; they primarily inhabit rivers and streams in the Far East.

Salmon in Alaska are usually anadromous, though some strictly freshwater populations occur here as well. The anadromous, or sea-run, variety are born in fresh water, migrate to salt water to feed for a few years, and eventually return to the river or stream of birth to spawn. The non-anadromous salmon come in two types. Some salmon are restricted to fresh water through natural means. An example is the red salmon, or Kokanee (which is the accepted name). This species may reproduce, given the right conditions. Also, freshwater lakes are often stocked for the purpose of expanding sport fishing opportunities. Here you'll usually find king or silver salmon. Southcentral and Interior Alaska boast both types of land-locked salmon. Usually they are significantly smaller than the sea-run variety.

When the mature salmon leave the Gulf of Alaska in the spring and summer, they begin to congregate in huge masses and move toward the coast in congregations of several hundred million fish. These masses consists of groups of salmon, called runs, which are each bound for specific watersheds. These runs of salmon migrate in great numbers along the coast as they home in on their spawning grounds.

Generally, the mighty king salmon is the first species to enter fresh water. They're closely followed by the red, then the pink and chum. The silver salmon appears last in line. This order of arrival is by no means true for all watersheds, however. In different areas, the species may switch places in the expected order. The roll call seems to be determined by the environment of the home river or stream, where the fish are going to spawn.

Some larger watersheds may include several tributaries, each with its own unique biological characteristics, such as water level and temperature, bottom structure, and food availability. Such watersheds often experience two runs of one species of salmon. Each run is timed to provide the adult salmon the safest passage possible, and to give the eggs the greatest chances of survival.

As the salmon close in on their spawning grounds, they change from the silvery ocean appearance to the typical breeding phase. This process usually takes just a few weeks in coastal areas, but it can take as long as a couple of months if the spawning stream is several hundred miles or more from the sea. It is also common for salmon, especially pink and chum, to change color at sea if their spawning process will take place near salt water.

As the exterior of the fish undergo physical changes during spawn, so does the interior. The flesh of a salmon in spawning condition typically is white and soft in texture, making it less desirable to eat. However, it is not unusual to catch salmon early in the run that is in advanced spawning condition on the outside, yet may still have high quality, orange-red flesh on the inside. At the tail end of a run, the opposite is often the case: the fish may appear bright silvery on the outside and yet have white, soft flesh on the inside.

After the salmon have completed reproduction, they will swim around, spent and exhausted, waiting to die. The fish literally begin to decompose: their skin wrinkles, their fins rot, and yellowish white tumors appear in growing numbers all over the fish. Within a week to ten days — occasionally longer — the fish will die. But the carcass is by no means wasted; it breaks up into tiny particles which will feed various organisms in the water, which eventually will become food for the newly hatched generation of salmon. The life cycle has been completed.

Following are more detailed facts on each species of Pacific salmon found in roadside waters in Alaska, their description and habits, and some basic sport fishing information.

KING SALMON

Scientific Name: *Oncorhynchus tshawytscha*
Other Common Names: Chinook, Spring, Blackmouth, Tyee, Quinnat, and Tule

IDENTIFICATION

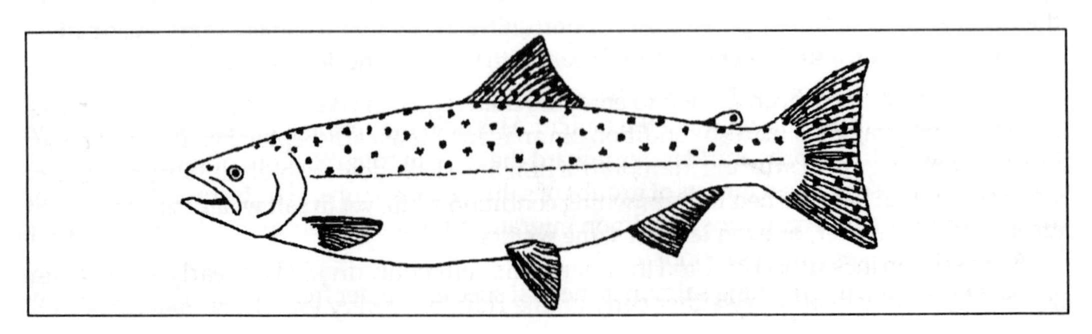

At sea, the king is recognized by the X -shaped black markings on its back and the black gums of the lower jaw. Also, the tail is covered with black spots on both tail lobes. The top of the head and back is greenish to blue-black, fading into silvery to white on the lower sides and belly. The meat is orange-red in color, with the exception of some saltwater populations, which may have a white flesh tone.

Just prior to and during spawning, the king have turned color from the previous silver bright hue to dark red, copper, or even almost black. Males have developed a kype and large teeth protrude from their jaws. The spine takes on a ridgeback form. Females retain their seagoing shape and are generally not quite as colorful as the males. At this point in the life cycle the flesh is white or yellowish and of soft texture.

SIZE

Upon entering coastal waters, mature kings may range anywhere from 10 or 15 inches up to 125 pounds or more. In most watersheds the largest king salmon would be around 45 to 65 pounds, with fish averaging between 20 and 30 pounds. A few rivers and streams, however, consistently produce kings of much greater proportions, but there are also waters where the kings are much smaller than average.

It is quite likely that some day an angler will break the 100-pound mark. Commercial catches of kings weighing more than 90 and 100 pounds are occasionally reported, with extreme weights of 125 and 135 pounds.

The Alaska record sport-caught king salmon was taken from the Kenai River in 1985 and weighed 97 pounds, 4 ounces.

DISTRIBUTION/ABUNDANCE

King salmon occur in the greatest numbers in the tributaries of the Susitna River drainage, the Copper River Valley, and in larger watersheds of the Kenai Peninsula in the Southcentral region. The Interior supports large numbers of fish, particularly in the Tanana River and a few of its tributaries. The Alaska Department of Fish & Game (ADF&G) has stocked many lakes and ponds with kings.

RUN TIMING - SALT WATER

Mature king salmon begin to appear along coastal waters as early as mid- to late April, and may continue arriving through late August. The number of fish peaks sometime during May and June, but as late as July in a few locations. Feeder kings — salmon that are not yet ready to enter fresh water to spawn — can be found in the ocean around southern Kenai Peninsula and Prince William Sound throughout the year.

RUN TIMING - FRESH WATER

A few scouts have been known to enter the tidal region of rivers and streams as early as late April, and stragglers in fresh condition can arrive as late as early September. But in general, the upstream surge peaks during the month of June and slows down rapidly as July progresses. King salmon that have turned into spawning condition while yet in salt water may appear as late as mid-September, or even later in some waters.

King salmon in Southcentral and the Interior are commonly divided into early and late run stocks. Most watersheds have either early or late runs, but a very few rivers may have both types. In Southcentral, most rivers boast early-run stocks that provide the best fishing during May and June. A few populations, however, are of the late run variety and peak during July and August. Stocks in the Interior, for the most part, are considered to be late-run fish appearing in July. These fish don't depart the ocean later than the early-run stocks, it just takes them longer — up to six weeks — to complete their journey from the coast to the spawning beds. These kings are quite dark in color upon arrival.

LIFE CYCLE

As spawning time approaches, the flesh grows paler in color and the fish takes on its traditional spawning hue. It usually takes from about two or three weeks up to three months for kings to completely change from the ocean bright hue to the spawning phase.

King salmon spawn in Southcentral and Interior rivers and streams during July and August in most areas, but a few watersheds may see spawners as early as mid-June or as late as mid-October, depending largely on the run timing of the stock. Spawned-out fish may occasionally survive long after the reproductive process, and some have been observed even in early November in certain drainages.

Each female deposits between 2,000 and 14,000 eggs in several redds, or depressions in the river bottom. Here the eggs lie buried until they hatch sometime in late winter or early spring. Most juvenile kings remain in fresh water until the following spring, feeding mainly on plankton and insects before heading out to sea. Then, having migrated to salt water, the salmon eat a large variety of small fish and other organisms. They grow rapidly and may double in weight during a single summer season. Adult kings feed primarily on fish, especially herring and other forage fish, and also on squid.

The kings begin returning to fresh water in their third, fourth, fifth, or sixth year of life, depending largely on the population. Some fish do return after one year, and some are as old as seven or even eight when they return to spawn. These are likely of trophy size.

SPORTFISHING FOR KING SALMON

King salmon are big, powerful fish that require at least a medium to heavy rod and reel with 20- to 30-pound test line.

Saltwater fishing for kings is best from mid-May to early July along tidal rips and near the mouths of clearwater rivers and streams. The best areas to seek out king salmon in fresh water are the mouths of rivers on an incoming tide, and in deep holes and pools further upstream where migrating fish school up. The confluence of a clearwater stream and a large glacial river is excellent. Best time generally runs from late May to mid-July.

Saltwater Lures: Bait and large, flashy spoons and spinners. Whole and cut herring or a hoochie skirt fished with or without a flasher is very effective, as are HotRod and Krocodile spoons and Vibrax and T-Spoon spinners. Salmon egg clusters or herring fished with a bobber work in some locations.

Freshwater Lures: King salmon have a particular fondness for medium- or large-sized flashy spoons, spinners, plugs, attractors, and bulky flies fished near the bottom. Proven lures include Pixie, Krocodile, and HotRod spoons; Vibrax and Mepps spinners; Flatfish, Hot Shot, Wiggle Wart, and Tadpolly plugs; Okie Drifter, Spin N Glo, and Cherry Drifter attractors; Teeny Nymph, Coho, Fat Freddy, Glo Bug, Hot Shot Pink, Alaska Mary Ann, Polar Shrimp, Two-Egg

Marabou, and Steelie Stopper flies. As for bait, a cluster of salmon eggs fished on or along the bottom is deadly.

KING SALMON HOT SPOTS

The following waters located in the Southcentral and Interior regions are considered to be some of the more productive king salmon fishing spots alongside the road system in Alaska. For more information on any individual hot spot, see the index in the back of this book for page number.

SOUTHCENTRAL

Anchor River
Caswell Creek*<+>
Cook Inlet Marine <+>
Deep Creek
Goose Creek
Gulkana River
Homer Spit Lagoon
Kasilof River
Kenai River <+>
Klutina River <+>
Little Susitna River <+>
Little Willow Creek
Montana Creek <+>
Ninilchik River
Peters Creek
Rabideux Creek*
Seward Harbor
Sheep Creek <+>
Sunshine Creek*
Willow Creek <+>

INTERIOR

Chatanika River
Salcha River

(*): The mouth of these streams only.
<+>: Trophy Water - catches of kings over 50 pounds possible.

Note: Due to the popularity the king salmon has among anglers, only a few selected rivers and streams that can handle large harvests of this species are open to king fishing. Please consult an official copy of the sport fishing rules and regulations, or contact the nearest Alaska Department of Fish & Game office for seasons, open areas, legal gear and methods, and bag limits before trying any of the above waters.

RED SALMON

Scientific Name: *Oncorhynchus nerka*
Other Common Names: Sockeye and Blueback. The land-locked type of this species is often referred to as Kokanee

IDENTIFICATION

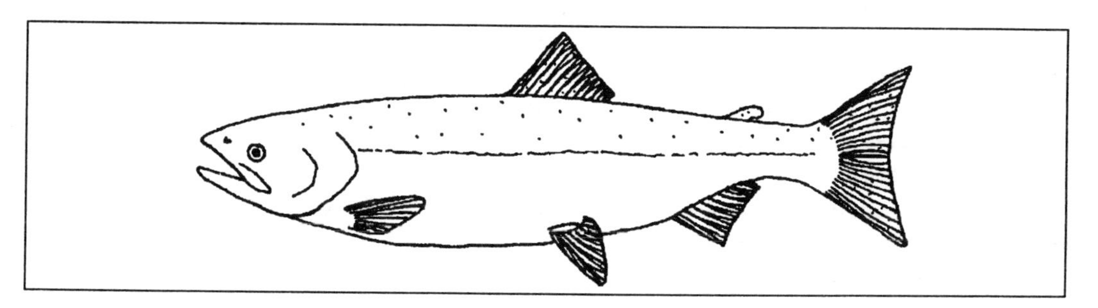

When at sea, the red salmon can be distinguished from other salmon because they lack the highly visible spots found on the majority of salmon species. Rather, they commonly have very minute black freckles, or, in the case of some populations, none at all. The fish are dark steel-blue to greenish blue on top of the head and back. The sides are silvery, fading to silvery white on the belly. Reds have larger scales in proportion to their body size than the other salmon species. The flesh is characteristically ruby red.

At spawning time, the fish turn a brilliant red with a distinctive olive green head and a creamy white jaw. Sometimes the large males will develop dark crimson stripes down their sides. Some individuals may become dirty brown, pale red, or even dark purplish to almost black. Males develop a slight humped back and a tooth-filled kype, while females retain their seagoing shape and are usually not as colorful as the opposite gender.

SIZE

When returning to coastal waters to spawn, reds can range in size from only two or three pounds to as much as 16 pounds or more. The maximum weight for most any watershed is about 10 or 12 pounds, but some drainages consistently produce fish in the 14- and 15-pound category. The average size varies between 4 and 8 pounds.

The land-locked version of red salmon, commonly called Kokanee, are noticeably smaller than the sea-run fish; their average length runs about 12 inches. Maximum weight rarely exceeds 2 pounds in Alaska.

The Alaska record sport-caught red salmon was taken from the Kenai River in 1974, and weighed 16 pounds, 0 ounces.

DISTRIBUTION/ABUNDANCE

Red salmon are most abundant in lake systems throughout the Southcentral region. Major runs occur in drainages on the Kenai Peninsula and Copper River Valley, and some smaller populations also are found in the Matanuska-Susitna Valley. Red salmon do not run into the Interior. Naturally occurring land-locked populations are very scarce, but at least one lake on the Kenai Peninsula has a significant population.

RUN TIMING - SALT WATER

Mature red salmon are present in coastal waters anytime between late April and early October, with most fish appearing during the months of May, June and July in the majority of areas.

RUN TIMING - FRESH WATER

Migration into fresh water usually occurs during June and July, when the runs are at peak strength, but scouts are sometimes seen in early May. Fresh stragglers have been known to enter rivers as late as mid-October, and an occasional bright fish has been caught in late October. However, most runs begin dissipating by August.

As with other salmon species, red salmon can be classified as early or late run fish. Both kinds are considered common in Southcentral, and a few drainages support both stock types. Early runs are found in fresh water during May and June, while late run fish are featured in July and August, and are perhaps slightly more dominant than early stocks.

LIFE CYCLE

After some time spent in fresh water, the previously mint-bright fish enter into the spawning phase, a process which may take anywhere from only two or three weeks to as long as three months.

From late June to early March, reds can be observed spawning in many streams and lakes throughout Southcentral. This reproductive activity generally peaks during July, August, and September, depending on run timing. Spawned-out fish are present for up to several weeks after they have completed the process.

Red salmon prefer watersheds that include one or more lakes, where they can find a variety of inlets, outlets, and streams in which to spawn. Drainages with no lakes have either a very small return of fish or none at all. In such instances, the few reds that are present make use of quiet stretches of water or side channels and sloughs for spawning. Springs or seepages are also frequently used in any population type. However, a few stocks are known to spawn in the main channel of large glacial rivers near the mouth of clearwater streams, none of which have a lakes in their drainages.

After the female has dug several nests along the bottom, she then deposits between 2,500 and 4,300 eggs. The eggs hatch from mid-winter to early spring, and the juvenile salmon remain in the fresh water of a lake or pond at least one year — usually two or three years — before migrating out to sea. While still in fresh water, the fish feed on insect larvae and other small organisms. As summer approaches, the young reds move downstream to salt water where their new diet consists of various zooplanktons. Adult fish feed mainly on crustaceans and small fishes.

The reds spend two to four years at sea before returning to fresh water to spawn. At spawning time, red salmon are four to six years old, though the length of time spent in fresh water and the ocean varies largely between populations.

SPORTFISHING FOR RED SALMON

Reds are superb fighters on light or medium rod and reel with 8- to 15-pound test line.

In fresh water, avoid fishing quiet stretches or still water. Concentrate your efforts on areas with medium to fast current, from the mouth of a river upstream to the headwaters. Remember, the fish usually travel close to shore in moderately shallow water so long casts are not required. The best time for reds is generally from mid-June to mid-August in fresh water. Saltwater angling is considered non-productive except for snagging.

Saltwater Lures: At present, there are no lures available that consistently yield catches of red salmon.

Freshwater Lures: Colorful flies in several variations work the best, but small- or medium-sized spoons and spinners or salmon egg clusters occasionally work, too. The most popular flies include the Coho, Teeny Nymph, Glo Bug, Alaska Mary Ann, Hot Shot Pink, Polar Shrimp, and Two-Egg Marabou.

RED SALMON HOT SPOTS

The following waters located in the Southcentral region are considered to be some of the more productive red salmon fishing spots adjacent to the road system in Alaska. The Interior does not support runs of red salmon. For more information on any individual hot spot, see the index in the back of this book for page number.

SOUTHCENTRAL

Byers Creek
Cottonwood Creek
Gulkana River
Moose River* <+>
Kasilof River <+>
Kenai River <+>
Klutina River
Jim Creek
Ninilchik River*
Russian River <+>

(*): The mouth or lower stretch of these rivers only.
<+>: Trophy Water - catches of reds over 12 pounds possible.

Note: As always, check the official sport fishing rules and regulations or contact the nearest Alaska Department of Fish & Game office for exact information on seasons, open areas, legal gear and methods, and bag limits before trying any of the above watersheds.

PINK SALMON

Scientific Name: *Oncorhynchus gorbuscha*
Other Common Names: Humpy and Humpback

IDENTIFICATION

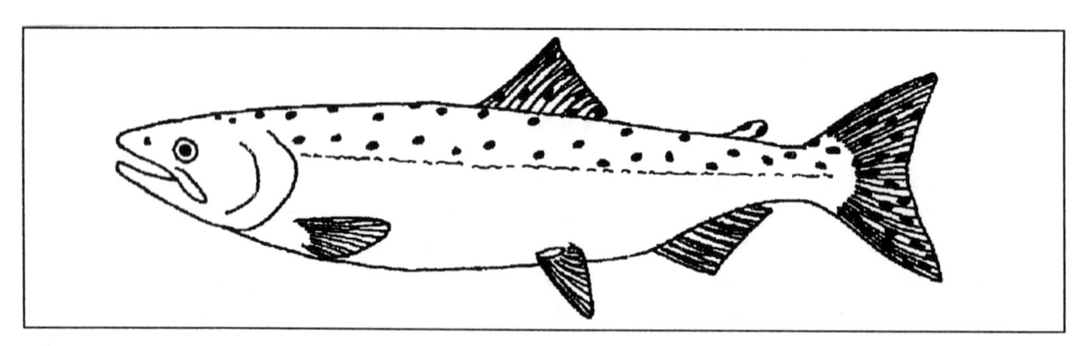

Fresh from the sea, the pink is a sleek and silvery fish with faint oval-shaped black spots on the back and tail. Its back and the top of its head are steel blue to blue green, fading into silver on the sides to white on the belly. The flesh is orange to a mere pink in color.

Just prior to and during spawning, the previously ocean-bright pink has turned dark or dirty brown on top of the head and back, and the sides turn a yellowish green. The belly and lower jaw remain white. Males develop a very distinctive humped back and an elongated, hooked snout, while the females retain their seagoing shape. Large, black oval spots are visible on the back and on both tail lobes. At this time, the flesh is white or yellowish white and of soft texture.

SIZE

The pink salmon is the smallest of the salmon species. In most rivers and streams these fish will average 2 to 4 pounds, and a fish of 6 or 7 pounds or more is considered a very large specimen. A few waters, however, produce pinks that are significantly heavier in both average and maximum weight and here fish of 6 to 8 pounds are not uncommon at all. In some places, exceptional weights of 12 to 14 pounds have been recorded.

The Alaska record sport-caught pink salmon was taken from the Moose River in 1974 and weighed 12 pounds, 9 ounces.

DISTRIBUTION/ABUNDANCE

Pink salmon are cyclic and appear in the heaviest numbers on even years —1992, 1994, 1996, and so on— in various rivers and streams on the Kenai Peninsula and in the Susitna River drainage. Odd years will see smaller returns of this fish. The Interior region does not support any runs of pink salmon.

RUN TIMING - SALT WATER

Pink salmon may begin appearing in coastal waters as soon as late May and continue to be present in some locations until mid-September. Most areas experience the peak numbers of fish sometime during July, with runs declining rapidly after the first of August.

RUN TIMING - FRESH WATER

Freshwater pink runs begin as early as early June and continue into late September, with peak migrations occurring in July in most places, or as late as August in others. Pinks in spawning condition can enter fresh water as late as early October.

As with other salmon species, pink salmon may be classified as early and late-run fish. The vast majority of runs in Southcentral are early and occur during June and July. The late runs appear in August and September.

LIFE CYCLE

Upon approaching the destined spawning grounds, pinks deteriorate very quickly. It is common for this species to change color and appearance even while still at sea, particularly if they are going to spawn close to saltwater. It is very common for pinks to spawn in tidal areas where fresh and salt water mix. This is possible because their eggs can withstand a high degree of salinity. The process of changing from ocean bright to spawning condition can take as little as a week to ten days, but usually two or three weeks is the norm.

Pink salmon spawn anytime between early July and mid-October, depending largely on the timing of the run. In most locations, however, the peak of reproductive activity occurs in August.

The female digs a shallow pit where she will deposit from 800 to 2,000 eggs. Spawning is usually on a one-to-one basis — each male fertilizes the eggs of a single female. The eggs hatch during the winter months and the young salmon will stay hidden in the gravel until spring arrives. As the ice disappears and the water temperature rises, the small fish emerge from the bottom. They almost immediately move downstream towards the sea, unlike other salmon species, which spend at least a few weeks to several years in fresh water first. At sea, it will feed on various zooplankton and eventually on smaller fish as it grows and matures.

Pink salmon usually spend two years at sea before returning to fresh water. Three-year old fish have been reported, though they're very rare. Thus, fish from odd-numbered years do not mix with fish from even-numbered years; they are two totally different stocks of pink salmon. Minor morphological differences may be observed between the stocks.

SPORTFISHING FOR PINK SALMON

Pink salmon, due to their smallish size, require ultra light or light rod and reel with 4- to 8-pound test line for the best sport.

Salt water action is most rewarding in coves and around the mouths of clearwater streams and rivers during July. Fishing for pinks in fresh water is best on incoming and receding tides in lower sections of rivers. In upstream areas, try deeper holes and pools for best success, as well as the confluence of clearwater tributaries and glacial rivers from mid-July to mid-August.

Saltwater Lures: Medium-sized flashy spoons and spinners and even some fly patterns work the best when fished quite close to shore. Pixie, HotRod, and Krocodile spoons and Vibrax and Mepps spinners are proven lures. Cut herring fished with a bobber also do the job.

Freshwater Lures: Small- and medium-sized flashy spoons and spinners and colorful flies are best. As in salt water, Pixie, HotRod, and Krocodile spoons, Vibrax and Mepps spinners, and fly patterns such as Coho, Hot Shot Pink, Alaska Mary Ann, and Polar Shrimp.

PINK SALMON HOT SPOTS

The following waters of the Southcentral region are considered to be some of the more productive pink salmon fishing spots adjacent to the road system. The Interior does not support runs of pink salmon. For more information on any individual hot spot, see the index in the back of this book for page number.

SOUTHCENTRAL

Allison Point
Anchor River
Bird Creek
California Creek
Caswell Creek*
Deep Creek
Fourth of July Creek Marine
Homer Spit
Homer Spit Lagoon
Kenai River <+>
Little Susitna River
Little Willow Creek
Montana Creek
Moose River* <+>
Ninilchik River
Portage Creek**
Resurrection Creek
Seward Harbor
Sheep Creek
Sixmile Creek*
Sunshine Creek*
Valdez Harbor
Willow Creek

(*): The mouth or lower section of these waters only.
(**): The tributaries of this drainage.
<+>: Trophy Water - catches of pinks over 8 pounds possible.

Note: As always, check the official sport fishing rules and regulations or the nearest Alaska Department of Fish & Game office for exact information on seasons, open areas, legal gear and methods, and bag limits before trying any of the above watersheds.

CHUM SALMON

Scientific Name: *Oncorhynchus keta*
Other Common Names: Calico, Dog, and Keta. Occasionally referred to as silver salmon in some locations in the Interior.

IDENTIFICATION

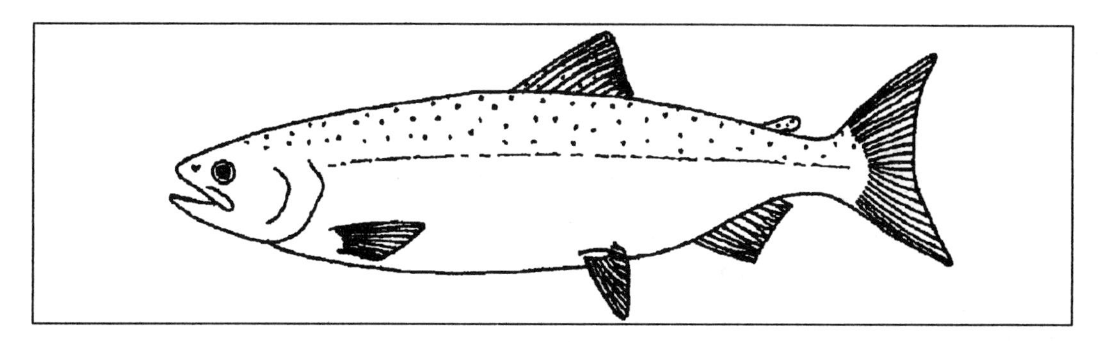

Ocean fresh chums are dark metallic blue on the head and back, silvery on the sides, and silver white on the belly. The iris of the eye is large and the base of the tail thin compared to king and silver salmon of same size. A fine dusting of small specks or spots are at times visible on the back and top of the head. Chums are also distinguishable at times by the very faint greyish vertical markings on the sides, even on sea bright fish. Some of the fins may have distinctive white tips. The flesh is orange to a soft pink.

When closing in on the spawning grounds, the chum salmon turns from bright silvery to a multi-colored spectacle. The sides display crimson markings in bright red, black, and dirty yellow. The belly is black or grey and the back of the fish is olive green to black or brown. The head is the same color, with the addition of yellowish gold on the cheeks. Pectoral, anal, and pelvic fins all have white tips. Males develop a hooked jaw, displaying a series of protruding canine-like teeth (hence the name dog salmon). Female chums often have a dark horizontal band across the sides and are not as brilliantly colored as the opposite gender.

SIZE

The chum salmon is the second largest species of the Pacific salmon family. Extreme weights of up to 40 pounds have been reported, though chums don't often exceed 18 or 20 pounds. Average weight is much more modest —from 6 to 10 pounds — with relatively few fish exceeding 15 pounds. A few locations, however, produce good numbers of chums of 12 pounds or more.

The Alaska record sport-caught chum salmon was taken at Caamano Point in 1985 and weighed 32 pounds, 0 ounces.

DISTRIBUTION/ABUNDANCE

Chum salmon are plentiful in many parts of the Southcentral, but perhaps are especially so in some parts of the Matanuska Valley and in the Susitna River drainage. Chums are scarce or absent from most Kenai Peninsula and Copper River waters. Major runs occur in the Interior region, primarily in tributaries and the main stem of the Tanana River.

RUN TIMING - SALT WATER

A few chums are known to enter coastal waters in late May and are occasionally present as late as late September. In most areas, however, the chums peak in July and runs dissipate quickly during the course of August.

RUN TIMING - FRESH WATER

Scouts might migrate into fresh water as soon as early June and fresh stragglers occasionally enter as late as early October. Peak months of abundance of bright fish is generally during July and August.

As with all other salmon species, the chum salmon often are categorized into early and late runs. In Southcentral, early-run chums are most numerous during June and July, and late-run fish during August and September. Although both types are quite common, more Southcentral watersheds probably have early-run fish.

The Interior, on the other hand, have a slightly different run timing. Early runs are present in July and August, while late runs peak during September, October, and November. Chums of the Interior, due to the distance travelled and the time it takes them from the coast to the Interior (about six weeks), are often dark and ready to spawn upon arrival at their spawning streams, especially with summer chums. However, fall fish are sometimes dime-bright even after the extensive journey. Both types of runs are equally common.

LIFE CYCLE

Like the pink salmon, chums deteriorate very quickly as they home in on the spawning grounds. It is common for these fish to change color and appearance while still in salt water.

From early July to early February chum salmon may be observed spawning in many rivers and streams in Southcentral and the Interior, from tidal regions to mountain springs. This spawning activity peaks in August and September in most areas, but not until November in others. Chum salmon prefer clearwater rivers, creeks, sloughs, and springs for spawning, but glacial waters are sometimes also home to a chum spawn.

Up to 2,700 eggs may be produced by some female chums in several redds, and the reproduction act is usually on a one-to-one basis. The eggs hatch in late winter or spring, and soon thereafter the small juvenile chums begin moving around feeding on insects and other small organisms. Chums do not migrate to the ocean as soon as the pink salmon fry, but tend to linger around the mouth of the river a few weeks. By the first summer after hatching, the fish have formed large schools and now venture out into the ocean where they feed on zooplankton. After their first year at sea, their diet expands to include small fishes and crustaceans.

After spending one to five years in salt water before reaching full maturity, the fish begin their journey back to the stream or river where they were born. At this point the fish are generally four or five years of age.

SPORTFISHING FOR CHUM SALMON

Fresh chum salmon are a stubborn species requiring light or medium rod and reel with 8- to 15-pound test line.

In salt water, look for chums around mouths of clearwater rivers and streams during the month of July. In fresh water, try deeper holes and pools with a slow or medium current from mid-July to mid-August. Fishing incoming and receding tides can also be very rewarding, as is the action at the confluences of clearwater streams and glacial rivers.

Saltwater Lures: Medium- and large-sized flashy spoons and spinners and certain patterns of flies. Pixie, HotRod, Krocodile, and Daredevle spoons, and Vibrax and Mepps spinners are all good. Plug cut herring sometimes work.

Freshwater Lures: Medium-sized spoons and spinners and colorful flies are effective, but certain types of plugs and attractor lures may work, too. Pixie, HotRod, Krocodile, and Daredevle spoons, Vibrax and Mepps spinners, and fly patterns such as Coho, Hot Shot Pink, Alaska Mary Ann, and Polar Shrimp. Occasionally, drifting salmon egg clusters take fish.

CHUM SALMON HOT SPOTS

The following waters of the Southcentral and Interior regions are considered to be some of the more productive chum salmon fishing spots available to the road system in Alaska. For more information on each individual hot spot, see the index in the back of this book for page number.

SOUTHCENTRAL

Allison Point	Jim Creek	Sheep Creek <+>
Bird Creek <+>	Jim Creek Flats	Sixmile Creek*
Caswell Creek*	Little Susitna River <+>	Sunshine Creek*
Eklutna Tailrace	Little Willow Creek	Willow Creek <+>
Fourth of July Creek Marine<+>	Montana Creek <+>	

INTERIOR

Chatanika River	Salcha River	Tanana River
Delta Clearwater River*		

(*): The mouth or lower section of these waters only.
<+>: Trophy Water - catches of chums over 15 pounds possible.

Note:.As always, check the official sport fishing rules and regulations or the nearest Alaska Department of Fish & Game office for exact information on seasons, open areas, legal gear and methods, and bag limits before trying any of the above watersheds.

SILVER SALMON

Scientific Name: *Oncorhynchus kisutch*
Other Common Names: Coho, Silverside, and Blueback

IDENTIFICATION

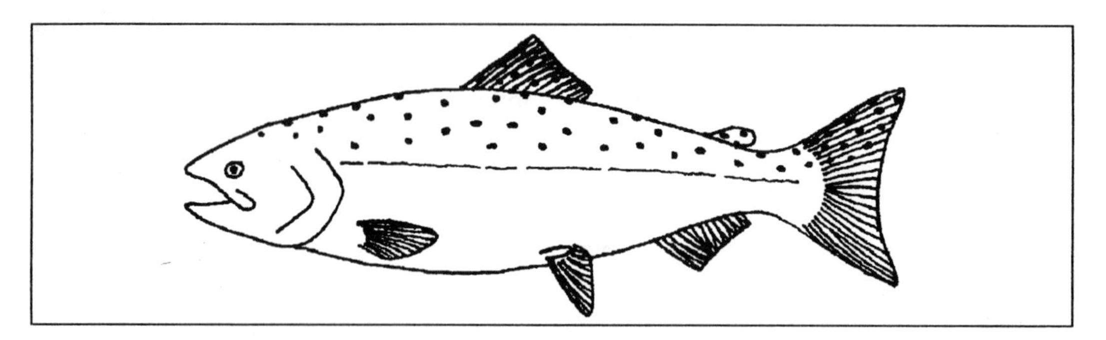

Silvers fresh from the sea are greenish to metallic blue on the back and top of the head, silvery on the sides, and white on the belly. The gumline is white, compared to kings, which have a black gumline. Moderately small black spots are seen covering the neck and back, sparingly on the dorsal fin, and across the upper tail lobe. The flesh is orange red in color.

Just prior to and during spawning, the silver salmon changes appearance from dime-bright to brilliant red on the head, sides and belly. Some populations have a darker skin tone, especially the females, and may appear bronze, greenish brown, or even almost black. The top of the head and back are dark olive green to a faded red or copper. The lower jaw and belly often are black. The males develop a very distinctive hooked snout, prolonged teeth, and a slightly humped back, while females retain their seagoing shape and are generally not as colorful as the opposite gender.

SIZE

Silver salmon average between 5 and 10 pounds, seldom weighing much more than 15 pounds in most drainages. Some rivers, however, consistently produce larger than average specimens of 12 to 18 pounds, and a few fish have reached to 22 pounds or more. The absolute maximum recorded size for a silver is 33 pounds, but fish of such dimensions are extremely rare.

Land-locked members of the silver salmon family also exist in many lakes and ponds around the state as a result of fish stocking programs conducted by the ADF&G. These fish are generally quite small, measuring between 7 and 16 inches long. Extreme weights of up to 10 pounds have been reported.

The Alaska record sport-caught silver salmon was taken in Icy Strait in 1976 and weighed 26 pounds, 0 ounces.

DISTRIBUTION/ABUNDANCE

Silver salmon are abundant in most areas of Southcentral, and thriving populations may be found in many waters of the Kenai Peninsula and Matanuska and Susitna Valleys. Smaller stocks of fish can be located in the Copper River drainage. In the Interior, silvers are rather scarce but a few tributaries of the Tanana River see quite significant returns. Land-locked silver salmon are common in both regions as a result of stocking programs by the ADF&G.

RUN TIMING - SALT WATER

Normally, silver salmon peak in coastal waters during July and August, or even in September in some areas, but have been known to show up as early as early June or as late as late December. In most locations, however, the number of fish present declines rapidly during September.

RUN TIMING - FRESH WATER

A few scouts may enter fresh water in mid-June, and fresh stragglers occasionally come in from the ocean as late as early January in certain drainages. Bright silvers have been reported in late February in at least one watershed. In general, runs peak during August and September, waning sharply during October.

Silver salmon display both early- and late-run characteristics, as do other salmon species. Early runs are common in Southcentral and occur during July and August in many drainages, while late runs peak in September and October. Late runs are not unusual in Southcentral, and seem to be the only run in the Interior. The Interior fish began their voyages at the same time as early-run fish but, due to the distance they've travelled, they arrive as late-run, spawn-condition fish six weeks later. A few rivers even have runs going strong in November.

LIFE CYCLE

Silver salmon, upon nearing their destined spawning grounds, change color quite slowly compared to pink and chum salmon. They are therefore often in good shape far up some inland rivers. However, the fish whose spawning beds are near saltwater may alter into the spawning phase while still at sea. The complete maturing process can take as little as two weeks or as long as three months.

The spawning time for silvers can vary greatly, depending on run timing, and may begin as early as early August or as late as mid-April. Spawned-out fish are occasionally observed in early May. Peak spawning activity in most locations tends to occur during September, October, or November, and reproduction generally is finished by December.

The female deposits her eggs in a shallow gravel pit and the mating is usually on a one-to-one basis. From about 1,400 to 5,700 eggs are laid in the redd. The young hatch in winter and spring and soon begin to feed on small insects and other tiny organisms. Most of the small fish stay in fresh water for one year, but a few may even hold out for two or three, and occasionally even four, years before finally deciding to migrate to sea. While there, silvers feed on zooplankton and eventually small fishes and crustaceans.

Silver salmon spend one to three years in the ocean before heading back to fresh water, generally at the age of two to five.

SPORTFISHING FOR SILVER SALMON

The gear most often used for silvers is a light or medium rod and reel with 8- to 15-pound test line.

Saltwater fishing is most productive along tidal rips and near the mouths of clearwater rivers and streams, primarily from early August to mid-September. In fresh water, concentrate efforts in deep holes and pools with slow or moderate flowing current, and at the confluence of clearwater streams and glacial rivers. The best time to fish silvers is from early August to early October.

Saltwater Lures: Bait and flashy spoons and spinners do the best. Plug cut or whole herring trolled with a flasher or fished with a bobber is exceptional. Pixie, HotRod, and Krocodile spoons, and Vibrax, T-Spoon, and Mepps spinners are proven lures. Salmon egg clusters do also take some fish.

Freshwater Lures: Bait, attractors, and flashy spoons and spinners. Salmon egg clusters fished on or along the bottom are deadly, as are Pixie, HotRod, and Krocodile spoons, and Vibrax and Mepps spinners. Okie Drifter and Spin-N-Glo attractors fished alone or with eggs are unbeatable in some waters. Fly patterns such as Coho, Hot Shot Pink, Fat Freddy, Glo-Bug, Alaska Mary Ann, and Polar Shrimp are all good.

SILVER SALMON HOT SPOTS

The following waters of the Southcentral and Interior regions are considered to be some of the more productive silver salmon fishing spots adjacent to the road system in Alaska. For more information on each individual hot spot, see the index in the back of this book for page number.

SOUTHCENTRAL

Allison Point
Anchor River
Bird Creek
Caswell Creek*
Cook Inlet Marine <+>
Cottonwood Creek*
Crooked Creek
Deep Creek
Eklutna Tailrace
Fish Creek
Homer Spit Lagoon
Jim Creek
Kasilof River
Kenai River <+>
Little Susitna River
Little Tonsina River
Little Willow Creek
Montana Creek
Ninilchik River
Placer River**
Portage Creek**
Rabideux Creek
Russian River
Seward Harbor
Sheep Creek
Sunshine Creek*
Swanson River
Valdez Harbor
Wasilla Creek
Willow Creek

INTERIOR

Clear Creek
Delta Clearwater River

(*): The mouth or lower section of these waters only.
(**): The tributaries of these drainages only.
<+>: Trophy Water - catches of silvers over 20 pounds possible.

Note: As always, check the official sport fishing rules and regulations or the nearest Alaska Department of Fish & Game office for exact information on seasons, open areas, legal gear and methods, and bag limits before trying any of the above watersheds.

King (Chinook) Salmon in spawning colors

Red (Sockeye) Salmon in spawning colors

Pink (Humpy) Salmon in spawning colors

Chum (Dog) Salmon in spawning colors

Silver (Coho) Salmon in spawning colors

Rainbow Trout

Dolly Varden Char

Lake Trout (Char)

CHAPTER 2

Trout and Char

This chapter covers two families of fishes that are closely related. The trouts and chars are widespread in the Southcentral and Interior regions of Alaska. They thrive well in both saltwater and freshwater environments, and occupy a variety of waters from the tidal areas of large glacial rivers to mere trickles of creeks in the high mountains.

The trout family are represented in Alaska by the rainbow and the cutthroat. The latter species is not found along the road system in Southcentral or Interior Alaska and therefore is excluded from this book. The rainbow trout, on the other hand, is a very common species that is present in two distinct varieties. One is the strictly freshwater form, and the other is the sea-run species of rainbow trout, popularly called the steelhead.

The char family is made up of two major species, the Arctic char / Dolly Varden and the lake trout. Arctic char and Dolly Varden are considered to be two slightly different variations of one species and both exhibit sea-run and land-locked tendencies. The two are grouped as one species because there are only a few very minor differences between them, none of which are really apparent to the untrained eye. Another char species, labeled erroneously as a trout, is the lake trout. This species is very common in certain areas of Southcentral, but do not appear in the numbers of the other char species, nor do they thrive in the same wide range of environments.

CHAPTER 2

Trout and Char

Following are more detailed facts on the char species found in roadside waters in Alaska, along with their description and habits in addition to basic sport fishing information.

STEELHEAD TROUT

Scientific Name: *Oncorhynchus mykiss*
Other Common Names: Steelie, Metalhead, Kelt, and Rainbow

IDENTIFICATION

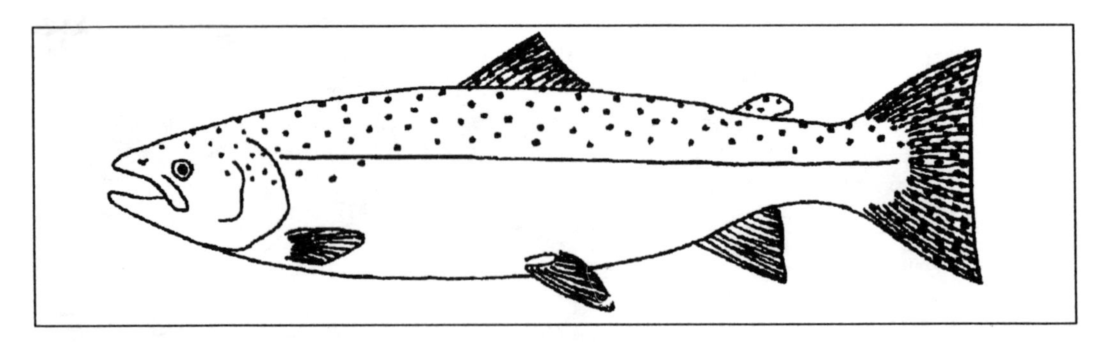

The steelhead in the ocean is a sleek, bright fish, resembling a salmon more than the rainbow trout it truly is. Its sides are silvery and light grey, with the back and the top of the head being almost black. Small black spots may be present but are usually only faintly visible on the head, sides, and tail fin. The belly is white. Flesh color is orange or orange red.

Once the fish have entered fresh water, or are in the vicinity of the stream mouth, they gradually lose their bright silvery shine. A pinkish red band soon appears on the trout's sides and cheeks, and numerous black spots become clearly visible covering the same areas, including the back and both tail lobes. It now begins to take on the appearance of a genuine rainbow trout.

During spawning activity, the steelhead may again resemble a salmon in its reddish color. Its sides and cheeks are dirty red, the back greenish yellow or grey, while the lower jaw and belly is grey. Sometimes, the previously small black spots may grow in size and become more pronounced, or they may almost disappear in the brilliant reddish hue.

SIZE

Although steelhead weighing as much as 45 pounds have been recorded, these sea-run rainbows only occasionally exceed 20 pounds. Specimens of 25 to 30 pounds are very rare. The average trout averages between 6 and 10 pounds, with fish up to 12 and 15 pounds being quite common.

The Alaska state record sport-caught steelhead trout was taken at Bell Island in 1970 and weighed 42 pounds, 3 ounces.

DISTRIBUTION/ABUNDANCE

Steelhead trout are found scattered sparingly in Southcentral Alaska, and are not found at all in the drainages of the Interior. Smaller populations of these fish are located in certain rivers and streams on the lower Kenai Peninsula and in the Copper River drainage; harvests of these fish are closely regulated. Stocking projects to introduce this species into new waters apparently have failed.

RUN TIMING - SALT WATER

The first few steelhead trout bound for their spawning streams begin to appear in coastal areas in late July. The runs build to a peak in September, and slow down after the first of October. A few fish will still be present in saltwater by November or December; these fish are fall-run trout and will spend the winter in fresh water. They return to the sea, spawned out, from mid-April through early August. The peak out-migration of post-spawn steelhead occurs during the month of June.

RUN TIMING - FRESH WATER

A few steelhead scouts occasionally show up as early as early August, but the bulk of the run generally migrates into fresh water in September. The number of fresh ocean fish decreases rapidly in October and very few will arrive in November and December. However, stragglers can show up as late as early January or even later in some waters.

Southcentral steelhead are generally considered to be fall-run fish, but there are indications that at least a few trout may occasionally enter fresh water between mid-April and mid-June. These spring arrivers may have spent the winter in salt water around the mouth of spawning streams, waiting for the ice to disappear and the spring floods to begin, or they may just be a very small, distinct run.

It is common for the steelhead trout to overwinter in deep holes and pools in the lower part of a river. After breakup, they move upstream to the spawning grounds in shallow areas of the river or in tributary creeks that run high with spring meltwater.

LIFE CYCLE

Soon after entering fresh water, and sometimes even before, the steelhead trout changes color from ocean bright to its dark spawning hue. This process usually takes about six months for fall-run fish, but may happen faster if the fish arrives late.

Spawning commences in the spring as water temperatures warm up to desired levels. Although a few fish may start the reproductive process in mid-March, most spawning occurs in May, and some individuals don't spawn until early July.

Steelhead prefer clear or semi-clear waters for spawning purposes with a course sand or gravel bottom structure. Glacial rivers and streams, though they're perhaps used for migration and over-wintering, are not used for spawning.

Most steelhead trout, depending on their age, will die after spawning, but some will survive to come back to spawn one more time or occasionally even two or three times. The fish that do survive drift downstream with the current into salt water where the fish will slowly begin to nourish itself to regain strength. At this time the fish, called kelts, are very thin and weak and the color has changed from the dark spawning hue to an almost silver bright appearance. This out-migration peaks in June.

Females deposit as few as 100 eggs or as many as 12,000 or more in several nests. Spawning can take place with one or more males. The eggs hatch in summer or early fall and the young remain in their natal stream for usually one or two years before heading out to the sea. A few are known to linger up to three or four years in fresh water, feeding on insects and other small organisms.

After entering salt water, steelhead will first feed on plankton and later on a variety of small fishes. Adult fish sustain themselves primarily on fishes and shrimp for two or three years before feeling the urge to return to fresh water to spawn. Some fish may only spend a few months or one year at sea, while other specimens stay up to four years.

SPORTFISHING FOR STEELHEAD TROUT

Steelhead are finicky, hard-fighting fish best tackled on light or medium road and reel with 8- to 15-pound test line.

Although sport fishing for steelhead in salt water is practically unexplored, a few fish are sometimes taken by anglers fishing for salmon. In fresh water, this species can be found in deeper holes and pools of rivers and streams from the tidal zone upstream to the headwaters. Incoming tides are usually a good bet; so is the confluence of a clearwater stream and a large glacial river. Best times are in May and early June, and in mid-September to mid-November.

Saltwater Lures: There are no lures with the distinction of catching steelhead trout in salt water on a regular basis.

Freshwater Lures: Steelhead have an undisputable reputation for liking various fly patterns and smaller attractor lures. Salmon egg clusters, fished on or along the bottom, are equally deadly, if not more so. Spoons and spinners are usually not well received. Flies such as the Egg Sucking Leech, Glo Bug, Alaska Mary Ann, Hot Shot Pink, Fenton Fly, and Polar Shrimp are proven effective, and corkies in sharp colors are good bets.

STEELHEAD TROUT HOT SPOTS

The following waters located in the Southcentral region are considered to be some of the more productive steelhead trout fishing spots along the road system in Southcentral Alaska. The Interior does not support populations of steelhead. For more information on each individual hot spot, see the index in the back of this book for the page number.

SOUTHCENTRAL

Anchor River <+>
Crooked Creek
Deep Creek
Kasilof River <+>
Ninilchik River

<+>: Trophy Water - catches of steelhead over 15 pounds possible.

Note: As always, check the official sport fishing rules and regulations or the nearest Alaska Department of Fish & Game office for exact information on seasons, open areas, legal gear and methods, and bag limits before trying in any of the above waters.

RAINBOW TROUT

Scientific Name: *Oncorhynchus mykiss*
Other Common Names: nickname "bow"

IDENTIFICATION

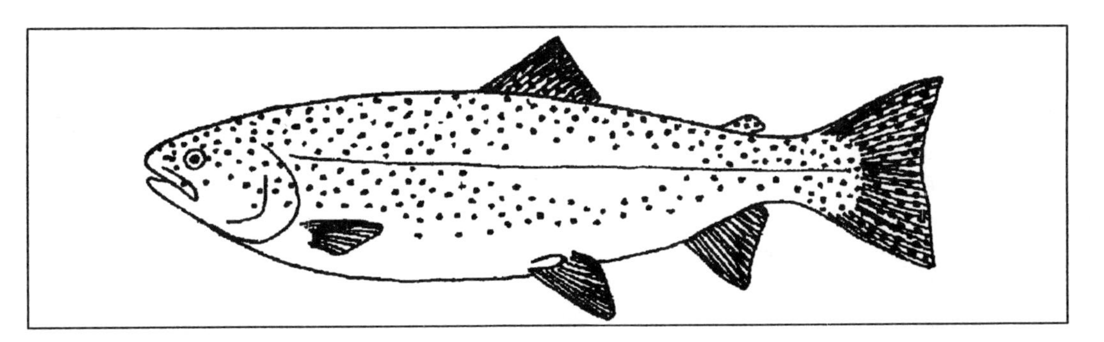

This species received the proper name from the horizontal pink or red band on the sides. The coloration of rainbow trout may vary greatly from stream to stream, or lake to lake. Some populations have a general dark appearance, as is common with small marshland lakes, ponds, and streams; fish of large lakes and rivers are often more silvery in appearance.

Rainbows boast numerous black spots the back and sides, top and sides of the head, and on the dorsal and tail fins. Older and larger fish have spots all around the head, including the jaw. The sides are silvery to copper, light brown or olive, depending on the stock, and have a light red stripe of varying width and pronunciation. The stomach is white or tan, and the back usually black or dark green.

Rainbow trout just prior to and during spawn are beautiful creatures in a wide range of color displays. How strong this coloration is depends on the age of the fish, and on the location of the stream or lake population. Mature trout are reddish pink on the sides as well as on the cheeks. The stomach is greyish or brown, and the back and top of head is black or dirty dark green. It is also common for some populations to have a copper or dirty yellowish color to its sides and head, or at times even to appear mostly black. The black spots on the fish may become enlarged and more pronounced during spawning phase.

SIZE

The typical size range for rainbows found in smaller lakes and streams is in the 8- to 15-inch category, with any fish approaching 4 or 5 pounds considered to be quite exceptional. However, many large rivers and lakes with an abundant supply of food commonly produce trout between 2 and 6 pounds, and sometimes up to 12 pounds. A few watersheds have produced rainbow trout weighing more than 20 pounds, which is thought to be the maximum size. Ocean trout, commonly referred to as steelhead trout, are generally larger than the strictly freshwater variety and may weigh, on average, twice as much.

The Alaska state record sport-caught rainbow trout, a sea-run fish (steelhead), was taken at Bell Island in 1970 and weighed 42 pounds, 3 ounces.

CHAPTER 2

Trout and Char

DISTRIBUTION/ABUNDANCE

Rainbow trout are quite abundant wherever they are found. Thriving populations are found in the Susitna River drainage, the major river systems on the Kenai Peninsula, and in lakes and ponds throughout the Southcentral region and the Interior. The Interior does not have naturally occurring populations of rainbows; the fish there have been stocked. This species has long been the subject of an intense stocking program by the ADF&G.

LIFE CYCLE

There is a similarity between rainbow and steelhead spawning migrations. The steelhead grows up in the sea and runs up into fresh water to spawn, while the rainbow trout typically over-winters in lakes and large rivers. When spring comes, they move into smaller tributaries to reproduce and feed for the summer and fall. When the temperature drops in the water just before freezeup, they move downstream to the traditional over-wintering areas.

But this is by no means the case in all populations. Some rainbows may just spawn and move out of the stream to feed in a lake or larger river during the rest of the year. Others, however, may choose to spend the winter suspended in deep holes or sloughs in the tributaries, or never leave its lake or river at all, but grow and spawn right there.

Rainbow trout begin their annual spawning migration or process anytime from March on into June, though most fish venture out in April and May. During the migration, the fish gradually turn darker and more mature as they prepare to spawn. The flesh grows paler in color from orange to a yellowish white. The female digs a redd and then, being joined by the dominant male, she drops somewhere of 200 up to 12,700 eggs in the pit or pits. Usually the larger and older the fish is, the more eggs it will produce.

Most of reproductive process occurs between May and early June, and is done by the end of June. After spawning, the spent fish may linger around the area for the summer and fall, or may begin a rapid migration to a feeding ground in another body of water.

The eggs hatch and the young emerge from the redds in late spring and summer. After the juvenile trout achieve a certain age and size, they start feeding on small insects and other organisms found in or on top of the water. The fish grow rapidly, and soon other small fishes and salmon eggs are also added to the diet.

Adult rainbows are aggressive fish. Some of the larger trout follow salmon up the rivers or into lakes to feed on spawn and even bits of decomposing salmon carcasses. Insects, other fishes, and even shrews and frogs are some of the more important food sources among large rainbows. The maximum age for rainbow trout is about nine years.

SPORTFISHING FOR RAINBOW TROUT

These acrobatic battlers are at their best on ultra light or light rod and reel with 4- to 12-pound test line.

Deep holes and pools or just behind spawning salmon are great places to find rainbow trout, as are the confluences of clearwater streams and large glacial rivers. Most rivers and lakes usually experience the best rainbow trout action from mid-May to mid-June and again from late August to early November.

Lures: Bait, colorful flies, and small flashy spoons and spinners are tops. Try colors in red, orange, and blue. Fjord and Krocodile spoons and Vibrax, Mepps, and Panther Martin spinners work well, as do fly patterns such as Glo Bug, Alaska Mary Ann, Hot Shot Pink, Polar Shrimp, Two-Egg Marabou, Boss, Comet, Wolly Worm, Egg-Sucking Leech, Thor, and Sculpin. Single salmon eggs or salmon egg clusters are unbeatable at times, and corn and shrimp secure catches, too. Attractor lures like Spin-N-Glo, Okie Drifter, and corkies are very effective in some waters.

RAINBOW TROUT HOT SPOTS

The following waters located in the Southcentral and Interior regions are considered to be some of the more productive rainbow trout fishing spots accessed by the road system in Alaska. For more information on each individual hot spot, see the index in the back of this book for the page number.

SOUTHCENTRAL

Breeze Lake
Canoe Lake
Cecille Lake
Crater Lake
Crystal Lake
Florence Lake
Forest Lake
Gulkana River
Honeybee Lake
Irene Lake
Jean Lake
Johnson Lake
Kalmbach Lake
Kenai River <+>
Kepler/Bradley Lakes
Knik Lake
Little Willow Creek
Longmere Lake
Lynne Lake
Matanuska Lake
Memory Lake
Montana Creek
Paddle Lake
Rainbow Lake
Reed Lake
Seymour Lake
Sheep Creek
Tex Smith Lake
Tolsona Lake
Vagt Lake
Watson Lake
Wik Lake
Willow Creek
Worthington Lake

INTERIOR

Birch Lake
Craig Lake
Jan Lake
Lisa Lake
Quartz Lake

<+>: Trophy Water - catches of rainbows over 15 pounds possible.

Note: As always, check the current sport fishing rules and regulations or the nearest Alaska Department of Fish & Game office for exact information on seasons, open areas, legal gear and methods, and bag limits before trying any of the above waters.

DOLLY VARDEN

Scientific Name: *Salvelinus malma*
Other Common Names: Dolly, Goldenfin, Golden Trout, and Char

IDENTIFICATION

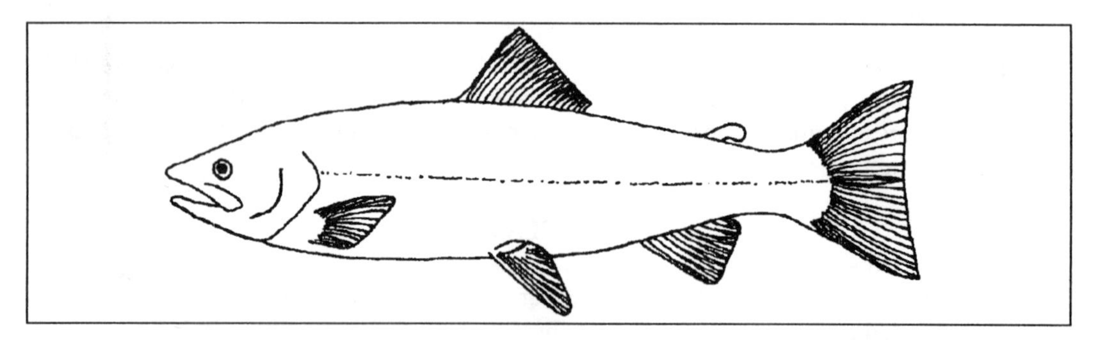

When found at sea, the Dolly Varden is black or dark greenish or blue on top of the head and back, silvery on the sides, and white on the lower jaw and belly. The sides may show faint pink or whitish spots, but sometimes none is visible. The flesh is light orange if the fish has spent a few weeks in salt water feeding, but may be white if it just out-migrated from fresh water.

Freshwater populations will always have a sign of pink spots on the sides, while the sides and back have a yellowish brown color. Sea-run dollies, having spent a few weeks in rivers and streams, will also show the same characteristics in coloration.

As spawning time draws near, the fish grows darker in color and flesh paler. Both male and female char display dirty-green or dark sides and backs as well as top of head. The lower sides and belly are bright orange or reddish. Large pink or red spots accent the dark sides. The male's lower jaw forms a kype and is orange or brownish in color. Pronounced teeth are common among the older and larger fish, especially the males. The pectoral, pelvic, anal, and tail fins are dusky with clear white edges.

SIZE

Sea-run Dolly Varden usually average between 10 and 18 inches, and fish in the 4- or 5-pound range are considered to be quite large specimens. Some populations, however, are known to produce significantly larger fish of up to 10 or 12, and even 15 pounds. Dollies of the land-locked variety in small lakes and streams seldom grow to more than 15 inches, and they average around 10 inches. As with sea-run fish, there are certain non-migrant populations in large-volume waters that can produce fish of several pounds.

The Alaska state record sport-caught char was taken in the Noatak River in 1991 and weighed 19 pounds, 12 ounces.

Note: This catch was of the variety Arctic Char, a very close relative of the Dolly Varden and officially considered the same species.

DISTRIBUTION/ABUNDANCE

Dolly Varden are abundant in Southcentral Alaska, occurring primarily in coastal rivers and streams on the Kenai Peninsula. These are fish of the sea-run variety, but land-locked char are found in good numbers in the Susitna River drainage, in a few lakes on the Kenai Peninsula, and in the Copper River Valley. In the Interior region, Dolly Varden are pretty scarce, though smallish populations do occur in the Tanana River drainage.

RUN TIMING - SALT WATER

The first few sea-run Dolly Varden begin to show in the vicinity of mouths of coastal rivers and streams just after breakup in late April or early May, but can, in some years, appear as early as February given the right weather conditions. The run peaks during June and July, and by August numbers of fish have decreased considerably. A few char, however, sometimes decide to continue feeding in the salt until at least the end of September before migrating back into fresh water to spawn. These are occasionally taken in the tidal regions of larger rivers as late as October.

RUN TIMING - FRESH WATER

Sea-run Dolly Varden move into rivers and streams to spawn anytime between late June and early October, with most fish appearing in July or August. The fish will spend the fall and winter spawning and schooling up in deeper stretches of rivers or lakes. As the ice breaks up and water temperatures rise, the fish will again begin a migration, this time to the ocean to feed for the summer. This out-migration, which can start as early as February in some years and locations, generally commences from mid-April to early June. Activity usually peaks during May.

Land-locked populations, obviously, are restricted to fresh water.

LIFE CYCLE

Dolly Varden soon begin to change color and appearance from ocean-bright to the spawning phase after entering fresh water, or when approaching the vicinity of the destined spawning ground. During this process, which takes a few weeks, the flesh color changes from orange to white.

Spawning takes place anytime from late August through late November, and peaks in most areas during September and October. A Dolly Varden will choose nearly any size and type water for spawning — from glacial to clear water, from large rivers to trickling streams. They prefer a coarse sand or gravel bottom. Unlike the salmon clan, dollies are not as strict about returning to the place of birth. They can spawn in completely different watersheds from year to year. Outlets and inlets of lakes and ponds may also be used for spawning.

After the reproduction process is complete, the fish will migrate into lakes and ponds, or deep holes or pools in rivers, to overwinter. Many of the char will spawn more than once, like the steelhead trout. The older and larger fish often die during the winter following the spawn, while younger specimens may reproduce three or four times more.

The sea-run female char buries between 700 to as many as 6,000 eggs in several redds, but land-locked fish only produce 350 eggs at most. Come spring, the eggs hatch and the young begin feeding on a variety of small insects and other organisms. Their first migration to sea will be after three or four years in fresh water. Fish eggs and other small fishes are soon added to the diet after the young char grow large enough.

At sea, the Dolly Varden feed on plankton, a large combination of fishes, and small crustaceans. The typical Dolly will reach sexual maturity at four to six years of age. From then on, the fish will spawn annually in the fall, or — as is the case with land-locked char in the far north — every other year.

SPORTFISHING FOR DOLLY VARDEN

The Dolly Varden is a flashy fighter best taken on an ultra-light or light road and reel with 4- to 6-pound test line.

Saltwater dollies are at their best from late May to mid-July, and are caught along gravel beaches or tidal rips near the mouths of clearwater rivers and streams. In fresh water, try deeper holes and pools, incoming tides, and behind spawning salmon for the best results. Mid-July to mid-November and the latter part of May are good times to target sea-run populations, but decent catches can be made through the summer in land-locked waters.

Saltwater Lures: Bait and small- to medium-sized spoons do the best, but certain fly patterns resembling bait fish work, too. Cut pieces of herring or Pixie, Fjord, and Krocodile spoons are known for their effectiveness. Small plugs such as the Rapala in a silvery finish can be deadly.

Freshwater Lures: Bait and small attractors, spoons, spinners, and flies are most popular. Single salmon eggs or salmon egg clusters fished along or on the bottom are good. So are Pixie, Fjord, and Krocodile spoons, Vibrax, Mepps, and Panther Martin spinners, and Spin-N-Glo, Okie Drifter, and corkie attractors. Famed fly patterns include Glo Bug, Fenton Fly, Two-Egg Marabou, Hot Shot Pink, Thor, Boss, Polar Shrimp, Alaska Mary Ann, Wolly Worm, Egg-Sucking Leech, and Sculpin.

DOLLY VARDEN HOT SPOTS

The following waters located in the Southcentral and Interior regions are considered to be some of the more productive Dolly Varden fishing spots by the road system in Alaska. For more information on each individual hot spot, see the index in the back of this book for the page number.

SOUTHCENTRAL

Anchor River
Big Lake
Crooked Creek
Deep Creek
Grouse Lake <+>
Homer Spit
Kasilof River
Kenai River <+>
Lower Summit Lake
Ninilchik River
Placer River*
Portage Creek*
Preacher Pond <+>
Ptarmigan Creek
Quartz Creek
Robe River
Russian River
Salmon Creek <+>
Swanson River
Talkeetna River
Trail River
20-Mile River*
Upper Summit Lake
West Resurrection Bay <+>

INTERIOR
Baker Creek

(*): Clearwater tributaries of these watersheds.
<+>: Trophy Water - catches of char over 10 pounds possible.

> **Note:** As always, check the official sport fishing rules and regulations or the nearest Alaska Department of Fish & Game office for exact information on seasons, open areas, legal gear and methods, and bag limits before trying in any of the above waters.

ARCTIC CHAR

Scientific Name: *Salvelinus alpinus*
Other Common Names: Blueback Char, Blueback Trout, and Char

IDENTIFICATION

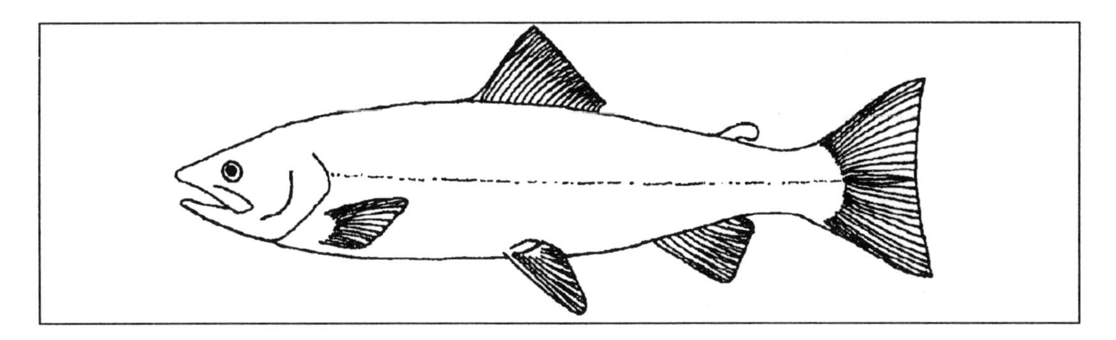

At sea, the Arctic char is bluish green on the back with silvery sides and a white belly. Faint white or slightly pink spots may be visible on the sides. Freshwater populations are very similar in color, with the back perhaps being just a shade darker, sort of brownish green, and the spots more pronounced on the sides. The eye is large and the scales are small.

Spawning fish are brilliant in coloration with orange red to bright red lower sides and belly, and similar shade on the pectoral, pelvic, and anal fins with the addition of creamy white tips and leading edges. The spots increase in intensity to pink or red, the ones along the lateral line often being larger than the pupil of the eye, as the sides and cheeks take on a golden shine. The tip of the lower jaw on males may turn orange or reddish brown.

SIZE

The sea-run arctic char can grow up to 25 or 30 pounds or more in some regions of the north, but generally do not grow to much more than 10 or 12 pounds in most areas with the average being around 3 or 4 pounds. Land-locked char, on the other hand, seldom grow to more than 5 pounds and averaging between 12 and 18 inches.

The Alaska state record sport-caught arctic char was taken in the Noatak River in 1991 and weighed 19 pounds, 12 ounces.

DISTRIBUTION/ABUNDANCE

Arctic char is a species that has been widely used for stocking programs by the ADF&G in lakes and ponds of the Interior where small scattered populations now exist. In the Southcentral region, however, the arctic char is less common with only a few isolated stocks present in lakes on the Kenai Peninsula.

LIFE CYCLE

Spawning may begin as early as September in populations to the north and extend into late December in areas to the south. Usually, however, spawning peaks during the months of October and November in the shallows of lakes and ponds, but also along quiet stretches of rivers and streams near a lake with a course sand or gravel bottom structure.

The female pair up with one or more males and lay between 200 and 6,000 eggs in several nests. After spawning, the char move into deeper parts of lakes and ponds to overwinter.

The eggs hatch in the spring and the young fish sustain on insects and other small organisms. Adult char feed on other small fishes, crustaceans, mollusks, worms, and even young char. The growth rate is slow among fish of all ages, but are known to reach at least 24 years of age.

Come summer, the arctic char, where possible, migrate into tributaries of lakes and ponds to feed on a variety of food items carried with the current. Land-locked char confined to lakes without access to flowing water, stay moderately deep throughout the summer months, only moving into the shallows in late summer and fall to complete the reproductive cycle.

SPORTFISHING FOR ARCTIC CHAR

The arctic char are colorful fighters taken on ultra light or light rod and reel with 4- to 6-pound test line.

Look for these fish on the edge of shallows where it drops off into deeper water in lakes and ponds. Also, try the mouths of clearwater creeks where they empty into the lake. Best time is from mid-August to mid-November.

Lures: Try bait, colorful flies, and flashy spoons and spinners. Salmon egg clusters, single salmon eggs, shrimp, and corn are all effective. Most popular flies include Boss, Comet, Wolly Worm, Thor, Alaska Mary Ann, Sculpin, and Polar Shrimp. As for hardware, Krocodile and Fjord spoons work, and Vibrax, Mepps, and Panther Martin spinners.

ARCTIC CHAR HOT SPOTS

The following waters located in the Southcentral and Interior regions are considered to be some of the more productive arctic char fishing spots accessed by the road system in Alaska. For more information on each individual hot spot, see the index in the back of this book for page number.

SOUTHCENTRAL

Dolly Varden Lake   Irene Lake   Rainbow Lake

INTERIOR

Backdown Lake	Harding Lake	Little Harding Lake
Brodie Lake	Ken's Lake	Rangeview Lake
Dick's Lake	Last Lake	Weasel Lake

Note: As always, check the official sport fishing rules and regulations or the nearest Alaska Department of Fish & Game office for exact information on seasons, open areas, legal gear and methods, and bag limits before trying any of the above waters.

LAKE TROUT

Scientific Name: *Salvelinus namaycush*
Other Common Names: Mackinaw, Grey Trout, and nickname Laker

IDENTIFICATION

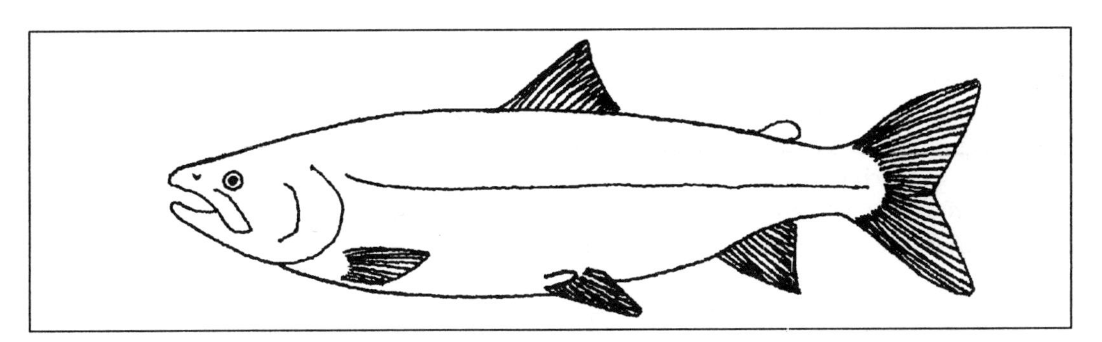

The lake trout's sides and back are dark green, greyish, brown, or at times even almost black. Whitish or yellowish spots are scattered throughout the body, including the head and some of the fins. The belly is white. As a rule, the color of the fish varies with geographical location and sometimes the type of food consumed by individual fish or populations.

Just prior to and during spawning, the lake trout begin to darken in color. A dark lateral band covers the sides of males and the back becomes lighter in color. In some populations the pectoral, pelvic, and anal fins take on a slight orange or red shade.

Unlike most other fish found in Alaska, the lake trout has a forked tail fin and the mouth extends well beyond the eye.

SIZE

The lake trout is Alaska's largest common fish limited strictly to fresh water. Extreme weights of more than 100 pounds have been recorded in some areas of the north, but do not exceed 50 or 60 pounds at most in Alaska. The average weight is considerably smaller, about 3 to 15 pounds, with fish up to 20 pounds not unheard of in some lakes.

The Alaska state record sport-caught lake trout was taken from Clarence Lake in 1970 and weighed 47 pounds, 0 ounces.

DISTRIBUTION/ABUNDANCE

Lake trout are found in large deep lakes of the Southcentral region, with major populations being present in the Copper River Valley and in a few lakes on the Kenai Peninsula. Some isolated lakes in the Susitna River drainage also support populations of this species. The Interior hosts a few scattered lakes and ponds that have been stocked with lake trout by the ADF&G, but very rarely occurs naturally in this region.

LIFE CYCLE

Lake trout are cold water fish that thrive best in deep high lying lakes. Their entire life is spent in the lake where they were born, but sometimes do move into tributary streams and rivers in search of food. These char prefer slow moving water and are rarely found in waters of fast flowing nature.

Come fall, spawning time has arrived. This activity may start as early as early September and continue into late November. Peak spawning usually occurs sometime in October in moderately shallow water around islands or the lake shore. During this period, both males and females are darker in color than any other time of the year.

Spawning is most often on a one-to-one basis and the female buries between 200 and 17,000 eggs in several rock and gravel redds. This activity only takes place at night, while the char are dispersed from the area during the day. Lake trout in far northern regions spawn every other year and populations to the south every year.

The eggs hatch in winter and early spring and the young, after having used up the yolk sack, begin to feed actively on plankton, insects, and other small organisms. The growth rate is fastest in summer when plenty of food is available, and slow in winter when food items may be limited.

Adult lake trout move around the lake in search of food such as small fishes and plankton. Sticklebacks, salmon smolts, and whitefish are high on the menu list. In the fall it is also common to see lake trout feeding on pieces of salmon carcasses.

During the summer months the char are located in deep water, either close to the bottom or suspended between the bottom and the surface, avoiding the warm temperatures of the upper layers. In the fall and spring, lake trout are most commonly found in shallow and moderately shallow water.

Lake trout are long-living fish. Sexual maturity is reached around 5 and 13 years of age, and some populations have fish estimated to be well over 40 years old. But older does not necessarily mean larger in this case. It all depends on the growing conditions in the specific watershed.

SPORTFISHING FOR LAKE TROUT

The robust lake trout is taken on light or medium rod and reel matched with 10- to 20-pound test line.

Fishing for this species is best from late September to late November and again from mid-May to mid-June in moderately shallow sections of lakes when larger specimens are present. Areas around lake inlets and outlets are often hot. Smaller fish can be caught through the summer in deep and slow moving water of larger rivers.

Lures: Bait, and medium- to large-sized flashy plugs, and spoons are most effective. Whole or cut whitefish, herring, or smelt fished near or on the bottom is great for larger lakers. Casting or trolling Rapala, Tadpolly, Flatfish, and Wiggle Wart plugs and Daredevle and Krocodile spoons take a lot of char. Large spinners or even flies may work at times.

LAKE TROUT HOT SPOTS

The following waters located in the Southcentral and Interior regions are considered to be some of the more productive lake trout fishing spots accessed by the road system in Alaska. For more information on each individual hot spot, see the index in the back of this book for page number.

SOUTHCENTRAL

Byers Lake
Glacier Lake
Hidden Lake <+>
Jack Lake
Lake Louise <+>
Little Swede Lake
Long Lake
Paxson Lake <+>
Round Tangle Lake
Rusty Lake
16.8-Mile Lake
Skilak Lake
Summit Lake <+>
36-Mile Lake

INTERIOR

Fielding Lake

<+>: Trophy Water - catches of lakers over 20 pounds possible.

Note: As always, check the current sport fishing rules and regulations or the nearest Alaska Department of Fish & Game office for exact information on seasons, open areas, legal gear and methods, and bag limits before trying any of the above waters.

CHAPTER 3

Grayling and Whitefish

This chapter deals with two major families of cold water fish—the grayling and the whitefishes. They are distantly related and often occupy the same lake and stream environment in addition to general similarities in physical appearance.

The arctic grayling is the only member of its family represented in Alaska and is believed to be an intermediate species between the trouts and whitefishes. It is typically found in clear and clean waters and has earned a solid reputation among anglers as being a superb sport fish due to its aerial antics and aggressiveness towards artificial lures.

The whitefish family covers three major kinds—the ciscos, the whitefishes, and the sheefish. All of these are closely related and share much the same habits and appearance. When grouping the cisco and whitefish together, there are ten species present in the state of Alaska of which six occur regularly along the road system in the Southcentral and Interior regions. While most of these species are strictly of the fresh water kind, some are anadromous and commit seasonal migrations much like steelhead trout and sea-run Dolly Varden.

The sheefish is by far the largest species of the whitefishes, but do not appear in the numbers which is characteristic for this family in the state's roadside waters and are generally quite scarce wherever found. It is a true sport fish that readily strike artificial lures, unlike most whitefishes, and has been nicknamed the "tarpon of the north." Sheefish populations are known in two varieties, sea-run and land-locked, both of which are common.

CHAPTER 3

Grayling and Whitefish

The following are more detailed facts, descriptions, and sport fishing information about the grayling, whitefish, and sheefish that are found along roadside waters in Alaska.

GRAYLING

Scientific Name: *Thymallus arcticus*
Other Common Name: Arctic Grayling

IDENTIFICATION

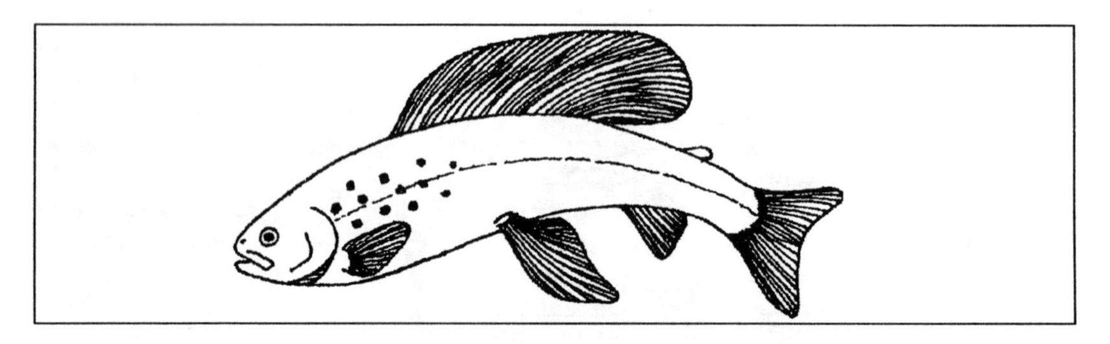

The grayling, especially the male, is characterized and easily distinguished from other species by having an exceptionally large dorsal fin which is sometimes referred to as a sail. Black or brownish spots spread from the gills to about midway down the fish. These spots vary to some degree in shape, size and number, depending on the age and geographical location of the fish. The grayling's body is elongate, with large scales and a small mouth. The tail is forked.

The coloration of grayling differs according to watershed and age of the fish. Most adults are silvery grey to a shade of brown or copper. The fins, most notably the dorsal and pelvic fins, are dusky or dark with vague spots or stripes. The belly is yellowish white. Flesh color is white.

Spawning fish are often darker, sometimes changing to deep purple or dark brown, with red and pink spots and stripes on the fins. The belly of a spawning grayling is bluish white.

SIZE

The grayling is a small fish, averaging 7 to 14 inches, and any specimen over 18 inches is considered very large. Although fish up to 5 pounds have been recorded, the maximum size tends to be closer to 2 pounds and 20 inches in length.

The Alaska state record sport-caught grayling was taken from Ugashik Narrows in 1981 and weighed 4 pounds, 13 ounces.

DISTRIBUTION/ABUNDANCE

Grayling are found in the greatest numbers in cold, clean rivers and streams at high altitudes throughout Southcentral and Interior Alaska. The largest populations are found in the Susitna River drainage, in clearwater tributaries of the Copper River, and in many rivers and creeks flowing into the Tanana and Yukon rivers. This species is also stocked in many lakes and ponds.

LIFE CYCLE

The grayling is a true cold-water fish, thriving in clear, cold mountain lakes and streams, most often in large schools. It is a surface and mid-depth feeder, only searching for food items along the bottom in the summer and fall, when there are salmon or other spawning fish present.

Grayling overwinter in large rivers and lakes, and start to move up into smaller tributary streams to spawn between early April and mid-June. The peak migration occurs just after breakup in late April or early May, but grayling sometimes are so eager to enter spawning streams they'll charge right up even if there is only a thin channel cut by overflow. Large schools of fish, sometimes numbering in the thousands, gather at the mouth of small muskeg-type creeks swollen with snow melt in the spring. They move *en masse* upstream as soon as temperatures and water flow permit.

Females produce around 4,700 eggs, depositing them in a shallow depression on the creek bottom. Males and females spawn one-to-one. The eggs develop rapidly buried in the gravelly creek bottom, and hatch in three weeks. After the young have used up the yolk sac, they start feeding on various organisms found along the stream bottom and in the current. The juvenile fish grow fast, taking full advantage of the activity of summer.

After spawning, usually by late May or early June, the adult grayling may either spend the summer in the stream area where they spawned, or move up- or downstream into a lake or another creek to feed for the remaining open-water season. Some of the spawning streams, though full of spring runoff during April and May, carry too little water to provide good feeding grounds for the summer. Adult grayling feed chiefly on insects and insect larvae from spring until fall. Their diet changes to aquatic organisms, salmon eggs, and small fishes from fall through winter.

Beginning in mid-August and continuing through early November, most grayling migrate out of the summer feeding areas to larger watersheds in anticipation of the coming winter. A few stragglers occasionally will stay behind in deep holes and pools until the following spring.

SPORTFISHING FOR GRAYLING

The feisty grayling justifies its reputation on an ultra-light rod and reel with 2- to 4-pound test line.

Grayling is a strictly freshwater species, thriving in deep holes, stretches, and pools with moderate to fast current in rivers and streams. They are less abundant in large, quiet sections. The outlets and inlets of lakes and confluences of clearwater streams and glacial rivers have always made for hot fishing. Muskeg-type streams can be outstanding during the annual spring spawning runs in May. Overall best time for this species is mid-May to mid-October.

Lures: Small, flashy spinners and insect imitation flies are most popular, but sometimes single salmon eggs or corn can work, too. Vibrax, Mepps, and Panther Martin spinners with a metallic, blue, black, yellow or brown finish are proven to bring success. Flies such as Mosquito, Boss, Dark Caddis, Stone Fly Nymph, Wolly Worm, Glo Bug, and Silver Hilton are dynamite.

GRAYLING HOT SPOTS

The following waters in Southcentral and Interior Alaska are considered to be some of the more productive grayling fishing spots nearby the road system in Alaska. For more information on each individual hot spot, see the index in the back of this book for the page number.

SOUTHCENTRAL

Brushkana River
Cache Creek
Canoe Lake
Clearwater Creek
Connor Lake
Crooked Creek
Fish Creek
George Lake
Glacier Lake
Goose Creek
Gulkana River
Gunn Creek
Gunsight Creek
Grayling Lake
Grays Creek
Indian River
June Lake
Lake Louise
Little Tonsina River
Little Tok River
Little Twin Lakes
Little Willow Creek
Mae West Lake
Meirs Lake
Mendeltna Creek
Mineral Lake
Montana Creek
Moose Creek
Mosquito Fork
O'Brien Creek
Octopus Lake
Paxson Lake
Poplar Grove Creek
Upper Tangle Lake <+>
Rock Creek
Rusty Lake
Round Tangle Lake <+>
Scottie Creek
Seventeenmile Lake
Sheep Creek
Sourdough Creek
Summit Lake
Tangle River
Teardrop Lake
Tolsona Creek
Tulsona Creek
Walker Fork
Willow Creek

INTERIOR

Birch Creek
Chatanika River
Delta Clearwater River
Fielding Lake
Hess Creek
North Fork Chena River
Tolovana River
Shaw Creek
Washington Creek
West Fork Tolovana River

<+> : Trophy water - catches of grayling over 3 pounds possible

Note: As always, check the current sport fishing rules and regulations or the nearest Alaska Department of Fish and Game office for exact information on seasons, open areas, legal gear and methods, and bag limits before trying any of the above waters.

WHITEFISH

Species: Round (*Prosopium cylindraceum*), Broad (*Coregonus nasus*), Lake (*Coregonus clupeaformis*), Alaska (*Coregonus nelsoni*), Bering Cisco (*Coregonus laurettae*), and Least Cisco (*Coregonus sardinaella*).

IDENTIFICATION

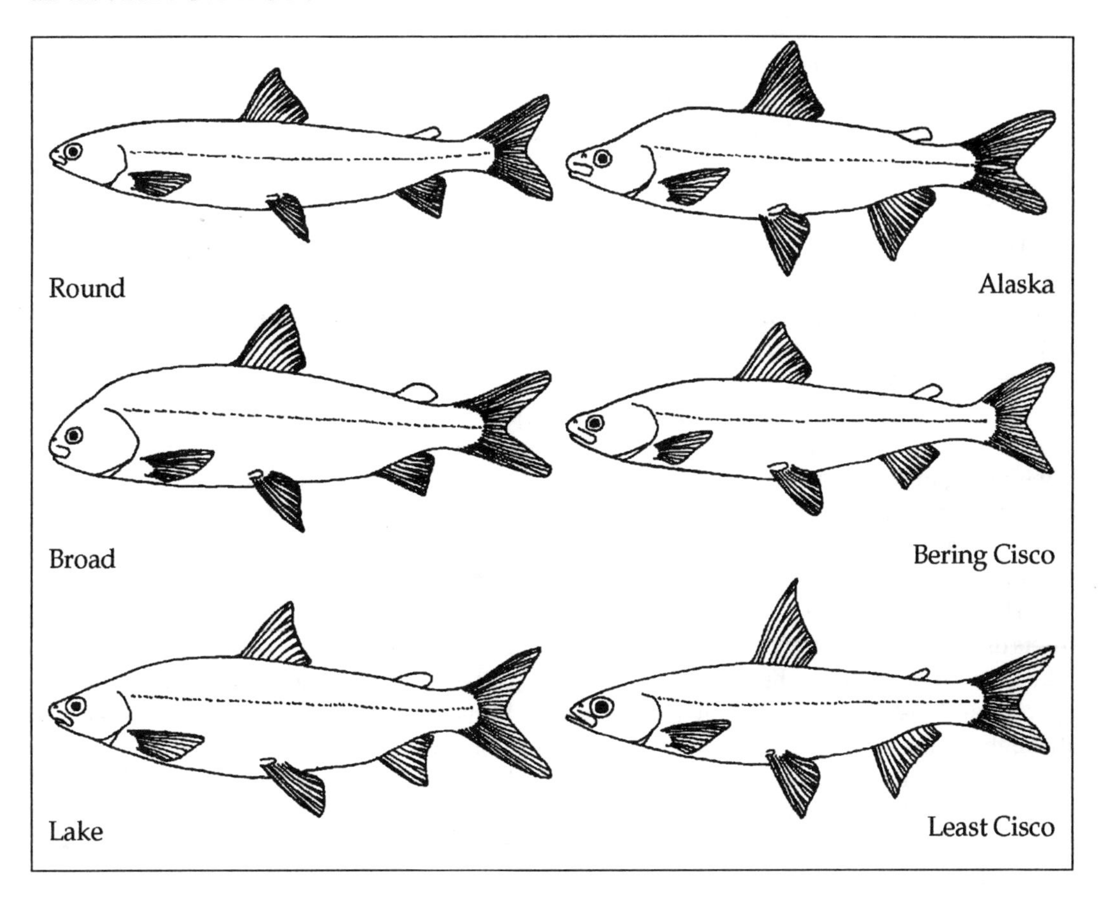

Different whitefish species vary considerably in body shape and size. Some are long and slender and rather tubular in shape; others are broad, thick, and compact; some even have a humpback appearance. The head is at times elongated, but in some species may be more round and compact. All species share large scales and a small mouth with very tiny teeth or no teeth at all.

Whitefish are usually silvery on the sides, dark grey or green on the back, and silvery white on the belly. The fins are dusky on some species, but more often plain white. During spawning, the fish turn a dirty brown on the back, light brown, yellowish, or bronze on the sides. The fins may at this time take on a slight orange coloration.

SIZE

The average length for whitefish vary from only about 10 inches up to 17 inches in most watersheds. The round whitefish are usually the shortest; the broad species usually reach greater lengths. Maximum length and weight for all species is as follows: Round, 16 inches and 3 pounds; Broad, 26 inches and 9 pounds; Lake, 21 inches and 5.5 pounds; Bering Cisco, 17 inches and 3.5 pounds; Alaska, 21 inches and 5.5 pounds; Least Cisco, 19 inches and 4.5 pounds.

The Alaska state record sport-caught whitefish was taken from the Tozitna River in 1989 and weighed 9 pounds, 0 ounces.

DISTRIBUTION/ABUNDANCE

Whitefish commonly share the same waters as pike, burbot, lake trout and grayling. They are locally abundant, and the greatest numbers are found in large lakes and mainstem rivers, and in the lower section of tributaries. The best areas are the Susitna and Copper river drainages of Southcentral, and the Yukon and Tanana river watersheds in the Interior.

LIFE CYCLE

Whitefish are nomadic to some extent. They frequently migrate from lakes or large rivers into smaller tributaries to feed during the summer or spawn in fall. Some populations have been known to move into salt water to feed during the summer and move back into fresh water in the fall to spawn and overwinter. All populations in Southcentral and Interior, however, are strictly fresh water forms.

As winter approaches, the fish migrate to deeper waters to overwinter. They usually seek out lakes, large glacial rivers, or deep holes, pools, and sloughs of rivers and streams.

Beginning in June, whitefish swim into selected spawning waters, but it is not before mid-September into December that the reproductive process itself takes place. Most spawning activity peaks between late September and November, but this varies according to species and location. The fish change into the spawning phase a few weeks before the process begins.

The actual spawning process occurs in areas with a gravel bottom, such as outlets and inlets of lakes, smooth-flowing stretches of creeks and rivers, sloughs, and the inshore areas of lakes. The female buries between 1,000 and 150,000 eggs (the number varies according to species and fish size) in several gravel nests. Whitefish usually gather in large schools throughout the spawning period and pair up on a one-to-one basis. Spawning is an annual event for most fish, but some species in the far north may only spawn every other year. Unlike salmon or steelhead trout, whitefish do not necessarily return to the same spawning stream every year. They are known to swim far from their natal watersheds, and don't necessarily return there to spawn.

Whitefish eggs hatch during the spring. The juvenile fish at first survive on the yolk sac until they are large enough to sustain themselves on small insects and other minute organisms. The growth rate is fast, especially in summer when food is plentiful.

Adult whitefish primarily feed on insects and fish eggs. Sexual maturity is commonly reached at about age five in most populations, and the maximum age ever recorded was a whitefish of at least 16 years.

SPORTFISHING FOR WHITEFISH

The finicky whitefish require an ultra-light or light rod and reel with 2- to 6-pound test line for the best results.

Whitefish are strictly freshwater fish in Southcentral and Interior Alaska. They are most often encountered in deep holes and pools of rivers and streams during the spawning run from mid-July to mid-November. The inlets and outlets of large lakes and the confluence of clearwater streams and glacial rivers can be very good spots to try.

Lures: Whitefish have small mouths, thus requiring small lures. Small, flashy spoons such as Krocodile or Fjord work well sometimes, as do some varieties of wet flies. Try Glo Bug, Wolly Worm, Steelie Stopper, Two-Egg Sperm Fly, Dark Caddis, and Stone Fly Nymph. Bait is often more reliable than artificials, and the fish will take single salmon eggs or small clusters of salmon eggs. Egg-imitation corkies allowed to drift along the bottom also fool some fish.

WHITEFISH HOT SPOTS

The following waters located in the Southcentral and Interior regions are considered to be some of the more productive whitefish spots nearby the road system in Alaska. For more information on each individual hot spot, see the index in the back of this book for the page number.

SOUTHCENTRAL

Kenai River
Little Susitna River
Montana Creek
Sheep Creek
Slana River
Willow Creek

INTERIOR

Chatanika River <+>
Hess Creek
Salcha River
West Fork Tolovana River

<+>: Trophy Water - catches of whitefish over 4 pounds possible.

Note: As always, check the current sport fishing rules and regulations or the nearest Alaska Department of Fish & Game office for exact information on seasons, open areas, legal gear and methods, and bag limits before trying any of the above waters.

SHEEFISH

Scientific Name: *Stenodus leucichthys*
Other Common Names: Inconnu

IDENTIFICATION

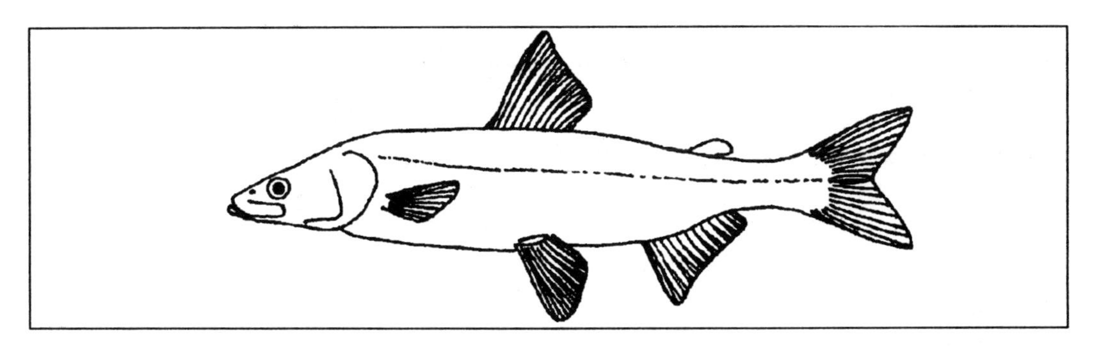

Sheefish have an elongated head and body, and their sides are covered with large scales. The large mouth contains a multitude of very small teeth above a protruding lower jaw. Their color is generally silvery, with green, blue, or pale brown on the back, silvery white on the belly, and pale or dusky fins. During spawning, the overall color may shift towards a very light shade of yellowish brown on the sides and back.

SIZE

The anadromous form of sheefish, common in some parts of the state, can reach up to 60 pounds, but the land-locked version seldom exceed 20 or 25 pounds. The average weight for freshwater sheefish is in the 8- to 12-pound category in larger watersheds, but those confined to smaller lakes with no inlet or outlet streams and limited forage are often considerably smaller — perhaps 3 to 6 pounds.

The Alaska state record sport-caught sheefish was taken from the Pah River in 1986 and weighed 53 pounds, 0 ounces.

DISTRIBUTION/ABUNDANCE

The sheefish appears in small numbers wherever it is found in roadside waters in the Interior, but is totally absent from all Southcentral watersheds. One of the larger populations inhabits the Minto Flats area and adjoining clearwater rivers, and a few fish also enter some of the larger streams in the Tanana and Yukon river drainages. Sheefish have been stocked in a few lakes to expand their range.

LIFE CYCLE

There are two forms of sheefish — anadromous and landlocked. The sea-run form migrate from their birthplace in inland rivers to the mouth of the watershed, and into the ocean. There they will grow to adults of reproductive age, and will return to fresh water to spawn. These fish are found in the Northwest region of the state, but not in the Interior.

The landlocked form, dominant in the Interior, spend their entire lives in large lakes and rivers, migrating to clearwater tributaries to spawn.

Adult sheefish begin to move out of the overwintering areas and into flowing water starting in June and July. The fish move slowly upstream towards the spawning grounds, and, unlike salmon, still feed during migration. By late August and September the fish reach their destination. Feeding slows to a halt and preparation for spawning commences.

Peak spawning activity occurs in late September and early October in most areas. Sheefish prefer clearwater rivers and streams with sand or gravel bottom structure for spawning. The female carry between 100,000 and 400,000 eggs, which she deposits in several redds. After spawning, the fish move downstream fairly rapidly before ice reclaims the water for winter. By November, all sheefish will have left the spawning grounds and begun feeding again for the long winter ahead.

The eggs hatch in late winter and early spring. The young fish feed mainly on plankton, insect larvae, and zooplankton. After one year or more, their diet shifts toward small fishes and eventually they are eating only fish. As adults, sheefish have a rich diet of various fish species, including king and chum salmon fingerlings, char, smelt, burbot, suckers, sticklebacks, blackfish, and sculpins. Individuals grow slowly and may reach 21 years of age or older.

SPORTFISHING FOR SHEEFISH

The sheefish are hard battlers and should be taken on light or medium road and reel with 8- to 15-pound test line.

All populations of sheefish along the Interior road system are land-locked, not sea-run. These fish are found on the edges of deep water in lakes throughout the year, and in deep holes and pools of clearwater rivers and streams during the fall spawning run. Best time is from mid-July to mid-October.

Lures: Medium- or large-sized flashy spoons and spinners with a metallic or blue finish, fished deep and slow, take fish the best. Daredevles and Krocodile are your top spoon choices, and Vibrax and Mepps are the most advantageous spinners. Large, colorful, bulky flies work at times.

SHEEFISH HOT SPOTS

The following waters are considered to be some of the more productive sheefish spots accessible by the road system in Alaska. As the populations in any of these watersheds may be quite small, the fishing is seldom better than fair at best for natural occurring fish, but may be good for stocked sheefish. For more information on each individual hot spot, see the index in the back of this book for the page number.

INTERIOR

Birch Creek	Four Mile Lake	Hess Creek*
Chatanika River	Harding Lake	40-Mile River

(*) The lower stretch of this stream only.

Note: As always, check the official sport fishing rules and regulations or contact the nearest Alaska Department of Fish & Game office for exact information on seasons, open areas, legal gear and methods, and bag limits before trying any of the above waters.

CHAPTER 4

Northern Pike and Burbot

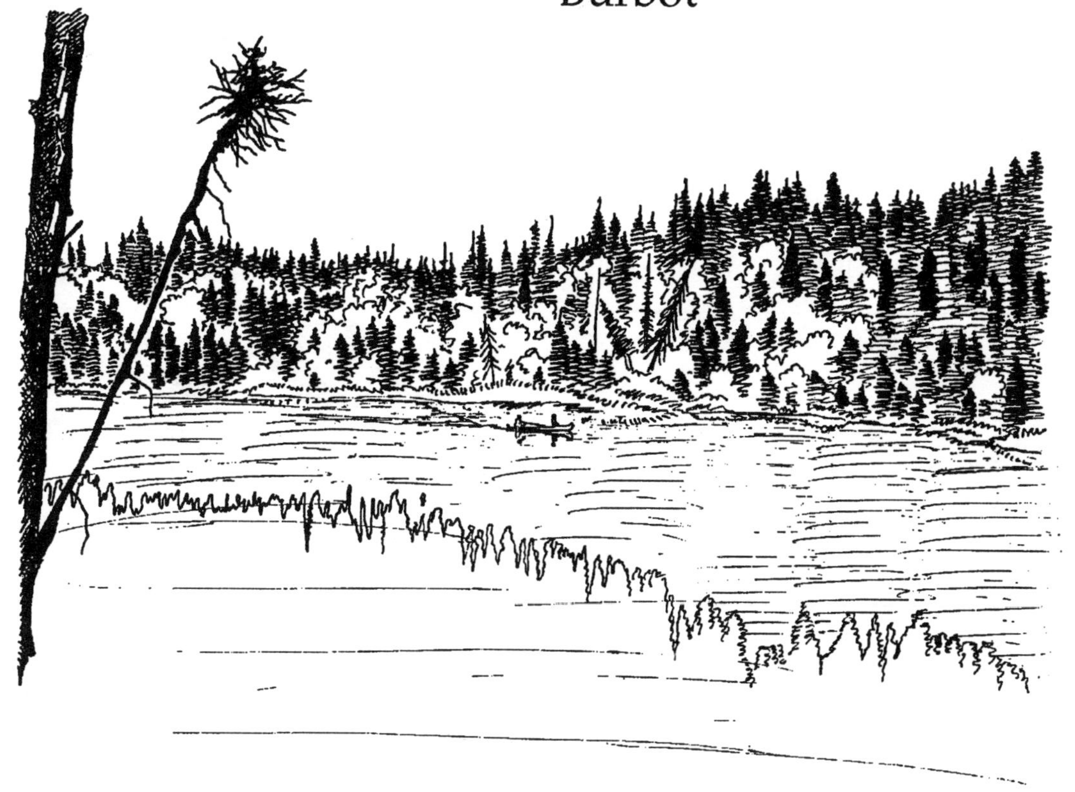

The northern pike and the burbot are in no respect related, but they frequently favor the same types of waters—slow moving or still rivers, streams, sloughs, and large lakes ranging from crystal clear to glacial silt. Both species are true cold water fish belonging to the northern hemisphere and occur for the most part in the Interior of Alaska but may also be quite abundant in certain locations of Southcentral.

Northern pike have long had a reputation of being an exceptionally aggressive species, thus making it a popular sport fish among a growing number of anglers. It has a veracious appetite and is considered a very serious predator of other game fish. Hence the nicknames "waterwolf" and "devil fish." Pike often use ambush tactics in catching its prey and are capable of outspeeding a salmon over shorter distances. Illegal introductions of this species has been made to small lakes with previous populations of only trout and char with the ending result being that the northern pike literally wiped out the entire native fish populations. However, larger lakes are better suited to absorb the predatory habits of these fish.

Burbot, on the other hand, are much more docile creatures and the only member of the codfish family strictly found in fresh water. It is primarily a bottomfish and is susceptible to bait fished still on the bottom. The burbot are usually encountered in the late fall, winter, or early spring as the fish move into slow moving waters in large concentrations to spawn. Despite its somewhat less appealing appearance, it is a popular quarry among many anglers who have labeled the fish "poor mans lobster."

CHAPTER 4

Northern Pike and Burbot

Following are more detailed facts on these species as they're found along roadside waters in Alaska, including a description, their habits, and basic sport fishing information.

NORTHERN PIKE

Scientific Name: *Esox lucius*
Other Common Names: Pike and Jackfish

IDENTIFICATION

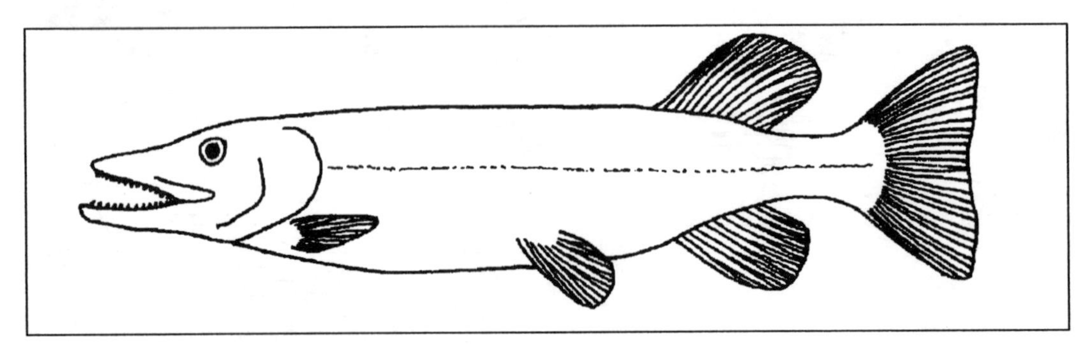

Pike have elongated and slender bodies with dorsal fins placed in a unique position far back on the body. Another characteristic is the long, flat duck-bill snout. Its scales are moderately small; its mouth is large and equipped with long, sharp teeth.

The color of an adult northern pike is dark grayish green to green or dark brownish on the back and sides, with creamy white or yellowish on the belly and lower jaw. Also, the sides display numerous yellow spots in irregular longitudinal rows. The fins are green to yellowish, sometimes more or less orange or red and marked with dark blotches. Young pike are of similar coloration, except the sides are marked with irregular pale vertical bars instead of spots.

SIZE

Maximum weight in Alaska is believed to be about 45 pounds, but any fish over 25 pounds is considered very large. Some larger lakes and rivers, where abundant feed is available year-round, consistently produce bigger-than-average pike, often between 15 and 20 pounds. The average weight, however, is in the order of 3 to 10 pounds or so.

The Alaska state record sport-caught northern pike was taken from Innoko Lake in 1991 and weighed 38 pounds, 8 ounces.

DISTRIBUTION/ABUNDANCE

Northern pike in the Southcentral region are found in small, scattered numbers in some lakes and streams in the Matanuska-Susitna Valley, and in a very few isolated lakes on the Kenai Peninsula. But it is in the Interior that this fish belongs, with major populations found in the larger watersheds of the Tanana River drainage.

LIFE CYCLE

Northern pike live in fresh water their entire lives, mainly in lakes and large rivers. Their favorite locations are quiet sloughs and stream mouths of glacial rivers, and moderately shallow waters of lakes.

Starting in May, the northern pike begins to move out of deep water and into the shallows in search of a suitable location for reproduction. If the fish are not strictly confined to one lake, they often move into quiet streams and rivers that are ice free, even if the main watershed is still frozen over, and frequently swim several miles up- or downstream.

Spawning takes place during June and July in marshy areas with shallow water, emergent vegetation, and mud bottoms covered with vegetation mats. These places may be along the shoreline of lakes or in sloughs and slow moving streams of both large rivers and lakes.

Females may deposit between 2,000 and 600,000 eggs, depending largely on the age and size of fish. The eggs are deposited into redds on the bottom, and hatch after about one month. Young pike feed on insects and zooplankton during the early stages of life, eventually switching to small crustaceans and fish.

After spawning, the fish move about in moderately shallow water through the summer, eventually seeking out deeper water for fall and winter. This migration may take the fish from shallow lakes into deep mainstem rivers, or from shallow, slow flowing rivers and streams into lakes of suitable depth. Some populations, however, may spend their whole lives in one single lake, if it offers no inlet or outlet streams.

Adult northern pike live on various species of fishes, such as whitefish, suckers, blackfish, burbot, and even jack salmon and smaller pike. Pike have a ferocious appetite and are fully capable of swallowing 25% of their body weight in just one meal — in fact they do so on a regular basis. Also included in the diet are large insects, mice, shrews, and, among larger pike, aquatic birds, primarily young ducks and geese. Pike may live up to 23 years of age or more.

SPORTFISHING FOR NORTHERN PIKE

Northern pike are furious fighters on a light or medium rod and reel with 6- to 15-pound test line. Use a wire leader with the lure.

Look for pike in slow moving water of deep rivers and streams and in adjoining sloughs in summer and fall, and in the weedy shallows of lakes and sloughs in the spring and early summer. Fish the moderately deep waters in winter. The fish are most active from late May to mid-October.

Lures: Medium- and large-sized spoons and plugs have always been effective, and bait is a very good bet also. Pixie, Krocodile, and Daredevle spoons are proven lures. Whole or cut whitefish, smelt, or herring fished with a bobber is especially hot at times.

NORTHERN PIKE HOT SPOTS

The following Interior waters are considered to be some of the more productive northern pike fishing spots nearby the road system in Alaska. Southcentral does not support good populations of this species within easy range of the road and is therefore not covered here. For more information on any individual hot spot, see the index in the back of this book for the page number.

INTERIOR

Birch Creek	Island Lake	Moose Creek
Deadman Lake	Mineral Lake	Yarger Lake
Eliza Lake	Minto Flats <+>	

<+>: Trophy Water - catches of pike over 15 pounds possible.

Note: As always, check the current sport fishing rules and regulations or the nearest Alaska Department of Fish & Game office for exact information on seasons, open areas, legal gear and methods, and bag limits before trying any of the above waters.

BURBOT

Scientific Name: *Lota lota*
Other Common Names: Ling, Freshwater Lush, Eelpout, and Ling Cod.

Note: The true ling cod is a saltwater species in the greenling family, while the burbot is the only fresh water member of the cod family.

IDENTIFICATION

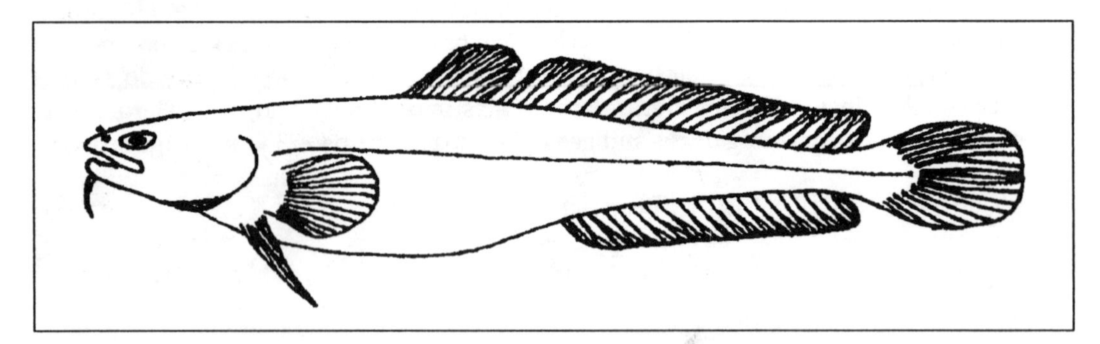

The burbot body is long and slender, its head wide and broad, and its mouth is large and adorned with the characteristic barbel — or chin whisker attached to the tip of the lower jaw — that is common to all members of the cod family. The dorsal and anal fins runs from the middle of the body almost to the tail, which is rounded rather than square or forked. The scales are very small, almost microscopic.

The coloration of burbot varies from area to area depending on the lake or river environment. A typical fish would be dirty yellow to brown or dark green on the back, top of head, and down the sides. The belly is usually of a lighter hue. Numerous markings in different shapes and sizes cover the back, sides, and belly in dirty yellow. Most of the fins are dark or dusky, and the pelvic fins are pale. The flesh is white.

SIZE

Although burbot up to a weight of 60 pounds and a length of 5 feet have been reported, they are uncommon. Most fish are in the 2- to 5-pound range, averaging 2 feet long. A specimen over 10 or 15 pounds would be large indeed, and a 20-pounder quite rare.

The Alaska state record sport-caught burbot was taken from Lake Louise in 1976 and weighed 24 pounds, 12 ounces.

DISTRIBUTION/ABUNDANCE

Burbot appear in moderate to large numbers in Southcentral Alaska, are common in the Susitna River and the confluence of clearwater tributaries, but are especially abundant in the Copper River drainage. In the Interior, burbot appear primarily in the mainstem Tanana river and in a few of the larger tributaries.

LIFE CYCLE

Burbot belong in cold, deep-water lakes and rivers, similar to lake trout. They thrive along the bottom, reportedly down to depths of as much as 700 feet, but usually around 10 to 50 feet where important foods are more abundant. Their preferred depth varies seasonally.

When spawning time draws near, in winter, the burbot start moving into moderately shallow water and congregate in a mass over selected areas. For spawning, they most often seek slow-flowing or quiet waters of deep rivers, streams, and sloughs, but will also move into lakes and ponds. Burbot often migrate several miles from large lakes or glacial rivers into ice-covered clearwater tributaries, with coarse sand or gravel bottoms, for spawning.

Most populations breed in late January and February, although spawning can start as early as mid-December or as late as early April. Up to 1.5 million eggs may be deposited by a single female; the average is about 600,000. The eggs develop on the bottom of lakes and rivers, and hatch in late winter and spring. Young burbot feed actively on insect larvae, plant material, and later, bottom-dwelling fish like small sculpins. They grow fast the first year, and more slowly as the fish ages.

The adult burbot feeds mainly on fish, especially whitefish, but its total diet is quite varied according to the season and water environment. Their varied menu includes mollusks, asellids, snails, fish eggs, shrews, and even smaller burbot. Even though the burbot is mainly a bottom scavenger, it is known to occupy the middle layers of water in search of schools of fish. The burbot may look sluggish and slow, but it can swim surprisingly fast in open water after a prey.

SPORTFISHING FOR BURBOT

The burbot is most often taken on medium rod and reel with 12- to 15-pound test line. Heavier line may be used for setting.

Although catches of this species can be made year-round, the fish are more active in winter just prior to, during, and right after the spawning run. Try the shallows of lakes from fall to spring, deeper water in summer. The confluences of glacial rivers and slow moving clearwater streams are especially good locations from mid-October to mid-April.

Lures: Burbot are usually caught using set lines with multiple baited hooks along the bottom of rivers and lakes, but a single baited hook used with a rod and reel works also. Most popular bait include chunks of whitefish, smelt, or herring. Only on occasions do these fish strike artificial lures such as spoons and spinners.

BURBOT HOT SPOTS

The following waters located in the Southcentral and Interior regions are considered to be some of the more productive burbot fishing spots adjacent to the road system in Alaska. For more information on each individual hot spot, see the index in the back of this book for the page number.

SOUTHCENTRAL

Big Lake
Big Twin Lake
Jack Lake
Little Susitna River
Long Lake
Mirror Lake
Paxson Lake <+>
Tolsona Lake
Round Tangle Lake
Summit Lake <+>
Teardrop Lake
Upper Tangle Lake

INTERIOR

Clearwater Lake
Fielding Lake
Minto Flats <+>
Moose Creek
Salcha River
Scottie Creek
Shaw Creek <+>
Tanana River <+>

<+>: Trophy Water - catches of burbot over 8 pounds possible.

Note: As always, check the current sport fishing rules and regulations or the nearest Alaska Department of Fish & Game office for exact information on seasons, open areas, legal gear and methods, and bag limits before trying any of the above waters.

CHAPTER 5

Halibut, Ling Cod, and Rockfish

What appeals to so many people about sport fishing in salt water is the unknown—especially when you're fishing along the bottom in deep water. What exactly you will hook is anyone's guess. The ocean contains a tremendous variety of fish and other creatures in all sizes, colors, and shapes imaginable. Most are non-sport species, yet a few of these, like cod and flounder, are actively sought after by some anglers. Fishing for these popular non-sport species is covered in chapter 6 dealing with bottomfish.

There are three species of bottomfish that are considered to be of sporting value to anglers. These include the monstrous halibut, ever-hungry ling cod, and colorful rockfish. They thrive in a wide range of bottom structures and provide good sport when hooked on the appropriate gear.

The mighty Pacific halibut is by far the most popular of the species due to its abundance, size, large distribution, and willingness to hit anglers offerings. As the fish migrate to the inshore waters in late spring and summer, boats of all proportions chase these behemoths along the cost until late fall when the halibut once again move out into deeper offshore waters. Shore anglers may also tie into halibut, though the fish are more often of scant size and commonly referred to as "chicken" halibut. In some coastal communities, the halibut even enjoys a greater popularity than the king salmon.

CHAPTER 5

Halibut, Ling Cod, and Rockfish

Ling cod and rockfish are two additional species that have gained popularity over the years. Both are found in the same structural type of environment and are distantly related. Ling cod are worthy challengers as they grow quite large and show little restraint in engulfing artificial lures and perhaps even less so when it comes to bait. The rockfish come in a large assortment of species that display a wide variety of sizes and colors and even in general appearance. The most productive angling for these two species can be experienced from boats in deeper offshore waters, but decent action can be had from shore in certain locations.

Following are more detailed facts on each species of salt water sport fish found in roadside waters in Alaska, along with a description, outline of fish habits, and sport fishing information.

HALIBUT

Scientific Name: *Hippoglossus stenolepis*
Other Common Names: Pacific Halibut, Northern Halibut, Right Halibut, and Albato

IDENTIFICATION

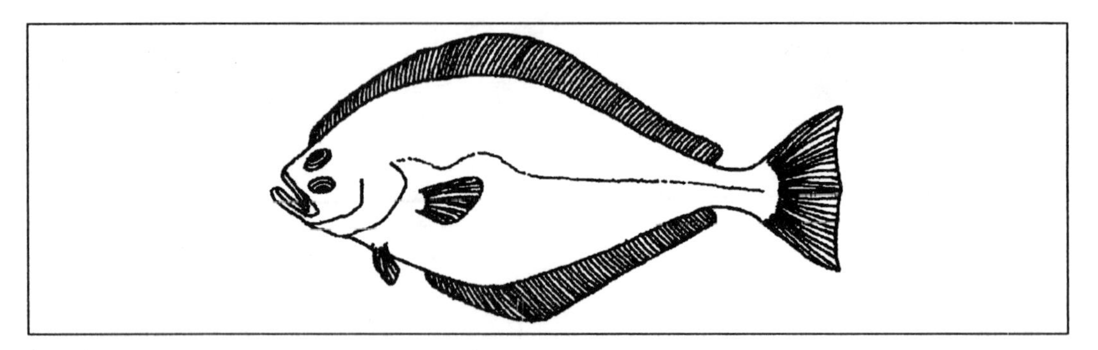

The halibut is dark brown or dirty brown with irregular blotches on the top side. The bottom is bright or dirty white. The body is somewhat elongated in shape, in contrast to other species of flounder, and the scales are small. Its lateral line extends from the base of the tail to the gills, curving over the pectoral fin. Its mouth is quite small, and contains well-developed teeth on both sides of the jaw. Like so many other ocean fish, halibut have a tendency to reflect the coloration of the bottom to camouflage themselves from potential predators. The flesh is white.

SIZE

Alaska's halibut are acclaimed as some of the largest in North America. Fish of 500 pounds, 9 feet in length, have been recorded, but any fish of over 350 pounds is thought to be exceptionally large. The average size of most halibut taken by sport anglers fall in the 20- to 50-pound category. Hundred-pounders are quite common, and fish above 250 pounds are not unheard of.

The Alaska state record sport-caught halibut was taken in Tutka Bay in 1984 and weighed 450 pounds, 0 ounces.

DISTRIBUTION/ABUNDANCE

Halibut are abundant throughout most of coastal Southcentral; large numbers of fish are found in most areas of Cook Inlet and around the Kenai Peninsula into Prince William Sound. They thrive best in clear or semi-clear inlets, passages, and bays in moderately deep water around islands and along beaches.

LIFE CYCLE

Halibut are mobile fish, known to travel as much as 2,000 miles along the coastline or across open ocean. This extensive migration is most common when the fish move from the spawning grounds to the feeding areas and back again. The largest of the flounder family, halibut thrive in depths ranging from about 50 feet down to an estimated 3,600 feet. The depth in which they may be found varies with the time of year and the age and size of the fish.

Come spawning time, the mature males and females move from the feeding grounds along the coast to the offshore spawning grounds, at the edge of the continental shelf in the Gulf of Alaska. Breeding begins in November in 900 to 3,000 feet of water and can last through March. Some of the smaller, immature halibut, however, may spend the winter in much more shallow water along nearshore areas.

One single female can produce between 2 and 3 million eggs, which she deposits along or near the bottom. The eggs hatch after ten days to two weeks and drift unrestrained in the ocean current. After a while the juvenile halibut settle in inshore waters and bays with gravel, mud, or sandy bottom structure. Their diet at this time consists of small organisms at first, switching to shrimp and other small crustaceans as the fish grow older and increase in size.

After spawning, the adult halibut move along the coast into moderately shallow water of bays, inlet passages, and coves. This migration occurs from March to July, with the larger fish appearing during June and July. Here they will begin a feeding frenzy to gain strength and weight. Their diet now consists of herring, cod fishes, flounders, sand lance, squid, and invertebrates such as shrimp and crab, and clams. Although halibut are mainly bottom dwellers, there are times when they move up towards the surface and chase schools of herring and other fishes. In open water a halibut can swim surprisingly quickly.

In August and September, many of the large halibut will move into shallow water at the mouth of salmon spawning streams and wait for salmon carcasses to come floating out. These carcasses are mainly pink and chum salmon, high on the list of favorite foods of a halibut in late summer and fall. But by October, the halibut begin migrating out into deeper water towards the spawning grounds in the North Pacific Ocean. They are usually gone from coastal areas by November. Some of the smaller fish, however, may linger around in deeper parts of bays and coves through the winter.

Halibut grow slowly but do get to be very old. Some fish estimated at about 45 years of age have been recorded, and still older specimens are thought to exist. Females live longer than males, and are larger in size. All trophy halibut are females; the males rarely exceed 40 pounds.

SPORTFISHING FOR HALIBUT

The halibut is a big, stubborn species that commands a heavy rod and reel with 40- to 80-pound test line. Use wire leader as an option.

Shore anglers occasionally hook up with halibut when fishing from docks or cliffs bordering on deep water in summer and fall. Those fish are generally small, 3 to 15 pounds, but fish up to 80 and 100 pounds are not unheard of. Boat anglers do considerably better, since they are able to target on spots with known concentrations of fish, like on shoals or in trenches in areas with a smooth bottom structure. Try between mid-May and late September, when action is best. Fishing near the mouth of clearwater rivers and streams can be very good in fall. Slack tides, high or low, are recommended, since the ocean currents are minimal.

Lures: Use bait or jigs fished on or right above the bottom. Whole or cut herring with a sliding sinker is an all-time favorite, while large jigs of the type Vi-Ki, YoHoHo, Sebastes, or Krocodile are at times very effective with or without bait. This species will seldom strike spoons or spinners.

HALIBUT HOT SPOTS

The following waters located in the Southcentral region are considered to be some of the more productive halibut fishing spots near the road system in Alaska. Since these fish are mainly taken by boaters, and are seldom found in any great numbers in shallow-water areas frequented by shore anglers, the following hot spots are for the offshore fishery only.

SOUTHCENTRAL

Cook Inlet Marine <+>
Kachemak Bay <+>
Resurrection Bay <+>
Valdez Arm

<+>: Trophy Water - catches of halibut over 250 pounds possible.

Note: As always, check the official sport fishing rules and regulations or contact the nearest Alaska Department of Fish & Game office for exact information on seasons, open areas, legal gear and methods, and bag limits before trying any of the above waters.

LING COD

Scientific Name: *Ophiodon elongatus*
Other Common Names: Cultus Cod, Blue Cod, Buffalo Cod, and Greenling. Also nicknamed ling.

Note: The true greenling is a smaller relative of the ling cod.

IDENTIFICATION

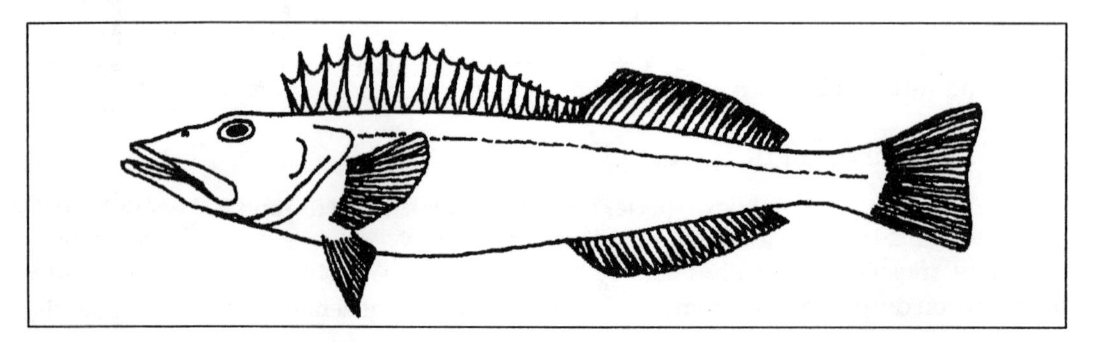

The ling cod head is large and broad with a wide mouth containing rows of canine-like teeth. Its body is slender, with a greyish narrow lateral band extending across the upper sides from the head to the base of the tail.

The color of a ling cod depends to some degree on the environment it inhabits. Fish found in areas with heavy growths of seaweed, kelp, or other plant material are likely to be greenish brown, all brown, or occasionally even slightly reddish in shade. Lings found in places with mostly rock and and hard-bottom structure tend to take on a dark greenish-blue or grey hue. All populations display numerous dark blotches and mottlings on the sides. The flesh can be white, bluish, or greenish, depending on the surrounding habitat and the diet of the individual fish.

SIZE

Lings will vary in size from just 2 or 3 pounds in shallow inshore areas to 15 or 20 pounds in deep offshore waters. Generally, a fish of 40 pounds or more is considered a very large specimen. The maximum size for ling cod is about 100 pounds and 5 feet in length.

The Alaska state record sport-caught ling cod was taken from Resurrection Bay in 1990 and weighed 66 pounds, 0 ounces.

DISTRIBUTION / ABUNDANCE

The greatest number of ling cod can be found in outer and inner bays and passages over hard-bottom environments along coastal Kenai Peninsula and in some areas of Prince William Sound.

LIFE CYCLE

Ling cod thrive best in areas with steep, rocky dropoffs and dense kelp growth. In such ideal environments, one can expect to find large numbers of fish, especially at depths of less than 350 feet. Generally, the smaller fish keep in shallow, inshore waters along hard bottom beaches around islands and the coastline, while the larger adult lings are more common in depths between 100 and 300 feet. Although the ling cod is basically a bottom dweller, it often can be found near the surface or in open water. These versatile fish are not totally limited to bottom structures of seaweed and rocks, but also are known to inhabit areas containing sand, pebble and mud, though they are not found in any abundance there.

Timing is important when targeting ling cod. They migrate each spring from deep water to shallow or moderately shallow water, and back again in the fall. Lings have been known to occupy depths of 1,400 feet in winter and as little as 6 feet in summer. The transitional migrations seem to occur during April and May, and again in September and October.

Ling cod spawn over kelp beds and reefs in moderately deep water from December to March. The eggs are adhesive and attach themselves in clusters to rocks, seaweed, and other bottom material and structures. It is the male ling cod that protects the spawning site to fend off potential intruders.

After hatching in the spring, the juvenile fish move into shallow coastal waters, around islands and shores. After using up the yolk sac, they begin eating small shrimp and other forms of crustaceans. The females grow about 30% faster than the males, but overall growth rate is quite slow and uneven. In time, the males may reach a maximum weight of 25 pounds and 3 feet in length; females may grow four times heavier than the males and 2 feet longer.

Adult ling cod are mainly bottom feeders and so are provided with a large variety of fishes to choose from. Rockfish are a favorite food, but octopus and squid are also high on the menu. Smaller ling cod are known to hunt for prey in shallow water, and at times are found chasing herring in the upper layers of water closer to the surface. It is common for lings to practice cannibalism.

SPORTFISHING FOR LING COD

The ling cod is a robust and aggressive species tackled with heavy rod and reel with 30- to 60-pound test line. Use wire leader as an option.

Shore anglers occasionally hook up with smaller ling cod during the summer while fishing in deep water off cliffs, docks, and points. Boat anglers do far better than shore fishermen, because they can reach the areas and depths where concentrations of ling are found. Try locations with a hard bottom structure and kelp from mid-May to mid-September.

Lures: Bait is the undisputed favorite with large ling cod, though heavy jigs are also very effective at times. Herring, smelt, and rockfish make the best bait and are fished with a sliding sinker on or just above the bottom. Jigs like Sebastes, YoHoHo, Vi-Ki, Krocodile, Bucktail, Wild Willie, and Flowering Floreo, fished in a similar manner, are all popular.

LING COD HOT SPOTS

The following waters in the Southcentral region are considered to be some of the more productive ling cod fishing spots near the road system in Alaska. Since these fish are mainly taken by boaters and are seldom found in any great numbers in areas frequented by shore anglers, the hot spots below are for the offshore fishery only.

SOUTHCENTRAL

Resurrection Bay <+>	Valdez Arm

<+>: Trophy Water - catches of lings over 45 pounds possible.

Note: As always, check the official sport fishing rules and regulations or the nearest Alaska Department of Fish & Game office for exact information on seasons, open area, legal gear and methods, and bag limit before trying any of the above waters.

ROCKFISH

Rockfish is a name commonly applied to a single species of fish, but in reality, it is a family name covering some 70 kinds of rockfish in North America. Of these, there are about 60 or more variations in Alaskan waters, ranging in abundance from very common to mere strays from more southern climates. In Southcentral, however, there are even fewer kinds present, and only a handful of those are common catches.

ish that make up the majority of catches among
rrimus), also known as red snapper or rasphead,
eferred to as black bass, black snapper, and black
v up in anglers' creels include Rougheye, Dusky,
: Ocean Perch among another dozen less frequent

found in the Atlantic Ocean, not the Pacific.

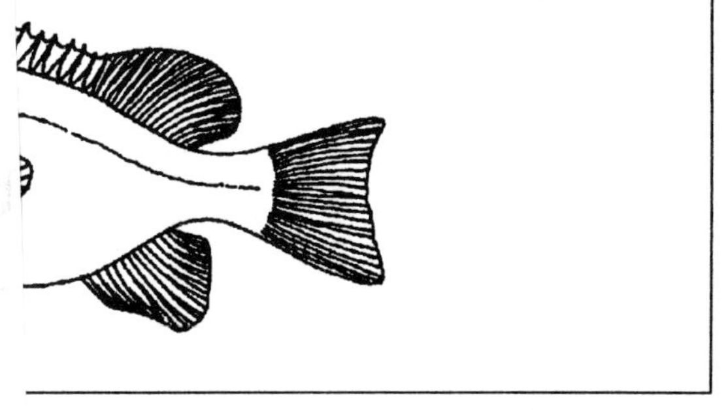

ge eyes, and varying shades of color according
ine-red to yellow or brown with orange, brown,
l line extends from the gills of both sides to the
include a high dorsal fin, large mouth, several
d, compared to the rest of the deep body, quite

tween 10 and 20 inches, seldom weighing more
-yelloweye, rougheye, and bocaccio, primarily
and weigh more than 30 pounds, but most any
upon as very large.
ish, a yelloweye, was taken in Kachemak Bay

...found in the greatest numbers in hard bottom areas around southern Kenai Peninsula and in Prince William Sound off points, islands, and dropoffs bordering on deep water.

LIFE CYCLE

Rockfish thrive the best in and around kelp beds, rocky areas, or in dense seaweed environments. They can, to some degree, take on the coloration of the surrounding environment to blend in and become less obvious to potential predators. This process may take as little as one minute.

The rockfish family is a typically deep water clan found in depths of 100 to 200 feet during summer, but rockfish can sometimes wander as deep as 2,000 feet in winter. Some kinds of rockfish are common in much more shallow water, especially in summer, and are accessible to shore anglers fishing in depths of 30 feet or less.

Rockfish spawn from March into June in moderately deep water, where the females deposit several thousand offspring along a thick kelp bottom. Unlike most species of fish, the rockfish gives birth to live young rather than eggs. Right after birth, the young rockfish begin to migrate into shallow water along the coast, where they stay to feed on various small organisms found on the bottom. Later in life their diet will consist more of other fishes like herring, needlefish and certain types of crustaceans.

Rockfish grow very slowly, about an inch or two a year, but do become very old. Most of the larger fish are likely between 20 and 70 years of age, while a few specimens may even be more than 100 years old.

SPORTFISHING FOR ROCKFISH

The rockfish give best accounts of themselves on a light or medium rod and reel with 12- to 20-pound test line. Use wire leader as an option.

Shore anglers fishing in areas with a hard bottom structure and kelp beds are sometimes rewarded with smaller-sized rockfish during June, July, and August. Boat anglers fishing the same type of structures and around islands have access to larger concentrations of rockfish. Although these fish may be taken year-round, the better action occurs from mid-May to mid-September.

Lures: Bait and small- to medium-sized jigs are most popular. Try cut herring or smelt, or metal jigs such as the Vi-Ki, YoHoHo, Sebastes, Flowering Floreo, Bucktail, Wild Willie, or Krocodile just above the bottom for best results.

ROCKFISH HOT SPOTS

The following waters of the Southcentral region are considered to be some of the more productive rockfish spots accessed by the road system in Alaska. Since these fish are mainly taken by boaters and are less frequently caught by shore anglers, the areas below are for the offshore fishery only.

SOUTHCENTRAL

Kachemak Bay <+> Resurrection Bay <+> Valdez Arm

<+>: Trophy Water - catches of rockfish over 18 pounds possible.

Note: As always, check the official sport fishing rules and regulations or the nearest Alaska Department of Fish & Game office for exact information on seasons, open areas, legal gear and methods, and bag limits before trying any of the above waters.

CHAPTER 6

Bottomfish

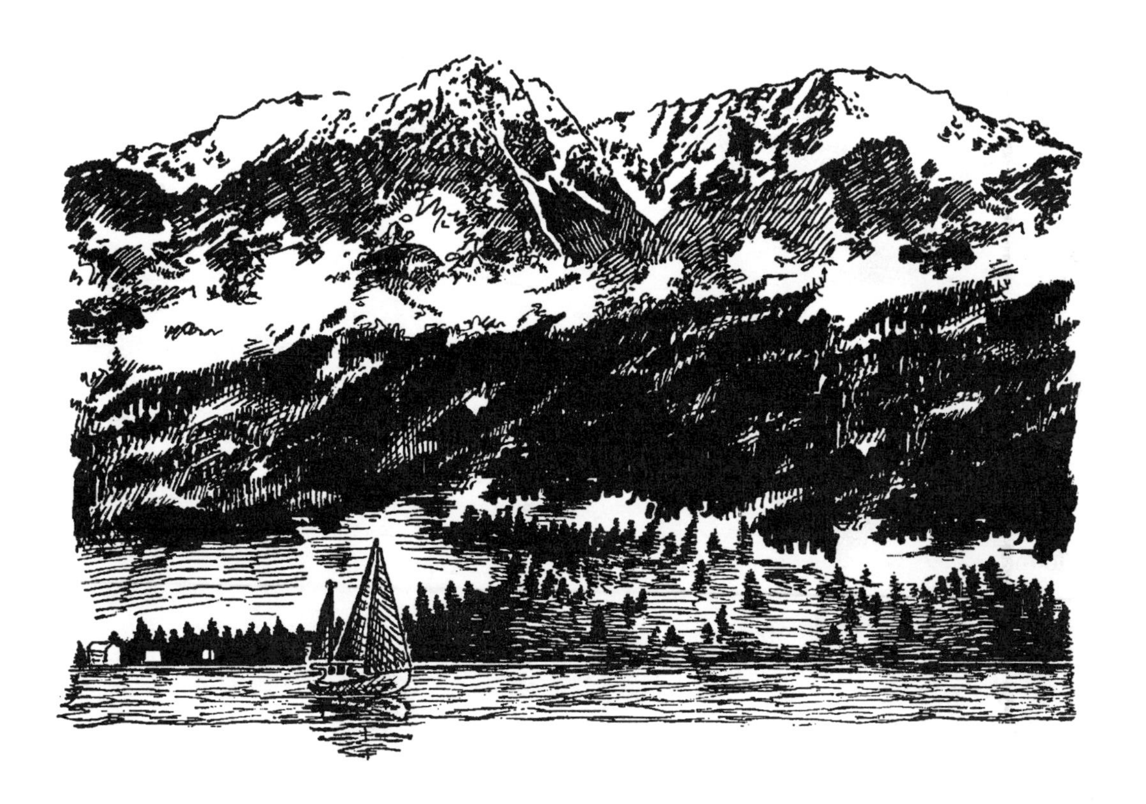

A multitude of species of bottomfish and other creatures inhabit the cold waters around the Kenai Peninsula and in Prince William Sound. Among these are tiny shrimp and sculpins measuring a mere few inches in length, crabs and clams, octopus and squid, in addition to odd-looking skates and even huge sharks that may exceed one thousand pounds. The most popular sport fish species, such as halibut, ling cod, and rockfish, are dealt with in detail in chapter 5. This chapter, however, covers the species more frequently encountered by anglers that are not considered to be on a sporting level, yet provide excitement just by their abundancy and lure-happy attitude.

Anglers fishing from boats and off beaches and docks regularly catch species such as cod, sablefish, flounder, and other non-sporting fish when seeking salmon, char, or halibut. But there are also those who look at the lesser bottomfish in terms of edibility rather than their lack of sport. However, some kinds of sharks, like the salmon shark, are fully capable of putting up a good fight—especially some of the larger specimens which may dwarf even the king of bottomfish, the halibut. The obvious drawback to this is that they are much less common than halibut and are therefore not of any importance to the angling community.

Also included in this chapter is the Irish Lord which, although being more abundant than many would like, is worthy to be mentioned here because of its originality and status as an all-time nuisance in Alaska's ocean fauna.

IDENTIFICATION

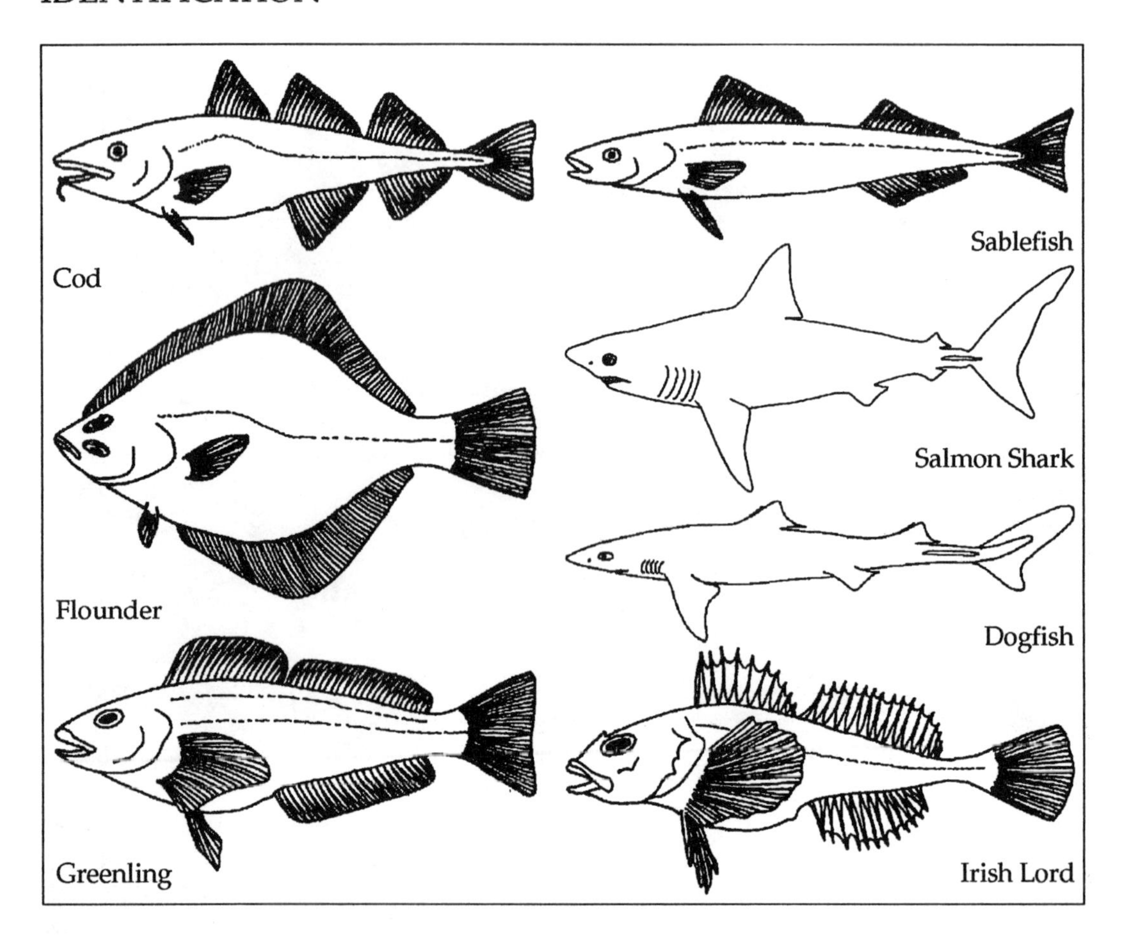

COD

There are four dominant species in this family which thrive in Southcentral. These are the Pacific cod (grey cod), tomcod, saffron cod, and pollock.

Most cod species found in shallow water are only around 8 to 18 inches long, but catches of Pacific cod sometimes approach 10 pounds or twice that in deeper waters offshore.

Cod prefer to swim and hunt along or near the bottom for smaller fish and crustaceans, preferring weed and kelp beds or any type of bottom structure containing rock, sand, gravel, or mud. It is not uncommon for these fish to venture into mouths of rivers and streams in search of food, but they do not generally swim much beyond the tidal zone. The winters are spent in moderately deep to very deep waters, where the fish spawn. They move inshore in the spring and summer.

Anglers do well to concentrate on depths between 15 and 100 feet from mid-April to mid-August, and between 100 and 200 feet during the rest of the year. Metal jigs and bait, particularly herring and shrimp, fished just above or on the bottom, are excellent.

FLOUNDER

The flounder family boasts many members in Southcentral Alaska, but the more common types taken by anglers are the rock sole, turbot, yellowfin sole, and the larger starry flounder.

Different species of flounder vary greatly in size, but most average between 10 and 15 inches long, the maximum length being 18 to 25 inches. The starry flounder is an exception: this species may reach up to 3 feet in length and 20 pounds in deeper waters.

Flounders are typically bottom dwellers, preferring a smooth bottom structure such as sand, pebble, and mud. They are very common in inshore waters around harbors, docks, and beaches. Starry flounders in particular, and commonly other flounder as well, are sometimes taken in the tidal area of rivers and streams. In a few large rivers, smaller flounders may be found several miles upstream in fresh water. Their most important foods include small crustaceans and worms; larger flounders also eat small fishes.

From mid-April to mid-September, angling from shore is best in water between 10 and 50 feet in depth. Boaters can catch flounders regularly throughout the year in deeper water, from 100 to 200 feet. Small metal jigs and herring bait are excellent when fished just above or on the bottom. Small spoons and spinners sometimes work well also.

GREENLING

The greenling family consists of two major species, the kelp greenling and the rock greenling. A sub-species, the ling cod, is described in more detail in Chapter 5 .

Both species of greenling average 10 to 15 inches in shallow inshore waters, slightly larger in deeper areas, and may reach 24 inches in length and a weight of 4 pounds.

Greenlings are true bottom dwellers, thriving in kelp and weed beds with rock, pebble, and sand structures. They are commonly found along rocky beaches and points, and off deep-water docks. Like most all other forms of marine fishes, the greenling migrate, moving into deep water down to 100 or 200 feet in winter, and into nearshore waters in summer.

Angling for greenling from shore is best between mid-May through late August. Small metal jigs and herring bait fished close to or on the bottom in 15 to 50 feet of water work best. Boaters can do well on this species year-round in deeper water.

SABLEFISH

The sablefish is the only one of its genus represented in Alaska. It is sometimes referred to as rock cod or black cod.

The sablefish is a sleek, fast swimmer attaining lengths of 3 feet and a weight of nearly 50 pounds. However, the size usually seen by shore anglers is about 12 to 18 inches, while boaters in deeper water frequently report fish of 5 to 10 pounds or more.

Sablefish thrive in the upper layers of water, and are regarded as a pelagic, or near-surface, species. The fish spend the long winter months at depths of around 100 feet along the coastline by the open ocean, and return to shallow inshore waters in late spring and summer. These fish may be found over any type of bottom structure around beaches, points, and docks where there is a considerable tidal movement and some wave action. They retreat into deeper offshore waters in the fall.

Shore anglers usually catch sablefish incidentally while fishing for salmon and bottomfish during June, July, and August. Boaters sometimes aim for the larger fish along the Gulf coast where they can be caught year-round. Bait such as herring works very well when fished a few feet below the surface down to about 50 feet. Flashy spoons or small jigs also work on occasions.

SHARK

There are two species of shark that are sometimes encountered by anglers along coastal Kenai Peninsula and Prince William Sound. They are the smallish but aggressive spiny dogfish and the often huge salmon shark.

The dogfish is a shark species of small proportions, averaging 2 to 3 feet in length and weighing in at 8 to 15 pounds. The body is long and slender with a sharp spine next to the dorsal fin. The salmon shark, on the other hand, displays very much the typical body shape of the common shark and average 5 to 7 feet in length, weighing a few hundred pounds. Some salmon sharks up to 12 feet long and 2,000 pounds have been reported.

Dogfish frequent cold waters in depths of 15 to 300 feet, but are sometimes observed in very shallow water by the surfline. This species is found over most types of bottom structures. They are commonly seen in huge schools of a few hundred up to several thousand fish. The salmon shark, much the same as the dogfish, thrive best in cold water around the Gulf coast and typically inhabit depths from the surface down to 100 feet.

Although shore anglers may occasionally hook into a dogfish, most are taken by boaters fishing for salmon and bottomfish. They can be quite a plague when they gather in great numbers. The salmon shark is occasionally caught by boaters fishing for other species. Like its name implies, it feeds actively on salmon and has been known to chase schools of the valuable sport fish into bays and coves. Salmon shark may even appear in shallow inshore waters.

Dogfish and salmon shark are most prone to strike natural bait like whole herring or squid, and will only rarely attack artificial lures. These fish are present year-round in southern Cook Inlet, outer Kachemak and Resurrection bays, and throughout most of Prince William Sound, including Valdez Arm.

IRISH LORD

The Irish Lord is one the 45 members of the sculpin family in Alaska. This bane of salmon and bottomfish fishermen is well known along coastal Kenai Peninsula and Prince William Sound.

Irish Lords come in all sizes. Most fall in the 8- to 15-inch category in nearshore waters, but 8- or 10-pounders are sometimes taken in summer. In deeper, offshore waters, however, a few specimens may reach 2.5 feet in length and weigh nearly 25 pounds.

The Irish Lord is basically a bottom hunter and scavenger, most common in areas with sand or pebble bottoms, but found also in rocky areas. This species prefers inshore waters around small boat harbors, gravel beaches, rocky points, and deep water docks during summer, inhabiting depths between 3 and 50 feet. In fall it moves out into deeper water, returning to the shallows again in the spring.

The Irish Lord is not a sport fish, despite its sometimes hefty appearance, and it does show more fright than fight when hooked. Shore anglers encounter them in shallow water using spoons, spinners, metal jigs, and bait from April through September, while boaters using the same types of lures may take them throughout the year in waters as deep as 100 to 300 feet.

CHAPTER 7

Fishing Tips

This chapter was written with the novice angler in mind but may also prove helpful with the intermediate. It briefly touches on some of the general aspects of fishing Alaskan waters and includes topics such as where to locate fish in certain types of water, fighting skills in hooking, playing, and landing fish, and a few points to consider in the art of catch and release. If the basics described here are applied correctly, your chances for success are much improved.

LOCATING THE FISH

It is well known that fish do have special preferences for the environment they choose to rest in, feed in, and migrate through. Knowing where and at what time in a river, lake, or bay to look for fish is at least as important — if not more so — as having the right gear and skill. To just walk up to a river and begin casting without any prior knowledge of habits of fish is a mistake many anglers make. But you must be able to "read" the water, or in other words, have enough basic information on fish habits to know exactly where a fish is most likely to be found. This is not such a difficult task at all, and, if mastered, can bring much success.

The following points illustrate the very basics in locating fish in the various types of water and the factors involved.

CHAPTER 7

Fishing Tips

RIVERS AND STREAMS

1. Keep the lure close to or near the bottom. Species such as salmon, large trout, char, whitefish, and others "hug" the bottom and will seldom move much of a distance to intercept a lure close to the surface. Lures fished on or near the surface will most likely take grayling and smaller trout and char, which feed mainly on insects. The fish along the bottom feed on larger foods, such as other small fishes, or — as is often the case with salmon and steelhead trout — they find security there while migrating upstream to the spawning grounds. Letting the lure or bait tumble downstream along the bottom will often stimulate one of the larger species to bite as it cruises through their line of vision.

2. Fish in deep and slow-moving water. Avoid the fast-flowing, shallow current of rivers and streams and concentrate efforts in deep holes, runs, pools, and eddies. Here, where the current is slower than the rest of the stream, you'll find fish of all species. Salmon school up and rest in such places on their way upstream. Deep pools provide ideal holding areas for feeding trout, char, grayling, and whitefish. Eddies can be found in many parts of a river or stream, such as behind bridge pillars, rocks and boulders (submerged or not), fallen trees, logs and in backwash of road pipes.

3. Try river and stream confluences. The confluence of clearwater streams and glacial rivers is a superb location to find all species of fish, provided it's the right time of year. Salmon school up and rest here on their way to the spawning grounds. A confluence is also a major holding area for feeding trout, char, grayling, whitefish, burbot, and pike. These fish wait here to intercept food particles that drift downstream with the current, or prepare for their spawning run upstream into the tributary.

3. Fish the tides. In coastal rivers and streams the fishing can vary greatly according to tidal movements. Working the mouth of these waters on an incoming tide is usually most productive because schools of salmon, steelhead trout, and char move upstream as the tide advances. On high tide, try the upper limit of tidal influence, or the "edge." This is where the fast river current meets the slack water of the tide. Deeper parts of the river, upstream from the mean high water mark, are most productive just following the high tide as an influx of fresh fish move through on their way to the spawning grounds. As the tide goes out, search out deep holes and runs where fish may school up as the water level drops. Salmon, in particular, are vulnerable at such times.

5. Fish during the low light hours. Although fishing for any species of fish can be productive at any time of the day, there are times when the action is usually better and more predictable. Trout, char, grayling, and other fresh water species feed most heavily during periods of low light, and salmon and steelhead trout respond with more enthusiasm to anglers' lures and bait when it's not too bright out. Shoot for the early morning and evening hours, or for cloudy conditions with perhaps a slight drizzle or light snow. Bright sunshine creates shadows on the water and high visibility for potential predators, often spooking the fish and making them avoid most any lure or bait an angler has to offer.

LAKES AND PONDS

1. Fish before or after break-up and freeze-up. The spring and fall months are considered to be the best time of the year to fish lakes and ponds. The water masses are neither too cold nor too warm. Heat and cold make fish lethargic and less responsive to lures and bait. The fish are often concentrated fairly close to shore in shallow or moderately shallow water as they prepare to spawn, jump into a feeding frenzy, or migrate to the summer feeding areas. Trout, char, pike, grayling, and land-locked salmon are all very active and vulnerable to anglers' offerings at this time.

2. Fish according to the seasons. As the water temperature increases or decreases with the seasons, so do the fish and their habits. Spring and fall are probably the best times to fish lakes and ponds, because the fish are active in most layers of water and eagerly respond to anglers' lures and bait. As the summer heat warms up the top layer of water, the fish become lethargic and move into deeper water with a more comfortable temperature range. By mid-summer they'll inhabit the mid-layer between the surface and the bottom. In early winter, the fish are suspended from near the ice surface down through the mid-layer of water, and are again actively feeding. Through the rest of the winter and early spring the fish remain at the same depth, but become lethargic and less interested in feeding as the water temperature and oxygen level drops. But as the spring sunshine begins to melt the ice and raise temperature and oxygen level, the fish will once again become very active.

3. Concentrate on the feeding areas. It is largely known that lake fish thrive best in certain areas of the lake at any given time of the year, only changing depth and level of activity. Where there is a concentration of feed, there is fish. Lake inlets, shorelines, and submerged structures are also very productive places to try. During windy conditions, do not seek out the calm side of a lake or pond, but rather concentrate efforts where the wind whips along the shoreline, tearing loose food particles for the fish to feed on.

4. Fish during the low light hours. Most fresh water fish are most active during the early morning and evening hours or cloudy conditions, especially in summer. In these conditions, fish will feed in moderately shallow water, moving to deeper parts of the lake or pond once the bright sunshine hits the surface.

SALT WATER

1. Fish the tides. Many species adjust their habits by the movement of the ocean tides. Salmon tend to move close to shore on incoming and high tides, probably in their search for fresh water. As the tide recedes, salmon move offshore into deeper or more open water. Permanent salt water species, such as bottomfish in shallow or moderately shallow water near shore, are most responsive to anglers' lures and bait on incoming and high tides. Boaters fishing for halibut, ling cod, rockfish, and other species do best right on the high or low (slack) tides. These tides provide anglers with the opportunity to fish in deep water without the strong current of incoming and outgoing tides, when it is easier to keep the lure or bait on the bottom without adding too much weight.

2. Concentrate on the feeding areas. Salmon, char, halibut, ling cod, rockfish, and other species found in salt water are often found in different types of bottom environment, but may share some feeding areas as well. Reefs, points, shoals, docks and the like, including the mouths of fresh water rivers and streams, provide excellent locations for feeding, migrating, and resting fish. All of these areas will offer a fish concentrations of food.

3. Fish during the low light hours. Salmon and char are most active in the early morning and evening, but all fish respond better to anglers' offerings during cloudy or rainy weather. Bright sunshine tend to drive salmon deep and slows the bite. Under windy conditions, however, the salmon may be found at most any depth, even in bright, mid-day sunshine.

FIGHTING SKILLS

The following is a short summary on the skill of hooking, playing, and landing fish. These points certainly apply to nearly any fish, but are particularly useful in battling salmon and large trout, char, and pike.

1.Keep hooks sharp. Dull hooks lose fish. Some fish, like king salmon, have very hard mouths and hooks must be sticky-sharp to penetrate and hold. Check the points after each hook-up or snag in the bottom to make sure they have not broken off or become dull in any way. Sharpen or change hooks as needed.

2. Set the hook hard. It does not matter how sharp a hook is if one does not set it properly - **hard!** When you feel the lure stop or hesitate for a moment, set the hook by jerking the rod upwards. This will make sure the needle-sharp point penetrates and holds. Do not wait to set the hook until you know for certain that a fish has grabbed your lure. By then it could be too late.

3. Play the fish carefully. After a solid hook-up, let the fish tire itself out before you try to bring it to shore. Let the rod and reel do most of the work for you. Keep the rod high so it can absorb the sharp and unpredictable movements of the fish. When the fish panics and runs, the drag of the reel should be loose enough to give out line, yet firm enough to provide resistance to the rampaging fish. Pump the rod with slow, even movements. Take in line with the reel when the fish begins to show signs of exhaustion, and let it take line back out when it wants to. Sooner or later the fish will give up and come to shore.

4. Let the fish come to the net. Do not thrash around in the water chasing the fish with the net. This will cause the fish to panic, and many times it will escape. The angler battling the fish must tire it out properly so it can be led to the net. Make sure the fish is netted head first. This will lessen the chances of the fish escaping the net, which is commonly the case when trying to net a fish from the side or tail first.

CATCH AND RELEASE TECHNIQUES

The following steps should be heeded in releasing a fish unharmed back into the water.

Step 1. Get the fish within reach to provide easy access to the point where it is hooked or snagged. Do not drag the fish up on shore through harsh sand or mud. The skin of the fish is a vital and sensitive organ — try not to damage it.

Step 2. Hold the fish gently under the belly in shallow water if possible. If the fish struggles intensely to free itself, grasp if firmly around the base of the tail with one hand. It may at times be necessary to remove the fish from the water (if legal) in order to gain control of the situation. Never insert any foreign objects into the gills of the fish, including fingers, sticks, etc. The gills are the breathing organ of the fish, and are extremely sensitive. The slightest touch can cause the gills to begin bleeding, which often results in death of the fish.

Step 3. Holding the fish steadily, grasp the shank of the hook(s) with a long-nosed plier or similar tool and remove the lure. Try to avoid using unnecessary force. If the fish is hooked deep in the throat (as common when fishing with bait), avoid making an attempt to remove the lure. Cut the line or leader instead. Leaving the hook in the fish is actually safer than trying to remove it.

Step 4. Once the hook has been removed, or the line cut, transfer the fish into water that is deep enough for it to move freely. With one hand clasping the base of the tail and the other supporting the fish under the belly, move the fish gently back and forth repeatedly until its strength returns. Make sure the head of the fish is facing into the current, so that fresh water can circulate through the mouth and gills. Never toss or kick a fish back into the water. Such actions will only cause further shock and possible internal injuries, which in turn means a slow death for the fish.

Step 5. When the fish starts struggling to get free from your hold, carefully let go and watch it swim off. But make sure the fish really does have the strength to continue once it is on its own. A fish that turns belly-up will almost certainly die.

CHAPTER 8

Hooligan Dipnetting

For many a dedicated angler in Southcentral Alaska, it is the hooligan that signal the start of the fishing season each spring. Just as the ice goes out on various glacial rivers around the region, these small, silvery smelt return to spawn in numbers from tens of thousands in some of the smaller drainages to perhaps as many as several million in the larger watersheds. At about that time, anglers line up along beaches and river banks dressed in hip boots, warm hats, gloves, and jackets and all armed with dip nets to intercept the fish.

The hooligan is a species which belongs to the smelt family. All member species are characterized by their smallish size, slender bodies, silvery shine, and forked tails. Altogether there are five species of smelt in Alaska, of which three occur in the Southcentral region. The most common and sought after is the eulachon, or hooligan as it's more popularly called, and lives an anadromous life history. The other smelt species may be strictly fresh water or salt water forms, or, like the hooligan, anadromous.

Much like some other sea-run species, the hooligan is born in fresh water, migrates to the unknown depths of the Pacific Ocean, then returns to the place of birth anytime between early spring and late fall depending largely on geographical location. And like the salmon, the hooligan usually die after spawning and become easy meals for waiting eagles, gulls, and predatory fish.

Following are more detailed facts on the hooligan found in Alaska's roadside waters along with their description and habits in addition to basic sport fishing information.

HOOLIGAN

Southcentral Name: *Thaleichthys pacificus*
Other Common Names: Eulachon, Candle Fish, and Smelt. The latter name is the family to which the hooligan belong.

IDENTIFICATION

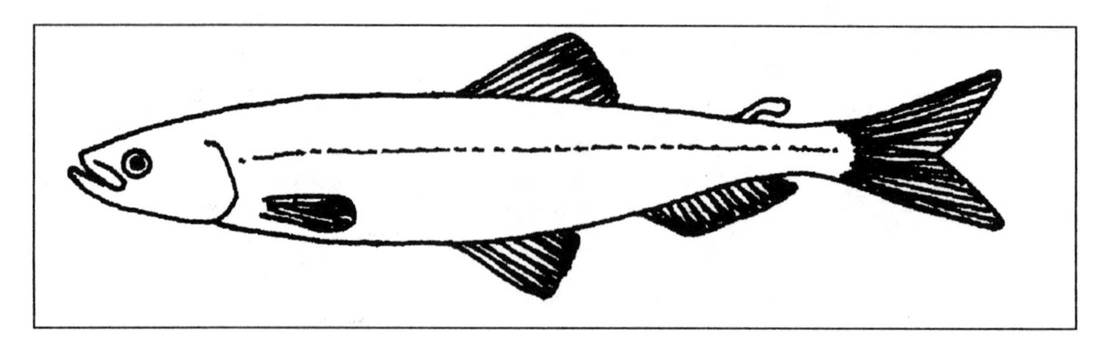

The hooligan is dark bluish, brown, or copper on the back, gradually fading to silvery white on the sides and white on the belly. The fins are transparent, though they may also be dusky.

Both males and females retain their sea-run shape throughout their life, color basically staying the same but perhaps a bit paler after spawning. The flesh is white and very oily.

SIZE

The average size for hooligan in Southcentral tends to be about 7 to 8 inches; 10 inches is about the maximum.

DISTRIBUTION

Hooligan are found in large glacial rivers throughout the Cook Inlet region of Southcentral, including Knik and Turnagain Arms, in Resurrection Bay, in Prince William Sound, and in the Copper River.

Major spawning runs enter the lower Susitna River in the Matanuska Valley, Kenai River on the Kenai Peninsula, 20-Mile River in the Portage area, and the Copper River delta. These runs see fish numbering from tens of thousand to several million. Smaller and less significant populations return to the Placer River, Little Susitna River, and Kasilof River.

RUN TIMING - SALT WATER

Hooligan begin appearing in coastal areas as early as mid-April, but generally do not appear in any great numbers until early or mid-May. Runs steadily decline in strength through June and end late in the month.

RUN TIMING - FRESH WATER

A few early hooligan may enter fresh water in late April. Runs steadily build to a peak sometime during mid- to late May in the tidal areas of rivers, though perhaps not until late May or early June in stretches further upstream. The males generally enter fresh water before the females. In most areas, the run of hooligan is over by late June, but an occasional fish may be present until mid-July.

LIFE CYCLE

Like salmon and steelhead trout, the hooligan is an anadromous species. It is born in fresh water, migrates to sea until it reaches sexual maturity, and then it proceeds to find its way back to the river where it was born.

Hooligan prefer rivers with coarse sand and pea-size gravel for spawning purposes. Look for them in large glacial rivers, and also in semi-clear streams. Although most hooligan only spawn once and then die shortly after, some may spawn twice.

The females produce from 17,000 to as many as 60,000 eggs, which they deposit in small redds. The eggs hatch after four or five weeks and the young stay in the river only a short time before being swept by river currents out to the sea. Here they stay for two or three years, feeding heavily on plankton. After they have reached full maturity, they will migrate towards coastal waters and back to their spawning grounds.

HOOLIGAN FISHING TIPS AND TECHNIQUES

The hooligan may be taken on small baited hooks or spoons, but the majority of anglers use a much more efficient method of catching these small fish: Long-handled dip nets. Hooligan are primarily a food fish, not a sport fish, due to their small size.

Hooligan are notorious for travelling in dense schools close to shore in the shallows, both in salt and fresh water. In salt water, it is often wise to choose a location close to a major spawning river, and to fish during incoming and high tides when the fish are on the move. Stretches of beach, or points having shallow or moderately shallow water, are best.

In fresh water, concentrate your efforts on the lower few river miles during incoming and high tides, which bring in large schools of migrating hooligan. Several miles upstream, near the spawning grounds, schools of hooligan can be spotted at any time of the day or tidal rhythm. In rivers with somewhat clear water, it is possible to see the fish moving upstream in long, black bands only a few feet from shore.

The following steps describe in more detail how the dip net should be used most effectively.

Step 1. Standing in shallow water, close to shore and facing the current, dip the net into the water at about a 45° angle. Force the net to the bottom as fast as possible. Hooligan travel about 2 to 15 feet from shore in 2 to 5 feet of water along the bottom.

Step 2. Pull the net, against the current, along the bottom until you decide to bring it out of the water. Bump the net on the bottom to get a feel of how the surrounding structure is and where fish may be holding or moving. Keep contact with the bottom throughout the sweep.

Step 3. When the net has reached a point of about 45 degrees behind and out from you, slowly twist the net so that the rim of it will be horizontal when it comes out of the water. This will keep the fish from escaping. Repeat the above steps as necessary.

Usually, you will bring up one or two fish in each dip — a catch of three or four isn't unusual. But if the runs are going strong, it's possible to snare up to a dozen fish in one scoop. Secure your catch in a safe spot, such as a sturdy bucket filled with two to four gallons of water. Place the bucket on the beach next to you so fish can be easily tossed into it. The water in the bucket will help balance it while keeping the fish fresh and cool.

HOOLIGAN HOT SPOTS

The following waters of the Southcentral region are considered to be some of the more productive hooligan fishing spots accessed by the road system in Alaska. The Interior does not support any runs or populations of hooligan.

SOUTHCENTRAL

1. **Kenai River**
Location: Kenai Peninsula. Lower section of river from Soldotna downstream to mouth of river in Kenai. Good to excellent fishing.

2. **Placer River**
Location: Portage area, head of Turnagain Arm. Section of river from one mile upstream of the highway bridge downstream to the mouth of the river in the arm. Fair fishing.

3. **Resurrection River**
Location: Town of Seward, head of Resurrection Bay on the Kenai Peninsula. Section of river from the highway bridge downstream to the mouth of river. Good fishing.

4. **Salmon Creek**
Location: Town of Seward, head of Resurrection Bay on the Kenai Peninsula. Lower stream section, from the Nash Road bridge downstream to its confluence with Resurrection River. Fair to good fishing.

5. **Turnagain Arm**
Location: That area from Kern Creek to the head of the arm; also the mouths of 20-Mile and Placer rivers. Good to excellent fishing.

6. **20-Mile River**
Location: Portage area, head of Turnagain Arm. Section of river from one mile upstream of the highway bridge downstream to the mouth of river in the arm. Good to excellent fishing.

Note: Hooligan fishing is open to Alaska residents only. Check the official sport fishing rules and regulations or the nearest Alaska Department of Fish & Game for exact information on seasons, open areas, legal gear and methods, and bag limits before trying any of the above waters.

CHAPTER 9

Clam Digging

In similarity to hooligan fishing, clam digging is one of the first outdoor activities to engage in after a long, cold Alaskan winter. As the spring temperatures rise to a comfortable level, more and more anglers flock to the sandy beaches of Cook Inlet and Prince William Sound in search of one of nature's true delicacies. Equipped with clam guns, shovels, and buckets they descend upon any one clam bed hot spot in the Southcentral region.

Clams, or razor clams, are available throughout the year as they do not commit to seasonal migrations like so many other marine species, and the only thing preventing anglers from enjoying digging for them is the weather which can be very harsh at times, especially during the winter months when strong winds, blowing snow, and below freezing temperatures are prevalent. But prior to the annual salmon runs, digging for razor clams can be very rewarding and stays productive through the spring and summer months.

There are twentyfive known kinds of clams in the state of Alaska, of which three member species are considered attractive and readily available to clam diggers. These include the Pacific and Northern clams, being the most abundant, and the butter clam which is also fairly often encountered. All are found in the same basic type of marine environment—surf-swept coastal beaches consisting of fine gravel or sand.

To further enhance an outing, many anglers along the coast turn to clam digging when the tide is out and the digging is best, waiting for the incoming tide bringing schools of salmon to the nearshore areas and up spawning streams.

Following is more detailed information on clams and clam digging along the road system in Alaska, including descriptions, habits, and how and when to dig for clams.

SPECIES

There are three types of clams that clam diggers may encounter on the beaches of Kenai Peninsula in Southcentral Alaska. The two more common species include Pacific Razor Clam (*Siliqual patual*) and Northern Razor Clam (*Siliqual alta*). The third, Butter Clam (*Saxidomus giganteus*), is somewhat less abundant than the others.

DESCRIPTION/SIZE

The Pacific razor clam has an olive-brown, brown or yellowish-brown pigment, and the shell is elongated in shape. The interior is glossy, white, or tinted purple. The neck and mantle skin is light in color. Length is up to 6 or 7 inches.

The Northern razor clam has an olive brown or dark brown pigment, with an elongated shell like the Pacific razor clam, but the shell ends are less rounded. The interior is chalky, white, or tinted purple. The neck and mantle skin is dark. Length is up to 5 or 6 inches.

The butter clam has a well-rounded white, gray, or black shell and a bulky appearance compared to razor clams. The interior is glossy, white, or tinted blue. Length is up to 5 or 6 inches.

LIFE CYCLE

Clams become sexually mature between the third and seventh growing season. Breeding takes place in shallow to moderately shallow water anytime between May and September, depending largely on seawater temperature. The males and females discharge eggs and sperm into the sand and water; fertilization occurs only by chance. A female clam may produce up to 10 million eggs per year.

The eggs float around with coastal currents until they hatch and the larvae begin free swimming. About sixteen weeks later, the clam larvae begin to develop shells and proceed to settle in areas with proper bottom environment.

Adult razor clams subsist on plant material and plankton, and may live up to 18 years of age or longer. The preferred areas for clams include surf-swept and somewhat protected coastal beaches with sand, mud, or pebble bottom structure. They can be found at depths from approximately 4 feet above the mean low water level down to 100 feet or more.

DISTRIBUTION

Major populations of Pacific and Northern razor clams can be found along the west and east shores of Cook Inlet, in suitable beaches around Kenai Peninsula, and in Prince William Sound. The butter clam is also quite abundant in much the same locations, but are less frequently caught than the other two species.

CLAM HOT SPOTS

Digging for clams in equally productive throughout the year, but table quality has a reputation for being somewhat better in the spring and summer months (April-August).

The following areas located in the Southcentral region are considered to be some of the more productive clam beaches accessed by the road system in Alaska.

1. **CLAM GULCH**

   Access: From MP 117.3 of the Sterling Highway. Turn west onto a gravel road leading to beach area with campground and facilities.

   Tides/Rating: The best clam digging in this area occurs on minus tides, preferable -2.0 feet or lower. Excellent.

2. **NINILCHIK RIVER**

   Access: From MP 135.1 of the Sterling Highway. Turn west onto a gravel road leading towards the village of Ninilchik. Take right fork at the "Y" and drive to the end of the road and the mouth of Ninilchik River. The clam beds are located just north of the river. The left fork of the road leads to the beach next to Ninilchik Harbor. The clam beds are located between Ninilchik River and Deep Creek just south of the harbor.

   Tides/Rating: The best clam digging in this area occurs on minus tides of at least -4.0 feet or lower. Good.

3. **DEEP CREEK**

   Access: From MP 137.0 of the Sterling Highway. Turn west onto a gravel road and drive about one mile to beach area and the mouth of Deep Creek. The best clam beds are located one mile due south of the creek and on to Happy Valley.

   Tides/Rating: The best clam digging occurs on minus tides, preferably -4.0 feet or lower. Good.

4. **WHISKEY GULCH**

   Access: From MP 152.7 of the Sterling Highway. Turn west onto a dirt road and drive about half a mile to beach area. Rough road.

   Tides/Rating: The best clam digging in this area occurs on minus tides of a least -4.0 feet or lower. Good.

5. **HOMER SPIT**

   Access: From the town of Homer at the end of Sterling Highway. Turn south on Spit Road and drive approximately five miles out on the spit. There are productive clam beds along most of the west side of Homer Spit.

   Tides/Rating: The best clam digging occurs on minus tides of at least -2.0 feet or lower. Also, a fair number of cockles can be found in Mud Bay on the East side of the spit.

HOW TO DIG FOR CLAMS

Before digging for clams in any area make sure that you have a valid Alaska sportfishing license in your possession and have studied an official copy of the sportfishing rules and regulations concerning clam digging. Get a tide booklet and find out when the next series of minus tides are scheduled. Bring a bucket — and fill it partly with cold seawater — and something to dig with, like the traditional clam shovel or the increasingly popular clam "gun."

The following steps are to help you find and catch clams on a regular basis on the beaches of Kenai Peninsula.

Step 1: Look for "dimples" or "shows" left on the sand surface. These small imprints are left as the clams withdraw their necks.

Step 2: Dig. Clams can only move vertically, or up or down, but not to the side. If you are using a curve-bladed clam shovel, dig fast where a dimple is present. Reach down into the hole with one hand and grab the clam as it tries to escape. This tool and method will work on any type of beach where clams are present.

Step 3: If you're using a clam gun, push the three- to four-foot long tube right over a dimple and force the tube into the sand with a rocking motion. When the clam gun is deep enough to have enclosed the clam, block the air vent at the top of the tube with a finger or thumb, thus creating a vacuum pressure in the tube. Pull it out of the sand and release the pressure from the air vent. The clam and a lot of sand should fall out onto the beach. The clam gun is most effective on silty beaches with sand and small scale gravel. It does not work well on beaches filled with large pebbles of gravel or rocks.

Step 4: Put the clam you have just caught in the bucket and find another dimple and repeat procedure.

HOW TO CLEAN A CLAM

Step 1: Remove the clam body from the shell by running a sharp knife blade or pointed scissor blade along the inner shell surface to cut away the muscle that connects it to the shell.

Step 2: Now remove the dark parts of the clam, which are the gills and digestive tract. Also cut away the tip of the neck and open both neck canals so sand can be removed.

Step 3: Wash the clam body in clean water and store or cook.

SHELLFISH TOXICITY

Always keep clams in a cool place until ready to eat. Clams that have been exposed to high temperatures during storage can cause illness when eaten.

Paralytic Shellfish Poisoning (PSP) is caused by clams' ingestion of a one-celled organism. This is a very serious illness when contracted, but is of no concern on the beaches of Kenai Peninsula, where PSP has not been reported. For more detailed information on PSP, contact the Alaska Department of Fish & Game.

CHAPTER 10

Alaska Highway

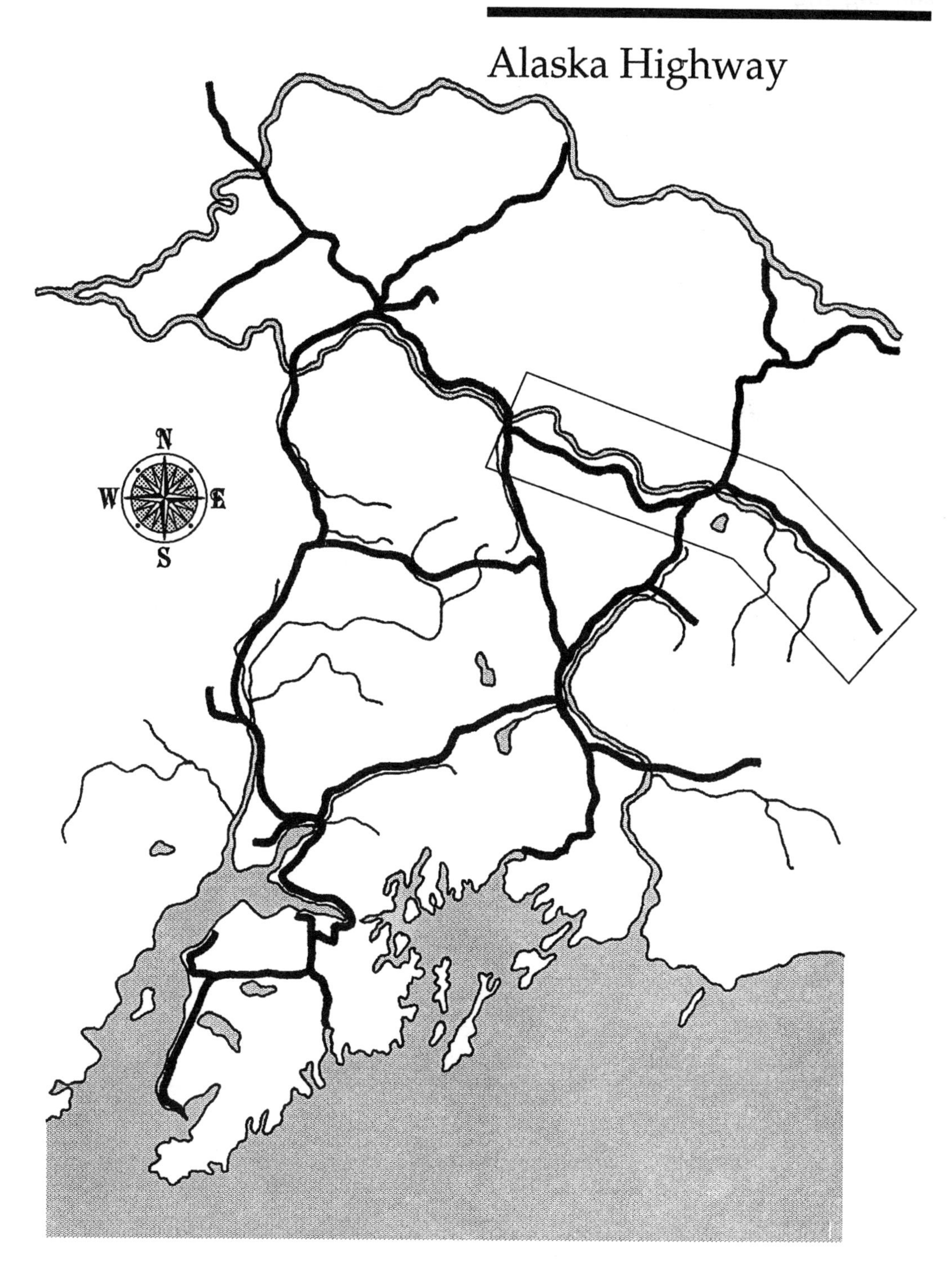

The Alaska Highway originates in Dawson Creek, British Columbia, and stretches into the interior of Alaska. This chapter covers that portion of the highway from the Canadian Border in the east to Delta Junction and the end of the road in the west. It serves as an important link between the state, Canada, and the Lower 48, with direct connections to Taylor, Tok Cutoff, and Richardson highways.

CHAPTER 10

Alaska Highway

The Alaska Highway more or less parallels two major glacial rivers, the Chisana and Tanana, and provides good access to several lakes and streams in the region. Major sport fish species in these waters include grayling, northern pike, and burbot. Chum, silver, and a few king salmon, along with whitefish, may also be encountered at the mouths of larger clearwater tributaries. Generally, the main fishing season lasts from about mid-May to mid-October when you'll find open water in most areas.

Important: Please be aware of the current sport fishing rules and regulations for the area covered in this chapter and abide by them. Remember, they have been applied to protect a fragile resource.

Following are the abbreviations used in this chapter for all the fish species and facility information:

KS - King Salmon	SF - Sheefish	P - Parking
CS - Chum Salmon	GR - Grayling	LP - Limited Parking
SS - Silver Salmon	WF - Whitefish	C - Camping
DV - Dolly Varden	NP - Northern Pike	T - Toilet
RT - Rainbow Trout	BB - Burbot	BL - Boat Launching

Time of Abundance/Availability Charts

These charts are designed to show the reader during which time of the year the indicated species are present or available in the most popular fishing streams, lakes, or regions. The charts correlate to when the fish are in their prime for both angling sport and consumption, unless otherwise noted. Species which are closed to sport fishing are also included on the charts just for the purpose of interest but are shown in all stages of maturity.

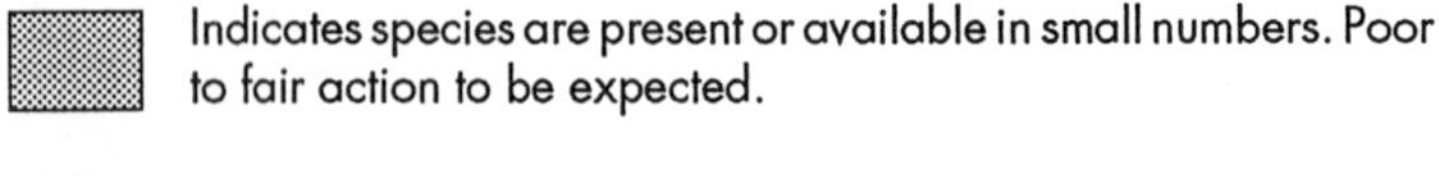

Indicates species are present or available in small numbers. Poor to fair action to be expected.

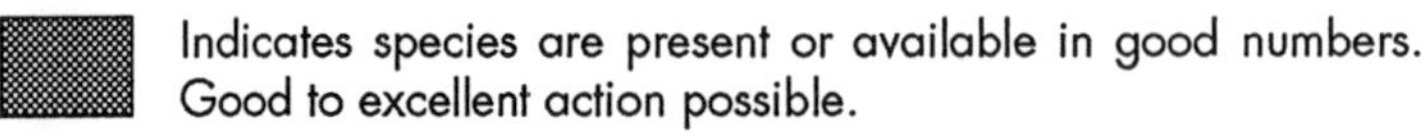

Indicates species are present or available in good numbers. Good to excellent action possible.

Note: The quality of fishing may vary due to certain fluctuations, such as weather conditions, angler experience, number of fish present, or other factors.

QUICK REFERENCE

This section of the chapter was designed to provide a quick view of all the fishing spots in the region, their map location and milepost, species available, facility information, and the page number on which to find detailed access and fishing information for any one watershed.

Note: All fish species shown within parenthesis are species that may be present but protected by law and/or are only occasionally seen or hooked by anglers fishing that particular watershed.

ALASKA HIGHWAY

	WATERSHED	MILE POST	SPECIES
1.	Scottie Creek Facilities: LP	1223.4 Page: 81	GR, NP, BB
2.	Desper Creek Facilities: P	1225.7 Page: 81	NP
3.	Island Lake Facilities: LP (trail)	1230.2 Page: 81	NP
4.	Gardiner Creek Facilities: P	1246.6 Page: 82	GR, NP
5.	Deadman Lake Facilities: P/C/T/BL	1249.4 Page: 82	NP
6.	Yarger Lake Facilities: P/C/T	1256.7 Page: 82	NP
7.	Eliza Lake Facilities: LP (trail)	1258.0 Page: 82	NP
8.	Moose Creek Facilities: LP	1264.0 Page: 82	NP, BB, (GR)
9.	Beaver Creek Facilities: LP	1268.1 Page: 82	GR
10.	Bitters Creek Facilities: LP	1280.3 Page: 82	GR
11.	Yerrick Creek Facilities: P	1333.6 Page: 83	DV, GR
12.	Robertson #2 Lake Facilities: P (trail)	1348.1 Page: 83	RT
13.	Jan Lake Facilities: P/T	1353.6 Page: 83	RT
14.	Bear Creek Facilities: LP	1357.3 Page: 83	DV, GR

CHAPTER 10

Alaska Highway

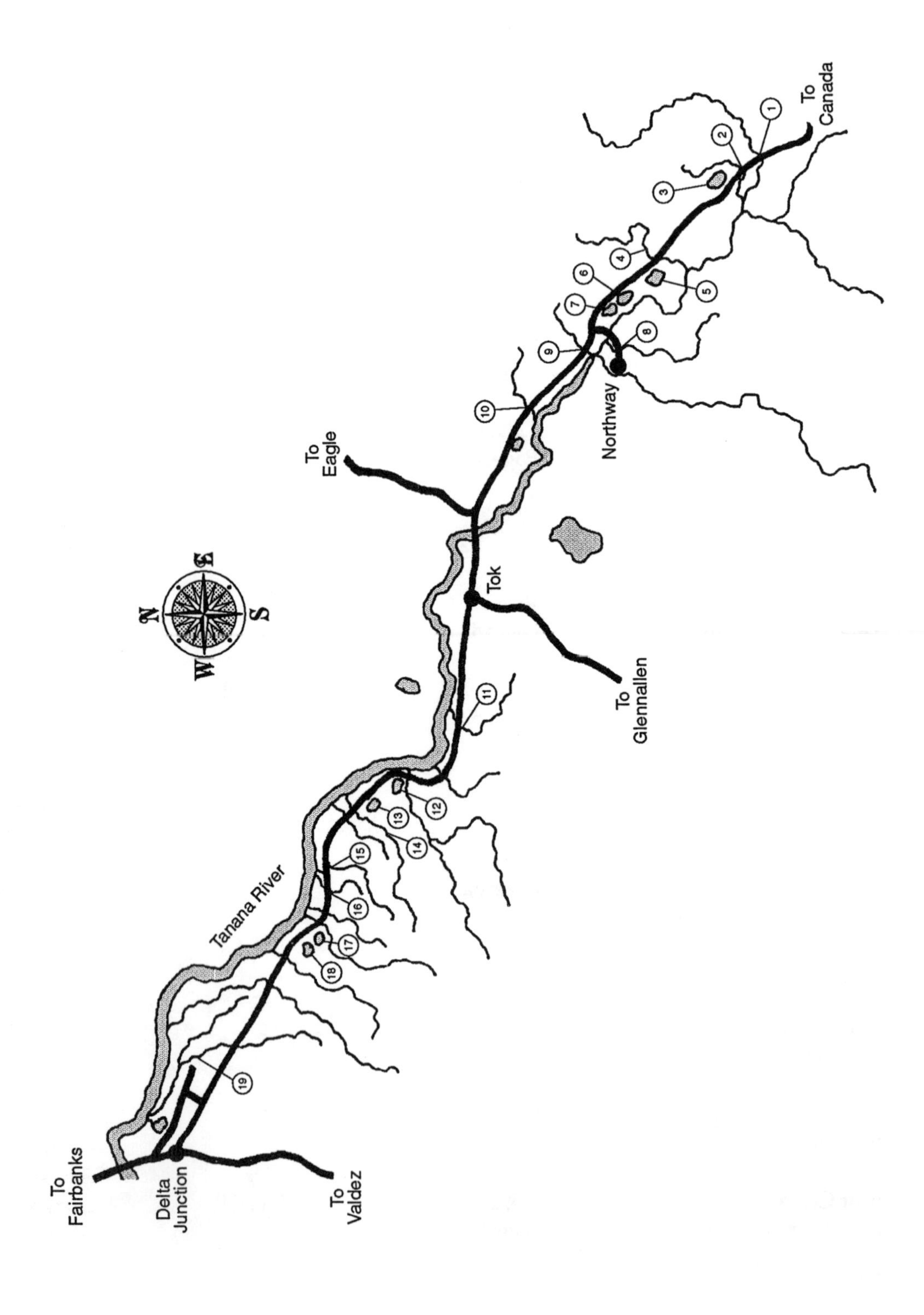

15. Berry Creek Facilities: P	1371.4 Page: 83	DV, GR
16. Sears Creek Facilities: LP	1374.5 Page: 83	GR
17. Lisa Lake Facilities: P (trail)	1381.0 Page: 83	RT
18. Craig Lake Facilities: LP (trail)	1383.7 Page: 83	RT
19. Delta Clearwater River Facilities: P/C/T/BL	1414.9 Page: 84	CS,SS,GR,WF, (KS,BB,NP)

AREA: TANANA RIVER DRAINAGE

Includes all water draining into and surrounding the Tanana River.
Time of Abundance:

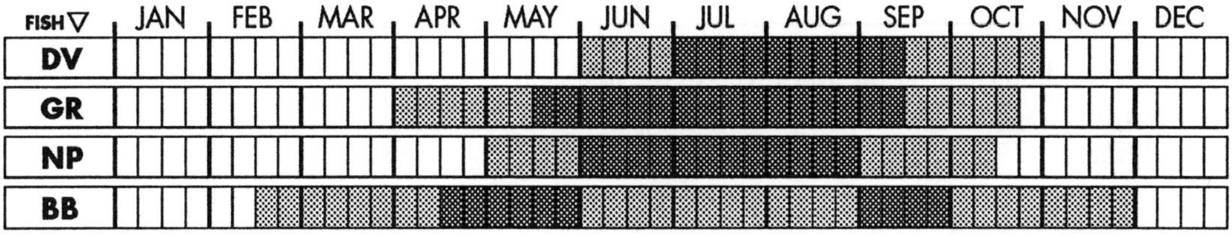

FISH▽	JAN	FEB	MAR	APR	MAY	JUN	JUL	AUG	SEP	OCT	NOV	DEC
DV												
GR												
NP												
BB												

Note: The above chart correlates to all tributaries flowing into the Tanana and Chisana Rivers.

1. **SCOTTIE CREEK**
   Access: The Alaska Highway crosses the stream at MP 1223.4
   Major Species:
   Grayling / fair to good / May and September / 7-15 in.
   Northern Pike / poor to fair / June through August / 2-5 lbs.
   Burbot / fair to good / April, May, September / 2-5 lbs.

2. **DESPER CREEK**
   Access: The Alaska Highway crosses the stream at MP 1225.7
   Major Species:
   Northern Pike / poor to fair / June through August / 2-5 lbs.

3. **ISLAND LAKE**
   Access: From MP 1230.2 of the Alaska Highway. Park and hike 0.5 miles due north-east to lake on old cat trail.
   Major Species:
   Northern Pike / fair / late May and June / 2-6 lbs.

4. **GARDINER CREEK**
Access: The Alaska Highway crosses the stream at MP 1246.6
Major Species:
Grayling / fair to good / May and September / 7-15 lbs.
Northern Pike / poor to fair / June through August / 2-5 lbs.

5. **DEADMAN LAKE**
Access: From MP 1249.4 of the Alaska Highway. Turn south onto a gravel road leading 1.2 miles to a campground and the lake.
Major Species:
Northern Pike / fair to good / late May and June / 2-6 lbs.

6. **YARGER LAKE**
Access: From MP 1256.7 of the Alaska Highway. Turn southwest onto gravel road leading 0.2 miles to a campground and the lake.
Major Species:
Northern Pike / fair to good / late May and June / 2-6 lbs.

7. **ELIZA LAKE**
Access: From MP 1258.0 of the Alaska Highway. Park and hike 0.25 miles due west to the lake. Also, turn onto rough dirt road at MP 1258.8 and drive due west 0.2 miles to end of road. Park and hike 100 yards to the lake.
Major Species:
Northern Pike / fair to good / late May and June / 2-6 lbs.

8. **MOOSE CREEK**
Access: From MP 1264.0 of the Alaska Highway. Turn southwest on gravel road towards town of Northway and drive 2.8 miles to confluence of Moose Creek and Fish Camp Creek on the right. Also, continue 2.5 miles to stream crossing.
Major Species:
Northern Pike / fair / June through August / 2-6 lbs.
Burbot / fair / May through / September / 2-5 lbs.

9. **BEAVER CREEK**
Access: The Alaska Highway crosses the stream at MP 1268.1.
Major Species:
Grayling / fair to good / mid-May to mid-September / 7-15 in.

10. **BITTERS CREEK**
Access: The Alaska Highway crosses the stream at MP 1280.3.
Major Species:
Grayling / fair to good / mid-May to mid-September / 7-15 in.

11. YERRICK CREEK
Access: The Alaska Highway crosses the stream at MP 1333.6.
Major Species:
Dolly Varden / poor to fair / July to mid-September / 7-12 in.
Grayling / fair to good / mid-May to mid-September / 7-15 in.

12. ROBERTSON #2 LAKE
Access: From MP 1348.1 of the Alaska Highway. Turn west onto a gravel road and drive 0.2 miles to a parking area. Find trail leading 0.25 miles to lake.
Major Species:
Rainbow trout / good / May and September, October / 8-16 in.

13. JAN LAKE
Access: From MP 1353.6 of the Alaska Highway. Turn west onto Jan Lake Road and drive 0.5 miles to the lake.
Major Species:
Rainbow trout / good / May and September, October / 8-18 in.

14. BEAR CREEK
Access: The Alaska Highway crosses the stream at MP 1357.3.
Major Species:
Dolly Varden / poor to fair / July to mid-September / 7-12 in.
Grayling / fair to good / mid-May to mid-September / 7-15 in.

15. BERRY CREEK
Access: The Alaska Highway crosses the stream at MP 1371.4.
Major Species:
Dolly Varden / poor to fair / July to mid-September / 7-12 in.
Grayling / fair to good / mid-May to mid-September / 7-15-in.

16. SEARS CREEK
Access: The Alaska Highway crosses the stream at MP 1374.5.
Major Species:
Grayling / fair to good / mid-May to mid-September / 7-15 in.

17. LISA LAKE
Access: From MP 1381.0 of Alaska Highway. Turn southwest onto pull-off and park. Hike 0.5 miles to the lake.
Major Species:
Rainbow trout / good / May and September, October / 8-16 in.

18. CRAIG LAKE
Access: From MP 1383.7 of the Alaska Highway. Turn southwest on gravel road and drive 1.1 miles to sign on right. Hike 0.25 miles to the lake.
Major Species:
Rainbow trout / good / May and September, October / 8-20 in.

19. DELTA CLEARWATER RIVER

Access: From MP 1414.9 of the Alaska Highway. Turn northeast on Clearwater Road, drive 5.3 miles to a "T" and turn right onto Remington Road, proceed 2.8 miles to gravel road on left next to a sign, and continue short distance to a campground and the river.

Fishing: See **page 123** for fishing information on Delta Clearwater River.

CHAPTER 11

Taylor Highway

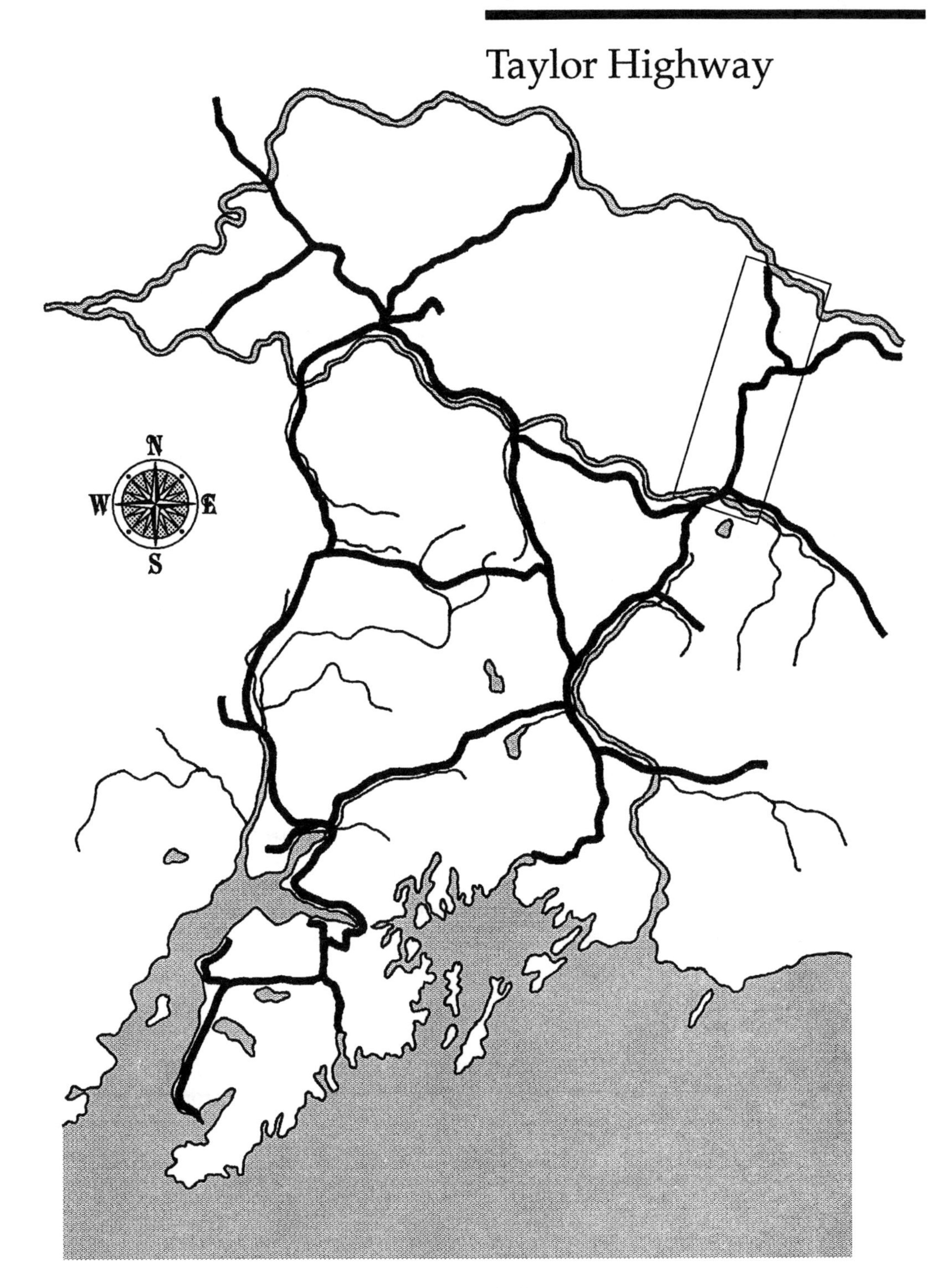

The Taylor Highway begins in Tetlin Junction, at Milepost 1301.7 of the Alaska Highway, and ends in the community of Eagle on the Yukon River. The gravel highway runs in a north-south direction with additional access to the Canadian Border.

CHAPTER 11

Taylor Highway

Taylor Highway provides good access to one lake, and to several clearwater tributaries of the large Forty-Mile River. Grayling, as the dominant sport fish species in the region, is available in all of the waters along the road. A few sheefish and whitefish sometimes are taken in larger watersheds. The main fishing season usually runs from about mid-May to mid-October, when open water is prevalent in the area.

Important: Please be aware of the current sport fishing rules and regulations for the area covered in this chapter, and abide by them. Remember, they have been applied to protect a fragile resource.

Following are the abbreviations used in this chapter for all the fish species and facility information:

SF - Sheefish
GR - Grayling
WF - Whitefish

P - Parking
LP - Limited Parking
C - Camping

T - Toilet
BL - Boat Launching

Time of Abundance/Availability Charts

These charts are designed to show the reader during which time of the year the indicated species are present or available in the most popular fishing streams, lakes, or regions. The charts correlate to when the fish are in their prime for both angling sport and consumption, unless otherwise noted. Species which are closed to sport fishing are also included on the charts just for the purpose of interest but are shown in all stages of maturity.

Indicates species are present or available in small numbers. Poor to fair action to be expected.

Indicates species are present or available in good numbers. Good to excellent action possible.

Note: The quality of fishing may vary due to certain fluctuations, such as weather conditions, angler experience, number of fish present, or other factors.

QUICK REFERENCE

This section of the chapter was designed to provide a quick view of all the fishing spots in the region, their map location and milepost, species available, facility information, and the page number on which to find detailed access and fishing information for any one watershed.

Note: The fish species shown in parentheses may be present but protected by law, and/or may only occasionally be seen or hooked in that particular watershed.

TAYLOR HIGHWAY

	WATERSHED	MILE POST	SPECIES
1.	Four Mile Lake Facilities: P (trail)	4.5 Page: 89	SF,RT
2.	Logging Cabin Creek Facilities: P	43.0 Page: 89	GR
3.	West Fork Dennison R. Facilities: P/C/T	49.2 Page: 89	GR
4.	Taylor Creek Facilities: LP	50.4 Page: 89	GR
5.	Mosquito Fork Facilities: P/T	64.3 Page: 89	GR
6.	40-Mile River Facilities: P/T	74.2-75.4 Page: 89	SF,GR,(WF,BB)
7.	Walker Fork Facilities: P/C/T	82.0 Page: 90	GR
8.	40-Mile River Facilities: P/T/BL	112.5 Page: 90	SF,GR,(WF,BB)
9.	O'Brien Creek Facilities: LP	113.2 Page: 90	GR
10.	Alder Creek Facilities: P	117.1 Page: 90	GR
11.	Columbia Creek Facilities: P	124.5 Page: 90	GR
12.	King Solomon Creek Facilities: P	133.9 Page: 90	GR
13.	N.F. King Solomon Cr. Facilities: LP	137.8 Page: 90	GR
14.	American Creek Facilities: LP	151.7-155.6 Page: 90	GR

Taylor Highway

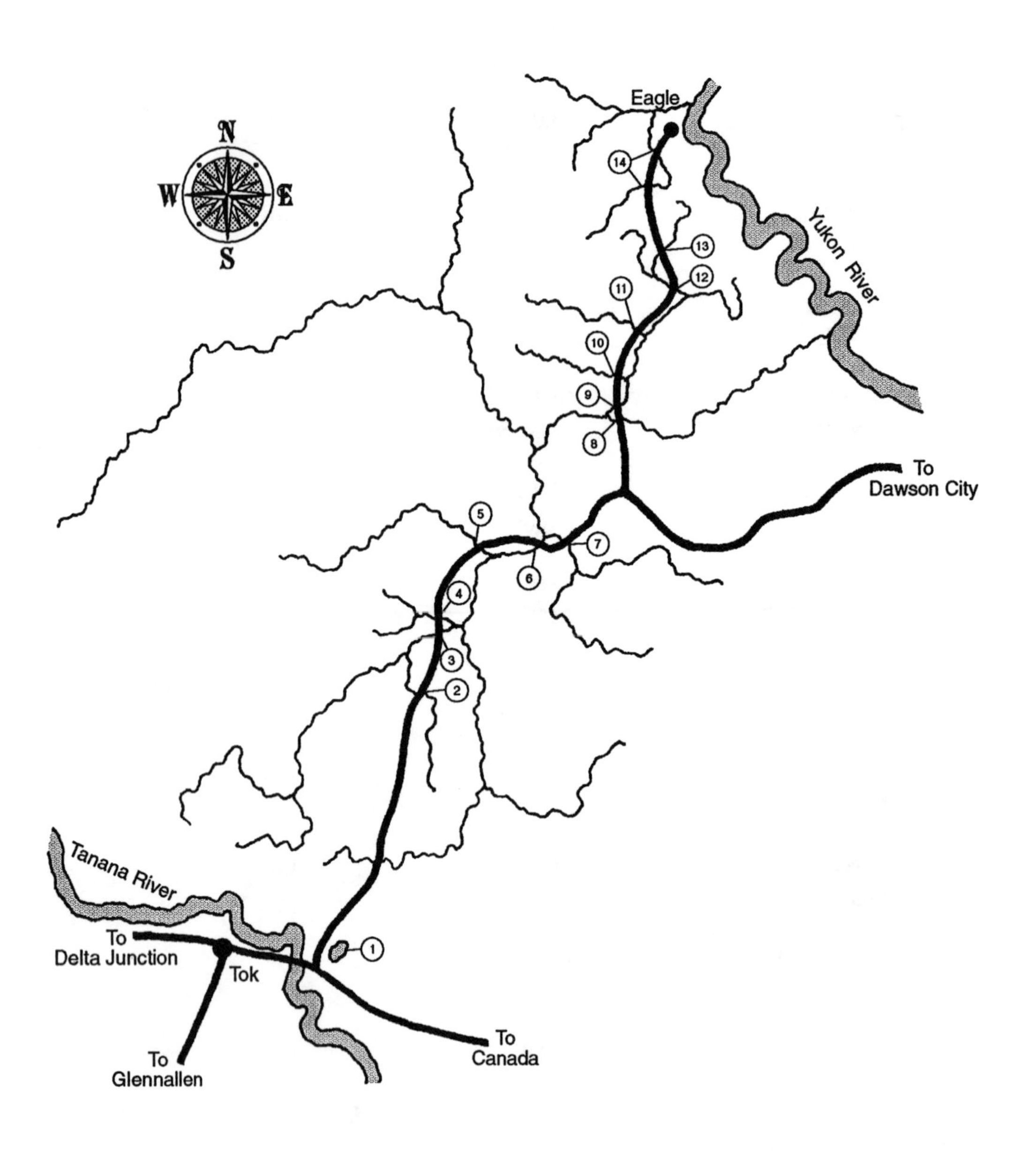

AREA: YUKON RIVER DRAINAGE

Includes all water draining into and surrounding the Yukon River along the Taylor Highway.

Time fo Abundance:

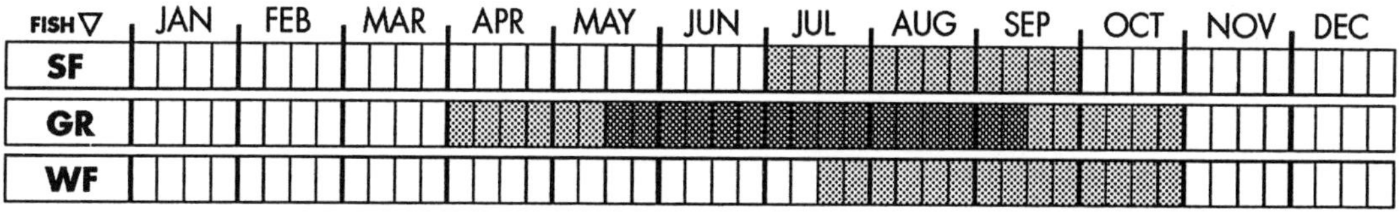

FISH ▽	JAN	FEB	MAR	APR	MAY	JUN	JUL	AUG	SEP	OCT	NOV	DEC
SF												
GR												
WF												

Note: The above chart correlates to all tributaries flowing into the Yukon River.

1. **FOUR MILE LAKE**
   Access: From MP 4.5 of the Taylor Highway. Park at pulloff east of road and find trail leading 0.75 miles to the lake.
   Major Species:
   Sheefish / fair to good / June through September / 2-5 lbs.
   Rainbow trout / good / May and September, October / 8-18 in.

2. **LOGGING CABIN CREEK**
   Access: The Taylor Highway crosses the stream at MP 43.0.
   Major Species:
   Grayling / poor to fair / mid-June to mid-September / 7-12 in.

3. **WEST FORK DENNISON RIVER**
   Access: The Taylor Highway crosses the river at MP 49.2.
   Major Species:
   Grayling / fair to good / June to September / 7-15 in.

4. **TAYLOR CREEK**
   Access: The Taylor Highway crosses the stream at MP 50.4.
   Major Species:
   Grayling / fair to good / June and September / 7-15 in.

5. **MOSQUITO FORK**
   Access: The Taylor Highway crosses the stream at MP 64.3.
   Major Species:
   Grayling / fair to good / June and September / 7-15 in.

6. **40-MILE RIVER**
   Access: The Taylor Highway parallels the river from MP 74.2 to 75.3, and crosses the river at MP 75.4.
   Major Species:
   Sheefish / poor to fair / August and September / 4-8 lbs.
   Grayling / fair to good / May and September / 7-15 in.

7. **WALKER FORK**
   Access: The Taylor Highway crosses the stream at MP 82.0.
   Major Species:
   Grayling / fair to good / June and September / 7-15 in.

8. **40-MILE RIVER**
   Access: The Taylor Highway crosses the river at MP 112.5.
   Major Species:
   Sheefish / poor to fair / August and September / 4-8 lbs.
   Grayling / fair to good / May and September / 7-15 in.

9. **O'BRIEN CREEK**
   Access: The Taylor Highway crosses the stream at MP 113.2.
   Major Species:
   Grayling / fair to good / June to mid-September / 7-15 in.

10. **ALDER CREEK**
    Access: The Taylor Highway crosses the stream at MP 117.1.
    Major Species:
    Grayling / fair to good / June to mid-September / 7-15 in.

11. **COLUMBIA CREEK**
    Access: The Taylor Highway crosses the stream at MP 124.5.
    Major Species:
    Grayling / fair to good / June to mid-September / 7-15 in.

12. **KING SOLOMON CREEK**
    Access: The Taylor Highway crosses the stream at MP 133.9.
    Major Species:
    Grayling / fair / June to mid-September / 7-12 in.

13. **NORTH FORK KING SOLOMON CREEK**
    Access: The Taylor Highway crosses the stream at MP 137.8.
    Major Species:
    Grayling / poor to fair / mid-June to mid-September / 7-12 in.

14. **AMERICAN CREEK**
    Access: The Taylor Highway parallels the stream from MP 151.7 to 155.6, crossing the stream in two locations.
    Major Species:
    Grayling / poor to fair / mid-May to mid-June / 7-12 in.

CHAPTER 12

Tok Cutoff Highway

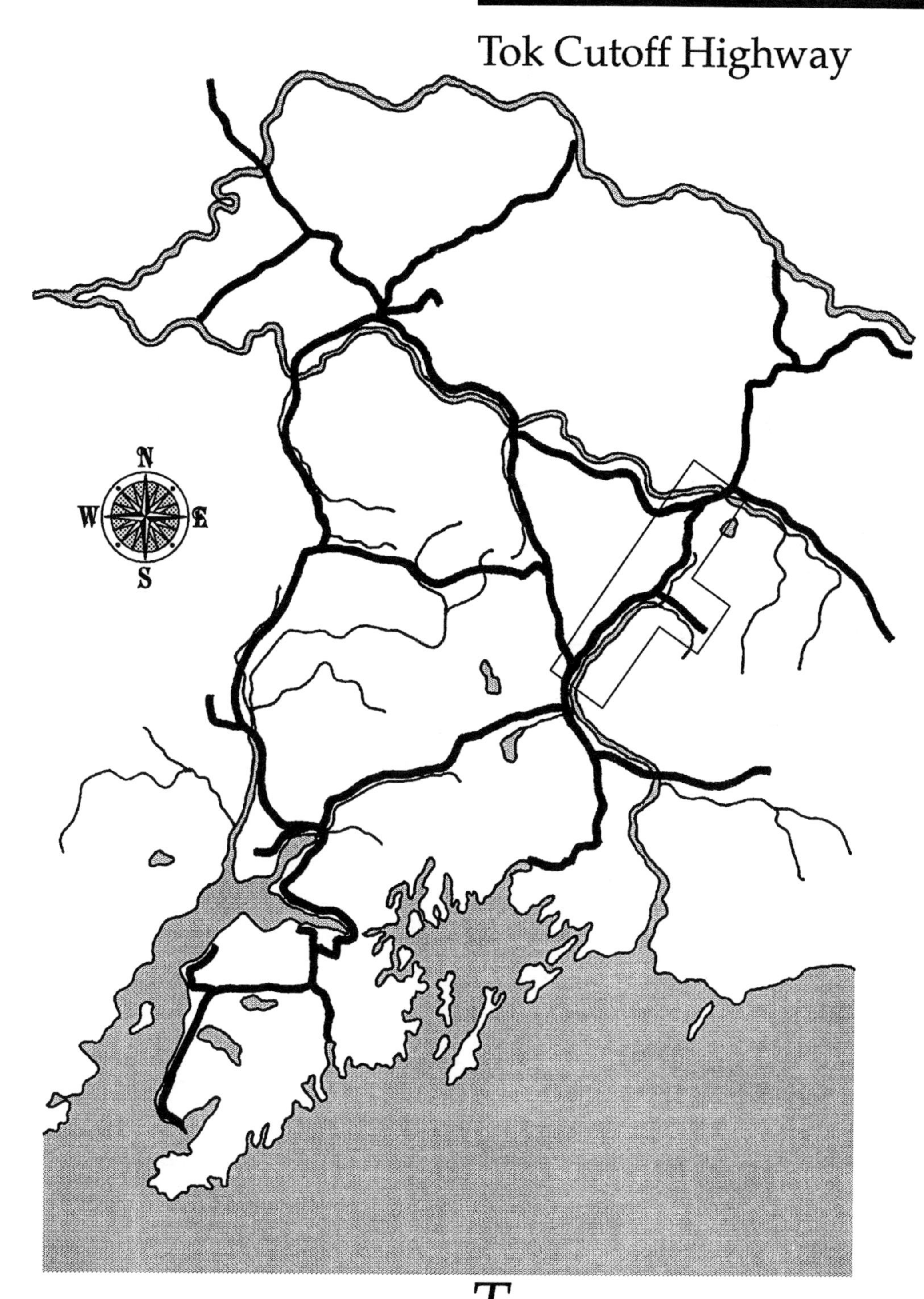

The Tok Cutoff Highway begins in Gakona Junction at Milepost 128.6 of the Richardson Highway and ends in Tok at mile 1314.2 of the Alaska Highway. This road initially was an extension of the Glenn Highway. It runs from southwest to northeast, and serves as a shortcut between the Alaska and Richardson Highways.

CHAPTER 12

Tok Cutoff Highway

The Tok Cutoff Highway parallels two large rivers, Tok and Slana, and a third major drainage, the Copper River. The road also provides good access to the region's lakes and streams. Grayling is by far the most abundant sport fish species, but fairly good numbers of lake trout, northern pike, burbot, and Dolly Varden are also present. A few king and red salmon and whitefish may at times be caught. The main fishing season lasts from mid-May to mid-October, when there's no ice.

Important: Please be aware of the current sport fishing rules and regulations for the area covered in this chapter, and abide by them. Remember, they have been applied to protect a fragile resource.

Following are the abbreviations used in this chapter for all the fish species and facility information:

KS - King Salmon
RS - Red Salmon
DV - Dolly Varden
LT - Lake Trout
RT - Rainbow Trout
GR - Grayling
WF - Whitefish
NP - Northern Pike
BB- Burbot

P - Parking
LP - Limited Parking
C - Camping
T - Toilet
BL - Boat Launch

Time of Abundance/Availability Charts

These charts are designed to show the reader during which time of the year the indicated species are present or available in the most popular fishing streams, lakes, or regions. The charts correlate to when the fish are in their prime for both angling sport and consumption, unless otherwise noted. Species which are closed to sport fishing are also included on the charts just for the purpose of interest but are shown in all stages of maturity.

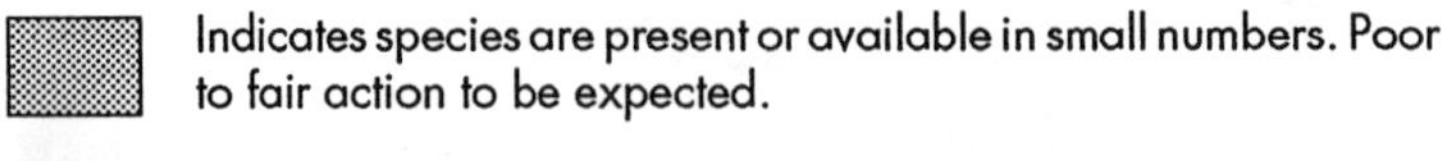
Indicates species are present or available in small numbers. Poor to fair action to be expected.

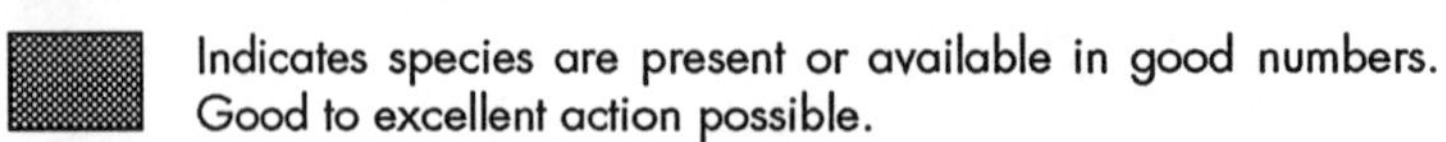
Indicates species are present or available in good numbers. Good to excellent action possible.

Note: The quality of fishing may vary due to certain fluctuations, such as weather conditions, angler experience, number of fish present, or other factors.

QUICK REFERENCE

This section of the chapter was designed to provide a quick view of all the fishing spots in the region, their map location and milepost, species available, facility information, and the page number on which to find detailed access and fishing information for any one watershed.

Note: All fish species shown within parentheses are species that may be present but protected by law and/or are only occasionally seen or hooked by anglers fishing that particular watershed.

TOK CUTOFF HIGHWAY

	WATERSHED	MILE POST	SPECIES
1.	Gakona River Facilities: P	1.9 Page: 96	GR,(KS,RS,WF,BB)
2.	Tulsona Creek Facilities: P	15.0-17.9 Page: 96	GR
3.	Gravel Pit Lake Facilities: P	30.0 Page: 96	GR
4.	Sinona Creek Facilities: LP	34.6 Page: 96	DV,GR,(KS,RS)
5.	Chistochina River Facilities: LP	35.4 Page: 96	GR,(KS,RS,WF,BB)
6.	Indian River Facilities: P	43.9 Page: 97	GR,(KS,RS,WF)
7.	Slana River Facilities: P	59.3 Page: 97	GR,WF,(KS,RS,DV,BB)
8.	Rufus Creek Facilities: LP	59.3 Page: 97	DV,GR
9.	Rock (Kettle) Lake Facilities: P	59.3 Page: 97	RT,GR
10.	Long Lake Facilities: LP	59.3 Page: 97	GR,BB
11.	Little Twin Lakes Facilities: LP (trail)	59.3 Page: 97	LT,GR,BB
12.	Big Twin Lakes Facilities: P	59.3 Page: 98	GR,BB
13.	Jack Lake Facilities: LP (trail)	59.3 Page: 98	LT,GR,BB
14.	Chalk Creek Facilities: LP	59.3 Page: 98	GR

15. Jack Creek 59.3 GR
Facilities: P Page: 98

16. Ahtell Creek 60.8 GR,(KS)
Facilities: P Page: 99

17. Porcupine Creek 64.2 GR
Facilities: P Page: 99

18. Slana River 65.0-74.4 GR,WF,(KS, RS,DV,BB)
Facilities: P Page: 99

19. Slana Slough 74.6-77.1 GR,(KS,RS,DV,WF,BB)
Facilities: P Page: 99

20. Mentasta Lake 81.0 GR,(RS, WF)
Facilities: P Page: 99

21. Mineral Lake 89.5 NP,GR,(DV)
Facilities: LP (trail) Page: 99

22. Little Tok River 91.0-98.0 GR,(DV)
Facilities: P Page: 99

23. Tok Overflow # 1 103.3 GR
Facilities: LP Page: 100

24. Tok River 103.8 GR,(DV)
Facilities: P Page: 100

25. Tok Overflow # 2 104.7 GR
Facilities: P Page: 100

26. Clearwater Creek 109.8 GR
Facilities: P/C/T Page: 100

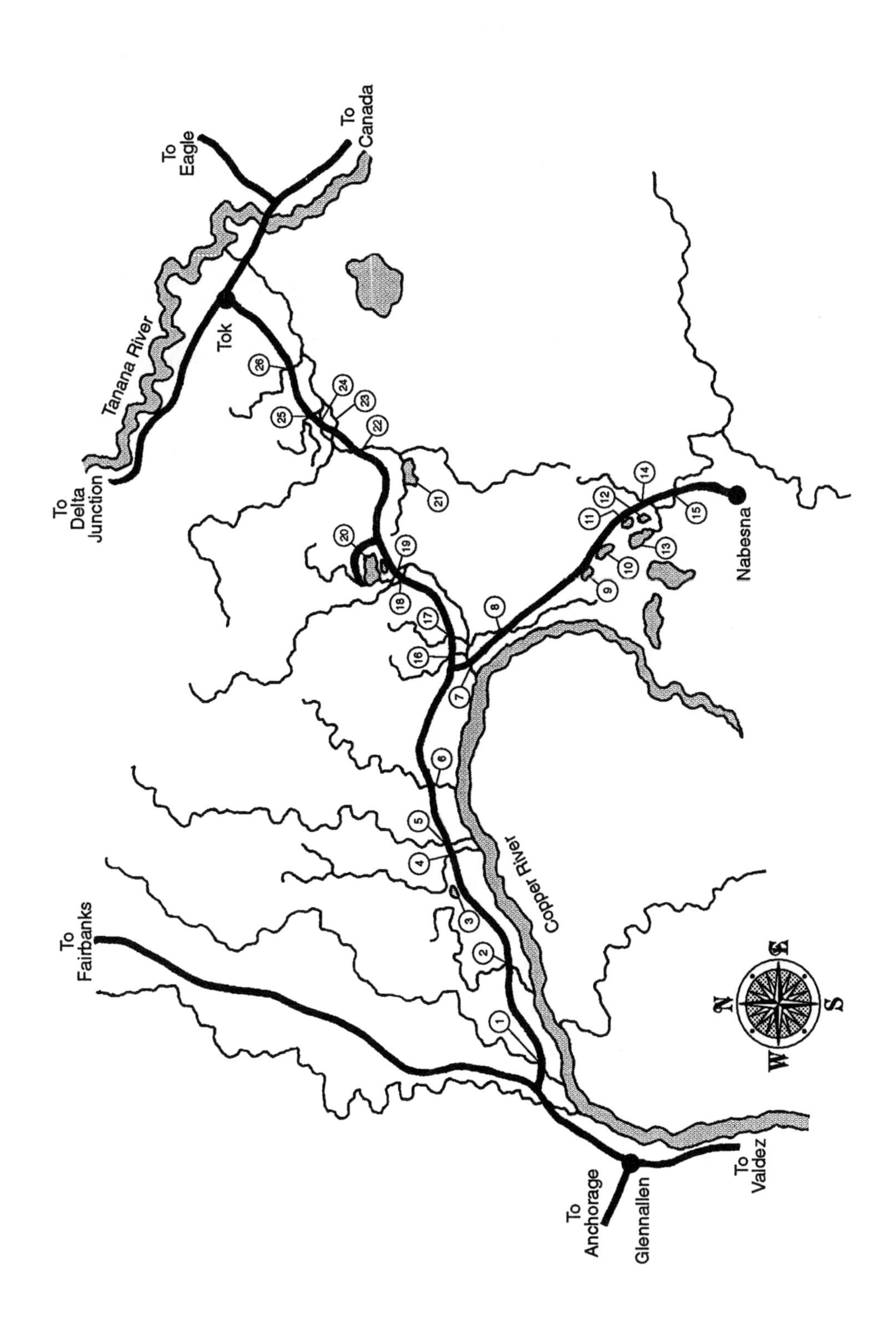
To Canada
To Eagle
Tanana River
Tok
To Delta Junction
Nabesna
Copper River
To Fairbanks
To Anchorage
Glennallen
To Valdez
N
E
S
W
1
2
3
4
5
6
7
8
9
10
11
12
13
14
15
16
17
18
19
20
21
22
23
24
25
26

AREA A: UPPER COPPER RIVER DRAINAGE

Includes all water draining into and surrounding the Copper River.

Time of Abundance:

FISH▽	JAN	FEB	MAR	APR	MAY	JUN	JUL	AUG	SEP	OCT	NOV	DEC
KS												
RS												
DV												
GR												
WF												
BB												

Note: The above chart correlates to all flowing waters of this region. The salmon of this region have travelled great distances from the ocean, and are generally in spawning condition upon entering area waters. The chart reflects the presence of salmon in all stages of the spawning run, except for post-spawning.

1. **GAKONA RIVER**
   Access: The Tok Cutoff Highway crosses the river at MP 1.9.
   Regulations: King salmon fishing prohibited from July 20 through December 31.
   Major Species:
   Grayling / fair / May and October / 7-15 in.

2. **TULSONA CREEK**
   Access: The Tok Cutoff Highway crosses and parallels the stream from MP 15.0 to 17.9.
   Major Species:
   Grayling / good / mid-May through September / 7-15 in.

3. **GRAVEL PIT LAKE**
   Access: From MP 30.0 of the Tok Cutoff Highway. Lake is located just north of the highway.
   Major Species:
   Grayling / fair to good / mid-May through September / 7-14 in.

4. **SINONA CREEK**
   Access: The Tok Cutoff Highway crosses the stream at MP 34.6.
   Regulations: King salmon fishing prohibited from July 20 through December 31.
   Major Species:
   Dolly Varden / fair / mid-July through September / 7-15 in.
   Grayling / fair / mid-May through September / 7-15 in.

5. **CHISTOCHINA RIVER**
   Access: The Tok Cutoff Highway crosses the river at MP 35.4.
   Regulations: King salmon fishing prohibited from July 20 through December 31.
   Major Species:
   Grayling / fair / May and September, October / 7-15 in.

6. **INDIAN RIVER**
Access: The Tok Cutoff Highway crosses the river at MP 43.9.
Regulations: King salmon fishing prohibited.
Major Species:
Grayling / good / June through September / 7-16 in.

AREA B: SLANA - NABESNA RIVER DRAINAGE

Includes all waters draining and surrounding the Slana River and Nabesna River region along the Nabesna Road.

7. **SLANA RIVER**
Access: From MP 59.3 of the Tok Cutoff Highway. Turn southeast on Nabesna Road and drive 1.5 miles to the river crossing.
Regulations: King salmon fishing prohibited from July 20 through December 31.
Major Species:
Grayling / fair / May and September, October / 7-15 in.
Whitefish / fair / late September and October / 10-18 in.

8. **RUFUS CREEK**
Access: From MP 59.3 of the Tok Cutoff Highway. Turn southeast on Nabesna Road and drive 7.1 miles to stream crossing.
Major Species:
Dolly Varden / fair / June through September / 7-12 in.
Grayling / fair / mid-May through June / 7-12 in.

9. **ROCK (KETTLE) LAKE**
Access: From MP 59.3 of the Tok Cutoff Highway. Turn southeast on Nabesna Road and drive 22.1 miles to lake on right.
Major Species:
Rainbow trout / fair / May, July through September / 7-12 in.

10. **LONG LAKE**
Access: From MP 59.3 of the Tok Cutoff Highway. Turn southeast on Nabesna Road and drive 23.2 miles to lake on right.
Major Species:
Grayling / fair to good / mid-May through September / 7-14 in.
Burbot / fair / March through December / 2-4 lbs.

11. **LITTLE TWIN LAKES**
Access: From MP 59.3 of the Tok Cutoff Highway. Turn southeast on Nabesna Road and drive 27.9 miles. Lake is located 0.3 miles south of road by trail.
Major Species:
Lake trout / fair / May, June, and September, October / 2-4 lbs.
Grayling / fair to good / mid-May through September / 7-15 in.
Burbot / fair / March through December / 2-4 lbs.

12. BIG TWIN LAKES

Access: From MP 59.3 of the Tok Cutoff Highway. Turn southeast on Nabesna Road and drive 28.1 miles to lake on right.

Major Species:

Grayling / fair to good / mid-May through September / 7-15 in.
Burbot / fair / March through December / 2-4 lbs.

13. JACK LAKE

Access: From MP 59.3 of the Tok Cutoff Highway. Turn southeast on Nabesna Road and drive 29.0 miles. Park and find old cat trail leading due south about 1.0 mile to lake.

Major Species:

Lake trout / fair / May, June, September, October / 2-5 lbs.
Grayling / fair to good / mid-May through September / 7-15 in.
Burbot / fair / March through December / 2-4 lbs.

14. CHALK CREEK

Access: From MP 59.3 of the Tok Cutoff Highway. Turn southeast on Nabesna Road and drive 32.2 miles to stream crossing.

Major Species:

Grayling / fair / June through September / 7-12 in.

15. JACK CREEK

Access: From MP 59.3 of the Tok Cutoff Highway. Turn southeast on Nabesna Road and drive 35.9 miles to the stream crossing.

Major Species:

Grayling / fair to good / June through September / 7-15 in.

AREA C: SLANA - TOK RIVER DRAINAGE

Includes all waters draining and surrounding the Slana River and Tok River region.

Time of Abundance:

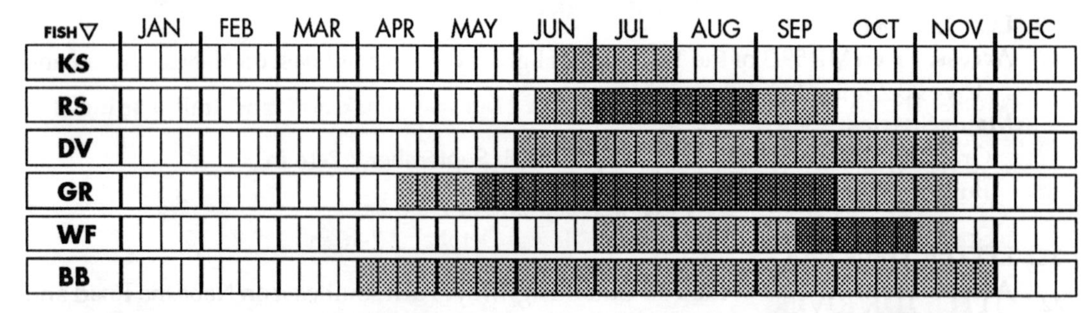

Note: The above chart correlates to all flowing waters of this region. The salmon of this region, because they've travelled a great distance from the ocean, are generally in spawning condition upon entering these waters. The chart above reflects the presence of salmon in all stages of the spawning run, except for post-spawning.

16. AHTELL CREEK
Access: The Tok Cutoff Highway crosses the stream at MP 60.8.
Regulations: King salmon fishing prohibited.
Major Species:
Grayling / fair to good / June through September / 7-15 in.

17. PORCUPINE CREEK
Access: The Tok Cutoff Highway crosses the stream at MP 64.2.
Major Species:
Grayling / poor to fair / June through September / 7-12 in.

18. SLANA RIVER
Access: The Tok Cutoff Highway parallels and crosses the river from MP 65.0 to 74.4.
Regulations: King salmon fishing prohibited from July 20 through December 31.
Major Species:
Grayling / fair / May and September, October / 7-15 in.
Whitefish / fair / late September and October / 10-18 in.

19. SLANA SLOUGH
Access: The Tok Cutoff Highway crosses or parallels various channels and slough of the Slana River from MP 74.6 to 77.1.
Regulations: King salmon fishing prohibited from July 20 through December 31.
Major Species:
Grayling / fair / May and September / 7-15 in.

20. MENTASTA LAKE
Access: From MP 81.0 of the Tok Cutoff Highway. Turn northwest onto paved road and drive 0.2 miles. Turn left on gravel road leading 7.1 miles to and through Mentasta Village ending at the bridge over Fish Creek. The inlet of the lake is located on the left side.
Regulations: Salmon fishing is prohibited in Fish Creek.
Major Species:
Grayling / fair to good / June through September / 7-15 in.

21. MINERAL LAKE
Access: From MP 89.9 of the Tok Cutoff Highway. Park and find trail leading due southeast 0.5 miles to the lake outlet.
Major Species:
Northern Pike / fair / June through September / 2-6 lbs.
Grayling / good to excellent / mid-May to October / 7-16 in

22. LITTLE TOK RIVER
Access: The Tok Cutoff Highway parallels and crosses the river from MP 91.0 to 98.0.
Major Species:
Grayling / good to excellent / June through September / 7-16 in.

23. TOK OVERFLOW # 1
Access: The Tok Cutoff Highway crosses the stream at MP 103.3.
Major Species:
Grayling / fair / mid-May through September / 7-14 in.

24. TOK RIVER
Access: The Tok Cutoff Highway crosses the river at MP 103.8.
Major Species:
Grayling / poor to fair / May and October / 7-16 in.

25. TOK OVERFLOW # 2
Access: The Tok Cutoff Highway crosses the stream at MP 104.7.
Major Species:
Grayling / fair / mid-May through September / 7-14 in.

26. CLEARWATER CREEK
Access: The Tok Cutoff Highway crosses the stream at MP 109.8.
Major Species:
Grayling / fair / May and September / 7-14 in.

CHAPTER 13

Richardson Highway

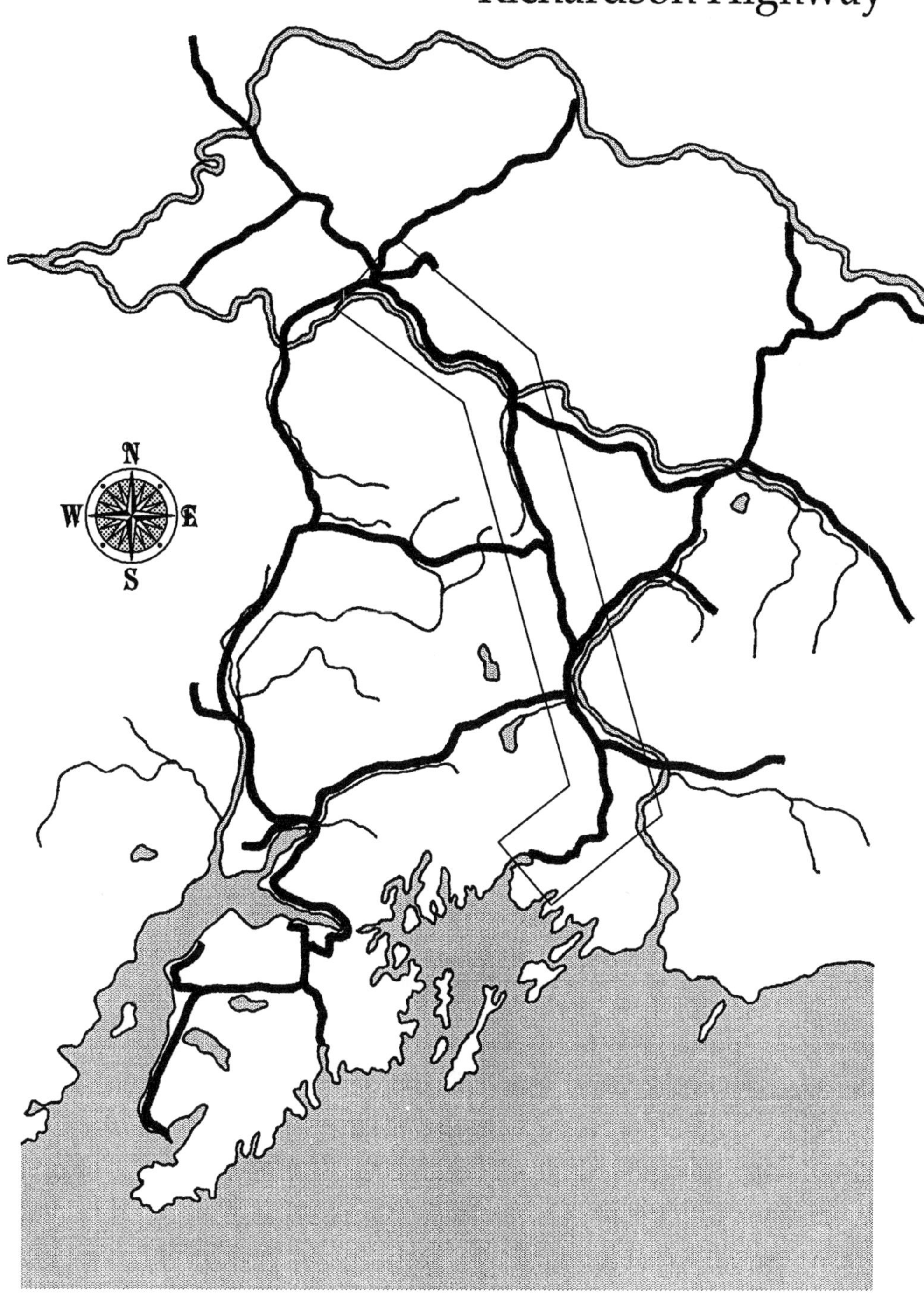

The Richardson Highway begins in the coastal community of Valdez, on northern Prince William Sound, and ends in the interior city of Fairbanks. The highway serves as a link between Glenn, Tok Cutoff, Denali, and Alaska Highways, and also connects to the Steese and Parks highways.

CHAPTER 13

Richardson Highway

The Richardson Highway parallels two major glacial rivers, the Copper and Tanana, and provides excellent access to lakes, rivers, and streams of the region as well as to saltwater fishing out of Valdez.

This region is rich in sport fishing opportunities. Highway anglers may find access to king, red, pink, chum, and silver salmon, Dolly Varden, lake trout, rainbow trout, grayling, and burbot, as well as lesser numbers of halibut, bottomfish, and Arctic char. A few sheefish, steelhead trout, whitefish, and northern pike are also present in certain areas. The main fishing season generally runs from mid-May to mid-October when area waters are open.

Important: Please be aware of the current sport fishing rules and regulations for the area covered in this chapter, and abide by them. Remember, they have been applied to protect a fragile resource.

Following are the abbreviations used in this chapter for all the fish species and facility information:

KS - King Salmon
RS - Red Salmon
PS - Pink Salmon
CS - Chum Salmon
SS - Silver Salmon
KO - Kokanee

SH - Steelhead Trout
DV - Dolly Varden
AC - Arctic Char
LT - Lake Trout
RT - Rainbow Trout
SF - Sheefish

GR - Grayling
WF - Whitefish
NP - Northern Pike
BB - Burbot
HB - Halibut
BF - Bottomfish

P - Parking
LP - Limited Parking

C - Camping
T - Toilet

BL - Boat Launching

Time of Abundance/Availability Charts

These charts are designed to show the reader during which time of the year the indicated species are present or available in the most popular fishing streams, lakes, or regions. The charts correlate to when the fish are in their prime for both angling sport and consumption, unless otherwise noted. Species which are closed to sport fishing are also included on the charts just for the purpose of interest but are shown in all stages of maturity.

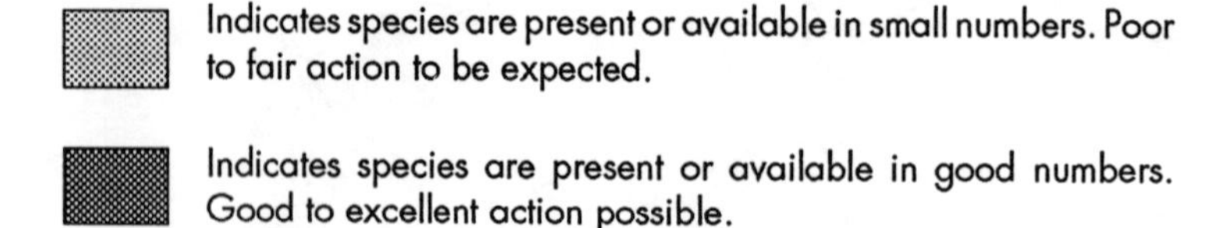
Indicates species are present or available in small numbers. Poor to fair action to be expected.
Indicates species are present or available in good numbers. Good to excellent action possible.

Note: The quality of fishing may vary due to certain fluctuations, such as weather conditions, angler experience, number of fish present, or other factors.

QUICK REFERENCE

This section of the chapter was designed to provide a quick view of all the fishing spots in the region, their map location and milepost, species available, facility information, and the page number on which to find detailed information for any one watershed.

Note: Shown in parentheses are fish species that may be present but protected by law, and/or are only occasionally seen or hooked by anglers fishing that particular watershed.

RICHARDSON HIGHWAY

	WATERSHED	MILE POST	SPECIES
1.	Valdez Harbor Facilities: P/BL	0.0 (Valdez) Page: 111, 112	PS,CS,SS,DV,BF,(KS,RS,HB)
2.	Robe River Facilities: LP	2.7 Page: 112	RS,PS,SS,DV,(KS,CS)
3.	Allison Point Facilities: P/T	2.8 Page: 112, 113	PS,CS,SS,DV,BF,(KS,RS)
4.	Lowe River Facilities: P	4.0-16.5 Page: 113	DV,(KS,RS,PS,CS,SS)
5.	Thompson Lake Facilities: P	23.5 Page: 113	GR
6.	Blueberry Lake Facilities: P/C/T	24.1 Page: 113	RT,GR
7.	Worthington Lake Facilities: P (trail)	27.3 Page: 113	RT
8.	Tiekel River Facilities: P	46.8-61.4 Page: 113	DV
9.	Little Tonsina River Facilities: P/C/T	65.0/68.2 Page: 114	SS,DV,GR,(KS,RS,RT,WF)
10.	Little Tonsina River Facilities: P	74.5 Page: 114	RS,SS,DV,GR,(KS,RT,WF)
11.	Tonsina River Facilities: LP	79.2 Page: 114	DV,GR,(KS,RS,SS,RT,WF)
12.	Squirrel Creek Pit Facilities: P/C/T	79.4 Page: 114	RT,GR

CHAPTER 13

Richardson Highway

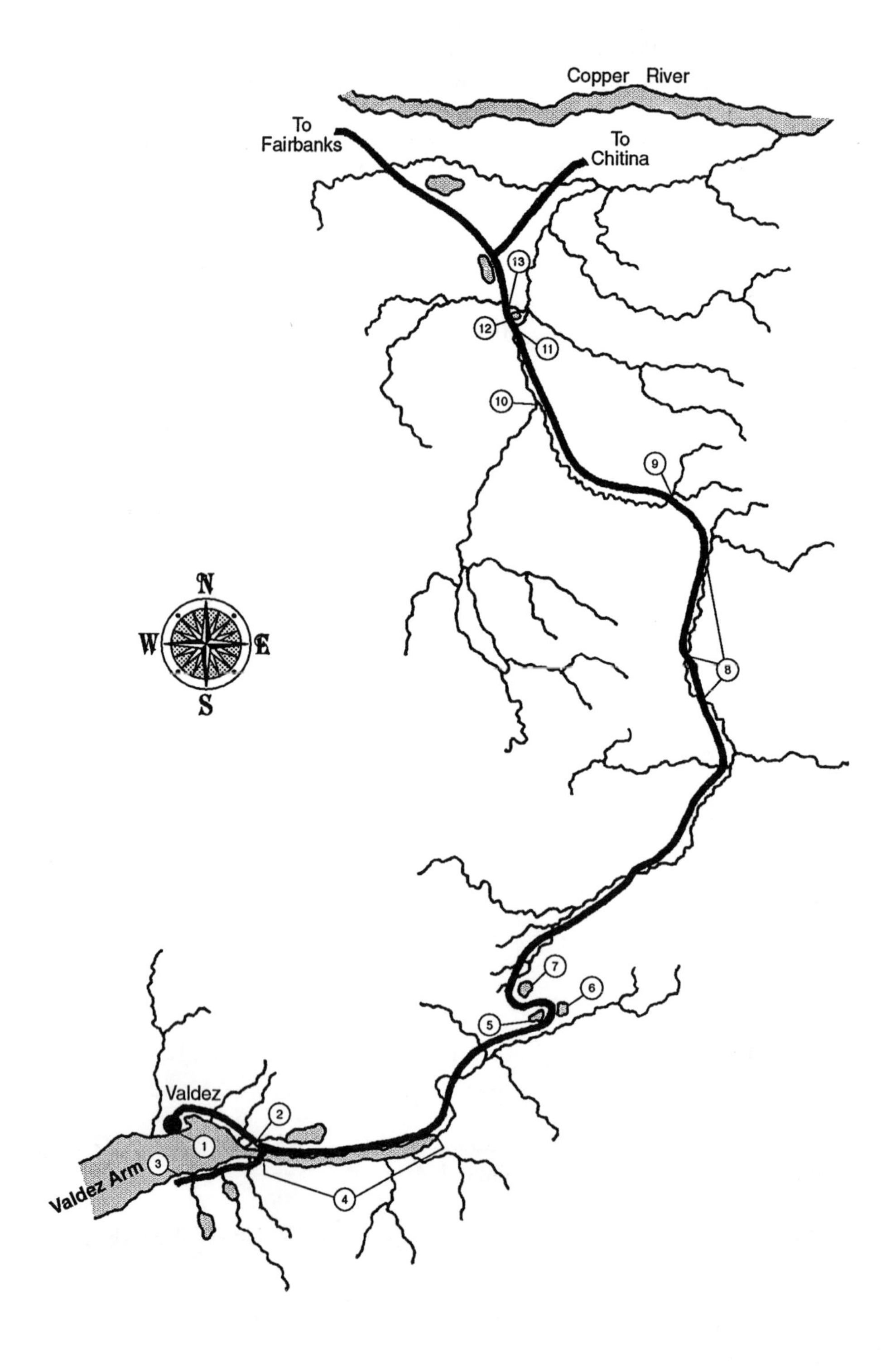

Richardson Highway

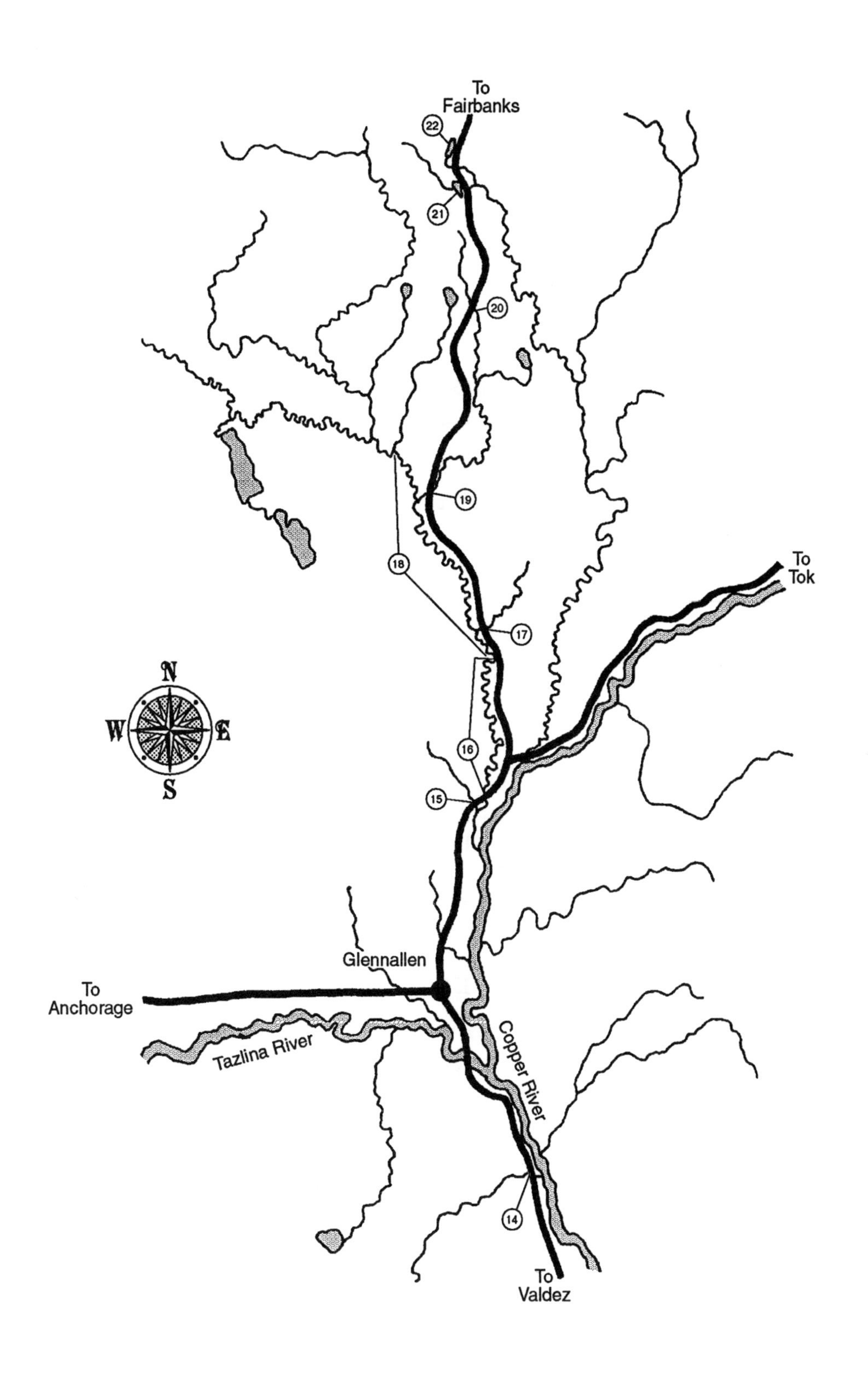

Location	Mile / Page	Species
13. Squirrel Creek Facilities: P/C/T	79.4 Page: 115	DV,GR,(KS,RS,SS)
14. Klutina River Facilities: P/C/T/BL	101.1/100.4 Page: 115	KS,RS,SS,DV,GR,(SH,RT,WF)
15. Bear Creek Facilities: P	125.9 Page: 115	GR
16. Gulkana River Facilities: P/C/T	126.9-129.3 Page: 116	KS,RS,SH,RT,GR,(WF,BB)
17. Poplar Grove Creek Facilities: P	138.3 Page: 116	GR
18. Gulkana River Facilities: P/C/T/BL	139.6-147.7 Page: 116, 117	KS,RS,SH,RT,GR,(WF,BB)
19. Sourdough Creek Facilities: P/C/T	147.7 Page: 117	GR
20. Haggard Creek Facilities: LP	161.0 Page: 117	GR
21. June Lake Facilities: P (trail)	166.5 Page: 117	GR
22. Meiers Lake Facilities: P	70.8 Page: 117	GR
23. Dick Lake Facilities: P	173.3 Page: 117, 118	GR
24. Paxson Lake Facilities: P/C/T/BL	175.0-182.5 Page: 118	RS,LT,RT,GR,BB,(KS,WF)
25. E. Fork Gulkana River Facilities: P	186.5-191.0 Page: 118	GR,(RS,RT,WF)
26. Fish Creek Facilities: P	190.5 Page: 118	GR,(RS,RT)
27. Summit Lake Facilities: P	191.0-196.0 Page: 118, 119	RS,LT,RT,GR,BB,(WF)
28. Gunn Creek Facilities: P	196.8 Page: 119	RS,GR,(RT, WF)

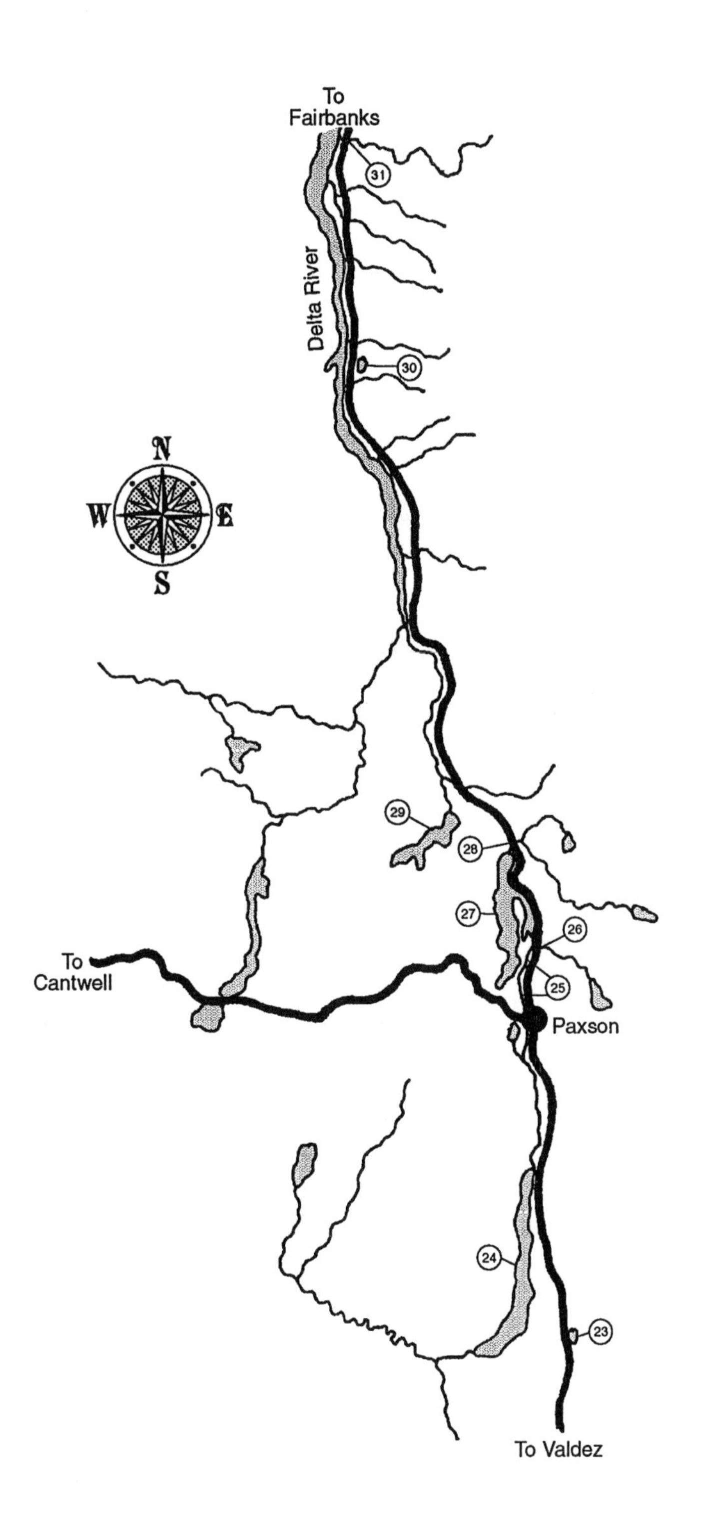
To
Fairbanks
31
Delta River
30
N
W
E
S
29
28
27
26
To
Cantwell
25
Paxson
24
23
To Valdez

29. Fielding Lake Facilities: P	200.5 Page: 119	LT,GR,BB,(WF)
30. Rapids Lake Facilities: P (trail)	225.4 Page: 119	RT
31. Donnelly Creek Facilities: P/C/T	238.0 Page: 120	GR
32. Coal Mine # 5 Lake Facilities: P (trail)	242.0 Page: 120	RT,LT
33. Backdown Lake Facilities: P (trail)	242.0 Page: 120	AC,RT
34. Last Lake Facilities: P (trail)	242.0 Page: 120	AC
35. Brodie Lake Facilities: P (trail)	242.0 Page: 120	AC,GR
36. Paul's Lake Facilities: LP	242.0 Page: 120	LT,GR
37. Rangeview Lake Facilities: LP	242.0 Page: 120	AC,GR
38. Dick's Lake Facilities: LP (trail)	242.0 Page: 121	AC
39. Ken's Lake Facilities: LP	242.0 Page: 121	AC,RT
40. Weasel Lake Facilities: P (trail)	242.8 Page: 121	KS,AC,RT
41. Donnelly Lake Facilities: P (trail)	244.6 Page: 121	KS,SS,RT
42. Ghost Lake Facilities: P (trail)	257.6 Page: 121	LT,RT
43. Nickel Lake Facilities: P	257.6 Page: 121, 122	RT,LT,GR
44. "J" Lake Facilities: P	257.6 Page: 122	GR

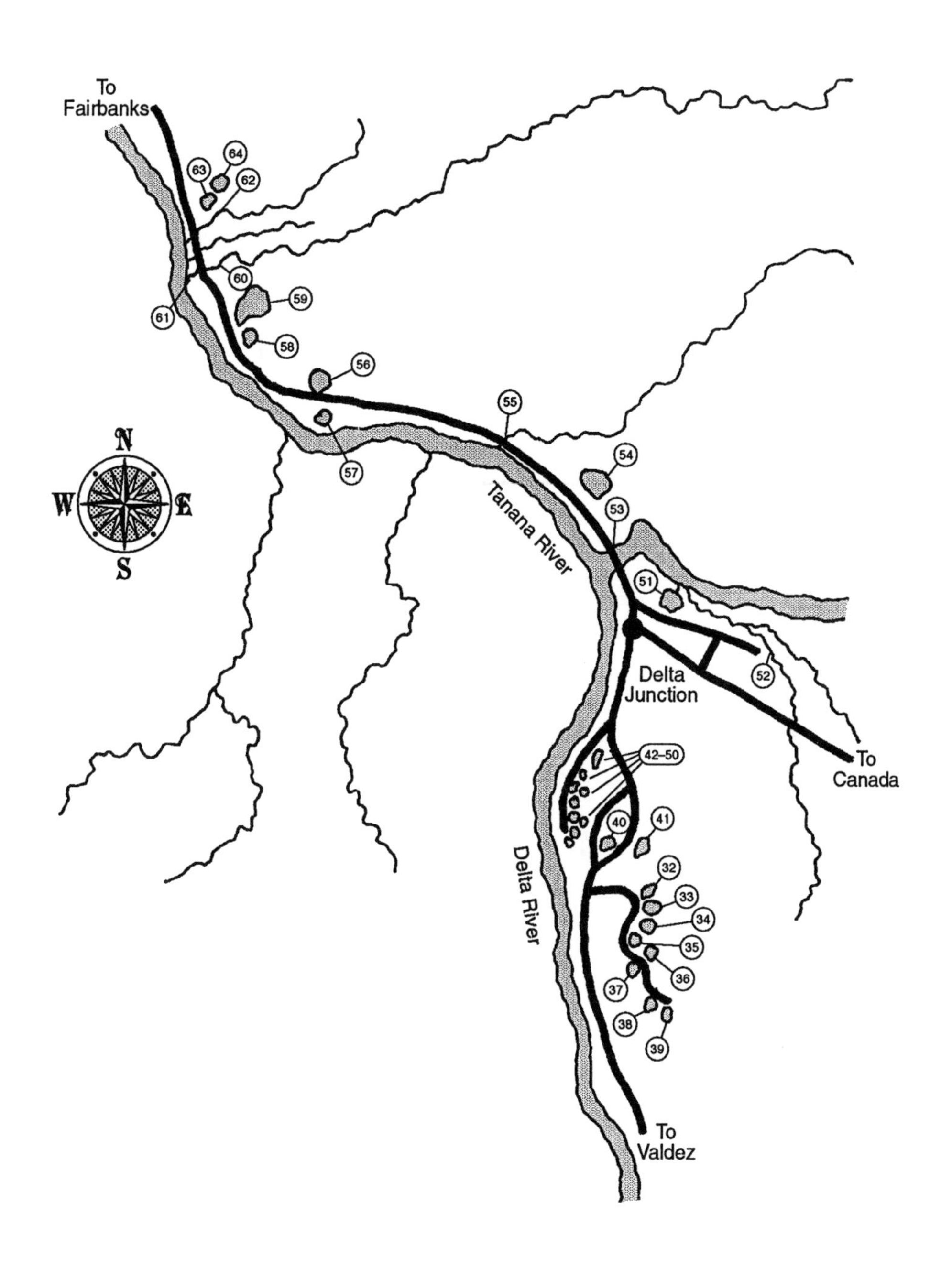
To
Fairbanks
64
63
62
60
59
61
58
56
55
57
N
W
E
S
54
53
Tanana River
51
Delta
Junction
52
To
Canada
42–50
40
41
32
33
34
35
36
37
38
39
Delta River
To
Valdez

45. Chet Lake Facilities: P	257.6 Page: 122	LT,RT,GR
46. Bolio Lake Facilities: P	257.6 Page: 122	KS,RT,LT,GR
47. Mark Lake Facilities: P	257.6 Page: 122	RT
48. North Twin Lake Facilities: P	257.6 Page: 122	KS,RT
49. South Twin Lake Facilities: P	257.6 Page: 123	KS,RT
50. No Mercy Lake Facilities: P (trail)	257.6 Page: 123	RT
51. Clearwater Lake Facilities: P/BL	268.2 Page: 123	CS,SS,GR,BB,(NP,WP)
52. Delta Clearwater River Facilities: P/C/T/BL	268.2 Page: 123, 124	CS,SS,GR,WF,(KS,BB,NP)
53. Tanana River Facilities: P/BL	275.3 Page: 124	CS,GR,BB,(KS,SS,NP,WF)
54. Quartz Lake Facilities: P/C/T/BL	277.8 Page: 124	SS,RT
55. Shaw Creek Facilities: P/BL	286.7 Page: 124	CS,SS,GR,BB,(KS,NP,WP)
56. Birch Lake Facilities: P	306.0 Page: 125	SS,RT
57. Lost Lake Facilities: LP/BL	306.2 Page: 125	SS,RT
58. Harding Lake Facilities: P/C/T/BL	321.6 Page: 125	RS,SF,AC,RT,(LT,NP,BB)
59. Little Harding Lake Facilities: P (trail)	319.5 Page: 125	AC,RT
60. Salcha River Facilities: P/C/T/BL	324.1 Page: 125, 126	KS,CS,GR,(SS,NP,WF,BB)

61. Salcha River Facilities: P (trail)	324.8 Pages: 126, 127	KS,CS,SS,NP,GR,WF,BB,(SF)
62. Little Salcha River Facilities: LP	327.8 Page: 127	GR,(KS,CS,NP)
63. Johnson Road # 1 Lake Facilities:	330.4 Page: 127	SS,RT,GR
64. Johnson Road #2 Lake Facilities: P	330.4 Page: 127	GR

AREA A: PORT VALDEZ DRAINAGE

Includes all water drainage into Port Valdez

Time of Abundance:

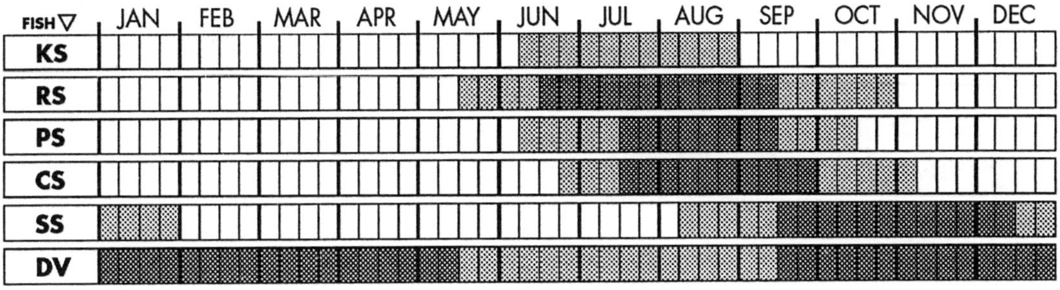

FISH▽	JAN	FEB	MAR	APR	MAY	JUN	JUL	AUG	SEP	OCT	NOV	DEC
KS												
RS												
PS												
CS												
SS												
DV												

Note: With the exception of Robe River, all waters draining into Port Valdez are closed to salmon fishing. The above chart depicts salmon and char of all stages of the life cycle, from ocean fresh to spawning condition.

1. VALDEZ HARBOR

Access: The Valdez Harbor is located on the northeast side of Port Valdez in front of the town of Valdez, at the beginning of the Richardson Highway.

Regulations: Salmon fishing is prohibited in all streams draining into the Valdez Harbor area.

Time of Abundance:

FISH▽	JAN	FEB	MAR	APR	MAY	JUN	JUL	AUG	SEP	OCT	NOV	DEC
KS												
RS												
PS												
CS												
SS												
DV												
HB												
BF												

Major Species:

Pink salmon / good to excellent / 2-4 lbs.,max. 7 lbs. / spoons and spinners.
Chum salmon / poor to fair / 6-12 lbs., max. 18 lbs. / spoons and spinners
Silver salmon / good to excellent / 7-12 lbs., max 18 lbs./ spoons, spinners, herring bait.
Dolly Varden / poor to fair / 8-15 in., max. 7 lbs. / spoons and spinners, herring bait.
Bottomfish / good / species include flounder, sole, cod, greenling, and sablefish / herring bait, spoons, jigs.

2. ROBE RIVER

Access: The Richardson Highway crosses the stream at MP 2.7.
Regulations: Flyfishing-only area. Check the sport fishing regulations for details.
Major Species:

Red salmon / poor to fair / mid- and late June / 4-6 lbs.
Pink salmon / poor to fair / late July, early August / 2-4 lbs.
Silver salmon / good / late September, early October / 6-12 lbs.
Dolly Varden / good / October and November / 8-20 in.

3. ALLISON POINT / SOLOMON GULCH CREEK MARINE

Access: From MP 2.8 of the Richardson Highway. Turn southwest on Dayville Road and drive about 5 miles to the Solomon Gulch Creek and Allison Point area.
Regulations: Salmon fishing is prohibited in Solomon Gulch Creek. Check the sport fishing regulations for details on open areas.
Time of Abundance:

FISH▽	JAN	FEB	MAR	APR	MAY	JUN	JUL	AUG	SEP	OCT	NOV	DEC
KS												
RS												
PS												
CS												
SS												
DV												
BF												

Major Species:
Pink salmon / excellent / 2-4 lbs., max. 6 lbs. / spoons and spinners, snag hooks.
Chum salmon / fair to good / 6-12 lbs., max. 18 lbs. / spoons and spinners, snag hooks.
Silver salmon / good / 6-12 lbs., max. 18 lbs. / spoons and spinners, herring bait, snag hooks.
Dolly Varden / poor to fair / 8-15 in., max. 7 lbs. / spoons and spinners, herring bait.
Bottomfish / poor to fair / species include flounder, sole, cod, sablefish, and greenling/ herring bait, spoons, jigs.

4. **LOWE RIVER**
Access: The Richardson Highway parallels the river from MP 4.0 to 16.5 with numerous access points.
Regulations: Salmon fishing prohibited.
Major Species:
Dolly Varden / fair / May, and October, November / 8-20 in.

5. **THOMPSON LAKE**
Access: From MP 23.5 of the Richardson Highway. Turn onto a gravel road and drive a short distance to the lake.
Major Species:
Grayling / good / June through September / 8-12 in.

6. **BLUEBERRY LAKE**
Access: From MP 24.1 of the Richardson Highway. Turn onto paved road and drive 0.8 miles to the lake.
Major Species:
Rainbow trout / good / May through October / 8-20 in.
Grayling / good / June through September / 8-12 in.

7. **WORTHINGTON LAKE**
Access: From MP 27.3 of the Richardson Highway. Park and hike 0.25 miles due southeast to the lake.
Major Species:
Rainbow trout / good / May through October / 8-20 in.

AREA B: TIEKEL - TONSINA RIVER DRAINAGE

Includes all waters of the Tiekel River and Tonsina River drainage.

8. **TIEKEL RIVER**
Access: The Richardson Highway parallels the Tiekel River between MP 46.8 and 61.4, crossing the river in two locations.
Major Species:
Dolly Varden / fair / mid-June to mid-September / 7-10 in.

9. LITTLE TONSINA RIVER

Access: The Richardson Highway crosses the Little Tonsina River at MP 65.0. Also, access from MP 68.2 by gravel road. Turn southwest onto gravel road leading 0.5 miles to small parking area. The river is located just beyond the hill.

Regulations: King salmon fishing prohibited.

Major Species:

Silver salmon / fair / mid- and late September / 5-12 lbs.
Dolly Varden / fair / July through mid-October / 8-15 in.
Grayling / fair to good / mid-May through September / 8-15 in.

10. LITTLE TONSINA RIVER / TONSINA RIVER CONFLUENCE

Access: From MP 74.5 of the Richardson Highway. Turn west onto gravel road and drive short distance to a "Y." Take the road on the right, which parallels the river from here. It's 0.3 miles to the confluence.

Regulations: King salmon fishing prohibited.

Time of Abundance:

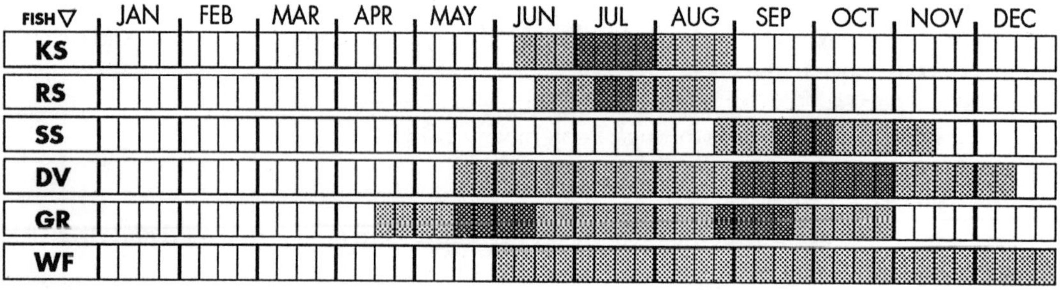

FISH▽	JAN	FEB	MAR	APR	MAY	JUN	JUL	AUG	SEP	OCT	NOV	DEC
KS												
RS												
SS												
DV												
GR												
WF												

Major Species:

Red salmon / poor to fair / 3-6 lbs., max. 10 lbs. / spoons and spinners, streamer flies.
Silver salmon / fair to good / 5-10 lbs., max 15 lbs. / spinners and salmon egg clusters.
Dolly Varden / fair / 8-15 in., max 3 lbs. / spinners and salmon egg clusters.
Grayling / fair to good / 8-15 in., max. 18 in. / spinners and flies.

11. TONSINA RIVER

Access: The Richardson Highway crosses the river at MP 79.2.

Regulations: King salmon fishing prohibited from July 20 through December 31.

Major Species:

Dolly Varden / poor to fair / June through October / 8-15 in.
Grayling / poor to fair / May and September / 8-15 in.

12. SQUIRREL CREEK PIT

Access: From MP 79.4 of the Richardson Highway. Turn east onto gravel road at the Squirrel Creek Campground and drive a short distance to lake on right.

Major Species:

Rainbow trout / fair to good / May, September, October / 8-15 in.
Grayling / good / May through September / 8-12 in.

13. SQUIRREL CREEK

Access: The Richardson Highway crosses the stream at MP 79.4. The confluence of Squirrel Creek and the Tonsina River can be reached through Squirrel Creek Campground.

Major Species:

Dolly Varden / poor to fair / September, October / 7-14 in.
Grayling / poor to fair / mid-May to mid-September / 7-14 in.

AREA C: MIDDLE COPPER RIVER DRAINAGE

Includes all waters draining into and surrounding the middle region of the Copper River.

14. KLUTINA RIVER

Access: The Richardson Highway crosses the river at MP 101.1. To reach the lower river and campgrounds, turn onto Loop Road at MP 100.4 heading east and drive 0.4 miles to the river.

Regulations: King salmon fishing prohibited from August 11 through December 31.

Time of Abundance:

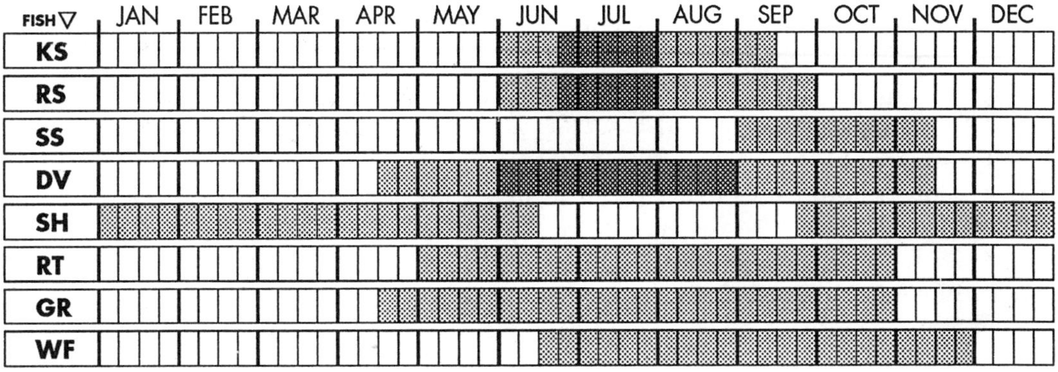

FISH▽	JAN	FEB	MAR	APR	MAY	JUN	JUL	AUG	SEP	OCT	NOV	DEC
KS												
RS												
SS												
DV												
SH												
RT												
GR												
WF												

Major Species:

King salmon / fair from shore, good from boat / 20-45 lbs., max. 75 lbs. / salmon egg clusters, attractor lures.
Red salmon / good to excellent / 4-8 lbs., max. 12 lbs. / egg imitation and streamer flies.
Silver salmon / poor to fair / 6-10 lbs., max. 15 lbs. / salmon egg clusters, spinners, attractor lures.
Dolly Varden / fair / 8-15 in., max. 5 lbs. / salmon egg clusters, attractor lures.
Grayling / poor to fair / 8-12 in., max. 18 in. / salmon egg clusters, spinners, attractor lures.

15. BEAR CREEK

Access: The Richardson Highway crosses the stream at MP 125.9.

Major Species:

Grayling / fair / early May to early June / 8-14 in.

16. GULKANA RIVER

Access: The Richardson Highway crosses the river at MP 126.9. Also, the river is accessible by trails and gravel roads due west from the highway at MP 129.1 and 129.3.

Regulations: King salmon fishing prohibited from August 1 through December 31. Flyfishing-only from the highway bridge downstream from June 1 through July 31. Catch-and-release only for rainbow/steelhead trout.

Time of Abundance:

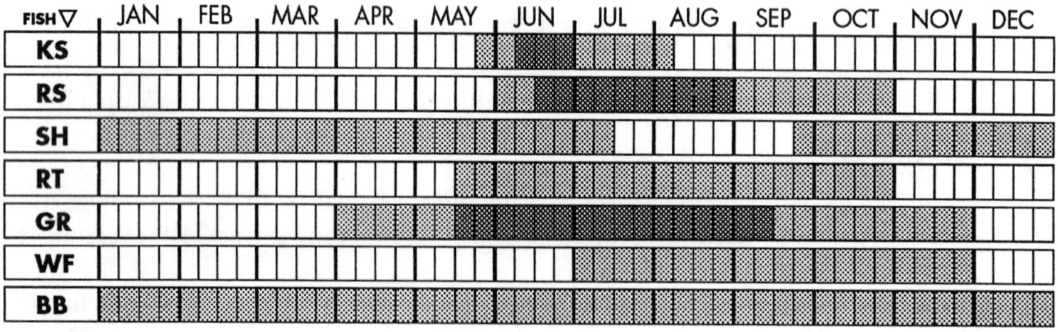

FISH▽	JAN	FEB	MAR	APR	MAY	JUN	JUL	AUG	SEP	OCT	NOV	DEC
KS												
RS												
SH												
RT												
GR												
WF												
BB												

Major Species:

King salmon / fair to good / 15-35 lbs., max. 60 lbs. / salmon egg clusters, attractor lures, egg imitation flies.

Red salmon / fair to good / 4-8 lbs., max 14 lbs. . egg imitation and streamer flies.

Steelhead trout / poor to fair / 5-8 lbs., max 12 lbs. / egg imitation and streamer flies, attractor lures.

Rainbow trout / poor to fair / 8-20 in., max. 6 lbs. / egg imitation flies, spinners.

Grayling / good / 7-14 in., max. 18 in. / spinners, dry and wet flies, single salmon eggs.

17. POPLAR GROVE CREEK

Access: The Richardson Highway crosses the stream at MP 138.3.

Major Species:

Grayling / good to excellent / early May to early June / 8-15 in.

18. GULKANA RIVER

Access: Trails leading from the highway due west to the river are found at MP 139.6, 141.4, and 146.5. Gravel roads leading about 0.25 to 0.50 miles to the river are found at MP 136.7 and 147.6.

Regulations: King salmon fishing prohibited from August 1 through December 31. Catch-and-release only for rainbow/steelhead trout.

Time of Abundance:

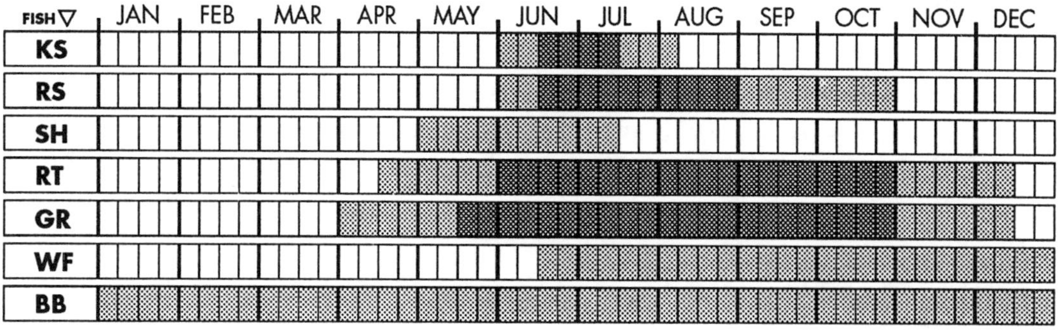

FISH▽	JAN	FEB	MAR	APR	MAY	JUN	JUL	AUG	SEP	OCT	NOV	DEC
KS												
RS												
SH												
RT												
GR												
WF												
BB												

Major Species:

King salmon / fair to good / 15-35 lbs., max. 60 lbs. / salmon egg clusters, attractor lures.
Red salmon / fair to good / 4-8 lbs., max 14 lbs. / egg imitation and streamer flies.
Steelhead trout / poor to fair / 5-8 lbs., max. 12 lbs. / egg imitation and streamer flies, attractor lures.
Rainbow trout / fair / 8-20 in., max 6 lbs. / egg imitation flies, spinners, corkies.
Grayling / good to excellent / 8-15 in., max. 18 in. / egg imitation, dry, and wet flies, and spinners.

19. SOURDOUGH CREEK

Access: The Richardson Highway crosses the stream at MP 147.7. Turn west into campground and follow trail about 0.25 miles to its confluence with the Gulkana River.
Major Species:
Grayling / good to excellent / early-May to mid-June / 8-17 in.

20. HAGGARD CREEK

Access: The Richardson Highway crosses the stream at MP 161.0.
Major Species:
Grayling / good / mid-May through early June / 7-15 in.

21. JUNE LAKE

Access: From MP 166.5 of the Richardson Highway. Park by road, find trail, and hike 0.25 miles due west to lake.
Major Species:
Grayling / good / late May through September / 7-15 in.

22. MEIER LAKE

Access: From MP 170.8 of the Richardson Highway. The lake is adjacent to the west side of highway.
Major Species:
Grayling / good / late May through September / 7-14 in.

23. DICK LAKE

Access: From MP 173.3 of the Richardson Highway. The lake is east of the highway.

Major Species:
Grayling / good / late May through September / 7-14 in.

24. PAXSON LAKE

Access: From MP 175.0 of the Richardson Highway. Turn at the sign onto a gravel road that runs due west. Drive 1.4 miles to a "Y," and follow sign a short distance to lake or campground. Also, there are numerous pull-offs west of the highway between MP 179.4 and 182.5.

Regulations: King salmon fishing prohibited. Check the sport fishing regulations for details on various restrictions.

Time of Availability:

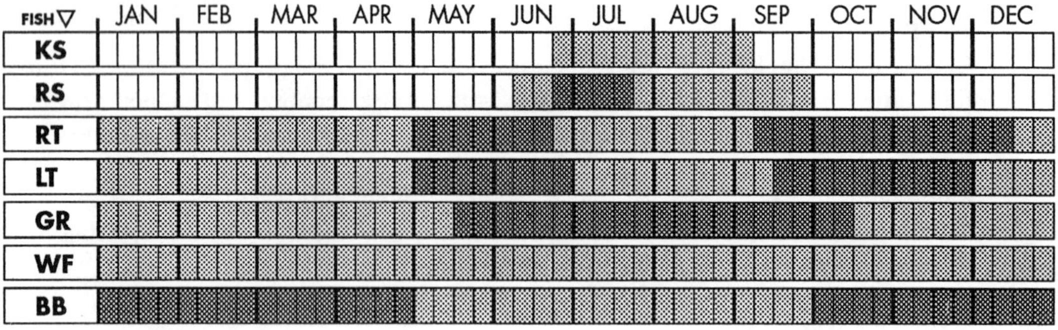

FISH ▽	JAN	FEB	MAR	APR	MAY	JUN	JUL	AUG	SEP	OCT	NOV	DEC
KS												
RS												
RT												
LT												
GR												
WF												
BB												

Major Species:
Red salmon / poor to fair / 4-8 lbs., max. 14 lbs., / spoons and spinners, streamer flies.
Lake trout / fair to good / 2-10 lbs., max 25 lbs. / spoons and spinners, fish bait.
Rainbow trout / fair / 8-20 in., max 6 lbs. / spoons and spinners salmon egg clusters, flies.
Grayling / good to excellent / 7-15 in., max. 20 in. / dry and wet flies, spinners.
Burbot / fair to good / 2-6 lbs., max 20 lbs. / herring smelt, and whitefish bait.

25. EAST FORK GULKANA RIVER

Access: The Richardson Highway parallels the river from MP 186.5 to the outlet of Summit Lake at MP 191.0.

Regulations: Salmon fishing prohibited.

Major Species:
Grayling / fair / mid-May through September / 7-15 in.

26. FISH CREEK

Access: The Richardson Highway crosses the stream at MP 190.5.

Regulations: Salmon fishing prohibited.

Major Species:
Grayling / fair / late May through mid-September / 7-12 in.

27. SUMMIT LAKE

Access: The Richardson Highway parallels the eastern shore of Summit Lake from MP 191.0 to 196.0.

Regulations: Check the sport fishing regulations for open times and areas for salmon fishing. Other restrictions may apply.
Time of Availability:

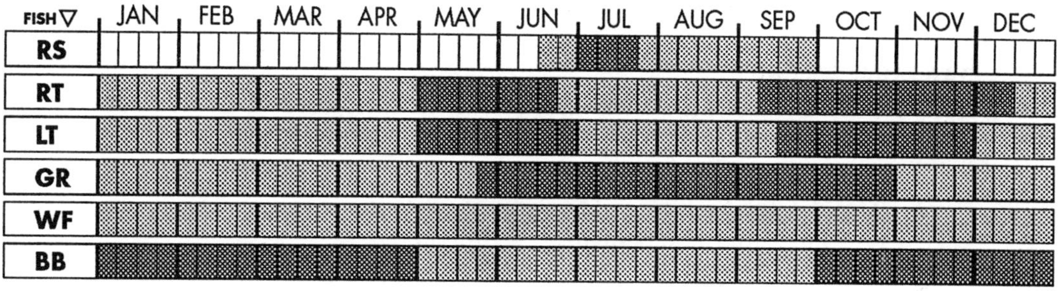

FISH▽	JAN	FEB	MAR	APR	MAY	JUN	JUL	AUG	SEP	OCT	NOV	DEC
RS												
RT												
LT												
GR												
WF												
BB												

Major Species:
Red salmon / poor to fair 4-8 lbs., max. 14 lbs. / spoons and spinners, streamer flies.
Lake trout / fair to good / 2-10 lbs., max. 25 lbs. / spoons and spinners, fish bait.
Rainbow trout / fair / 8-20 in., max. 5 lbs. / spoons and spinners, salmon egg clusters, flies.
Grayling / good to excellent / 7-15 in., max. 20 in. / dry and wet flies, spinners.
Burbot / fair to good / 2-6 lbs., max. 20 lbs. / herring, smelt, and whitefish bait.

28. GUNN CREEK
Access: The Richardson Highway crosses the stream at MP 196.8.
Regulations: Salmon fishing prohibited from January 1 through July 31.
Major Species:
Red salmon / poor to fair / early and mid-August / 4-8 lbs.
Grayling / good / September and early October / 7-15 in.

AREA D: DELTA RIVER DRAINAGE

Includes all waters draining into and surrounding the Delta River.

29. FIELDING LAKE
Access: From MP 200.5 of the Richardson Highway. Turn southwest onto a gravel road and drive 2.1 miles to the outlet of the lake.
Regulations: No set lines may be used.
Major Species:
Lake trout / fair to good / June and September / 2-6 lbs.
Grayling / good / June through September / 8-15 in.
Burbot / fair / March, April, November, December / 2-5 lbs.

30. RAPIDS LAKE
Access: From MP 225.4 of the Richardson Highway. Park and hike 0.25 miles due north to lake.
Major Species:
Rainbow trout / fair / June and September / 8-16 in.

CHAPTER 13

Richardson Highway

31. DONNELLY CREEK
Access: The Richardson Highway crosses the stream at MP 238.0.
Major Species:
Grayling / fair through September / 7-14 in.

32. COAL MINE # 5 LAKE
Access: From MP 242.0 of the Richardson Highway. Turn east onto Coal Mine Road and drive 1.6 miles. Park and follow trail due east 0.5 miles to the lake.
Major Species:
Rainbow trout / good / June and September / 8-15 in.
Lake trout / fair / June and September / 10-18 in.

33. BACKDOWN LAKE
Access: From MP 242.0 of the Richardson Highway. Turn east onto Coal Mile Road and drive 1.6 miles to foot trail. Park and hike 0.5 mile due east to lake.
Major Species:
Arctic char / fair to good / August and September / 8-16 in.
Rainbow trout / good / June and September / 8-18 in.

34. LAST LAKE
Access: From MP 242.0 of the Richardson Highway. Turn east onto Coal Mine Road and drive 1.9 miles and park. Lake is located 100 yards east of road.
Major Species:
Arctic char / fair to good / August and September / 8-16 in.

35. BRODIE LAKE
Access: From MP 242.0 of the Richardson Highway. Turn east onto Coal Mine Road and drive 2.1 miles. Lake is located 100 yards east of road.
Major Species:
Arctic char / fair to good / August and September / 8-20 in.
Grayling / good / June through September / 7-14 in.

36. PAUL'S LAKE
Access: From MP 242.0 of the Richardson Highway. Turn east onto Coal Mine Road and drive 2.6 miles. Lake is located 50 yards east of road.
Major Species:
Lake trout / fair / June and September / 7-12 in.
Grayling / good / June through September 7-14 in.

37. RANGEVIEW LAKE
Access: From MP 242.0 of the Richardson Highway. Turn east onto Coal Mine Road and drive 2.7 miles. Lake is located 10 yards south of road.
Major Species:
Arctic char / fair to good / August and September / 8-16 in.
Grayling / good / June through September / 7-14 in.

38. DICK'S LAKE

Access: From MP 242.0 of the Richardson Highway. Turn east onto Coal Mine Road and drive 4.1 miles. Lake is located 0.5 mile south of road.

Major Species:

Arctic char / fair to good / August and September / 8-20 in.

39. KEN'S LAKE

Access: From MP 242.0 of the Richardson Highway. Turn east onto Coal Mine Road and drive 4.7 miles. Lake is located 0.5 mile south of road.

Major Species:

Arctic char / fair to good / August and September / 8-20 in.
Rainbow trout / good / June and September / 8-18 in.

40. WEASEL LAKE

Note: Weasel Lake is located on military property and a permit is required for access. Call 873-1111 for information.

Access: From MP 242.8 of the Richardson Highway. Turn east onto gravel road and drive 0.7 miles and park. Lake is located 100 yards due east of road.

Major Species:

King salmon / good / June through December / 7-15 in.
Arctic char / fair / August and September / 8-12 in.
Rainbow trout / good / June and September / 8-20 in.

41. DONNELLY LAKE

Access: From MP 244.6 of the Richardson Highway. Lake is located 0.5 miles east of road.

Major Species:

King salmon / good / June through December / 7-15 in.
Silver salmon / good / June through December / 7-15 in.
Rainbow trout / good / June and September / 8-15 in.

42. GHOST LAKE

Note: Ghost Lake is located on military property and a permit is required for access. Call 873-1111 for information.

Access: From MP 257.6 of the Richardson Highway. Turn south on gravel road and drive 5.1 miles. Turn north and drive 0.2 miles and park. Follow ATV trail 0.5 miles due west to lake.

Major Species:

Rainbow trout / good / June and September / 8-15 in.
Lake trout / fair / June and September / 7-12 in.

43. NICKEL LAKE

Note: Nickel Lake is located on military property and a permit is required for access: Call 873-1111 for information.

Access: From MP 257.6 of the Richardson Highway. Turn south on gravel road and drive 5.4 miles and park. Lake is located adjacent to the road.

Major Species:

Rainbow trout / good / June and September / 8-15 in.

Lake trout / fair / June and September / 8-12 in.
Grayling / good / June through September / 7-14 in.

44. "J" LAKE

Note: "J" Lake is located on military property and a permit is required for access. Call 873-1111 for information.

Access: From MP 257.6 of the Richardson Highway. Turn south on gravel road and drive 5.4 miles to the lake. The lake is located adjacent to the road.

Major Species:
Grayling / good / June through September / 7-14 in.

45. CHET LAKE

Note: Chet Lake is located on military property and a permit is required for access. Call 873-1111 for information.

Access: From MP 257.6 of the Richardson Highway. Turn south on gravel road and drive 5.6 miles and park. Lake is located adjacent to the road.

Major Species:
Rainbow trout / good / June and September / 8-15 in.
Lake trout / fair / June and September / 8-12 in.
Grayling / good / June through September / 7-14 in.

46. BOLIO LAKE

Note: Bolio Lake is located on military property and a permit is required for access. Call 873-1111 for information.

Access: From MP 257.6 of the Richardson Highway. Turn west onto Meadows Road and drive 2.0 miles. Turn on Bolio Lake Road and follow 0.5 miles to lake.

Major Species:
King salmon / good / June through December / 7-15 in.
Rainbow trout / good / June and September / 7-15 in.
Lake trout / fair / June and September / 7-15 in.
Grayling / good / June through September / 7-10 in.

47. MARK LAKE

Note: Mark Lake is located on military property and a permit is required for access. Call 873-1111 for information.

Access: From MP 257.6 of the Richardson Highway. Turn west on Meadows Road and drive 5.3 miles. Turn on Mark Road and drive 0.3 miles to the lake.

Major Species:
Rainbow trout / good / June and September / 7-18 in.

48. NORTH TWIN LAKE

Note: North Twin Lake is located on military property and a permit is required for access. Call 873-1111 for information.

Access: From MP 257.6 of the Richardson Highway. Turn west on Meadow Road and drive 5.6 miles to Twin Lake turn-off. Continue 1.4 miles to the lake.

Major Species:
King salmon / good / June through December / 7-15 in.
Rainbow trout / good / June and September / 7-18 in.

49. SOUTH TWIN LAKE

Note: South Twin Lake is located on military property and a permit is required for access. Call 873-1111 for information.

Access: From MP 257.6 of the Richardson Highway. Turn west on Meadows Road and drive 5.6 miles to the Twin Lakes turn-off. Continue 1.4 miles to lake.

Major Species:
King salmon / good / June through December / 7-15 in.
Rainbow trout / good / June and September / 7-18 in.

50. NO MERCY LAKE

Note: No Mercy Lake is located on military property and a permit is required for access. Call 873-1111 for information.

Access: From MP 257.6 of the Richardson Highway. Turn west onto Meadows Road and drive 5.6 miles to the Twin Lakes turnoff. Continue 1.4 miles to Twin Lake. Trailhead begins between the Twin Lakes. Hike 0.5 miles due east to fork in trail. Take left fork and go 150 yards to the lake.

Major Species:
Rainbow trout / good / June and September / 7-18 in.

AREA E: TANANA RIVER DRAINAGE

Includes all waters draining into and surrounding the Tanana River.

51. CLEARWATER LAKE

Access: From MP 268.2 of the Richardson Highway. Turn east onto Jack Warren Road and follow to MP 9.3. Turn left on Triple H Road and proceed 1.3 miles to parking area and the lake.

Major Species:
Chum salmon / poor to fair / late September / 5-12 lbs.
Silver salmon / fair to good / early October / 5-12 lbs.
Grayling / fair to good / July through September / 7-15 lbs.
Burbot / fair to good / November through April / 2-6 lbs.

52. DELTA CLEARWATER RIVER

Access: From MP 268.2 of the Richardson Highway. Turn east onto Jack Warren Road and follow paved section 11.5 miles to campground sign on the left. Turn onto gravel road leading short distance to the river. Another access: continue 0.2 miles to the end of the road and the lodge. Find dirt road leading a short distance to the river.

Regulations: Only unbaited artificial lures may be used. Catch-and-release only for grayling from April 1 to the first Saturday in June. Check the sport fishing regulations.

Time of Availability:

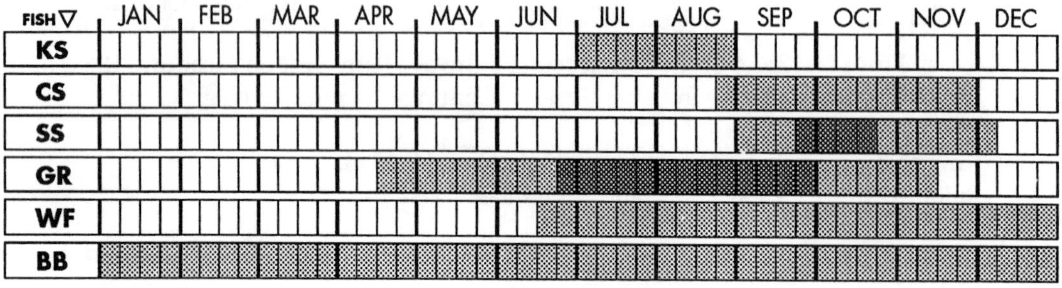

FISH ▽	JAN	FEB	MAR	APR	MAY	JUN	JUL	AUG	SEP	OCT	NOV	DEC
KS												
CS												
SS												
GR												
WF												
BB												

Note: For salmon, the chart reflects fish of all stages of maturity up to spawning condition.

Major Species:

Chum salmon / poor to fair / 5-10 lbs., max., 15 lbs. / spoons and spinners.
Silver salmon / good to excellent / 5-10 lbs., max. 15 lbs. / spoons and spinners, attractor lures.
Grayling / fair to good / 8-14 in., max. 18 in. / dry and wet flies, and spinners.
Whitefish / poor to fair / 10-18 in., max. 5 lbs. / wet and egg imitation flies.

53. TANANA RIVER

Access: The Richardson Highway crosses the river at MP 275.3.

Major Species:

Chum salmon / poor to fair / early November / 5-12 lbs.
Grayling / fair / mid-May and late October / 7-15 in.
Burbot / good / November through April / 2-8 lbs

Note: During the summer months the Tanana River is thick with silt and therefore unsuitable for sport fishing. The spring, fall, and winter months are better, when the water clears up a bit due to low precipitation.

54. QUARTZ LAKE

Access: From: MP 277.8 of the Richardson Highway. Turn east onto Quartz Lake Road and drive 2.6 miles to the lake.

Major Species:

Silver salmon / good / March through December / 8-16 in.
Rainbow trout / good / June and September / 8-24 in.

55. SHAW CREEK

Access: The Richardson Highway crosses the stream at MP 286.7.

Regulations: Catch-and-release only for grayling between April 1 and the first Saturday in June. Only unbaited artificial lures above the bridge. Check the sportfishing regulations for more details.

Major Species:

Chum salmon / poor to fair / early November / 5-12 lbs.
Silver salmon / fair / late September, early October / 5-12 lbs.
Grayling / good to excellent / May and early June / 7-15 in.
Burbot / fair / October through April / 2-8 lbs.

56. BIRCH LAKE

Access: From MP 306.0 of the Richardson Highway. The lake is adjacent to the north side of the road.

Major Species:

Silver salmon / good / March through December / 8-16 in.
Rainbow trout / good / June and September / 8-24 in.

57. LOST LAKE

Access: From MP 306.2 of the Richardson Highway. Turn south on Lost Lake and drive 0.5 miles to "Y," and turn right to the lake.

Major Species:

Silver salmon / good / March through December / 8-15 in.
Rainbow trout / good / June and September / 8-15 in.

58. HARDING LAKE

Access: From MP 321.6 of the Richardson Highway. Turn east on Harding Drive and continue 1.4 miles to a "Y." Turn right to the lake shore, left to the campground.

Time of Availability:

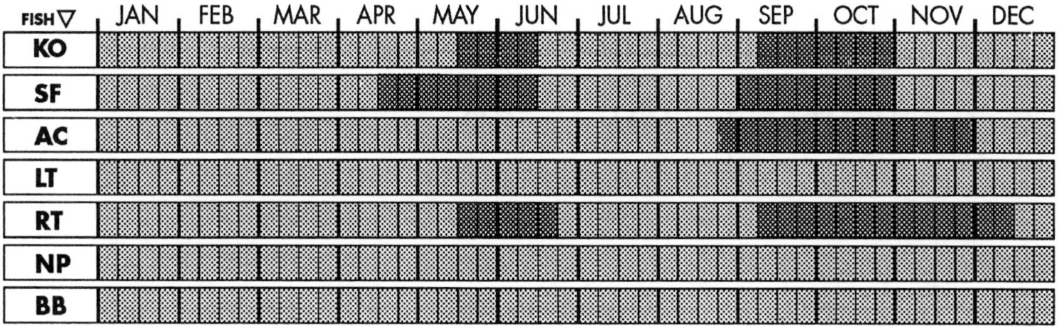

FISH▽	JAN	FEB	MAR	APR	MAY	JUN	JUL	AUG	SEP	OCT	NOV	DEC
KO												
SF												
AC												
LT												
RT												
NP												
BB												

Major Species:

Kokanee / fair / 7-10 in., max. 12 in. / spoons, shrimp, worm, and single salmon egg bait.
Sheefish / fair / 17-22 in., max. 5 lbs. / spoons and spinners, plugs, streamer flies.
Arctic char / fair to good / 8-24 in., max. 6 lbs. / spoons, salmon egg clusters.
Rainbow trout / good / 7-12 in., max. 18 in. / salmon egg clusters, spinners, flies.

59. LITTLE HARDING LAKE

Access: From MP 319.5 of the Richardson Highway. Turn onto paved road by sign and drive 0.4 miles to a "T." Turn right and continue 0.4 miles to access road on right next to sign, then drive a short distance to small parking area. Follow trail 100 yards to lake.

Major Species:

Arctic char / fair / August and September / 8-15 in.
Rainbow trout / good / June and September / 8-15 in.

60. SALCHA RIVER

Access: The Richardson Highway crosses the river at MP 324.1. The river and campground is reached by gravel road from MP 324.3.

Regulations: Catch-and-release only for grayling between April 1 and the first Saturday in June.

Time of Abundance:

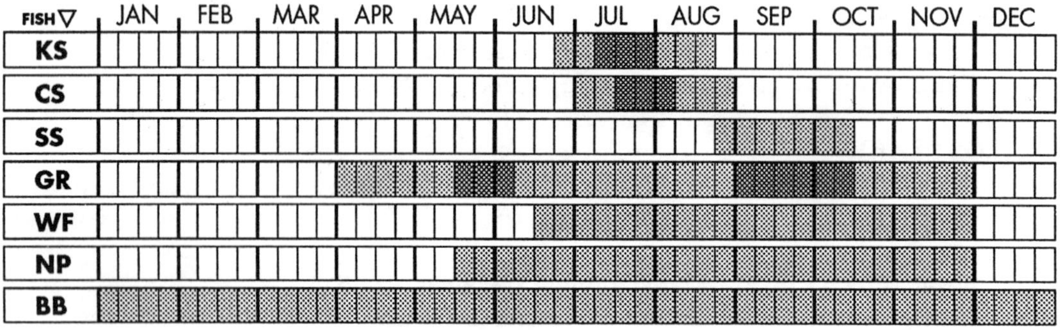

FISH▽	JAN	FEB	MAR	APR	MAY	JUN	JUL	AUG	SEP	OCT	NOV	DEC
KS												
CS												
SS												
GR												
WF												
NP												
BB												

Note: Salmon in this region have travelled quite far from the sea. The chart above reflects all the stages of maturity of the fish up to spawning.

Major Species:

King salmon / fair / 15-30 lbs., max, 45 lbs. / spoons and spinners, attractor lures, streamer flies.

Chum salmon / fair / 5-10 lbs., max. 15 lbs. / spoons and spinners, streamer flies.

Grayling / fair to good / 7-15 in., max. 18 in. / spinners, dry and wet flies.

61. SALCHA RIVER / TANANA RIVER CONFLUENCE

Access: From MP 324.8 of the Richardson Highway. Park at turnoff next to Munsons Slough, find trail on the other side of the highway leading 0.5 miles to the confluence.

Regulations: Catch-and-release only for grayling between April 1 and the first Saturday in June.

Time of Abundance:

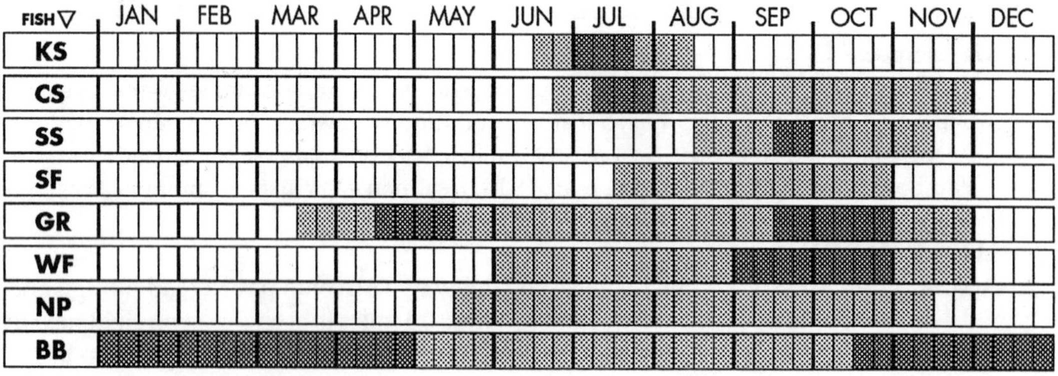

FISH▽	JAN	FEB	MAR	APR	MAY	JUN	JUL	AUG	SEP	OCT	NOV	DEC
KS												
CS												
SS												
SF												
GR												
WF												
NP												
BB												

Note: Salmon in this region have travelled quite far from the sea. The chart above reflects all the stages of maturity of the fish up to spawning.

Major Species:

King salmon / fair to good / 15-30 lbs., max. 45 lbs, / spoons and spinners, attractor lures.

Chum salmon / fair / 5-10 lbs., max. 15 lbs. / spoons and spinners, attractor lures.

Silver salmon / poor to fair / 5-10 lbs., max. 15 lbs. / spoons and spinners, attractor lures.

Northern Pike / poor to fair / 2-7 lbs., max. 15 lbs. / spoons, spinners, plugs.

Grayling / good / 7-15 in., max. 18 in. / spoons, spinners, and flies.

Whitefish / poor to fair / 10-20 in., max. 4 lbs. / salmon egg clusters, corkies.
Burbot / fair / 2-8 lbs., max. 15 lbs. / herring, smelt, and whitefish bait.

62. LITTLE SALCHA RIVER

Access: The Richardson Highway crosses the river at MP 327.8.

Major Species:

Grayling / fair / mid-May through September / 7-15 in.

63. JOHNSON ROAD # 1 LAKE

Access: From MP 330.4 of the Richardson Highway. Turn north onto Johnson Road and drive 0.3 mile. Turn left, take an immediate right, and drive 0.4 miles. Turn left and drive a short distance to the pond.

Major Species:

Silver salmon / fair / March through December / 7-15 in.
Rainbow trout / good / June and September / 8-15 in.
Grayling / good / June through September / 7-12 in.

64. JOHNSON ROAD # 2 LAKE

Access: From MP 330.4 of the Richardson Highway. Turn north onto Johnson Road and drive 0.3 miles. Turn left, take an immediate right, and drive 0.4 miles. Turn left and drive 0.4 miles to pond.

Major Species:

Grayling / good / June through September / 7-14 in.

CHAPTER 14

Edgerton Highway

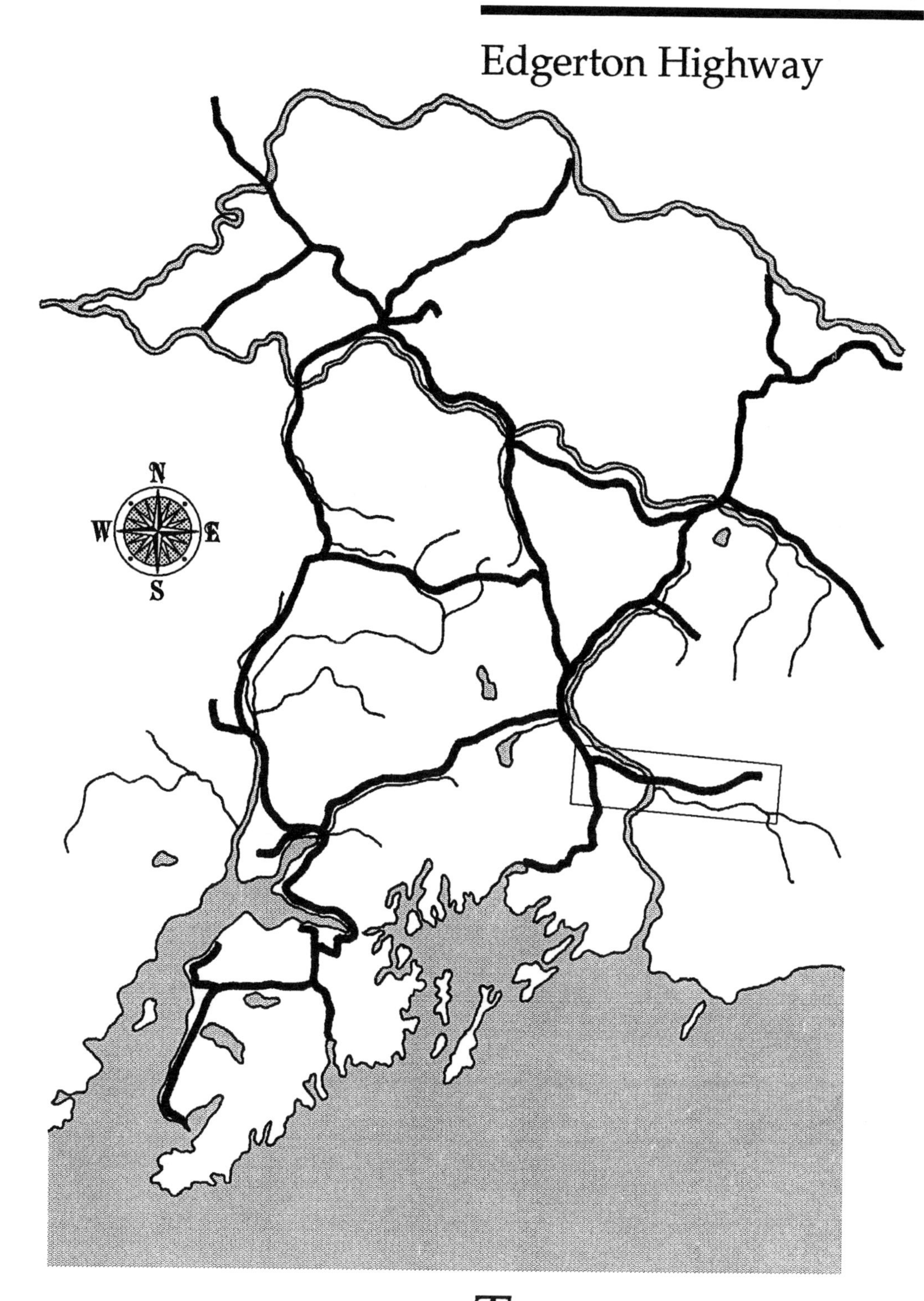

The Edgerton Highway begins at Milepost 82.6 of the Richardson Highway and runs west to east to the settlement of Chitina. Here the pavement ends and the highway becomes the McCarthy Road, continuing in the same general direction to the mining area of Kennicott River.

Edgerton Highway

Edgerton Highway (including McCarthy Road) crosses the large glacial Copper River and runs parallel to Chitina River, providing good access to the region's lakes and streams. This road offers sport fishing for several species, including grayling, Dolly Varden, rainbow trout, and landlocked silver salmon. Also present in smaller numbers are king, red, and silver salmon, and lake trout and burbot. The main fishing season is from breakup in mid-May until freeze-up in mid-October.

Important: Please be aware of the current sport fishing rules and regulations for the area covered in this chapter, and abide by them. Remember, they have been applied to protect a fragile resource.

Following are the abbreviations used in this chapter for all the fish species and facility information:

KS - King Salmon	DV - Dolly Varden	GR - Grayling
RS - Red Salmon	LT - Lake trout	BB - Burbot
SS - Silver Salmon	RT - Rainbow trout	
P - Parking	C - Camping	BL - Boat Launch
LP - Limited Parking	T - Toilet	

Time of Abundance/Availability Charts

These charts are designed to show the reader during which time of the year the indicated species are present or available in the most popular fishing streams, lakes, or regions. The charts correlate to when the fish are in their prime for both angling sport and consumption, unless otherwise noted. Species which are closed to sport fishing are also included on the charts just for the purpose of interest but are shown in all stages of maturity.

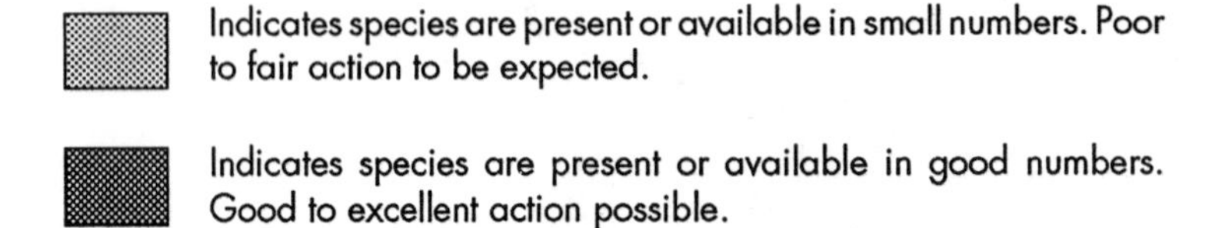
Indicates species are present or available in small numbers. Poor to fair action to be expected.
Indicates species are present or available in good numbers. Good to excellent action possible.

Note: The quality of fishing may vary due to certain fluctuations, such as weather conditions, angler experience, number of fish present, or other factors.

QUICK REFERENCE

This section of the chapter was designed to provide a quick view of all the fishing spots in the region, their map location and milepost, species available, facility information, and the page number on which to find detailed information for any one watershed.

EDGERTON HIGHWAY

Note: Mileposts in parentheses indicate McCarthy Road log.

	WATERSHED	MILE POST	SPECIES
1.	Willow Creek Facilities: LP	5.5 Page: 133	GR
2.	Tonsina River Facilities: LP	19.4 Page: 133	DV, GR,(KS,RS,SS,RT,WF)
3.	Liberty Falls Creek Facilities: P/C/T	23.6 Page: 133	GR
4.	3-Mile Lake Facilities: P	29.9 Page: 133	RT,GR
5.	2-Miles Lake Facilities: P	30.6 Page: 133	RT,GR
6.	Chitina Lake Facilities: P	33.4 Page: 134	GR
7.	Strelna Lake Facilities: P (trail)	(8.3) Page: 134	SS,(RT)
8.	Silver Lake Facilities: P/C	(9.3) Page: 134	RT
9.	Van Lake Facilities: P (trail)	(9.3) Page: 134	RT
10.	Sculpin Lake Facilities: P/C	(10.8) Page: 134	RT
11.	Strelna Creek Facilities: P/C	(13.3) Page: 134	DV,(GR)
12.	Lou's Lake Facilities: P (trail)	(23.5) Page: 134	SS,GR
13.	Long Lake Facilities: P	(44.7) Page: 135	DV,LT,GR,BB,(RS,SS)

Edgerton Highway

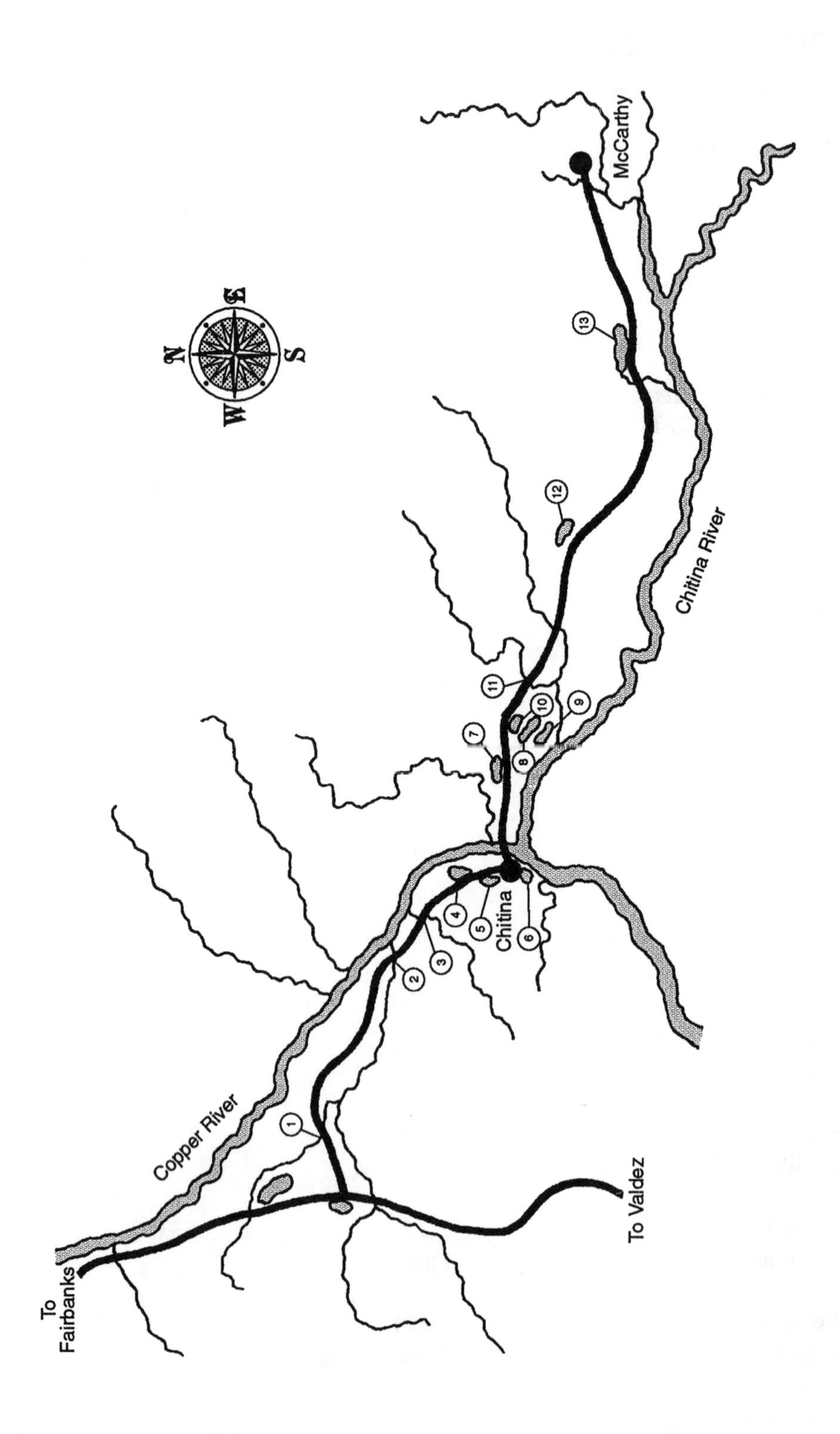

AREA: COPPER - CHITINA RIVER REGION

Includes all waters draining into and surrounding Copper and Chitina Rivers along the Edgerton Highway, including McCarthy Road.

Time of Abundance:

FISH▽	JAN	FEB	MAR	APR	MAY	JUN	JUL	AUG	SEP	OCT	NOV	DEC
KS												
RS												
SS												
DV												
RT												
GR												
WF												

Note: This chart reflects the abundance of fish in flowing water only, with the exception of salmon, which are represented in both lakes and streams in all stages of the life cycle.

1. **WILLOW CREEK**
   Access: The Edgerton Highway crosses the stream at MP 5.5.
   Major Species:
   Grayling / fair to good / mid-May to mid-June / 7-14 in.

2. **TONSINA RIVER**
   Access: The Edgerton Highway crosses the river at MP 19.4.
   Regulations: King salmon fishing prohibited from July 20 through December 31.
   Major Species:
   Dolly Varden / poor to fair / June through October / 8-15 in.
   Grayling / poor to fair / May through September / 8-15 in.

3. **LIBERTY FALLS CREEK**
   Access: The Edgerton Highway crosses the stream at MP 23.6.
   Major Species:
   Grayling / fair / mid-June through August / 7-12 in.

4. **3-MILE LAKE**
   Access: The Edgerton Highway parallels the lake at MP 29.9.
   Major Species:
   Rainbow trout / fair / June, September, October / 8-15 in.
   Grayling / fair / June through September / 7-14 in.

5. **2-MILE LAKE**
   Access: The Edgerton Highway parallels the lake at MP 30.6.
   Major Species:
   Rainbow trout / fair / June, September, October / 8-15 in.

6. **CHITINA (TOWN) LAKE**
Access: The Edgerton Highway parallels the lake at MP 33.4.
Major Species:
Grayling / fair / June through September / 7-15 in.

7. **STRELNA LAKE**
Access: From the end of Edgerton Highway. Continue on McCarthy Road 8.3 miles to trailhead of left. Park and follow trail due north about 0.3 miles to lake.
Major Species:
Silver salmon / good / March through December / 7-15 in.

8. **SILVER LAKE**
Access: From the end of Edgerton Highway. Continue on McCarthy Road 9.3 miles access site on right.
Major Species:
Rainbow trout / good / June and September, October / 8-15 in.

9. **VAN LAKE**
Access: From the end of Edgerton Highway. Continue on McCarthy Road 9.3 miles to Silver Lake access site on right. Find trail leading 0.25 miles due south to lake.
Major Species:
Rainbow trout / good / June and September, October / 8-15 in.

10. **SCULPIN LAKE**
Access: From the end of Edgerton Highway. Continue on McCarthy Road 10.8 miles to access site on right and drive a short distance to camping area and the lake.
Major Species:
Rainbow trout / good / June and September, October / 8-15 in.

11. **STRELNA CREEK**
Access: From the end of Edgerton Highway. Continue on McCarthy Road 13.3 miles to stream crossing.
Major Species:
Dolly Varden / fair / July to mid-September / 7-15 in.

12. **LOU'S LAKE**
Access: From the end of Edgerton Highway. Continue on McCarthy Road 23.5 miles to trail on left. Hike 0.75 miles due north to lake.
Major Species:
Silver salmon / good / March through December / 7-15 in.
Grayling / good / June through September / 7-14 in.

13. LONG LAKE

Access: From the end of Edgerton Highway. Continue on McCarthy Road 44.7 miles to access site on left.

Major Species:

Dolly Varden / fair / late August to mid-October / 7-15 in.
Lake trout / fair / June, September through December / 2-6 lbs.
Grayling / fair to good / June through September / 7-14 in.
Burbot / fair / October through April / 2-4 lbs.

CHAPTER 15

Denali Highway

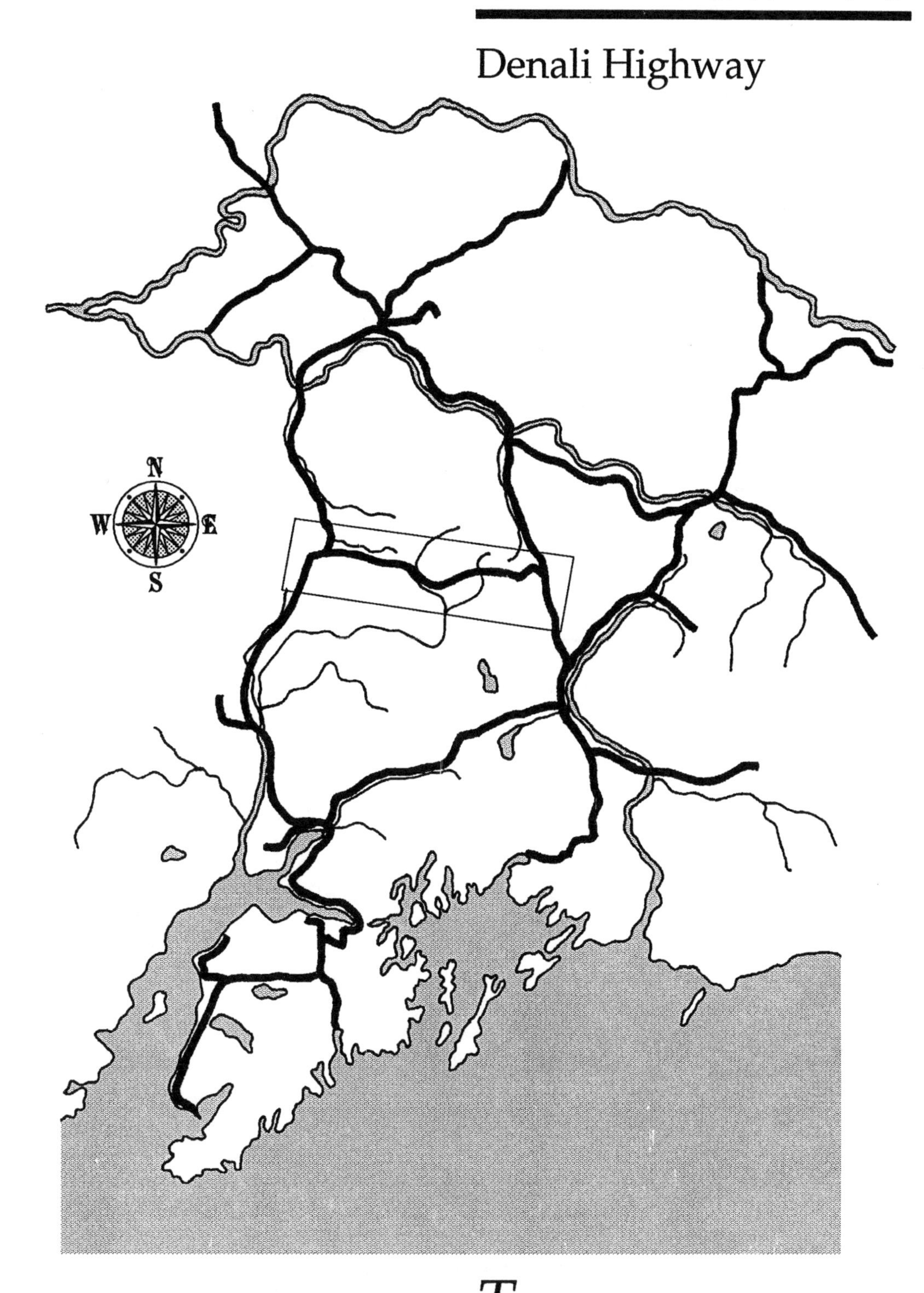

The Denali Highway stretches from Paxson in the east, Milepost 185.5 of the Richardson Highway, to Cantwell in the west, Milepost 209.9 of the Parks Highway. The entire road is of gravel, except for the far ends, which are paved for a few miles.

CHAPTER 15

Denali Highway

Denali highway is unique in that the surrounding waters drain into three different regions. The road crosses or parallels the major drainages of Maclaren, Susitna, and Nenana rivers. Some of the waters drain into Prince William Sound through Copper River, others into Cook Inlet by the way of Susitna River, and also into the Bering Sea through Yukon River. The most common sport fish species along the road is the grayling, which inhabits just about any size lake or stream, but lake trout and burbot are also very common in some of the lakes. Anglers also may run across red salmon, rainbow trout, whitefish, and Dolly Varden.

The main fishing season generally begins in late May and ends sometime in Mid-October.

Important: Please be aware of the current sport fishing rules and regulations of the area covered in this chapter and abide by them. Remember, they have been applied to protect a fragile resource.

Following are the abbreviations used in this chapter for all the fish species and facility information:

RS - Red Salmon	RT- Rainbow Trout	WF - Whitefish
DV - Dolly Varden	GR - Grayling	BB - Burbot
LT - Lake Trout		

P - Parking	C - Camping	BL - Boat Launch
LP - Limited Parking	T - Toilet	

Time of Abundance/Availability Charts

These charts are designed to show the reader during which time of the year the indicated species are present or available in the most popular fishing streams, lakes, or regions. The charts correlate to when the fish are in their prime for both angling sport and consumption, unless otherwise noted. Species which are closed to sport fishing are also included on the charts just for the purpose of interest but are shown in all stages of maturity.

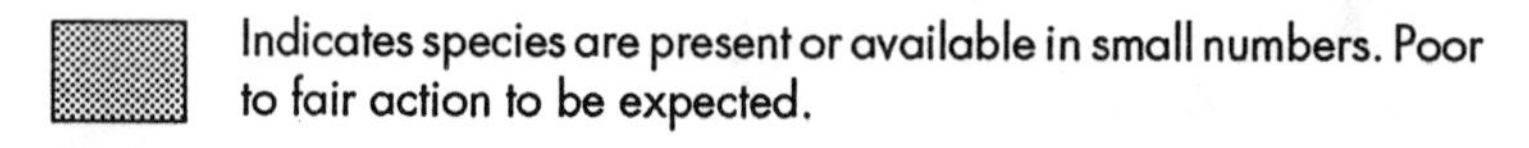
Indicates species are present or available in small numbers. Poor to fair action to be expected.

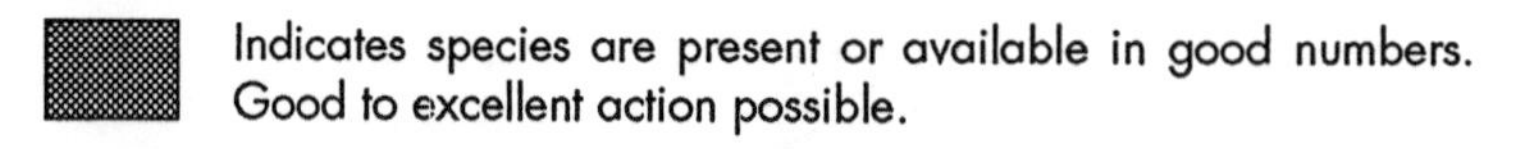
Indicates species are present or available in good numbers. Good to excellent action possible.

Note: The quality of fishing may vary due to certain fluctuations, such as weather conditions, angler experience, number of fish present, or other factors.

QUICK REFERENCE

This section was designed to provide a quick view of all the fishing spots in the region, their map location and milepost, species available, facility information, and the page number on which to find detailed access and fishing information for any one watershed.

Note: Species shown in parentheses may be present but are protected by law, and/or are only occasionally seen or hooked by anglers fishing that particular watershed.

DENALI HIGHWAY

	WATERSHED	MILE POST	SPECIES
1.	E. Fork Gulkana River Facilities: P	0.2 Page: 142	GR,(RS,RT,WF)
2.	Mud Lake Facilities: P	0.3 Page: 142	GR,(RS,RT)
3.	Seven-Mile Lake Facilities: P/T	6.9 Page: 142	LT
4.	Ten-Mile Lake Facilities: P/T	9.9 Page: 142	LT,GR,BB, (WF)
5.	Teardrop Lake Facilities: P	10.4 Page: 143	LT,GR,BB,(RS)
6.	Octopus Lake Facilities: LP (trail)	11.0 Page: 143	LT,GR, (RS)
7.	Little Swede Lake Facilities: P (trail)	16.8 Page: 143	LT
8.	16.8 Mile Lake Facilities: LP (trail)	16.8 Page: 143	LT,GR
9.	Rusty Lake Facilities: LP (trail)	6.8 Page: 143	LT,GR
10.	Round Tangle Lake Facilities: P/C/T/BL	21.5 Page: 143	LT,GR,BB,(WF)
11.	Tangle River Facilities: P	21.6 Page: 143	GR
12.	Upper Tangle Lake Facilities: P	21.7 Page: 143, 144	LT,GR,BB,(WF)
13.	Rock Creek Facilities: P	25.3 Page: 144	GR
14.	Glacier Lake Facilities: P (trail)	31.0 Page: 144	LT,GR, (WF)

15. 36-Mile Lake — 36.0 — LT,GR
    Facilities: LP (trail) — Page: 144

16. Crooked Creek — 46.9-49.0 — GR
    Facilities: P — Page: 144

17. 49.9-Mile Lake — 47.2 — GR
    Facilities: P — Page: 144

18. 50-Miles Lake — 49.0-50.0 — GR
    Facilities: P — Page: 144

19. Clearwater Creek — 59.4 — GR
    Facilities: P — Page: 144

20. No Name Lake — 77.5 — GR
    Facilities: LP — Page: 145

21. No Name Creek — 79.2 — GR
    Facilities: LP — Page: 145

22. Stevenson's Lake — 84.0 — GR
    Facilities: LP (trail) — Page: 145

23. Canyon Creek — 94.8 — GR
    Facilities: LP — Page: 145

24. Brushkana River — 104.3 — DV,GR
    Facilities: P/C/T — Page: 145

25. Seattle Creek — 111.7 — DV,GR
    Facilities: LP — Page: 145

26. Jerry Lake — 125.4 — GR
    Facilities: P — Page: 145

27. Joe Lake — 125.4 — GR
    Facilities: P — Page: 145

28. Fish Creek — 127.6 — GR
    Facilities: LP — Page: 146

29. Fish Creek — 132.3 — GR
    Facilities: LP — Page: 146

CHAPTER 15

Denali Highway

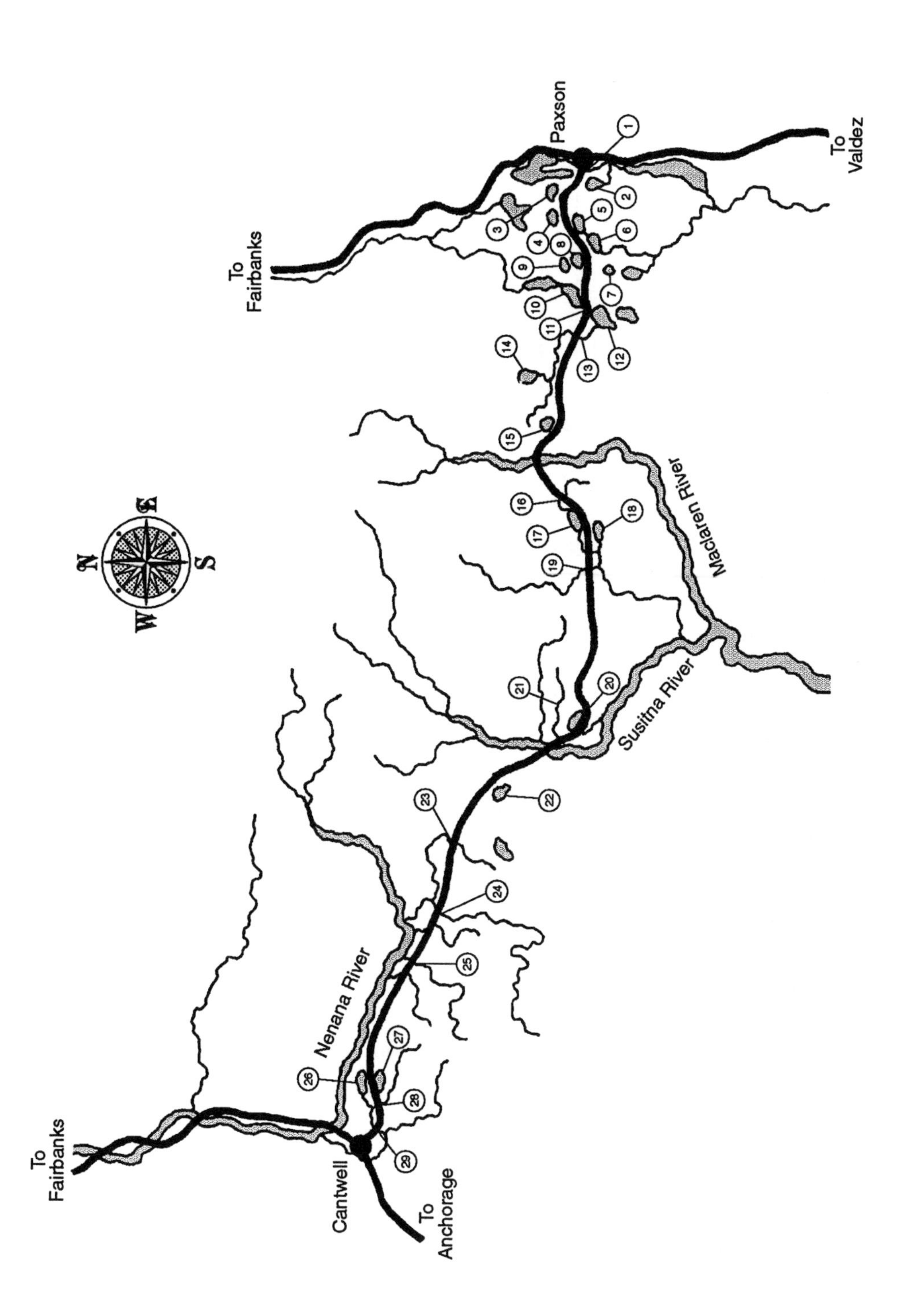

AREA: DENALI

Includes all waters draining into and surrounding the Delta, Copper, Maclaren, Susitna, and Nenana Rivers along the Denali Highway.

Time of Abundance:

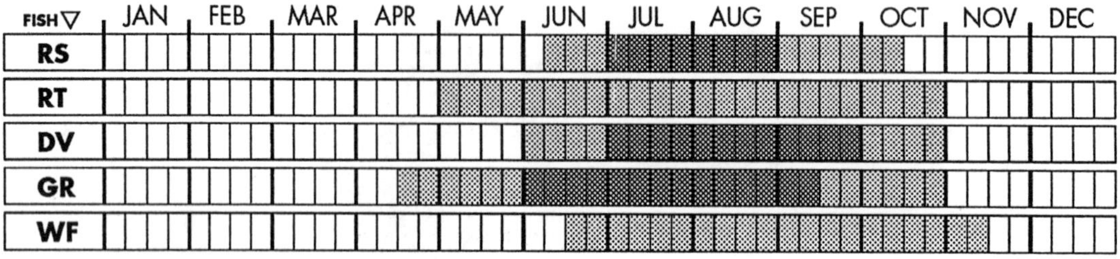

FISH▽	JAN	FEB	MAR	APR	MAY	JUN	JUL	AUG	SEP	OCT	NOV	DEC
RS												
RT												
DV												
GR												
WF												

Note: The above chart correlates to flowing waters only, except for salmon, which is represented in both lakes and streams in all stages of the life cycle.

1. **EAST FORK GULKANA RIVER**

   Access: The Denali Highway crosses the river at MP 0.2.
   Regulations: Salmon fishing prohibited.
   Major Species:
   Grayling / fair / June through September / 7-15 in.

2. **MUD LAKE**

   Access: From MP 0.3 of the Denali Highway. Turn south onto a gravel road leading 0.6 miles to stream draining out of Mud Lake. Walk short distance upstream along creek to reach lake outlet.
   Regulations: Salmon fishing prohibited from January 1 through September 9; catch-and-release only for rainbow/steelhead trout in stream draining Mud Lake.
   Major Species:
   Grayling / good / late May and June / 7-14 in.

3. **SEVEN-MILE LAKE**

   Access: From MP 6.9 of the Denali Highway. Turn north onto gravel road and drive 0.6 miles to the lake.
   Major Species:
   Lake trout / good / June, August, and September / 2-5 lbs.

4. **TEN-MILE LAKE**

   Access: From MP 9.9 of the Denali Highway. Turn south onto gravel road and drive 0.3 miles to the lake.
   Major Species:
   Lake trout / fair / June, August, and September / 2-5 lbs.
   Grayling / good / June through September / 7-15 in.
   Burbot / fair / March through December / 2-4 lbs.

5. **TEARDROP LAKE**
Access: From MP 10.4 of the Denali Highway. Park and hike short distance down steep hill due south to the lake.
Major Species:
Lake trout / fair / June, August, and September / 2-5 lbs.
Grayling / good / June through September / 7-15 in.
Burbot / fair / March through December / 2-4 lbs.

6. **OCTOPUS LAKE**
Access: From MP 11.0 of the Denali Highway. Park by road and hike 0.25 miles due south to lake through open terrain.
Major Species:
Lake trout / fair / June, August, and September / 2-5 lbs.
Grayling / good / June through September / 7-15 in.

7. **LITTLE SWEDE LAKE**
Access: From MP 16.8 of the Denali Highway. Turn south onto gravel road and drive 0.2 miles to parking area on right next to sign. Follow cat trail 2.5 miles to lake.
Major Species:
Lake trout / excellent / June, August, and September / 2-6 lbs.

8. **16.8 MILE LAKE**
Access: From MP 16.8 of the Denali Highway. Park and hike 200 yards due north up creek to lake.
Major Species:
Lake trout / fair / June, August, and September / 2-4 lbs.
Grayling / good / June through September / 7-15 in.

9. **RUSTY LAKE**
Access: From MP 16.8 of the Denali Highway. Park and hike 0.5 miles beyond 16.8 Miles Lake in a northwesterly direction.
Major Species:
Lake trout / fair / June, August, and September / 2-4 lbs.
Grayling / good / June through September / 7-15 in.

10. **ROUND TANGLE LAKE**
Access: The Denali Highway runs parallel to the lake at MP 21.5.
Major Species:
Lake trout / good / June, August, and September / 2-5 lbs.
Grayling / excellent / June through September / 7-18 in.
Burbot / fair / March through December / 2-4 lbs.

11. **TANGLE RIVER**
Access: The Denali Highway crosses the river at MP 21.4.
Major Species:
Grayling / good / July through September / 7-15 in.

12. UPPER TANGLE LAKE
Access: The Denali Highway runs parallel to the lake at MP 21.7.
Major Species:
Lake trout / fair / June, August, September / 2-4 lbs.
Grayling / good / June through September / 7-15 in.
Burbot / fair / March through December / 2-4 lbs.

13. ROCK CREEK
Access: The Denali Highway crosses the stream at MP 25.3.
Major Species:
Grayling / fair to good / June through September / 7-15 in.

14. GLACIER LAKE
Access: From MP 31.0 of the Denali Highway. Park and hike 2.0 miles due north on cat trail to lake.
Major Species:
Lake trout / good / June, August, and September / 2-6 lbs.
Grayling / excellent / June through September / 7-16 in.

15. 36-MILE LAKE
Access: From MP 36.0 of the Denali Highway. Park and hike 0.5 miles due north to lake.
Major Species:
Lake trout / fair / June, August, and September / 2-5 lbs.
Grayling / good / June through September / 7-15 in.

16. CROOKED CREEK
Access: The Denali Highway parallels the stream from MP 46.9 to 49.0.
Major Species:
Grayling / good to excellent / June through September / 7-15 in.

17. 46.9 MILE LAKE
Access: From MP 47.2 of the Denali Highway. Park and hike short distance due north to lake.
Major Species:
Grayling / excellent / June through September / 7-17 in.

18. 50-MILE LAKE
Access: The Denali Highway runs parallel to the lake from MP 49.0 to 50.0.
Major Species:
Grayling / fair / June through September / 7-15 in.

19. CLEARWATER CREEK
Access: The Denali Highway crosses the stream at MP 59.4.
Major Species:
Grayling / good to excellent / June through September / 7-15 in.

20. NO NAME LAKE
Access: The Denali Highway runs parallel to the lake and crosses outlet stream at MP 77.5.
Major Species:
Grayling / fair / June through September / 7-15 in.
Note: The small stream draining the lake can also be productive for grayling in summer.

21. NO NAME CREEK
Access: The Denali Highway crosses the stream at MP 79.2.
Major Species:
Grayling / fair / June through September / 7-12 in.

22. STEVENSON'S LAKE
Access: From MP 84.0 of the Denali Highway. Park and hike 0.5 miles due south through open country to lake.
Major Species:
Grayling / good / June through September / 7-15 in.

23. CANYON CREEK
Access: The Denali Highway crosses the stream at MP 94.8.
Major Species:
Grayling / fair to good / June through September / 7-15 in.

24. BRUSHKANA RIVER
Access: The Denali Highway crosses the river at MP 104.3.
Major Species:
Dolly Varden / fair / July through September / 7-12 in.
Grayling / fair to good / June through September / 7-15 in.

25. SEATTLE CREEK
Access: The Denali Highway crosses the stream at MP 111.7.
Major Species:
Dolly Varden / fair / July through September / 7-12 in.
Grayling / fair to good / June through September / 7-15 in.

26. JERRY LAKE
Access: From MP 125.4 of the Denali Highway. Park and hike short distance on trail due north to lake.
Major Species:
Grayling / fair to good / June through September / 7-15 in.

27. JOE LAKE
Access: From MP 125.4 of the Denali Highway. Park and hike short distance on trail due south to lake.
Major Species:
Grayling / fair to good / June through September / 7-15 in.

28. FISH CREEK
Access: The Denali Highway crosses the stream at MP 127.6.
Major Species:
Grayling / fair to good / June through September / 7-15 in.

29. FISH CREEK
Access: The Denali Highway crosses the stream at MP 132.3.
Major Species:
Grayling / good to excellent / June through September / 7-15 in.

CHAPTER 16

Glenn Highway

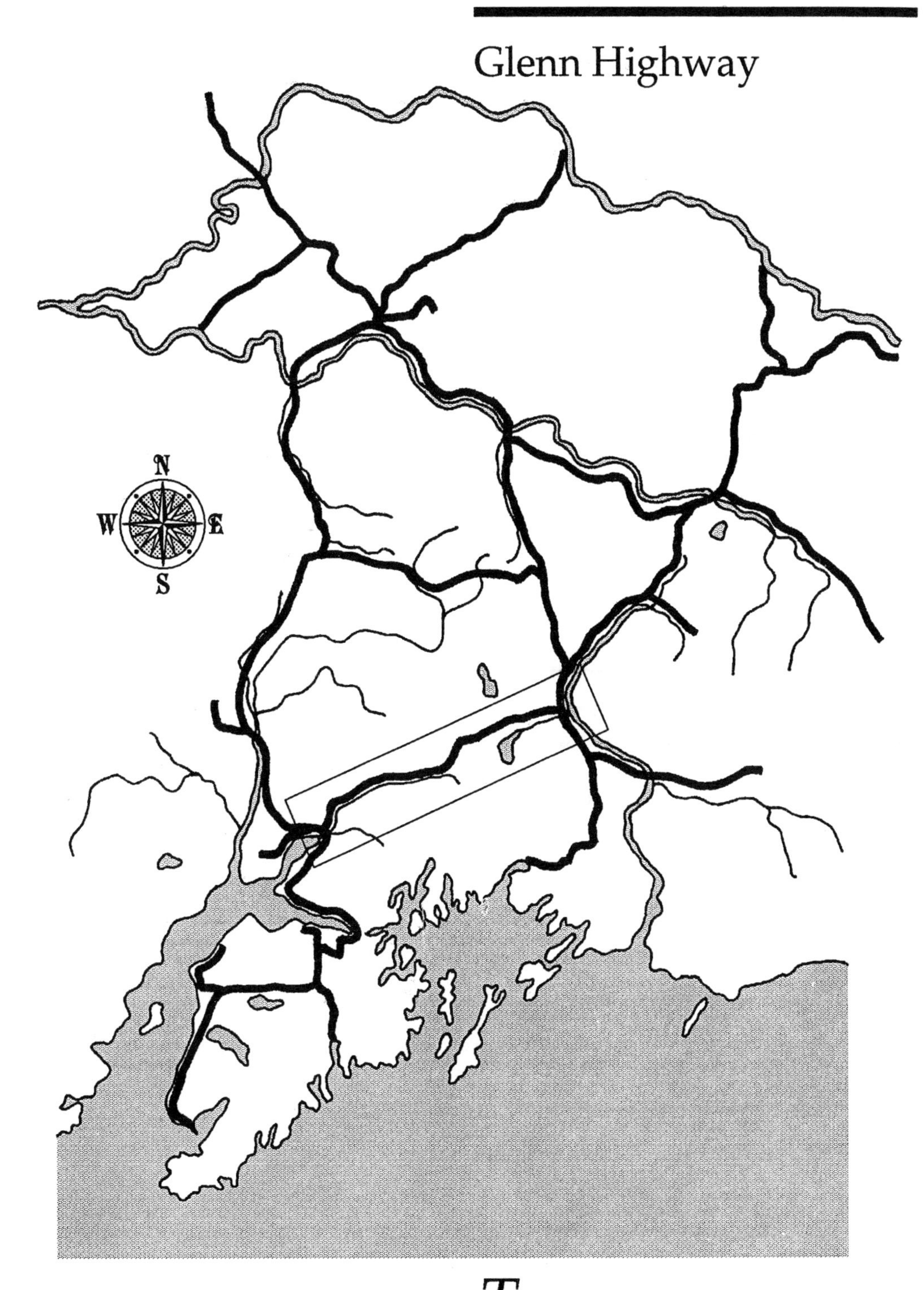

The Glenn Highway begins in the city of Anchorage and heads off in a northeasterly direction to Glennallen, where it intersects the Richardson Highway at Milepost 115.0. It is the link between Alaska's largest city and the Lower 48. The Glenn Highway also connects with the Parks Highway at mile post 35.3. This chapter covers the area from Eklutna, at the head of Knik Arm, to Glennallen.

CHAPTER 16

Glenn Highway

The Glenn Highway passes three large glacial rivers — the Knik, Matanuska, and Tazlina — with good access to many of the region's lakes and streams. Major sport fish species include rainbow trout and grayling, with good numbers of Dolly Varden and chum and silver salmon in some areas. You also may find king, pink, and red salmon, arctic char, whitefish, lake trout, and burbot here. The fishing season starts in mid-May and is usually over by mid-October in most areas, but ice fishing on some of the lakes is also popular in winter.

Important: Please be aware of the current sport fishing rules and regulations for the area covered in this chapter, and abide by them. Remember, they have been applied to protect a fragile resource.

Following are the abbreviations used in this chapter for all the fish species and facility information:

KS - King Salmon	SS - Silver Salmon	RT - Rainbow Trout
RS - Red Salmon	DV - Dolly Varden	GR - Grayling
PS - Pink Salmon	AC - Arctic Char	WF - Whitefish
CS - Chum Salmon	LT - Lake Trout	BB - Burbot

P - Parking	C - Camping	BL - Boat Launch
LP - Limited Parking	T - Toilet	

Time of Abundance/Availability Charts

These charts are designed to show the reader during which time of the year the indicated species are present or available in the most popular fishing streams, lakes, or regions. The charts correlate to when the fish are in their prime for both angling sport and consumption, unless otherwise noted. Species which are closed to sport fishing are also included on the charts just for the purpose of interest but are shown in all stages of maturity.

Indicates species are present or available in small numbers. Poor to fair action to be expected.

Indicates species are present or available in good numbers. Good to excellent action possible.

Note: The quality of fishing may vary due to certain fluctuations, such as weather conditions, angler experience, number of fish present, or other factors.

QUICK REFERENCE

This section was designed to provide a quick overview of all the fishing spots in the region, their map locations and milepost numbers, species available, facility information, and the page number on which to find detailed access and fishing information for any one watershed.

Note: Species shown in parentheses may be present but are protected by law, and/or are only occasionally seen or hooked by anglers fishing that particular watershed.

GLENN HIGHWAY

	WATERSHED	MILEPOST	SPECIES
1.	Eklutna Tailrace Facilities: P	29.5 Page: 155	PS,CS, SS, (KS,RS,DV)
2.	Jim Creek Facilities: P (trail)	29.5 Page: 155, 156	RS,CS,SS,DV,(KS,PS,BB,WF)
3.	Jim Creek Flats Facilities: P	29.5 Page: 156	RS,CS,SS,DV,(KS,PS,BB,WF)
4.	Wasilla Creek Facilities: P	33.9 Page: 156, 157	PS,CS,SS,DV,RT(KS,RS)
5.	Wasilla Creek Facilities: LP	34.7 Page: 157	PS,SS,DV,RT,(KS,RS,CS)
6.	Matanuska Lake Facilities: P/T	36.4 Page: 157	SS,RT,GR
7.	Echo Lake Facilities: P/T	37.0 Page: 157	SS,RT
8.	Kepler / Bradley Lakes Facilities: P	37.3 Page: 158	RT,GR
9.	Victor Lake Facilities: P (trail)	37.3 Page: 158	SS
10.	Canoe Lake Facilities: P/T	38.0 Page: 158	RT,GR
11.	Irene Lake Facilities: P	38.0 Page: 158	RT,AC
12.	Long Lake Facilities: P/T	38.0 Page: 158	RT
13.	Meirs Lake Facilities: P	39.2 Page: 158, 159	RT,GR
14.	Moose Creek Facilities: P/C/T	54.6 Page: 159	RS,CS,SS,DV,RT,(KS,PS,WF)

CHAPTER 16
Glenn Highway

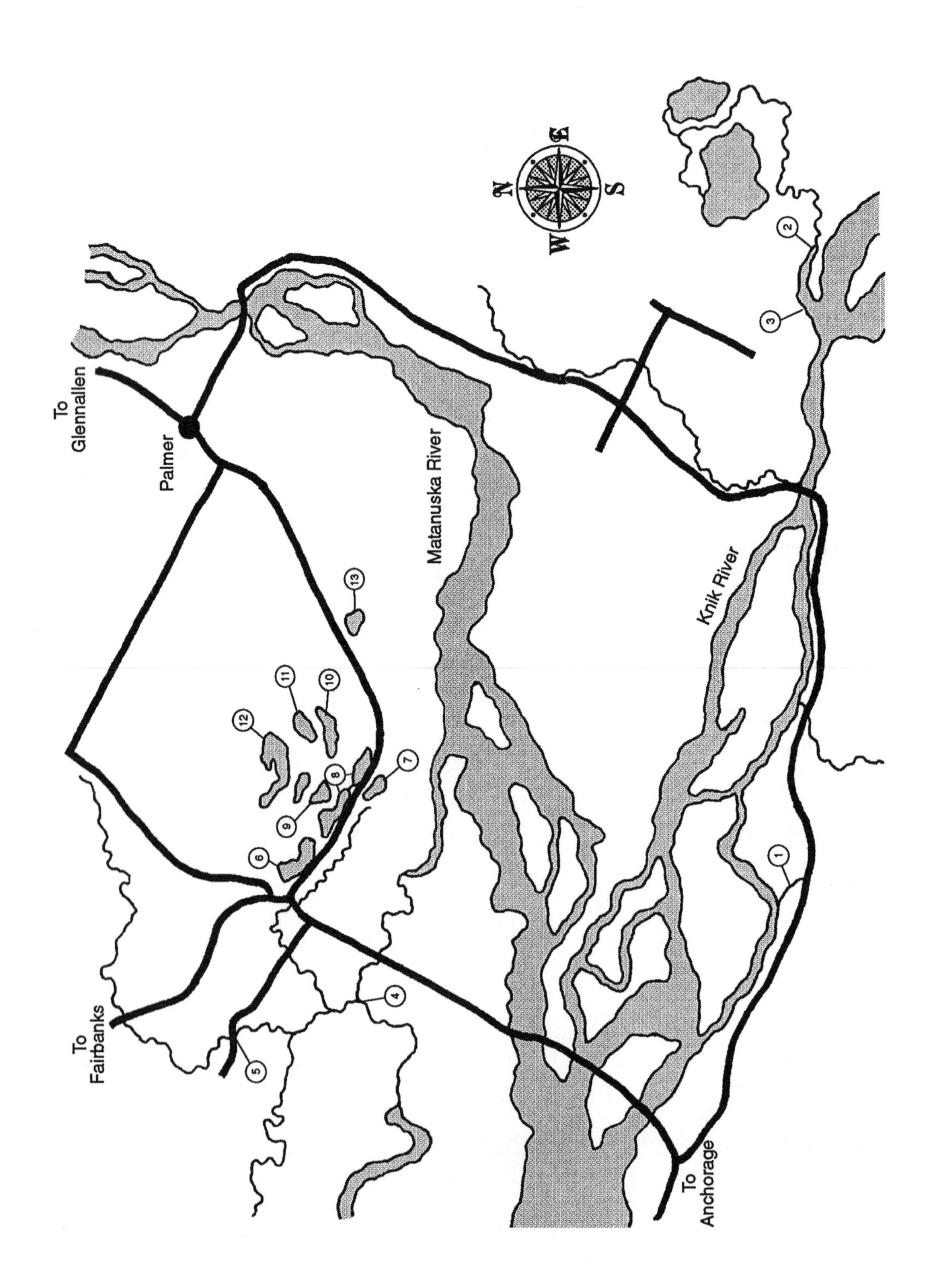

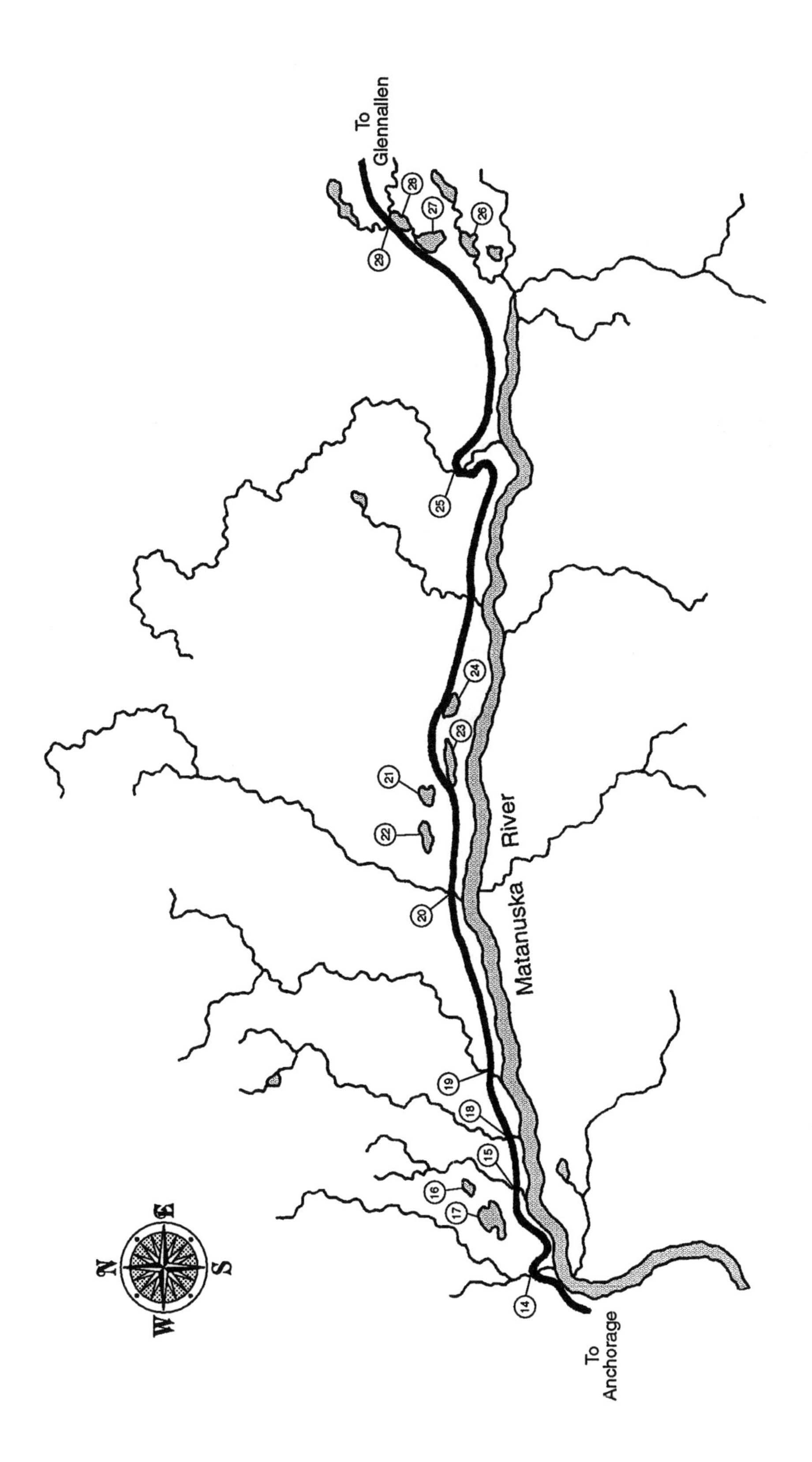
To Glennallen
Matanuska River
To Anchorage
N
E
S
W

Location	Mile / Page	Species
15. Eska Creek Facilities: LP	60.8 Page: 159	DV,(CS,SS,RT)
16. Slipper Lake Facilities: LP (trail)	61.0 Page: 159,160	RT
17. Seventeenmile Lake Facilities: P	61.0 Page: 160	RT,GR
18. Granite Creek Facilities: P	62.4 Page: 160	DV,RT,(KS,RS,CS,SS,GR,WF)
19. Kings River Facilities: P	66.5 Page: 160	DV,RT,(KS,RS,CS,SS,GR,WF)
20. Chickaloon River Facilities: P	77.7 Page: 160	DV,(KS,RS,CS,SS,RT,GR,BB,WF)
21. Ravine Lake Facilities: P	83.3 Page: 160	RT
22. Lower Bonnie Lake Facilities: P/T	83.3 Page: 160	RT,GR
23. Long Lake Facilities: P/T	85.4 Page: 161	GR,BB
24. Weiner Lake Facilities: P	88.5 Page: 161	RT,GR
25. Caribou Creek Facilities: P	106.9 Page: 161	DV,(KS,CS,SS,RT,GR,BB,WF)
26. Trail Lake Facilities: LP	18.4 Page: 161	DV
27. Leila Lake Facilities: P	121.2 Page: 161	GR,BB
28. Tahneta Lake Facilities: P	122.0 Page: 162	GR
29. Gunsight Creek Facilities: LP	123.5 Page: 162	GR

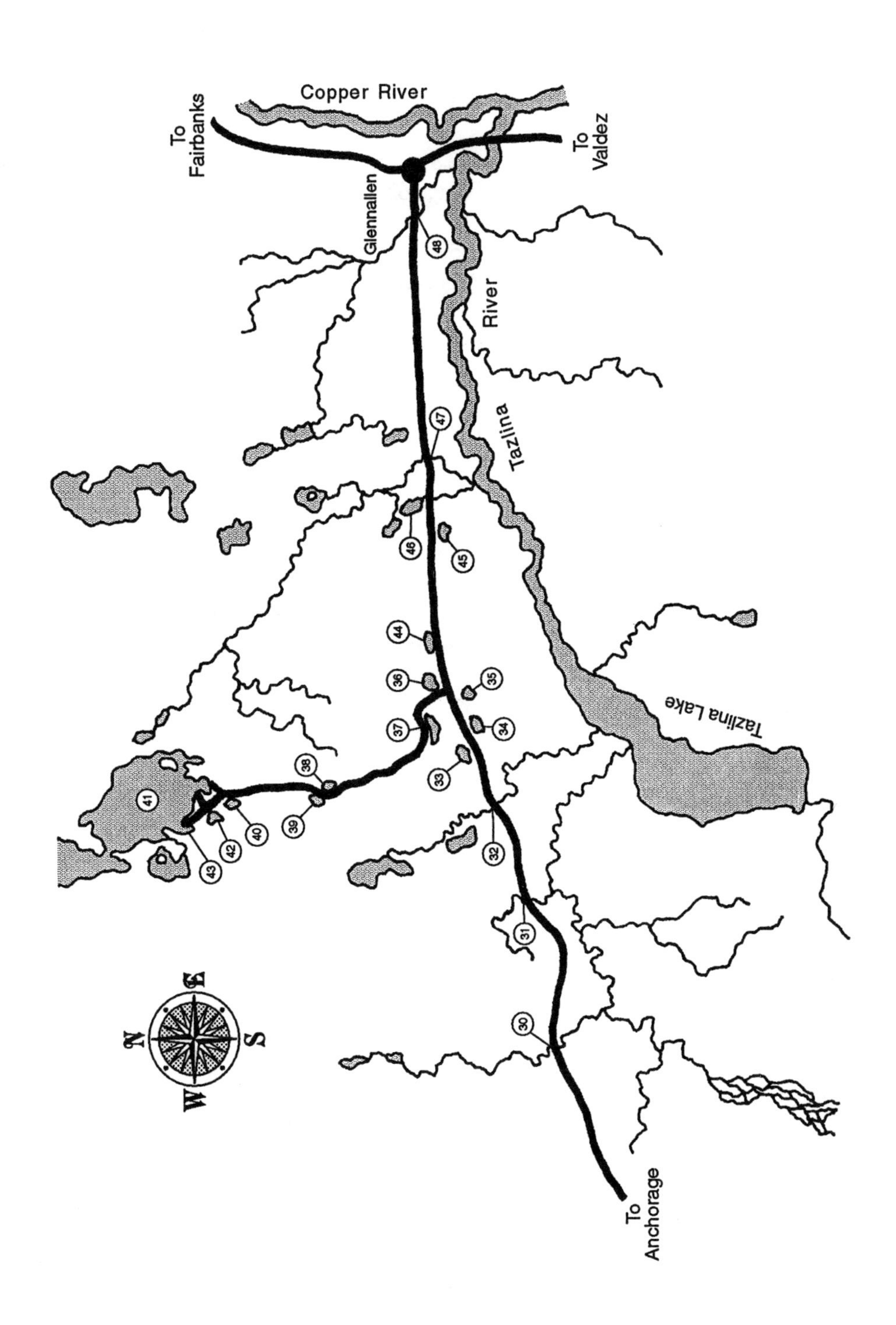
Copper River
To Fairbanks
To Valdez
Glennallen
Tazlina River
Tazlina Lake
To Anchorage
N
E
S
W
30
31
32
33
34
35
36
37
38
39
40
41
42
43
44
45
46
47
48

30. Little Nelchina River Facilities: P/C/T	137.6 Page: 162	GR
31. Cache Creek Facilities: LP	147.1 Page: 162	GR
32. Mendeltna Creek Facilities: P/C/T	152.8 Page: 162	GR,(KS,RS,WF,BB,RT)
33. Arizona Lake Facilities: LP (trail)	155.4 Page: 162	GR
34. Buffalo Lake Facilities: P	156.2 Page: 162	RT
35. Little Junction Lake Facilities: LP (trail)	159.8 Page: 162	GR
36. Junction Lake Facilities: P	159.9 Page: 162, 163	SS,GR
37. Crater Lake Facilities: P (trail)	159.9 Page: 163	RT
38. Elbow Lake Facilities: LP	159.9 Page: 163	GR
39. Caribou Lake Facilities: LP	159.9 Page: 163	GR
40. Connor Lake Facilities: LP (trail)	159.9 Page: 163	GR
41. Lake Louise Facilities: P/C/T/BL	159.9 Page: 163	LT,GR,(WF,BB)
42. George Lake Facilities: P (trail)	159.9 Page: 164	GR
43. Dinty Lake Facilities: P	159.9 Page: 164	GR
44. Tex Smith Lake Facilities: P	162.0 Page: 164	SS,RT
45. Mae West Lake Facilities: P (trail)	169.3 Page: 164	GR

46. Tolsona Lake Facilities: P/C/BL	170.5 Page: 164	RT,GR,BB
47. Tolsona Creek Facilities: P/C/T	173.7 Page: 164	GR
48. Moose Creek Facilities: LP	186.0 Page: 164	GR

AREA A: MATANUSKA VALLEY

Includes all lakes and streams of upper Knik Arm and tributaries of the Knik River.

1. EKLUTNA TAILRACE

Access: From MP 29.5 of the Glenn Highway. Turn onto the Old Glenn Highway and drive to MP 4.1 and the stream crossing. Or, turn left onto one of two dirt roads at MP 3.9 to access the confluence of the tailrace and Knik River.

Regulations: King salmon fishing prohibited.

Time of Abundance:

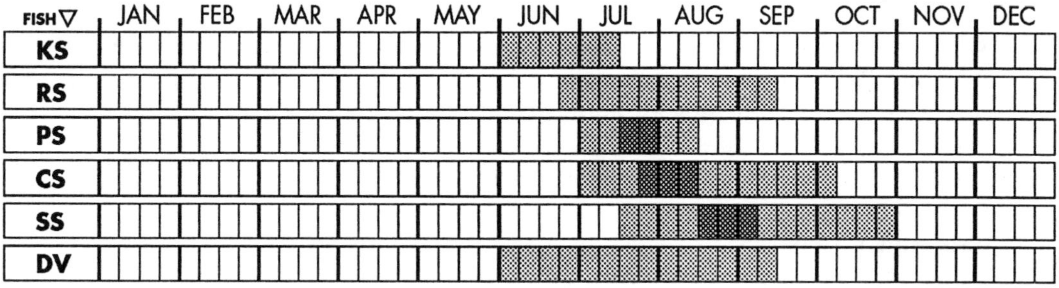

FISH▽	JAN	FEB	MAR	APR	MAY	JUN	JUL	AUG	SEP	OCT	NOV	DEC
KS												
RS												
PS												
CS												
SS												
DV												

Major Species:

Chum salmon / good to excellent / 6-12 lbs., max. 18 lbs. / spoons and spinners, attractor lures.

Silver salmon / good / 6-12 lbs. max. 18 lbs. / spinners, salmon egg clusters, attractor lures.

Pink salmon / poor to fair / 2-4 lbs., max. 6 lbs. / spoons and spinners.

2. JIM CREEK

Access: From MP 29.5 or Arctic Avenue in Palmer from the Glenn Highway. Turn east and drive to MP 11.5 of the Old Glenn Highway. Turn east again onto Plumley Road and drive 1.2 miles to a "T," turn right on Caudill Road and drive 0.5 miles to Walling Road on left. Take first dirt road on immediate right and drive 1.9 miles to a parking area. Hike upstream along Knik River 0.25 miles to the mouth of Jim Creek.

Regulations: King salmon fishing prohibited.

Time of Abundance:

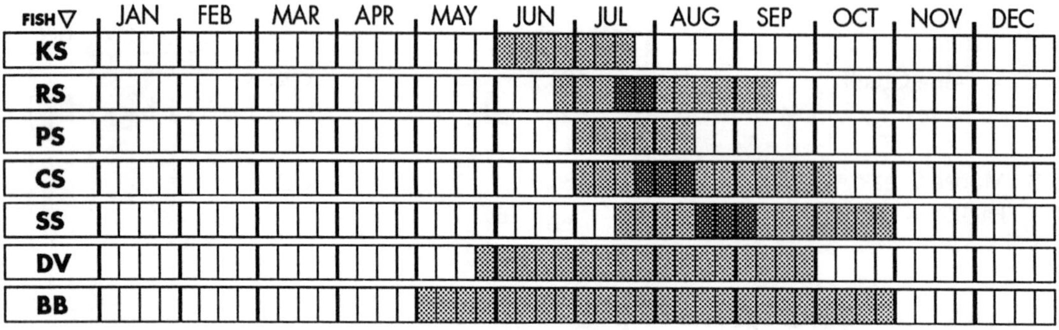

FISH ▽	JAN	FEB	MAR	APR	MAY	JUN	JUL	AUG	SEP	OCT	NOV	DEC
KS												
RS												
PS												
CS												
SS												
DV												
BB												

Major Species:

Red salmon / fair to good / 4-8 lbs. max. 12 lbs. / spoons and spinners, streamer flies.

Chum salmon / good to excellent / 6-12 lbs., max. 18 lbs. / spoons and spinners, salmon egg clusters.

Silver salmon / good / 6-12 lbs., max 18 lbs. / spoons and spinners, salmon egg clusters, attractor lures.

Dolly Varden / poor to fair / 7-12 in., max. 3 lbs. / spoons and spinners, salmon egg clusters.

3. JIM CREEK FLATS

Access: From MP 29.5 of the Glenn Highway or Arctic Avenue in the town of Palmer. Turn east onto Old Glenn highway and drive to MP 11.5. Turn east on Plumley road and drive 1.2 miles to a "T." Turn right on Caudill Road and drive 1.3 miles to a gravel and dirt road on left, continue 1.8 miles to the flats.

Regulations: King salmon fishing prohibited.

Major Species:

Red salmon / poor to fair / late July, early August / 4-8 lbs.

Chum salmon / fair to good / early August / 6-12 lbs.

Dolly Varden / poor to fair / July and August / 7-15 in.

4. WASILLA CREEK / RABBIT SLOUGH

Access: From MP 33.9 of the Glenn Highway. Turn west at pull-off and find dirt road leading 0.6 miles to Wasilla Creek and the confluence with Rabbit Slough.

Regulations: King salmon fishing prohibited. Closed to all fishing from April 15 through June 14. Check the sport fishing regulations for other restrictions.

Time of Abundance:

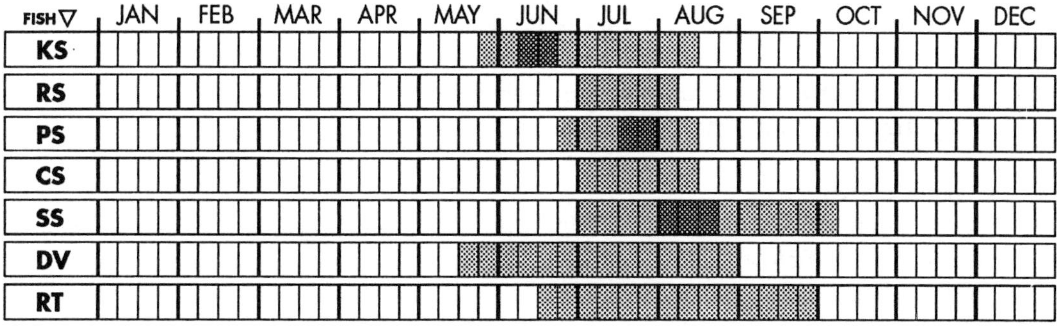

FISH▽	JAN	FEB	MAR	APR	MAY	JUN	JUL	AUG	SEP	OCT	NOV	DEC
KS												
RS												
PS												
CS												
SS												
DV												
RT												

Major Species:

Pink salmon / poor to fair / 2-4 lbs., max. 6 lbs. / spoons and spinners.
Chum salmon / poor to fair / 6-12 lbs., max. 15 lbs. / spoons and spinners.
Silver salmon / good to excellent / 4-10 lbs., max. 15 lbs. / salmon egg clusters, spinners.
Dolly Varden / fair / 7-12 in., max. 17 in. / salmon egg cluster, single salmon eggs, spoons.
Rainbow trout / poor to fair / 7-12 in., max. 15 in. / salmon egg clusters, single eggs, spinners.

5. WASILLA CREEK

Access: From MP 34.7 of the Glenn Highway. Turn west onto Nelson Road and drive 2.2 miles to the stream crossing.

Regulations: King salmon fishing prohibited. Closed to all fishing from April 15 through June 14. Check the sport fishing regulations for other restrictions.

Major Species:

Pink salmon / poor to fair / late July / 2-4 lbs.
Silver salmon / fair / early and mid-August / 4-10 lbs.
Dolly Varden / fair / July and August / 7-14 in.
Rainbow trout / poor to fair / June through August / 7-12 in.

6. MATANUSKA LAKE

Access: From MP 36.4 of the Glenn Highway. Turn north onto a gravel road leading 0.2 miles to lake on the left and a parking area.

Major Species:

Silver salmon / good / March through December / 7-15 in.
Rainbow trout / good / June and September, October / 8-20 in.
Grayling / fair / June through September / 7-14 in.

7. ECHO LAKE

Access: From MP 37.0 of the Glenn Highway. Turn south onto a gravel road and follow 0.3 miles to a pull-off and the lake.

Major Species:

Silver salmon / good / March through December / 7-15 in.
Rainbow trout / good / June and September, October / 7-18 in.

8. **KEPLER / BRADLEY LAKES**
Access: From MP 37.3 of the Glenn Highway. Turn onto gravel road leading short distance to the lakes. Kepler Lake is on the left, Bradley Lake on the right.
Major Species:
Rainbow trout / good / June and September, October / 7-25 in.
Grayling / fair / June through September / 7-14 in.

9. **VICTOR LAKE**
Access: From MP 37.3 of the Glenn Highway. Turn onto gravel road leading to parking area at Kepler/Bradley Lakes. Inquire at office for information about using the road and trail leading 1.0 mile to lake.
Major Species:
Silver salmon / good / March through December / 7-15 in.

10. **CANOE LAKE**
Access: From MP 38.0 of the Glenn Highway. Turn north on Colleen Street and drive short distance and turn left on Bradley Lake Avenue. Continue 0.2 miles and turn right on Green Jade Place, drive short distance to Killarney Drive and turn left. Proceed 0.2 miles to the lake on the right. Short hike to lake.
Major Species:
Rainbow trout / fair / June and September, October / 7-15 in.
Grayling / fair / June through September / 7-14 in.

11. **IRENE LAKE**
Access: From MP 38.0 of the Glenn Highway. Turn north onto Colleen Street, drive short distance and turn left on Bradley Lake Avenue. Continue 0.2 miles and turn right on Green Jade Place. Proceed short distance to Killarney Drive and turn left, drive 0.4 miles to a parking area. Hike short distance to the lake.
Major Species:
Rainbow trout / good / June and September, October / 7-18 in.
Arctic char / poor to fair / August through October / 7-15 in.

12. **LONG LAKE**
Access: From MP 38.0 of the Glenn Highway. Turn north on Colleen Street, drive short distance and turn left on Bradley Lake Avenue. Continue 0.2 miles and turn right on Green Jade Place. Proceed short distance to Killarney Drive, turn left, and drive 0.7 miles to end of road. Park and hike short distance to lake.
Regulations: Unbaited, single hook, artificial lures only. Catch-and-release fishing for rainbow trout.
Major Species:
Rainbow trout / good / June and September, October / 7-20 in.

13. **MEIRS LAKE**
Access: From MP 39.2 of the Glenn Highway. Turn east on Outer Springer Loop and drive 0.3 miles to access road on left. Park and hike short distance to lake.

Major Species:
Rainbow trout / fair / June and September / 7-15 in.
Grayling / good / May, June, and September / 7-12 in.

AREA B: MATANUSKA RIVER DRAINAGE

Includes all waters draining into and surrounding the Matanuska River.
Time of Abundance:

FISH▽	JAN	FEB	MAR	APR	MAY	JUN	JUL	AUG	SEP	OCT	NOV	DEC
KS												
RS												
PS												
CS												
SS												
DV												
RT												
BB												

Note: All tributaries of the Matanuska River are closed to king salmon fishing.

14. MOOSE CREEK
Access: The Glenn Highway crosses the stream at MP 54.6. Hike along the stream on faint trail for 0.5 miles to the confluence of Moose Creek and Matanuska River.
Regulations: King salmon fishing prohibited. Only unbaited artificial lures from September 1 through December 31.
Major Species:
Red salmon / poor to fair / late July, early August / 4-7 lbs.
Chum salmon / poor to fair / early August / 6-12 lbs.
Silver salmon / fair / late August, early September / 5-10 lbs.
Dolly Varden / fair to good / July and August / 7-15 in.
Rainbow trout / poor to fair / June through August / 7-15 in.

15. ESKA CREEK
Access: The Glenn Highway crosses the stream at MP 60.8.
Regulations: King salmon fishing prohibited. Only unbaited artificial lures from September 1 through December 31.
Major Species:
Dolly Varden / fair / July and August / 7-12 in.

16. SLIPPER LAKE
Access: From MP 61.0 of the Glenn Highway. Turn north on Jonesville Road and drive 1.7 miles. Turn left on gravel road, continue 0.4 miles and park. Hike 150 yards due north to lake.

Major Species:
Rainbow trout / fair / June and September / 7-14 in.

17. **SEVENTEENMILE LAKE**
Access: From MP 61.0 of the Glenn Highway. Turn north on Jonesville Road and drive 1.7 miles. Turn left on gravel road, continue 0.5 miles to a "T." Turn left and proceed 0.2 miles and turn right at the "Y". Drive 2.1 miles and turn left at the "Y" and continue a short distance to the lake.
Major Species:
Rainbow trout / fair / June and September / 7-15 in.
Grayling / good / June through September / 7-14 in.

18. **GRANITE CREEK**
Access: The Glenn Highway crosses the stream at MP 62.4.
Regulations: King salmon fishing prohibited. Only unbaited artificial lures from September 1 through December 31.
Major Species:
Dolly Varden / poor to fair / July and August / 7-12 in.
Rainbow trout / poor to fair / May and June / 7-15 in.

19. **KINGS RIVER**
Access: The Glenn Highway crosses the river at MP 66.5.
Regulations: King salmon fishing prohibited. Only unbaited artificial lures from September 1 through December 31.
Major Species:
Dolly Varden / poor to fair / July and August / 7-12 in.
Rainbow trout / poor to fair / May and June / 7-15 in.

20. **CHICKALOON RIVER**
Access: The Glenn Highway crosses the river at MP 77.7.
Regulations: King salmon fishing prohibited. Only unbaited artificial lures from September 1 through December 31.
Major Species:
Dolly Varden / poor to fair / July and August / 7-15 in.

21. **RAVINE LAKE**
Access: From MP 83.3 of the Glenn Highway. Turn north onto a gravel road and drive 0.8 miles to access area on right.
Major Species:
Rainbow trout / good / June and September, October / 7-15 in.

22. **LOWER BONNIE LAKE**
Access: From MP 83.3 of the Glenn Highway. Turn north onto a gravel road and drive 1.2 miles to dirt road on right, continue 0.8 miles to lake wayside on left.
Major Species:
Rainbow trout / fair / June and September, October / 7-15 in.
Grayling / fair / June through September / 7-14 in.

23. LONG LAKE

Access: From MP 85.4 of the Glenn Highway. Turn into parking area next to lake.

Major Species:

Grayling / fair / June through September / 7-14 in.
Burbot / fair / November through April / 15-22 in.

24. WEINER LAKE

Access: From MP 88.5 of the Glenn Highway. The lake is located adjacent to the road.

Major Species:

Rainbow trout / fair / June and September, October / 7-15 in.
Grayling / fair / June through September / 7-14 in.

25. CARIBOU CREEK

Access: The Glenn Highway crosses the stream at MP 106.9.

Regulations: King salmon fishing prohibited. Unbaited artificial lures only from September 1 through December 31.

Major Species:

Dolly Varden / poor to fair / July and August / 7-15 in.

26. TRAIL LAKE

Access: From MP 118.4 of the Glenn Highway. Turn southeast onto a gravel road leading 2.9 miles to lake on left.

Major Species:

Dolly Varden / poor to fair / June through October / 7-12 in.

AREA C: TAZLINA LAKE / RIVER DRAINAGE

Include all waters draining into and surrounding Tazlina Lake and River.

Time of Abundance:

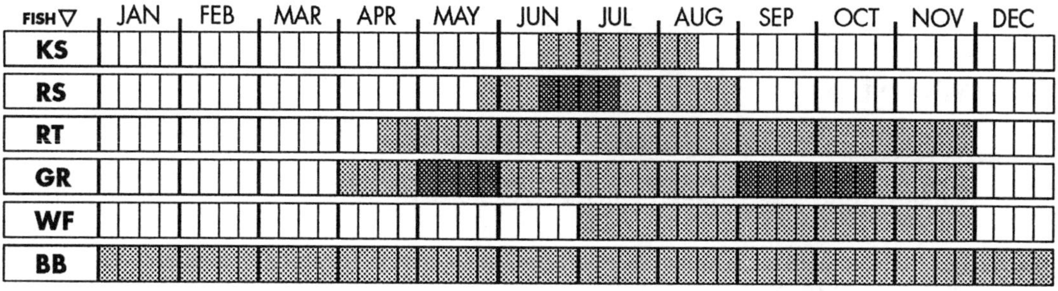

FISH▽	JAN	FEB	MAR	APR	MAY	JUN	JUL	AUG	SEP	OCT	NOV	DEC
KS												
RS												
RT												
GR												
WF												
BB												

27. LEILA LAKE

Access: From MP 121.2 of the Glenn Highway. Turn southeast on a dirt road leading 0.2 miles to the lake.

Major Species:

Grayling / good / June through September / 7-14 in.
Burbot / fair / November through April / 15-22 in.

CHAPTER 16

Glenn Highway

28. TAHNETA LAKE

Access: From MP 122.0 of the Glenn Highway. The lake is adjacent to the road.

Major Species:

Grayling / good / May and June / 7-14 in.

29. GUNSIGHT CREEK

Access: The Glenn Highway crosses the stream at MP 123.5.

Major Species:

Grayling / good / mid-May to mid-June / 7-14 in.

30. CACHE CREEK

Access: The Glenn Highway crosses the stream at MP 137.6. Turn onto gravel road just east of bridge and follow 0.3 miles to a campground and the river.

Major Species:

Grayling / fair / mid-May through August / 7-14 in.

31. CACHE CREEK

Access: The Glenn Highway crosses the stream at MP 147.1.

Major Species:

Grayling / good / early and mid-May / 7-14 in.

32. MENDELTNA CREEK

Access: The Glenn Highway crosses the stream at MP 152.8.

Regulations: Salmon fishing prohibited.

Major Species:

Grayling / excellent / May, September, early October / 7-15 in.

33. ARIZONA LAKE

Access: From MP 155.4 of the Glenn Highway. Park by road and find trail leading 0.25 miles to the lake.

Major Species:

Grayling / good / June through September / 7-14 in.

34. BUFFALO LAKE

Access: From MP 156.2 of the Glenn Highway. Find dirt road due south 0.2 miles to lake.

Major Species:

Rainbow trout / fair / June, September, October / 7-14 in.

35. LITTLE JUNCTION LAKE

Access: From MP 159.8 of the Glenn Highway. Park and follow trail 0.25 miles due south to lake.

Major Species:

Grayling / good / June through September / 7-14 in.

36. JUNCTION LAKE

Access: From MP 159.9 of the Glenn Highway. Turn north onto Lake Louise Road and drive 0.5 miles to the lake on right.

Major Species:
Silver salmon / fair / March through December / 7-15 in.
Grayling / fair / June through September / 7-14 in.

37. CRATER LAKE

Access: From MP 159.9 of the Glenn Highway. Turn north onto Lake Louise Road and drive 1.3 miles. Park and hike 200 yards due west to lake.

Major Species:
Rainbow trout / good / June and September, October / 7-15 in.

38. ELBOW LAKE

Access: From MP 159.9 of the Glenn Highway. Turn north onto Lake Louise Road and drive 11.6 miles to lake on right.

Major Species:
Grayling / fair to good / June through September / 7-14 in.

39. CARIBOU LAKE

Access: From MP 159.9 of the Glenn Highway. Turn north onto Lake Louise Road and drive 11.6 miles to access road on left. Proceed short distance to a "T" and turn right. Follow gravel road 0.7 miles to lake on left.

Major Species:
Grayling / fair / June through September / 7-14 in.

40. CONNOR LAKE

Access: From MP 159.9 of the Glenn Highway. Turn north onto Lake Louise Road and drive 16.9 miles to trail on left leading 300 yards to lake.

Major Species:
Grayling / good / June through September / 7-14 in.

41. LAKE LOUISE

Access: From MP 159.9 of the Glenn Highway. Turn north onto Lake Louise Road and drive 17.3 miles to a "Y." Turn left at the "Y" and drive 0.2 miles to access road on right leading to campground and the lake. Turn right at the "Y" and drive 0.5 miles to the lake and a campground.

Regulations: Minimum legal size limit for lake trout is 18 inches. Burbot fishing is prohibited.

Time of Availability:

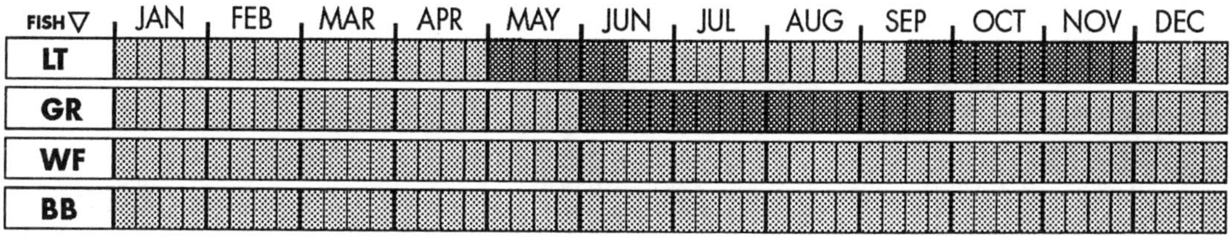

FISH▽	JAN	FEB	MAR	APR	MAY	JUN	JUL	AUG	SEP	OCT	NOV	DEC
LT												
GR												
WF												
BB												

Major Species:
Lake trout / good / 3-8 lbs., max. 27 lbs. / spoons and spinners, plugs.
Grayling / good / 7-14 in., max. 18 in. / dry and wet flies, and spinners.

Glenn Highway

42. GEORGE LAKE

Access: From MP 159.9 of the Glenn Highway. Turn north onto Lake Louise Road and drive 17.6 miles. Park and find trail leading 0.25 miles due west to lake.

Major Species:

Grayling / good / June through September / 7-14 in.

43. DINTY LAKE

Access: From MP 159.9 of the Glenn Highway. Turn north onto Lake Louise Road and drive 19.3 miles to the end of the road. The lake is located on the left, Lake Louise on the right.

Major Species:

Grayling / fair / June through September / 7-12 in.

44. TEX SMITH LAKE

Access: From MP 162.0 of the Glenn Highway. The lake is located adjacent to the north side of the road.

Major Species:

Silver salmon / fair / March through December / 7-14 in.
Rainbow trout / good / June and September, October / 7-14 in.

45. MAE WEST LAKE

Access: From MP 169.3 of the Glenn Highway. Park and find trail leading 0.25 miles due south to lake.

Major Species:

Grayling / good / June through September / 7-14 in.

46. TOLSONA LAKE

Access: From MP 170.5 of the Glenn Highway. Turn north onto a gravel road and drive 0.7 miles to the lake.

Major Species:

Rainbow trout / good / June and September, October / 8-18 in.
Grayling / good / June to mid-October / 7-14 in.
Burbot / good / November through April / 2-6 lbs.

47. TOLSONA CREEK

Access: The Glenn Highway crosses the stream at MP 173.7.

Major Species:

Grayling / good / mid and late May / 7-14 in.

48. MOOSE CREEK

Access: The Glenn Highway crosses the stream at MP 186.0.

Major Species:

Grayling / good / mid- and late May / 7-14 in.

CHAPTER 17

Parks Highway

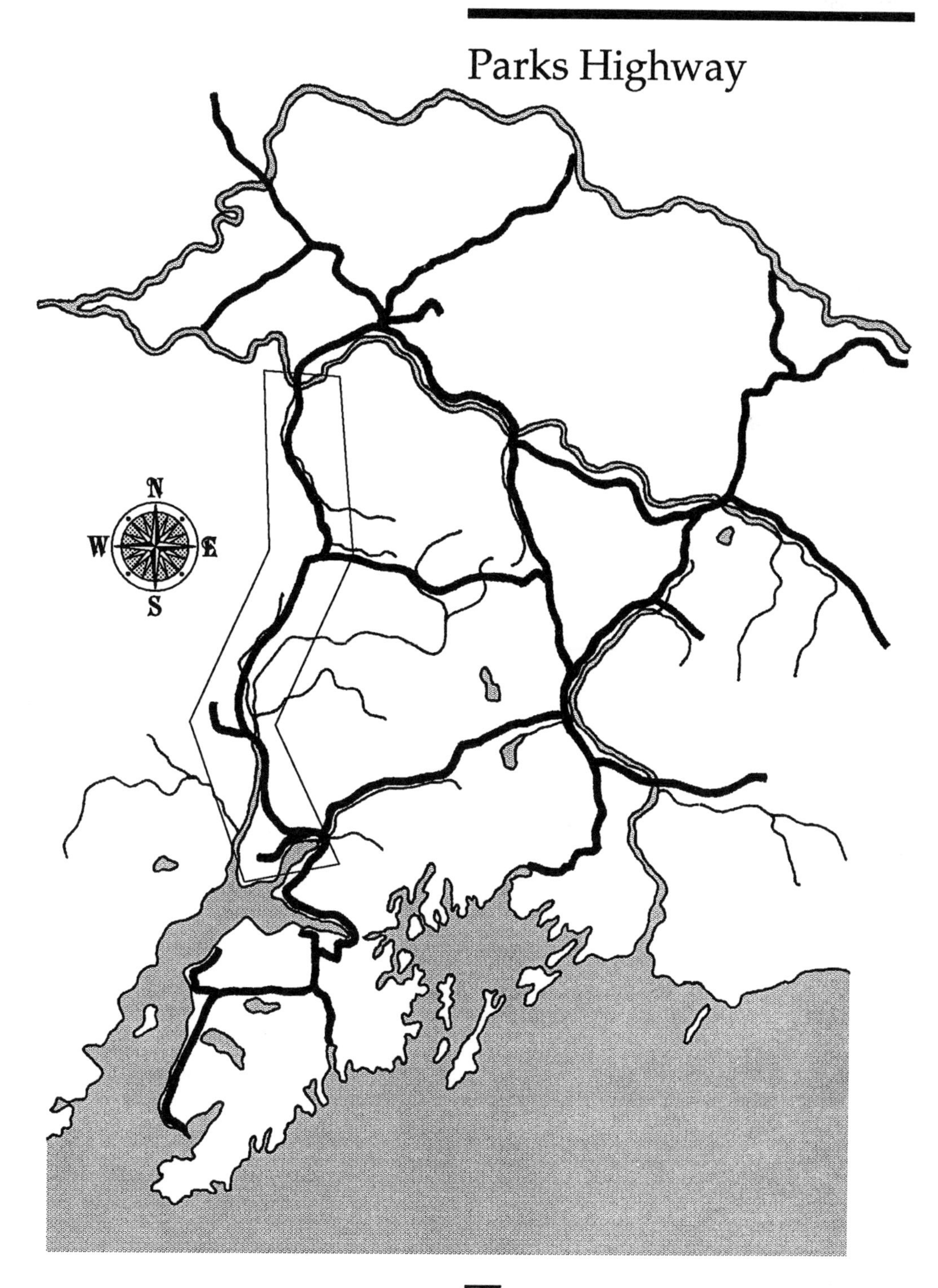

The Parks Highway begins just southeast of Wasilla at Milepost 35.3 of the Glenn Highway, and runs northwards to the interior city of Fairbanks. After diverting from the Glenn Highway, it joins up with the Denali Highway at Cantwell, and also connects with the Richardson and Steese highways in Fairbanks. The Parks Highway is a vital link between Alaska's two largest cities, Anchorage and Fairbanks.

CHAPTER 17

Parks Highway

The Parks Highway crosses and parallels three major glacial rivers, the Susitna, Chulitna, and Nenana. From the road there are a multitude of lakes and streams to fish, many with excellent access. Major sport fish species include king, pink, chum, and silver salmon, rainbow trout, grayling, and land-locked silver salmon. You'll also find other common species: red salmon, lake trout, Dolly Varden, and burbot. A few whitefish occasionally are taken. The fishing season may last throughout the year, but most activity occurs between mid-May and mid-October when area waters are ice-free.

Important: Please be aware of the current sport fishing rules and regulations for the area covered in this chapter, and abide by them. Remember, they have been applied to protect a fragile resource.

Following are the abbreviations used in this chapter for all the fish species and facility information:

KS - King Salmon	SS - Silver Salmon	GR - Grayling
RS - Red Salmon	DV - Dolly Varden	WF - Whitefish
PS - Pink Salmon	LT - Lake Trout	BB - Burbot
CS - Chum Salmon	RT - Rainbow Trout	

P - Parking	C - Camping	BL - Boat Launch
LP - Limited Parking	T - Toilet	

Time of Abundance/Availability Charts

These charts are designed to show the reader during which time of the year the indicated species are present or available in the most popular fishing streams, lakes, or regions. The charts correlate to when the fish are in their prime for both angling sport and consumption, unless otherwise noted. Species which are closed to sport fishing are also included on the charts just for the purpose of interest but are shown in all stages of maturity.

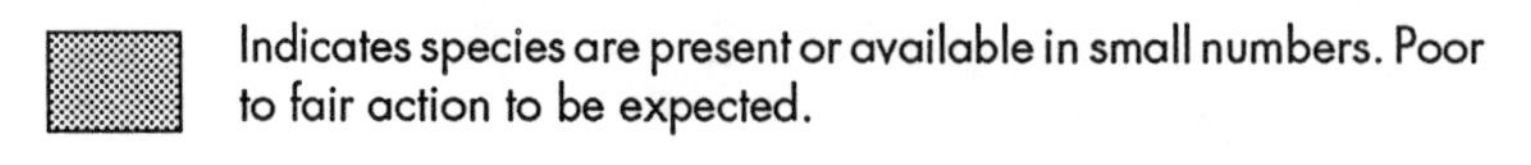

Indicates species are present or available in small numbers. Poor to fair action to be expected.

Indicates species are present or available in good numbers. Good to excellent action possible.

Note: The quality of fishing may vary due to certain fluctuations, such as weather conditions, angler experience, number of fish present, or other factors.

QUICK REFERENCE

This section was designed to provide a quick overview of all the fishing spots in the region, their map locations and milepost numbers, species available, facility information, and the page number on where to find detailed access and fishing information for any one specific watershed.

Note: Species shown in parentheses may be present but are protected by law, and/or are only occasionally seen or hooked by anglers fishing that particular watershed.

PARKS HIGHWAY

	WATERSHED	MILEPOST	SPECIES
1.	Walby Lake Facilities: P	35.6 Page: 175	RT
2.	Cornelius Lake Facilities: P	35.6 Page: 176	DV,RT,(RS,SS)
3.	Wolf Lake Facilities: P/T (trail)	35.6 Page: 176	SS
4.	Neklason Lake Facilities: P	35.6 Page: 176	DV,RT,(RS,SS)
5.	Finger Lake Facilities: P/C/T/BL	35.6 Page: 176	SS,RT,GR
6.	Cottonwood Lake Facilities: P	35.6 Page: 176	RT,(RS,SS,DV)
7.	Loberg Lake Facilities: P	35.7 Page: 176, 177	SS,RT
8.	Wasilla Creek Facilities: LP	37.8 Page: 177	SS,DV,RT,(KS,RT,PS,CS)
9.	Cottonwood Creek Facilities: LP	40.9 Page: 177	DV,RT,(RS,PS,CS,SS)
10.	Wasilla Lake Facilities: P/T/BL	(Wasilla) Page: 177	SS,DV,RT,(RS,PS)
11.	Cottonwood Creek Facilities: P	(Wasilla) Page: 177, 178	RS,SS,DV,(KS,PS,CS,RT)
12.	Knik Lake Facilities: P	(Wasilla) Page: 178	SS,RT,GR
13.	Fish Creek Facilities: P	(Wasilla) Page: 178, 179	RS,PS,SS,DV,RT,(KS,CS,WF)
14.	Little Susitna River Facilities: P/C/T/BL	(Wasilla) Page: 179, 180	KS,RS,PS,CS,SS,DV,RT,BB,WF, (LT,GR)

15. Lake Lucille Facilities: P	(Wasilla) Page: 180	SS,RT
16. Memory Lake Facilities: P	(Wasilla) Page: 180	SS,RT
17. Reed Lake Facilities: LP	(Wasilla) Page: 180	RT
18. Beverly Lake Facilities: P	48.7 Page: 180	RT
19. Kalmbach Lake Facilities: P	48.7 Page: 180	RT
20. Seymour Lake Facilities: P	48.7 Page: 180, 181	RT
21. Rocky Lake Facilities: P/C	52.3 Page: 181	SS,RT
22. Big Beaver Lake Facilities: P	52.3 Page: 181	RT
23. Big Lake Facilities: P/BL	52.3 Page: 181	DV,RT,BB, (KS,RS,PS,CS,SS,LT,WF)
24. Dawn Lake Facilities: P	52.3 Page: 182	RT
25. Marion Lake Facilities: LP (trail)	52.3 Page: 182	RT
26. Bear Paw Lake Facilities: P	54.8 Page: 182	SS,RT
27. Loon Lake Facilities: LP (trail)	54.8 Page: 182	SS,RT
28. Prator Lake Facilities: P	54.8 Page: 182	SS,RT
29. Little Susitna River Facilities: P/T	56.0/57.1 Page: 182, 183	KS,PS,CS,SS,DV,RT,GR,WF (RS,BB)

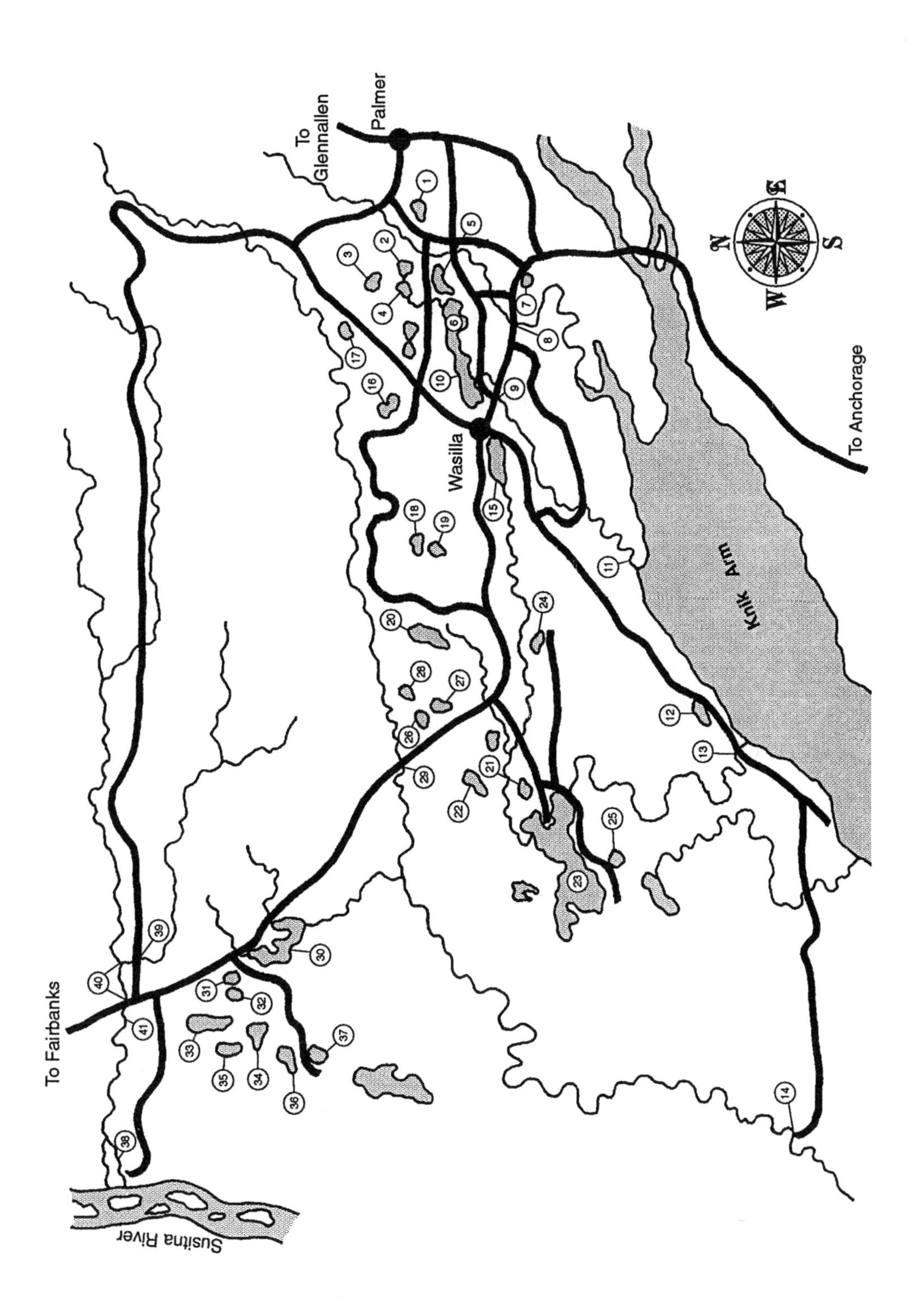
To Glennallen
Palmer
Wasilla
To Anchorage
Knik Arm
To Fairbanks
Susitna River
N
E
S
W

30.	Nancy Lake Facilities: P/C/T/BL	66.6/64.4 Page: 183, 184	RS,SS,DV,RT,(KS,PS,CS,LT,GR,WF,BB)
31.	Lynne Lake Facilities: LP	67.2 Page: 184	RT
32.	Honeybee Lake Facilities: LP	67.2 Page: 184	RT
33.	Long Lake Facilities: P	67.2 Page: 184, 185	RT
34.	Crystal Lake Facilities: P	67.2 Page: 185	RT
35.	Florence Lake Facilities: P	67.2 Page: 185	RT
36.	North Rolly Lake Facilities: P (trail)	67.2 Page: 185	RT
37.	South Rolly Lake Facilities: P/C/T/BL	67.2 Page: 185	RT
38.	Willow Creek Facilities: P/C/T	70.7 Page: 185, 186	KS,RS,PS,CS,SS,DV,RT,GR,WF,(BB)
39.	Deception Creek Facilities: P	71.2 Page: 186	RT,GR,(KS,PS,CS,SS,DV,WF)
40.	Willow Creek Facilities: P/C/T	71.2 Page: 186, 187	CS,SS,RT,GR,(KS,RS,PS,DV,WF)
41.	Willow Creek Facilities: P/C/T/BL	71.4 Page: 187	KS,PS,CS,SS,DV,RT,GR,WF,(RS,BB)
42.	Little Willow Creek Facilities: P	74.7 Page: 187, 188	KS,PS,CS,SS,RT,DV,GR,(RS,WF,BB)
43.	Kashwitna Lake Facilities: P	76.4 Page: 188	RT,(RS,SS,DV)
44.	Grays Creek Facilities: P	81.0 Page: 188	GR,(RT,DV)
45.	Kashwitna River Facilities: P/T/BL	83.2/82.5 Page: 188, 189	KS,PS,CS,SS,DV,RT,GR,(RS,WF,BB)

Parks Highway

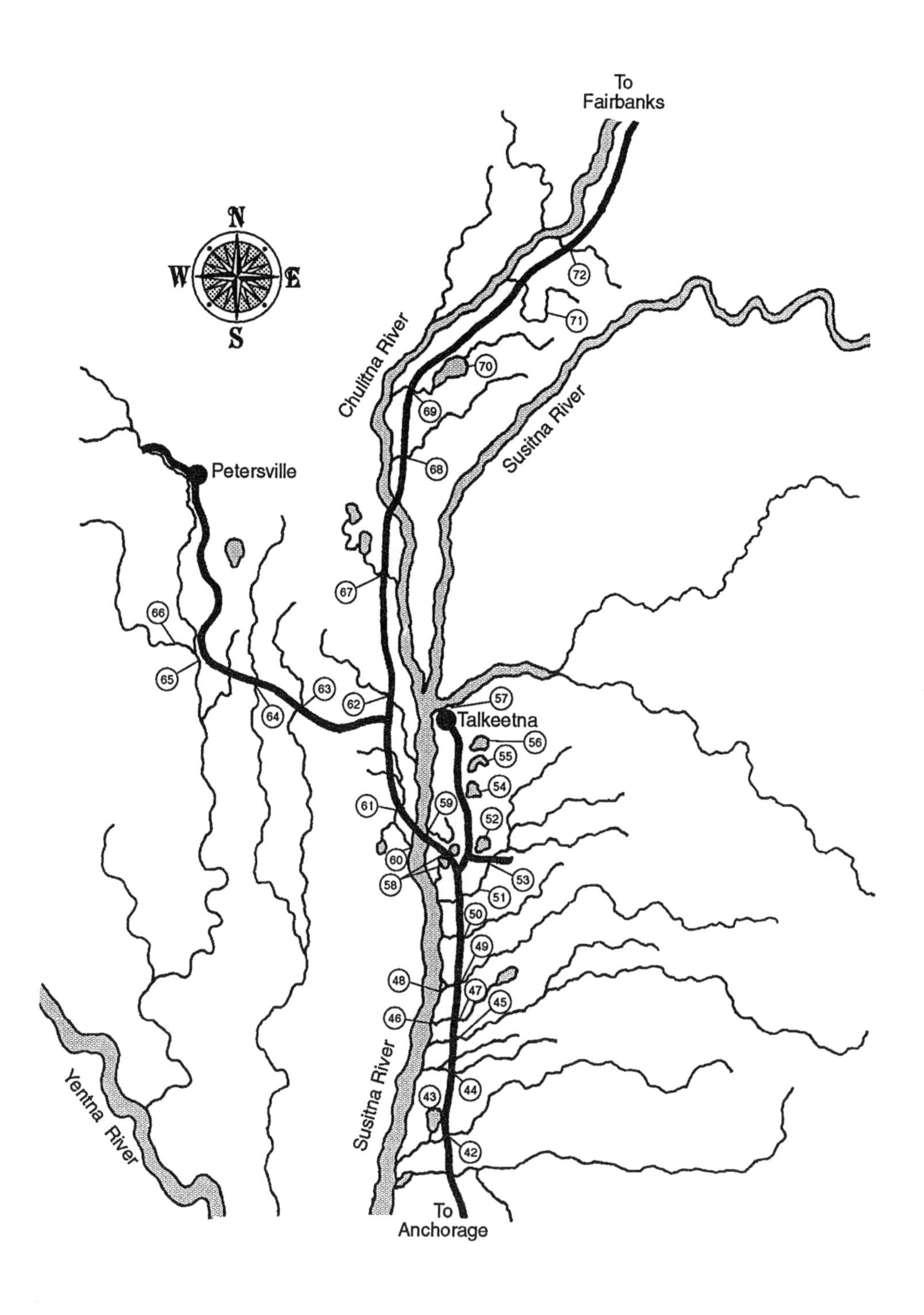

Site	Mile / Page	Species
46. Caswell Creek Facilities: P	84.1 Page: 189	KS,PS,CS,SS,RT,GR,(RS,DV,WF,BB)
47. Caswell Creek Facilities: P	84.9 Page:189, 190	GR (KS,RS,PS,CS,SS,DV,RT)
48. Sheep Creek Slough Facilities: P/T	85.8 Page: 190	KS,PS,CS,SS,DV,RT,GR,(RS,WF,BB)
49. Sheep Creek Facilities: P	88.6 Page: 190, 191	KS,PS,CS,SS,RT,DV,GR,WF,(RS,BB)
50. Goose Creek Facilities: P	92.7 Page: 191, 192	KS,PS,CS,SS,DV,RT,GR,(RS,WF,BB)
51. Montana Creek Facilities: P/C/T	96.5 Page: 192, 193	KS,PS,CS,SS,DV,RT,GR,WF(RS,BB)
52. Benka Lake Facilities: P/T/BL	98.7 Page: 193	SS,DV,RT
53. Montana Creek Facilities: P	98.7 Page: 193, 194	RT,GR,(KS,RS,PS,CS,SS,DV,WF)
54. Tigger Lake Facilities: P (trail)	98.7 Page: 194	RT
55. "Y" Lake Facilities: LP (trail)	98.7 Page: 194	RT
56. Christiansen Lake Facilities: P/T/BL	98.7 Page: 194	SS,RT
57. Talkeetna River Facilities: P/T/BL	98.7 Page: 194	KS,PS,CS,SS,DV,RT,GR,(RS,WF,BB)
58. S./N. Friend Lakes Facilities: LP	99.2 Page: 195	RT,(RS,SS,DV)
59. Sunshine Creek Facilities: P	102.5 Page: 195	KS,RS,PS,CS,SS,RT,GR,(DV,WF,BB)
60. Rabideux Creek Facilities: P	104.4 Page: 195, 196	KS,PS,CS,SS,RT,GR,(RS,DV,WF,BB)
61. Rabideux Creek Facilities: LP	105.8 Page: 196	PS,SS,RT,GR,(KS,RS,CS,DV,WF)

62. Trapper Creek Facilities: LP	115.6 Page: 196	SS,RT,GR,(KS,RS,PS,CS,DV)
63. Moose Creek Facilities: LP	114.8 Page: 197	SS,RT,GR,(KS,RS,PS,CS,DV)
64. Kroto Creek Facilities: P	114.8 Page: 197	SS,RT,GR,(KS,RS,PS,CS,DV)
65. Peters Creek Facilities: P	114.8 Page: 197, 198	KS,SS,RT,GR,(RS,PS,CS,DV,WF)
66. Martin Creek Facilities: P (trail)	114.8 Page: 198	KS,SS,RT,GR,(PS,CS,DV)
67. Sunny Creek Facilities: P	128.5 Page: 198, 199	RS,SS,DV,RT,GR,(KS,PS,CS)
68. Troublesome Creek Facilities: P/T	137.4 Page: 199	RS,PS,CS,SS,RT,GR,(KS,DV,WF)
69. Byers Creek Facilities: LP	143.9 Page: 199	RS,SS,RT,GR,(KS,PS,CS,DV,WF)
70. Byers Lake Facilities: P/C/T/BL	147.2 Page: 199	DV,LT,GR,BB,(KS,RS,PS,SS,RT,WF)
71. Horseshoe Creek Facilities: LP	159.8 Page: 199, 200	RS,SS,RT,GR,(KS,PS,CS,DV)
72. Coal Creek Facilities: LP	161.3 Page: 200	SS,RT,GR,(KS,RS,PS,CS,DV)
73. Honolulu Creek Facilities: P	178.1 Page: 200	SS,GR,(KS,PS,CS,DV,RT,WF)
74. E. Fork Chulitna River Facilities: P/C/T	184.8 Page: 200	KS,SS,RT,GR,WF,(CS,DV)
75. M. Fork Chulitna River Facilities: P	194.5 Page: 200	RT,GR,(KS,CS,SS,DV,WF)
76. Summit Lake Facilities: P	200.1 Page: 201	LT,GR,BB
77. Mirror Lake Facilities: LP (trail)	202.0 Page: 201	LT,GR,BB

CHAPTER 17

Parks Highway

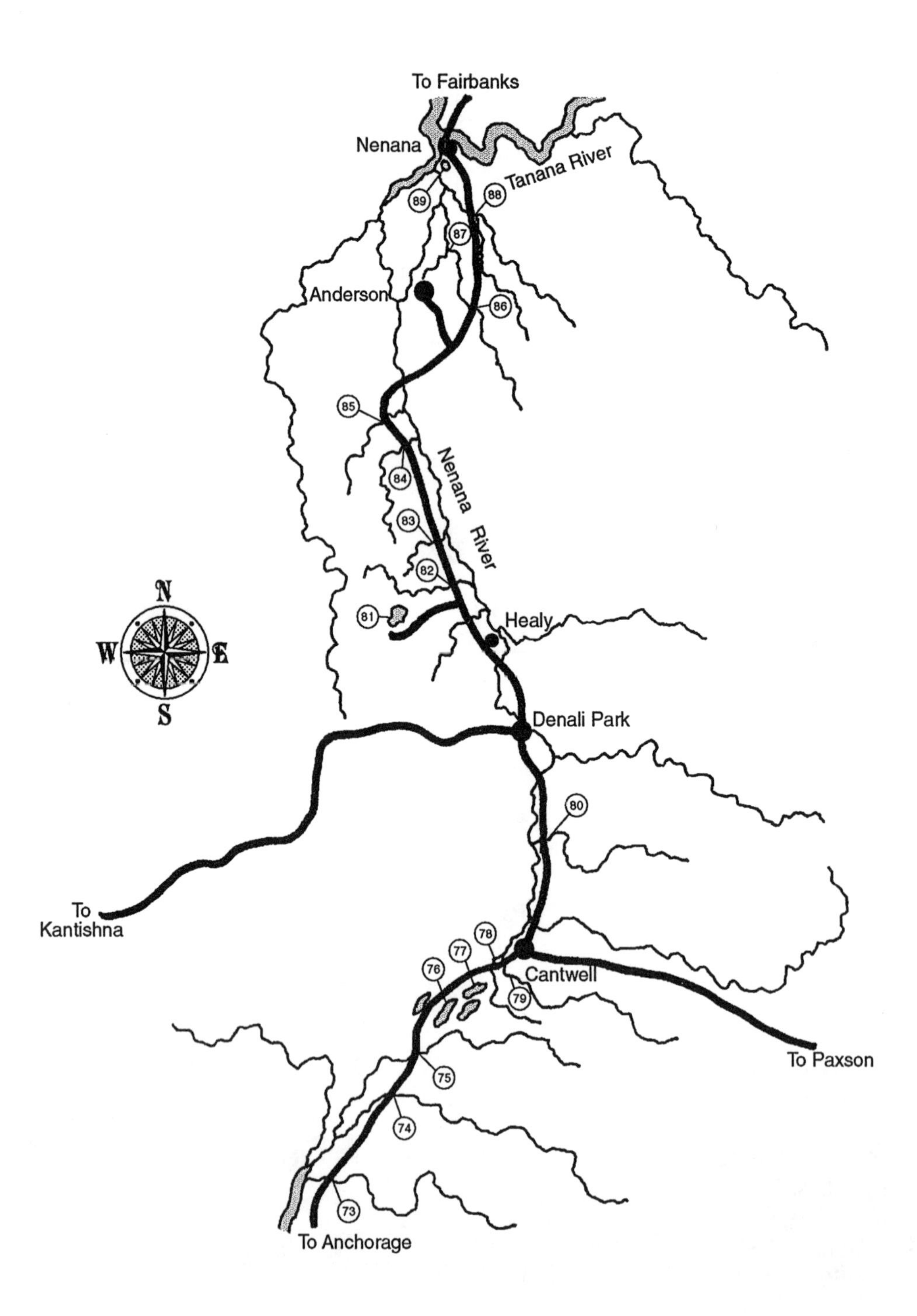

78. Pass Creek Facilities: P	208.0 Page: 201	GR
79. Jack River Facilities: P	209.6 Page: 201	GR,(WF)
80. Carlo Creek Facilities: P	223.9 Page: 201	GR
81. Eightmile Lake Facilities: P (trail)	251.2 Page: 201	GR
82. Panguingue Creek Facilities: P	252.4 Page: 201	GR
83. Slate Creek Facilities: LP	257.8 Page: 201	GR
84. Bear Creek Facilities: LP	269.3 Page: 202	GR
85. Birch Creek Facilities: LP	272.5 Page: 202	GR
86. Julius Creek Facilities: LP	285.6 Page: 202	GR
87. Julius Creek Facilities: LP (trail)	295.2 Page: 202	SS,GR,(CS,WF)
88. Fish Creek Facilities: LP	296.6 Page: 202	GR
89. Nenana Pond Facilities: P/C/T	303.4 Page: 202	SS

AREA A: MATANUSKA VALLEY DRAINAGE

Includes all waters draining into and surrounding Knik Arm and upper Cook Inlet.

1. WALBY LAKE

Access: From MP 35.6 of the Parks Highway. Turn north onto Trunk Road, drive 5.1 miles to Tern Drive on right, proceed 0.6 miles to access road on right.

Major Species:

Rainbow trout / fair / May and September, October / 7-12 in.

2. **CORNELIUS LAKE**
Access: From MP 35.6 of the Parks Highway. Turn north onto Trunk Road, drive 4.2 miles and turn left on Bogard Road, continue 0.5 miles to Engstrom Road and turn right, proceed 1.0 mile to lake on the right.
Regulations: Salmon fishing prohibited.
Major Species:
Dolly Varden / fair / August through October / 7-14 in.
Rainbow trout / fair / May and September, October / 7-15 in.

3. **WOLF LAKE**
Access: From MP 35.6 of the Parks Highway. Turn north onto Trunk Road, drive 4.2 miles and turn left on Bogard Road. Continue 0.5 miles to Engstrom Road, turn right, and proceed 2.6 miles to the end of the road. Park and hike 100 yards to lake.
Major Species:
Silver salmon / good / March through December / 7-12 in.

4. **NEKLASON LAKE**
Access: From MP 35.6 of the Parks Highway. Turn north onto Trunk Road, drive 4.2 miles and turn left on Bogard Road. Continue 0.5 miles to Engstrom Road, turn right, and proceed 0.8 miles to Zephyr Drive. Turn left, drive 0.3 miles to Breezewood Drive on the right. Continue 0.2 miles to a "T," take the right fork and proceed 0.2 miles to the lake.
Regulations: Salmon fishing prohibited.
Major Species:
Dolly Varden / fair / August through October / 7-14 in.
Rainbow trout / fair / May and September, October / 7-15 in.

5. **FINGER LAKE**
Access: From MP 35.6 of the Parks Highway. Turn north onto Trunk Road, drive 4.2 miles and turn left on Bogard Road. Continue 1.8 miles to sign on left, and follow gravel road 0.4 miles to the lake.
Major Species:
Silver salmon / good / March through December / 7-15 in.
Rainbow trout / fair / May and September, October / 7-16 in.
Grayling / fair / June through September / 7-14 in.

6. **COTTONWOOD LAKE**
Access: From MP 35.6 of the Parks Highway. Turn north onto Trunk Road, drive 4.2 miles and turn left on Bogard Road. Continue 2.1 miles to East Cottonwood Drive, turn left, and proceed 0.8 miles to Spruce Drive. Turn left and drive 0.3 miles to the lake.
Regulations: Salmon fishing prohibited.
Major Species:
Rainbow trout / fair / May and September, October / 7-16 in.

7. **LOBERG LAKE**
Access: From MP 35.7 of the Parks Highway. The lake is located beside the road to the southwest.

Major Species:
Silver salmon / fair / March through December / 7-14 in.
Rainbow trout / fair / May and September, October / 7-14 in.

8. WASILLA CREEK

Access: The Parks Highway crosses the stream at MP 37.8. Park on southwest side of creek and fish downstream.
Regulations: King salmon fishing prohibited. Closed to all fishing from April 15 through June 14.
Major Species:
Silver salmon / fair / early and mid-August / 4-10 lbs.
Dolly Varden / fair / August and September / 7-12 in.
Rainbow trout / poor to fair / July and August / 7-12 in.

9. COTTONWOOD CREEK

Access: The Parks Highway crosses the stream at MP 40.9. Or, turn northwest onto the Palmer Wasilla Highway in the town of Wasilla. Drive to MP 15.6 and stream crossing and outlet of Wasilla Lake.
Regulations: Salmon fishing prohibited. Closed to all fishing from April 15 through June 14.
Major Species:
Dolly Varden / poor to fair / July through September / 7-14 in.
Rainbow trout / fair / July through October 7-15 in.

10. WASILLA LAKE

Access: The lake is adjacent to the Parks Highway right in Wasilla. Or, turn onto Palmer Wasilla Highway and drive to MP 15.6 and the lake outlet.
Regulations: Salmon fishing prohibited.
Major Species:
Silver salmon / fair / March through December / 7-15 in.
Rainbow trout / fair / May and September, October / 7-16 in.
Dolly Varden / poor to fair / August through October / 7-15 in.

11. COTTONWOOD CREEK

Access: From the town of Wasilla. Turn south on Main Street (Knik Goose Bay Road), drive 4.0 miles to Fairview Loop Road and turn left. Continue 1.9 miles to a sharp turn in the road and proceed straight on the gravel road 1.3 miles. Turn left on dirt road leading 0.5 miles to parking area and the stream.
Regulations: King salmon fishing prohibited. Closed to all fishing from April 15 through June 14. Weekend-only fishery.

Time of Abundance:

FISH▽	JAN	FEB	MAR	APR	MAY	JUN	JUL	AUG	SEP	OCT	NOV	DEC
KS												
RS												
PS												
CS												
SS												
DV												
RT												

Major Species:

Red salmon / fair to good / 4-8 lbs., max. 12 lbs. / egg imitation and streamer flies, salmon egg clusters.

Silver salmon / fair to good / 5-10 lbs., max. 15 lbs. / egg imitation flies, salmon egg clusters.

Dolly Varden / poor to fair / 7-15 in., max. 3 lbs. / egg imitation flies, salmon egg clusters, attractor lures.

12. KNIK LAKE

Access: From the town of Wasilla. Turn south on Main Street (Knik Goose Bay Road) and drive 13.6 miles. Turn right at Public Access sign and follow series of signs a short distance to the lake.

Major Species:

Silver salmon / fair / March through December / 7-12 in.

Rainbow trout / good / May and September, October / 7-18 in.

Grayling / fair / May through September / 7-14 in.

13. FISH CREEK

Access: From the town of Wasilla. Turn south on Main Street (Knik Goose Bay Road) and drive 21.0 miles to stream crossing.

Regulations: King salmon prohibited. Closed to all fishing from January through July. Check sport fishing regulations closely for detail on openings and areas.

Time of Abundance:

FISH▽	JAN	FEB	MAR	APR	MAY	JUN	JUL	AUG	SEP	OCT	NOV	DEC
KS												
RS												
PS												
CS												
SS												
DV												
RT												
WF												

Major Species:

Red salmon / poor to fair / 4-8 lbs., max. 12 lbs. / streamer flies and spinners.
Pink salmon / poor to fair / 2-4 lbs., max 6. lbs. / spoons and spinners, streamer flies.
Silver salmon / good / 5-10 lbs., max. 15 lbs. / streamer flies, spinners, salmon egg clusters.
Dolly Varden / fair / 8-15 in., max. 3 lbs. / spoons, flies, salmon egg clusters, single salmon eggs.
Rainbow trout / fair to good / 7-15 in., max. 5 lbs. / flies, spinners, single salmon eggs, salmon egg clusters.

14. LITTLE SUSITNA RIVER

Access: From the town of Wasilla. Turn south on Main Street (Knik Goose Bay Road), drive 17.2 miles and turn right on Point Mackenzie Road. Continue 7.6 miles to a "T" and turn right. Proceed a short distance to another "T" and turn on Ayrshire Road. Drive 2.7 miles to a "Y" and turn right on Little Su Access Road. Drive 3.3 miles to campground and the river.

Regulations: King salmon fishing prohibited from July 14 through December 31. Check the sport fishing regulations closely for various other restrictions.

Time of Abundance:

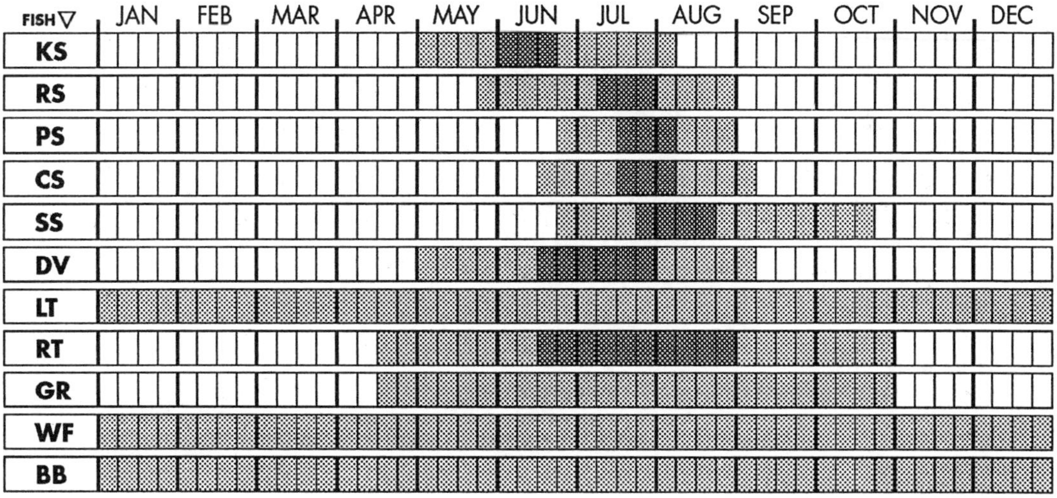

FISH ▽	JAN	FEB	MAR	APR	MAY	JUN	JUL	AUG	SEP	OCT	NOV	DEC
KS												
RS												
PS												
CS												
SS												
DV												
LT												
RT												
GR												
WF												
BB												

Major Species:

King salmon / good to excellent / 15-45 lbs., max. 70 lbs. / salmon egg clusters, attractor lures, spinner.
Red salmon / poor to fair / 4-8 lbs., max. 12 lbs. / streamer flies, salmon egg clusters, spinners.
Pink salmon / good to excellent / 2-5 lbs., max. 7 lbs. / spoons and spinners, attractor lures.
Chum salmon / good excellent / 6-12 lbs., max. 18 lbs. / spoons and spinners, attractor lures, salmon egg clusters.
Silver salmon / good to excellent / 5-12 lbs., max. 18 lbs./ salmon egg clusters, attractor lures, spinners.

Dolly Varden / fair / 8-15 in., max. 4 lbs. / salmon egg clusters, single salmon eggs, flies, spinners.
Rainbow trout / fair / 7-15 in., max. 3 lbs. / salmon egg clusters, spinners, flies, single salmon eggs.
Burbot / poor to fair / 15-22 in., max. 6 lbs. / herring, smelt, and whitefish bait.
Whitefish / poor to fair / 10-15 in., max. 17 in. / single salmon eggs, salmon egg clusters, wet flies, corkies.

15. LAKE LUCILLE

Access: From the town of Wasilla. Turn south on Main Street, drive a short distance and turn right on Susitna Avenue. Continue 0.3 miles to the lake.

Major Species:
Silver salmon / fair / March through December / 7-14 in.
Rainbow trout / fair / May and September, October / 7-15 in.

16. MEMORY LAKE

Access: From the town of Wasilla. Turn north on Main Street (Wasilla Fishhook Road), drive 3.0 miles and turn left on Schrock Road. Continue 1.1 mile to Hebrides Drive and turn right. Proceed 0.2 miles to a "T" and turn left on Inverness Drive. Continue a short distance to access road on right leading to the lake.

Major Species:
Silver salmon / good / March through December / 7-14 in.
Rainbow trout / fair / May and September, October / 7-16 in.

17. REED LAKE

Access: From the town of Wasilla. Turn north on Main Street (Wasilla Fishhook Road), drive 7.3 miles and turn left on Welch road. Proceed 0.35 miles to access trail on right.

Major Species:
Rainbow trout / good / May and September, October / 7-16 in.

18. BEVERLY LAKE

Access: From MP 48.7 of the Parks Highway. Turn north on Pittman Road, drive 1.3 miles to Beverly Lake Road and turn right. Proceed 3.1 miles to trail on right. Short hike to the lake.

Major Species:
Rainbow trout / fair / May and September, October / 7-16 in.

19. KALMBACH LAKE

Access: From MP 48.7 of the Parks Highway. Turn north on Pittman Road, drive 1.3 miles to Beverly Lake Road and turn right, proceed 3.1 miles to small parking area on right. Park and hike short distance to the lake.

Major Species:
Rainbow trout / good / May and September, October / 7-18 in.

20. SEYMOUR LAKE

Access: From MP 48.7 of the Parks Highway. Turn north on Pittman Road, drive 1.8 miles to Meadow Lake Road and turn left. Continue 0.9 miles to Juliana Drive and turn right.

Proceed 0.1 mile to a "T" and turn right on Alma Drive. Go a short distance to Louise Road and drive 0.1 mile to the lake.

Major Species:

Rainbow trout / good / May and September, October / 7-18 in.

21. ROCKY LAKE

Access: From MP 52.3 of the Parks Highway. Turn southwest on Big Lake Road and drive 3.4 miles to Beaver Lake Road on the right. Proceed 0.4 miles and turn left by sign on Rocky Street. Take first left to campground and the lake.

Major Species:

Silver salmon / fair / March through December / 7-14 in.
Rainbow trout / fair / May and September, October / 7-15 in.

22. BIG BEAVER LAKE

Access: From MP 52.3 of the Parks Highway. Turn southwest on Big Lake Road and drive 3.4 miles to Beaver Lake Road on the right. Proceed 4.2 miles to Wilma Street and turn right. Continue short distance to the lake on right.

Major Species:

Rainbow trout / fair / May and September, October / 7-18 in.

23. BIG LAKE

Access: From MP 52.3 of the Parks Highway. Turn southwest on Big Lake Road and drive 3.5 miles to a "Y." Take right fork and drive 1.6 miles to a wayside and the lake. Follow left fork and drive 1.7 miles to gravel road on the right leading to the lake.

Regulations: Salmon fishing prohibited.

Time of Availability:

FISH▽	JAN	FEB	MAR	APR	MAY	JUN	JUL	AUG	SEP	OCT	NOV	DEC
KS												
RS												
PS												
CS												
SS												
DV												
LT												
RT												
WF												
BB												

Major Species:

Dolly Varden / fair to good / 7-20 in., max. 7 lbs. / spoons and spinners, single salmon eggs, salmon egg clusters.
Rainbow trout / fair to good / 7-20 in., max. 10 lbs. / flies, spinners, single salmon eggs, salmon egg clusters.
Burbot / fair / 15-22 in., max. 8 lbs. / herring, smelt, and whitefish bait.

24. DAWN LAKE

Access: From MP 52.3 of the Parks Highway. Turn southwest on Big Lake and drive 4.1 miles to Hollywood Road. Turn left and drive 4.0 miles to Johnson Road on the left. Proceed a short distance and turn right on Dawn Lake Drive. Continue 0.6 miles to Dawn Lake Road and turn left into parking area. Short hike to lake.

Major Species:

Rainbow trout / good / May and September, October / 7-16 in.

25. MARION LAKE

Access: From MP 52.3 of the Parks Highway. Turn southwest on Big Lake Road and drive 8.9 miles to Marion Drive on left. Proceed a short distance and turn left. Continue 0.5 miles to access trail on the right by sign. Hike 100 yards to the lake.

Major Species:

Rainbow trout / good / May and September, October / 7-18 in.

26. BEAR PAW LAKE

Access: From MP 54.8 of the Parks Highway. Turn east on Cheri Lake Road, drive 0.8 miles and turn left on White Rabbit Drive. Proceed 0.1 mile to Enchanted Drive and turn left. Continue 0.2 miles straight to the end of the road and the lake.

Major Species:

Silver salmon / fair / March through December / 7-14 in.
Rainbow trout / fair / May and September, October / 7-16 in.

27. LOON LAKE

Access: From MP 54.8 of the Parks Highway. Turn east on Cheri Lake Road, drive 1.3 miles and turn right on Anthony Road. Proceed 1.0 mile to access trail on the right. Hike 200 yards to the lake.

Major Species:

Silver salmon / good / March through December / 7-14 in.
Rainbow trout / fair / May and September, October / 7-16 in.

28. PRATOR LAKE

Access: From MP 54.8 of the Parks Highway. Turn north on Cheri Lake Road, drive 1.3 miles and turn left on Anthony Road. Proceed 0.3 miles to Prince Charming Drive and turn right. Continue 0.4 miles to access road on right.

Major Species:

Silver salmon / fair / March through December / 7-14 in.
Rainbow trout / fair / May and September, October / 7-16 in.

29. LITTLE SUSITNA RIVER

Access Point A: Millers Reach - From MP 56.0 of the Parks Highway. Turn southwest on Millers Reach Road and drive 2.0 miles to sharp bend in road where it joins Rapalla Street. Continue straight 0.5 miles to end of the road. Park and hike 100 yards by trail to river.

Access Point B: Parks Highway Bridge - The Parks Highway crosses the river at MP 57.1. Parking is available by bridge or to the south from MP 57.4.

Access Point C: Alaska Railroad Trestle Bridge - From MP 58.0 of the Parks Highway. Turn west onto dirt road leading 0.5 miles to parking area. Hike along railroad tracks about 200 yards to the river and bridge.

Regulations: King salmon fishing prohibited from July 14 through December 31. Salmon fishing is prohibited year-round above the highway bridge. Check the sport fishing regulations for details on various restrictions.

Time of Abundance:

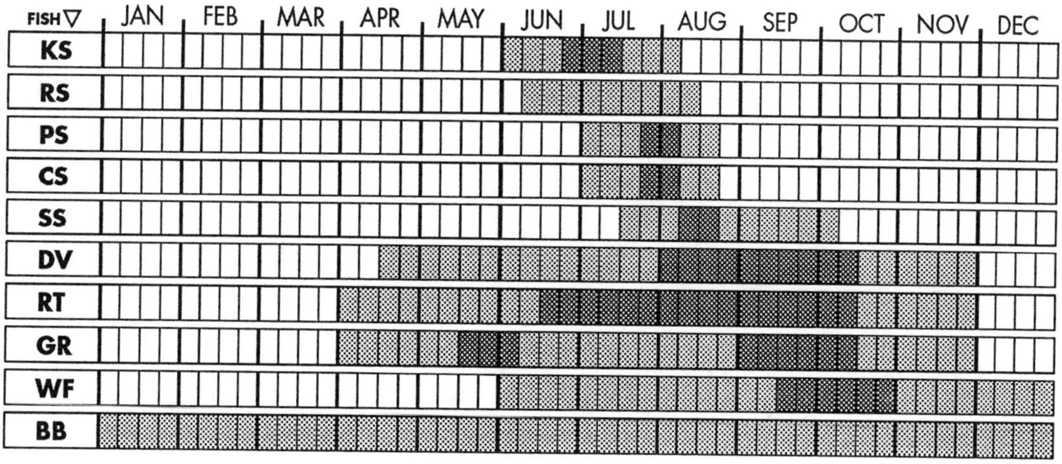

FISH ▽	JAN	FEB	MAR	APR	MAY	JUN	JUL	AUG	SEP	OCT	NOV	DEC
KS												
RS												
PS												
CS												
SS												
DV												
RT												
GR												
WF												
BB												

Major Species:

King salmon / fair to good / 15-45 lbs., max 70 lbs. / salmon egg clusters, egg imitation flies, attractor lures.

Pink salmon / fair to good / 2-5 lbs., max. 7 lbs. / spoons and spinners.

Chum salmon / good / 6-12 lbs. max. 18 lbs. / spoons and spinners, plugs.

Silver salmon / fair to good / 5-12 lbs., max. 18 lbs. / salmon egg clusters, spinners, and plugs.

Dolly Varden / fair / 7-15 in., max 4 lbs. / salmon egg clusters, single salmon eggs, spinners, flies.

Rainbow trout / fair / 7-15 in., max. 3 lbs. / salmon egg clusters, single salmon eggs, flies, spinners.

Grayling / fair / 7-14 in., max. 17 in./ flies, spinners, single salmon eggs.

Whitefish / poor to fair / 10-15 in., max. 17 in. / salmon egg clusters, single salmon eggs, flies.

30. NANCY LAKE

Access: From MP 66.6 of the Parks Highway. Turn south on gravel road and follow signs 0.6 miles to the lake. Also, turn west onto a gravel road leading a short distance to Nancy Lake Marina from MP 64.4 of the Parks Highway.

Regulations: King salmon and Burbot fishing prohibited.

Time of Availability:

FISH▽	JAN	FEB	MAR	APR	MAY	JUN	JUL	AUG	SEP	OCT	NOV	DEC
KS												
RS												
PS												
CS												
SS												
DV												
LT												
RT												
GR												
WF												
BB												

Major Species:

Red salmon / poor to fair / 4-8 lbs., max. 12 lbs. / spoons and spinners, streamer flies.
Silver salmon / fair to good / 5-12 lbs., max. 15 lbs. / spoons and spinners, salmon egg clusters.
Dolly Varden / fair / 8-15 in., max. 3 lbs. / salmon egg clusters, spinners, flies.
Rainbow trout / fair to good / 8-18 in., max. 5 lbs. / spoons and spinners, flies, salmon egg clusters.

31. LYNNE LAKE

Access: From MP 67.2 of the Parks Highway. Turn southwest on Nancy Lake Parkway and drive 0.7 miles to Long Lake Road on right. Proceed about 0.7 miles to dirt road on right and continue 0.6 miles and park. Hike a short distance to the lake located on the right.

Major Species:

Rainbow trout / good / May and September, October / 7-18 in.

32. HONEYBEE LAKE

Access: From MP 67.2 of the Parks Highway. Turn southwest onto Nancy Lake Parkway and drive 0.7 miles to Long Lake Road on right. Proceed about 0.7 miles to dirt road on right and continue 0.7 miles and park. Hike a short distance due west to the lake.

Major Species:

Rainbow trout / good / May and September, October / 7-18 in.

33. LONG LAKE

Access: From MP 67.2 of the Parks Highway. Turn southwest onto Nancy Lake Parkway and drive 0.7 miles to Long Lake Road on the right. Proceed 1.8 miles to Crystal Lake Road and turn left, continue 0.3 miles to small parking area on the right. Hike 50 yards following small stream to lake.

Regulations: Fishing prohibited in creek draining the lake from April 15 through June 14.

Major Species:
Rainbow trout / good / May and September, October / 7-18 in.

34. CRYSTAL LAKE

Access: From MP 67.2 of the Parks Highway. Turn southwest onto Nancy Lake Parkway, drive 0.7 miles to Long Lake Road and turn right. Proceed 1.8 miles to Crystal Lake Road and turn left. Drive 0.5 miles to a "Y" and turn right. Continue 1.4 miles to Crystal View Drive and turn left. Proceed 0.9 miles to access road on left leading a short distance to the lake.

Major Species:
Rainbow trout / good / May and September, October / 7-18 in.

35. FLORENCE LAKE

Access: From MP 67.2 of the Parks Highway. Turn southwest onto Nancy Lake Parkway, drive 0.7 miles to Long Lake Road on the right. Proceed 1.8 miles to Crystal Lake Road and turn left. Continue 0.5 miles to a "Y," turn right, and drive 1.7 miles to lake on the right.

Major Species:
Rainbow trout / good / May and September, October / 7-18 in.

36. NORTH ROLLY LAKE

Access: From MP 67.2 of the Parks Highway. Turn southwest onto Nancy Lake Parkway and drive 5.0 miles and park. Find trail on right side of road leading 200 yards due north to lake.

Major Species:
Rainbow trout / fair / May and September, October / 7-18 in.

37. SOUTH ROLLY LAKE

Access: From MP 67.2 of the Parks Highway. Turn southwest onto Nancy Lake Parkway and drive 6.8 miles to the end of the road. The lake and campground are located on the left.

Major Species:
Rainbow trout / fair / May and September, October / 7-18 in.

AREA B: SUSITNA RIVER DRAINAGE

Includes all waters draining into the middle Susitna River and the surrounding area.

38. WILLOW CREEK / SUSITNA RIVER CONFLUENCE

Access: From MP 70.7 of the Parks Highway. Turn west on Willow Creek Parkway and drive 3.9 miles to the end of the road. Park and hike along trail about 0.25 miles to the confluence area.

Regulations: Check the sport fishing regulations closely for open dates. Only unbaited, artificial lures may be used from September 1 through December 31.

Time of Abundance:

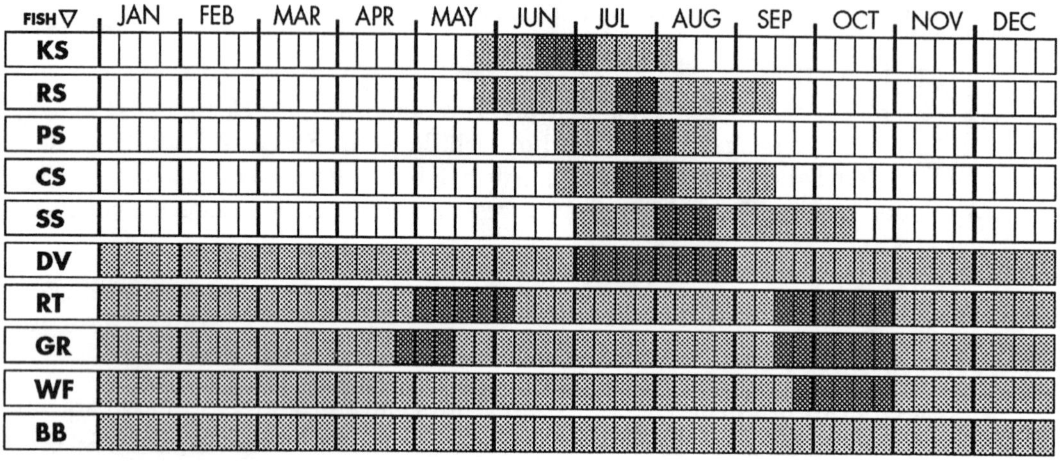

FISH ▽	JAN	FEB	MAR	APR	MAY	JUN	JUL	AUG	SEP	OCT	NOV	DEC
KS												
RS												
PS												
CS												
SS												
DV												
RT												
GR												
WF												
BB												

Major Species:

King salmon / good to excellent / 15-45 lbs., max. 75 lbs. / attractor lures, spoons, salmon egg clusters.
Red salmon / poor to fair / 4-8 lbs., max. 12 lbs. / streamer flies, spoons, and spinners.
Pink salmon / good to excellent / 2-4 lbs., max. 6 lbs. / spoons and spinners.
Chum salmon / good to excellent / 6-12 lbs., max. 18 lbs. / spoons and spinners, salmon egg clusters.
Silver salmon / good to excellent / 5-12 lbs., max. 15 lbs. / salmon egg clusters, spoons, and spinners.
Dolly Varden / fair / 7-15 in., max. 4 lbs. / salmon egg cluster, spoons, spinners, single salmon eggs.
Rainbow trout / fair to good / 7-18 in., max. 12 lbs. / egg imitation flies, salmon egg clusters, spinners.
Grayling / fair to good / 7-15 in., max. 18 in. / flies and spinners.
Whitefish / poor to fair / 10-15 in., max. 17 in. / salmon egg clusters, single salmon eggs, wet flies.

39. DECEPTION CREEK

Access: From MP 71.2 of the Parks Highway. Turn east onto Hatcher Pass Road and drive to MP 48.1 and stream crossing. The confluence of Deception and Willow creeks is accessible through the campground north of the road just before the bridge.

Regulations: Salmon fishing prohibited. Closed to all fishing from April 15 through June 14.

Major Species:

Rainbow trout / fair / June and September / 8-20 in.
Grayling / fair / June through September / 7-15 in.

40. WILLOW CREEK

Access: From MP 71.2 of the Parks Highway. Turn east onto Hatcher Pass Road and drive to Deception Creek Wayside on the left, MP 48.2. Find trail leading a short distance from the parking area to the river.

Regulations: King salmon fishing prohibited. Only unbaited, artificial lures may be used from September 1 through December 31.

Major Species:

Chum salmon / poor to fair / late July / 6-12 lbs.
Silver salmon / fair to good / mid-August / 5-12 lbs.
Rainbow trout / fair to good / September, October / 8-25 in.
Grayling / fair to good / June through September / 7-15 in.

41. WILLOW CREEK

Access: The Parks Highway crosses the river at MP 71.4.

Regulations: King salmon fishing prohibited upstream from the highway bridge. Check the sport fishing regulations closely for open dates. Only unbaited, artificial lures may be used from September 1 through December 31.

Time of Abundance:

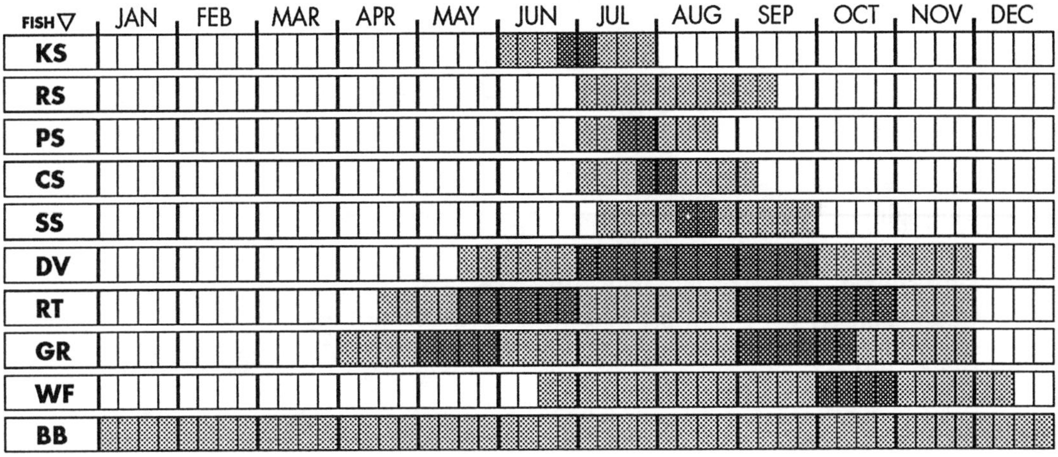

FISH▽	JAN	FEB	MAR	APR	MAY	JUN	JUL	AUG	SEP	OCT	NOV	DEC
KS												
RS												
PS												
CS												
SS												
DV												
RT												
GR												
WF												
BB												

Major Species:

King salmon / good / 15-45 lbs., max. 75 lbs. / spoons and spinners, salmon egg clusters, streamer flies.
Pink salmon / fair to good / 2-4 lbs., max. 6 lbs. / spoons and spinners.
Chum salmon / good / 6-12 lbs., max. 18 lbs. / spoons and spinners, salmon egg clusters.
Silver salmon / good / 5-12 lbs., max. 15 lbs. / salmon egg clusters, spoons, spinners.
Dolly Varden / fair / 8-15 in., max. 5 lbs. / spoons, spinners, salmon egg clusters, single salmon eggs.
Rainbow trout / fair to good / 8-20 in., max. 12 lbs. / egg imitation flies, spinners, salmon egg clusters.
Grayling / fair to good / 7-15 in., max. 18 in. / flies and spinners, single salmon eggs.
Whitefish / poor to fair / 10-15 in., max. 17 in. / single salmon egg, wet flies, salmon egg clusters.

42. LITTLE WILLOW CREEK

Access: The Parks Highway crosses the stream at MP 74.7.

Regulations: King salmon fishing prohibited upstream from the highway bridge. Check the sport fishing regulations closely for opening dates below the highway for king salmon. Only unbaited, artificial lures may be used from September 1 through December 31.

Time of Abundance:

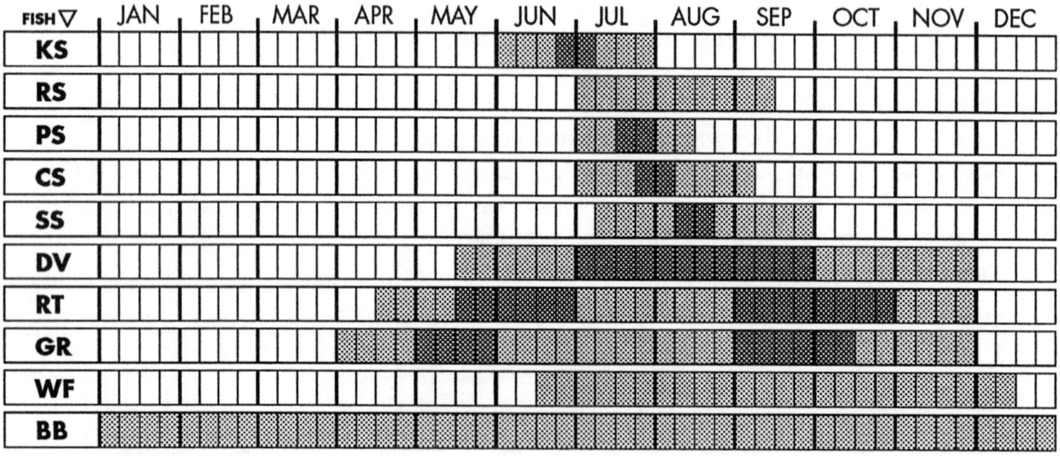

FISH▽	JAN	FEB	MAR	APR	MAY	JUN	JUL	AUG	SEP	OCT	NOV	DEC
KS												
RS												
PS												
CS												
SS												
DV												
RT												
GR												
WF												
BB												

Major Species:

King salmon / fair / 15-45 lbs., max. 65 lbs. / salmon egg clusters, spoons, spinners, attractor lures.

Pink salmon / fair / 2-4 lbs., max. 6 lbs. / spoons and spinners, streamer flies.

Chum salmon / fair / 6-12 lbs., max. 18 lbs. / spoons and spinners, salmon egg clusters.

Silver salmon / fair to good / 5-10 lbs., max. 15 lbs. / salmon egg clusters, spinners, spoons.

Rainbow trout / fair to good / 8-20 in., max. 12 lbs. / spinners, single salmon eggs, salmon egg clusters.

Dolly Varden / poor to fair / 8-15 in., max. 5 lbs. / spoons and spinners, single salmon eggs, salmon egg clusters.

Grayling / fair to good / 7-15 in., max. 18 in. / flies and spinners, single salmon eggs.

43. KASHWITNA LAKE

Access: The lake is located adjacent to the west side of the Parks Highway at MP 76.4.

Major Species:

Rainbow trout / fair / May and September, October / 7-16 in.

44. GRAYS CREEK

Access: The Parks Highway crosses the stream at MP 81.0.

Major Species:

Grayling / good to excellent / May and September / 7-15 in.

45. KASHWITNA RIVER

Access: The Parks Highway crosses the river at MP 83.2. Also, the confluence of Kashwitna and Susitna rivers may be reached through a gravel road heading west at MP 82.5. It leads 0.6 miles to the Susitna Landing.

Regulations: Check the sport fishing regulations closely for details on open areas and dates for king salmon. Only unbaited, artificial lures may be used from September 1 through December 31.

Major Species:

King salmon / poor to fair / late June, early July / 15-45 lbs.
Pink salmon / poor to fair / late July / 2-4 lbs.
Chum salmon / poor to fair / late July / 6-12 lbs.
Silver salmon / fair / early and mid-August / 5-12 lbs.
Dolly Varden / fair / July and August / 8-15 in.
Rainbow trout / fair to good / September, October / 8-20 in.
Grayling / fair / September and October / 7-15 in.

46. CASWELL CREEK / SUSITNA RIVER CONFLUENCE

Access: From MP 84.1 of the Parks Highway. Turn west on a dirt road leading 0.4 miles to a camping area. Short hike to the confluence area.

Regulations: Check the sport fishing regulations for details on open dates and areas for king salmon. Only unbaited, artificial lures may be used from September 1 through December 31.

Time of Abundance:

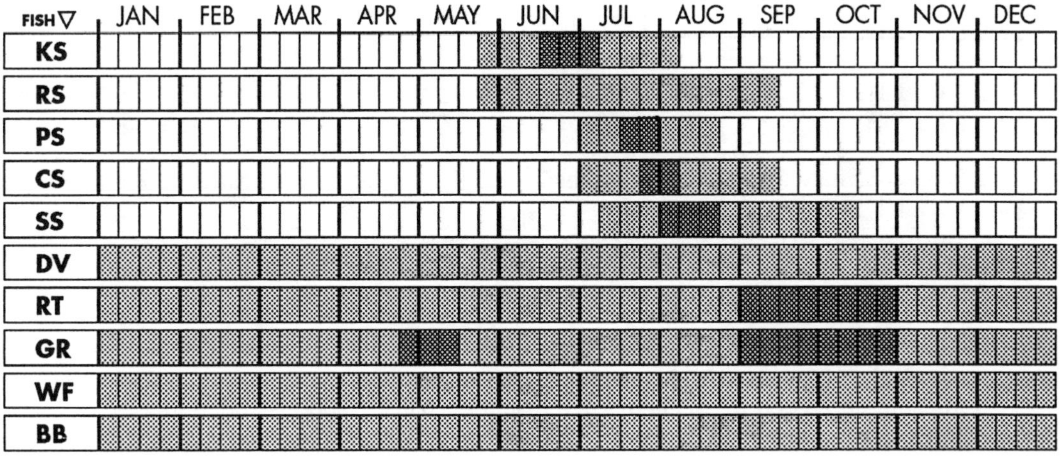

FISH▽	JAN	FEB	MAR	APR	MAY	JUN	JUL	AUG	SEP	OCT	NOV	DEC
KS												
RS												
PS												
CS												
SS												
DV												
RT												
GR												
WF												
BB												

Major Species:

King salmon / good / 15-45 lbs., max. 75 lbs. / attractor lures, salmon egg clusters, spoons, spinners.
Pink salmon / good / 2-4 lbs., max. 6 lbs. / spoons and spinners, attractor lures.
Chum salmon / good / 6-12 lbs., max. 18 lbs. / spoons and spinners, salmon egg clusters.
Silver salmon / good / 5-12 lbs., max. 15 lbs. / salmon egg clusters, spinners, spoons.
Rainbow trout / fair to good / 8-20 in., max. 12 lbs. / egg imitation flies, spinners, salmon egg cluster.
Grayling / fair to good / 7-15 in., max. 18 in. / single salmon eggs, spinners, flies.

47. CASWELL CREEK

Access: The parks Highway crosses the stream at MP 84.9.

Regulations: Check the sport fishing regulations closely for open areas and times for king salmon. Only unbaited, artificial lures may be used from September 1 through December 31.

Major Species:

Grayling / fair / mid-May to mid-September / 7-12 in.

48. SHEEP CREEK SLOUGH

Access: From MP 85.8 of the Parks Highway. Turn west on Resolute Drive and proceed on gravel road to a "Y." Continue straight to large parking area, which is 1.4 miles from the highway. Hike 100 yards by trail to the confluence area.

Regulations: Check the sport fishing regulations closely for details on open dates for king salmon. Only unbaited, artificial lures may be used from September 1 through December 31.

Time of Abundance:

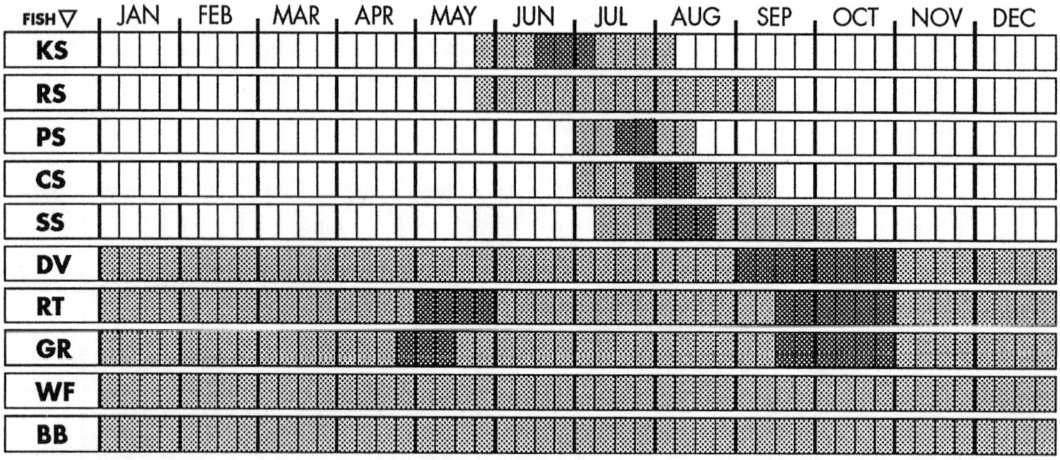

FISH▽	JAN	FEB	MAR	APR	MAY	JUN	JUL	AUG	SEP	OCT	NOV	DEC
KS												
RS												
PS												
CS												
SS												
DV												
RT												
GR												
WF												
BB												

Major Species:

King salmon / good to excellent / 15-45 lbs., max. 75 lbs. / attractor lures, salmon egg clusters, spoons, spinners.

Pink salmon / good to excellent / 2-4 lbs., max. 6 lbs. / spoons and spinners.

Chum salmon / good to excellent / 6-12 lbs., max. 18 lbs. / spoons and spinners, salmon egg clusters.

Silver salmon / good to excellent / 5-12 lbs., max. 15 lbs. / salmon egg clusters, spinners, spoons.

Dolly Varden / poor to fair / 8-15 in., max. 5 lbs. / salmon egg clusters, single salmon eggs, spoons.

Rainbow trout / fair to good / 8-20 in., max. 12 lbs. / salmon egg clusters, single salmon eggs, spinners.

Grayling / fair to good / 7-15 in., max. 18 in. / spinners, single salmon eggs.

49. SHEEP CREEK

Access: The Parks Highway crosses the stream at MP 88.6.

Regulations: Check the sport fishing regulations closely for details on open season and area for king salmon. Only unbaited, artificial lures may be used from September 1 through December 31.

Time of Abundance:

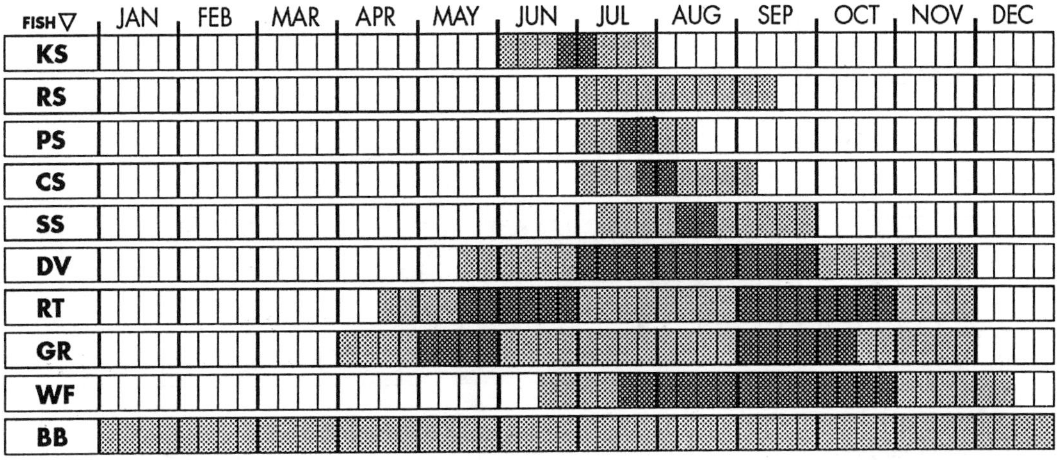

FISH▽	JAN	FEB	MAR	APR	MAY	JUN	JUL	AUG	SEP	OCT	NOV	DEC
KS												
RS												
PS												
CS												
SS												
DV												
RT												
GR												
WF												
BB												

Major Species:

King salmon / fair to good / 15-45 lbs., max. 75 lbs. / spoons, attractor lures, salmon egg clusters, streamer flies.
Pink salmon / fair to good 2-4 lbs., max. 6 lbs. / spoons and spinners.
Chum salmon / good to excellent / 6-12 lbs., max. 18 lbs. / spoons and spinners, streamer flies.
Silver salmon / fair to good / 5-12 lbs., max. 15 lbs. / salmon egg clusters and spinners.
Dolly Varden / poor to fair / 7-15 in., max. 5 lbs. / spoons, spinners, salmon egg clusters, single salmon eggs.
Rainbow trout / fair to good / 7-20 in., max. 12 lbs. / egg imitation flies, single salmon eggs, spinners.
Grayling / fair to good / 7-15 in., max. 18 in. / spinners, flies, single salmon eggs.
Whitefish / poor to fair / 10-15 in., max. 17 in. / salmon egg clusters, single salmon, wet flies.

50. GOOSE CREEK

Access: The Parks Highway crosses the stream at MP 92.7. To reach the confluence with the Susitna River, hike along the stream some 1.0 mile downstream from the highway.
Regulations: Check the sport fishing regulations closely for details on open season and area for king salmon. Only unbaited, artificial lures may be used from September 1 through December 31.

Time of Abundance:

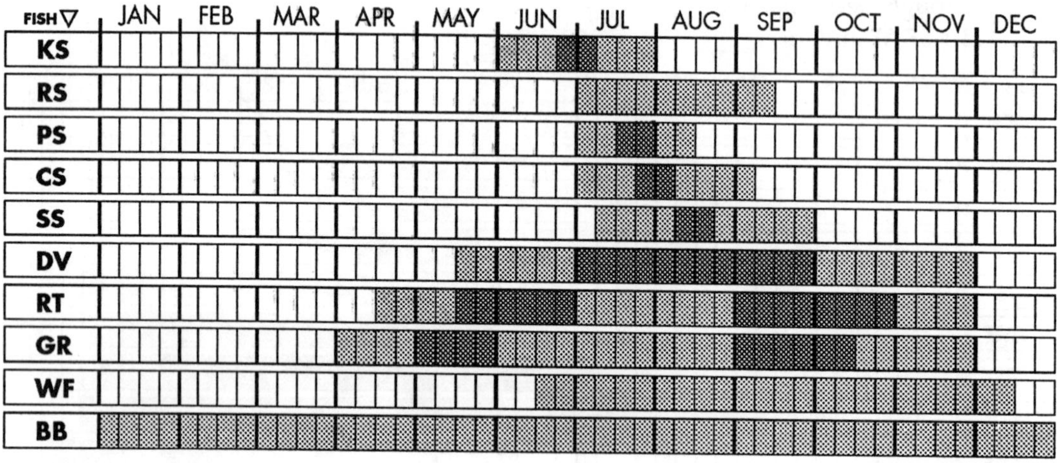

FISH▽	JAN	FEB	MAR	APR	MAY	JUN	JUL	AUG	SEP	OCT	NOV	DEC
KS												
RS												
PS												
CS												
SS												
DV												
RT												
GR												
WF												
BB												

Major Species:

King salmon / fair / 15-45 lbs., max. 65 lbs. / attractor lures, streamer flies, spoons, salmon egg clusters.

Pink salmon / fair to good / 2-4 lbs., max. 6 lbs. / spoons and spinners, streamer flies.

Chum salmon / fair to good / 6-12 lbs., max. 18 lbs. / spoons and spinners, streamer flies.

Silver salmon / fair to good / 5-12 lbs., max. 15 lbs. / salmon egg clusters, spoons, spinners.

Dolly Varden / poor to fair / 7-15 in., max. 5 lbs. / salmon egg clusters, single salmon eggs, flies.

Rainbow trout / fair to good / 7-20 in., max. 12 lbs. / egg imitation flies, salmon egg clusters, spinners.

Grayling / fair to good / 7-15 in., max. 18 in. / spinners, flies, single salmon eggs.

51. MONTANA CREEK

Access: The Parks Highway crosses the stream at MP 96.5. Turn west into parking area at MP 96.4 to access the lower stream and its confluence with the Susitna River. Trails lead about 0.25 miles to the mouth.

Regulations: Check the sport fishing regulations closely for open season and areas for king salmon. Only unbaited, artificial lures may be used from September 1 through December 31.

Time of Abundance:

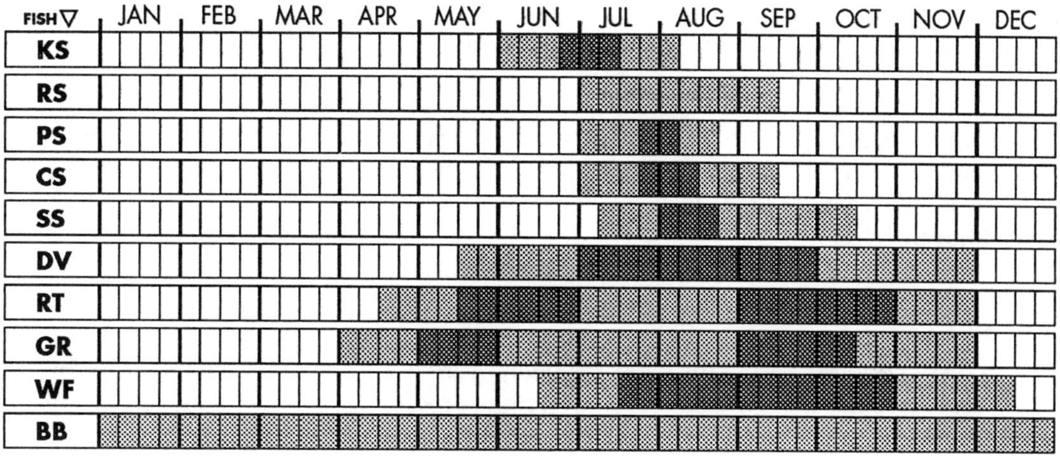

FISH▽	JAN	FEB	MAR	APR	MAY	JUN	JUL	AUG	SEP	OCT	NOV	DEC
KS												
RS												
PS												
CS												
SS												
DV												
RT												
GR												
WF												
BB												

Major Species:

King salmon / good to excellent / 15-45 lbs., max. 75 lbs. / attractor lures, spoons, salmon egg clusters, spinners.
Pink salmon / good to excellent / 2-4 lbs., max. 6 lbs. / spoons and spinners.
Chum salmon / good to excellent / 6-12 lbs., max. 18 lbs. / spoons and spinners, salmon egg clusters.
Silver salmon / good to excellent / 5-12 lbs., max. 15 lbs. / salmon egg clusters, spoons, and spinners.
Dolly Varden / poor to fair / 7-15 in., max. 5 lbs. / salmon egg clusters, single salmon eggs, spoons.
Rainbow trout / fair to good / 7-20 in., max. 12 lbs. / egg imitation flies, single salmon eggs, salmon egg clusters.
Grayling / fair to good / 7-15 in., max. 18 in. / spinners, flies, single salmon eggs.
Whitefish / poor to fair / 10-15 in., max. 17 in. / single salmon eggs, wet flies, salmon egg clusters.

52. BENKA LAKE

Access: From MP 98.7 of the Parks Highway. Turn north onto Talkeetna Spur Highway and drive 3.1 miles to Yoder Road on right. Proceed 0.5 miles to gravel road on left and continue straight 0.4 miles to the lake.

Major Species:

Silver salmon / poor to fair / March through December / 7-14 in.
Dolly Varden / poor to fair / August and December / 8-15 in.
Rainbow trout / poor to fair / September, October / 7-16 in.

53. MONTANA CREEK

Access: From MP 98.7 of the Parks Highway. Turn north onto Talkeetna Spur Highway and drive 3.1 miles to Yoder Road on right. Proceed 2.7 miles to the stream crossing.

Regulations: Salmon fishing prohibited. Only unbaited, artificial lures may be used from September 1 through December 31.

Major Species:
Rainbow trout / fair to good / August, September / 8-20 in.
Grayling / fair to good / June through September / 7-15 in.

54. TIGGER LAKE
Access: From MP 98.7 of the Parks Highway. Turn north onto Talkeetna Spur Highway and drive 11.0 miles to gravel road on right leading into a gravel pit. Park and find trail leading 0.25 miles to the lake.
Major Species:
Rainbow trout / poor to fair / September, October / 8-16 in.

55. "Y" LAKE
Access: From MP 98.7 of the Parks Highway. Turn north onto Talkeetna Spur Highway and drive 12.0 miles to Comsat Road on right, proceed 0.8 miles to public access trail on right.
Major Species:
Rainbow trout / fair / May and September, October / 7-16 in.

56. CHRISTIANSEN LAKE
Access: From MP 98.7 of the Parks Highway. Turn north onto Talkeetna Spur Highway and drive 12.0 miles to Comsat Road on right. Follow this road 0.8 miles to gravel road on left, continue 0.9 miles and turn right. Drive 0.1 miles to a "Y" and turn right on access road leading a short distance to the lake.
Major Species:
Silver salmon / good / March through December / 7-14 in.
Rainbow trout / fair / May and September, October / 7-16 in.

57. TALKEETNA RIVER
Access: From MP 98.7 of the Parks Highway. Turn north onto Talkeetna Spur Highway and drive 14.0 miles to the town of Talkeetna. The town borders on the south bank on the Talkeetna River and its confluence with Susitna River.
Regulations: King salmon fishing prohibited from July 14 through December 31. Only unbaited, artificial lures may be used from September 1 through December 31.
Major Species:
King salmon / poor to fair / early July / 15-45 lbs.
Pink salmon / fair / late July, early August / 2-4 lbs.
Chum salmon / fair / late July, early August / 6-12 lbs.
Silver salmon / fair to good / mid-August / 5-12 lbs.
Dolly Varden / fair to good / May and October / 8-20 in.
Rainbow trout / fair / May, September, October / 7-20 in.
Grayling / fair / May, September, October / 7-15 in.

Note: The Talkeetna River generally runs grayish green in color during the summer months, making sport fishing in the river itself somewhat limited. But, barring heavy rain showers or long periods of warm weather, the river may clear up enough to yield catches. Early spring and fall months usually see low and moderately clear water conditions.

58. SOUTH FRIEND / NORTH FRIEND LAKES

Access: From MP 99.2 of the Parks Highway. The lakes are located adjacent to the north and south side of the highway, connected by a small stream which the road crosses.

Major Species:

Rainbow trout / fair / May and September, October / 7-16 in.

59. SUNSHINE CREEK

Access: From MP 102.5 of the Parks Highway. Turn northeast onto a gravel road by sign and drive 0.6 miles to parking area. Hike 100 yards to the stream and its confluence with the Susitna River.

Regulations: Check the sport fishing regulations closely on open season and areas for king salmon. Only unbaited, artificial lures may be used from September 1 through December 31.

Time of Abundance:

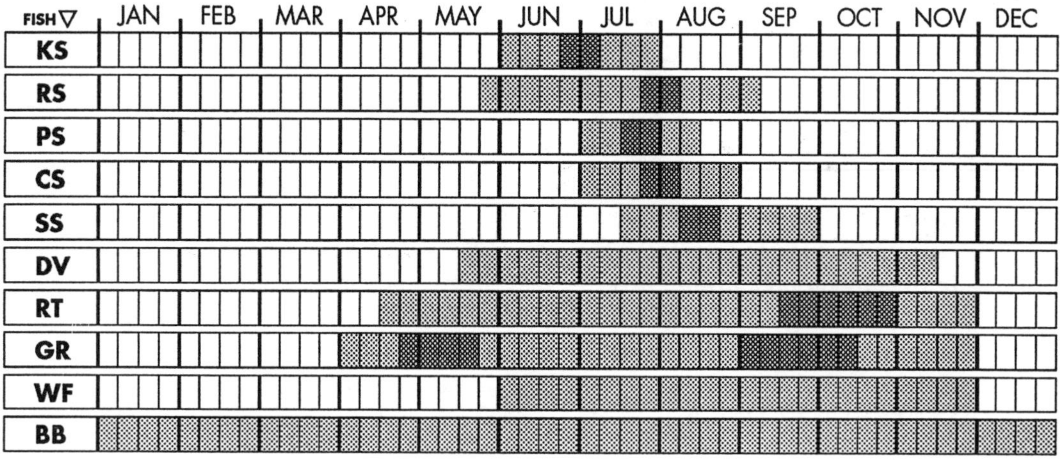

FISH ▽	JAN	FEB	MAR	APR	MAY	JUN	JUL	AUG	SEP	OCT	NOV	DEC
KS												
RS												
PS												
CS												
SS												
DV												
RT												
GR												
WF												
BB												

Major Species:

King salmon / good / 15-40 lbs., max. 70 lbs. / attractor lures, salmon egg clusters, spoons, spinners.

Red salmon / poor to fair / 4-8 lbs., max. 12 lbs. / spoons and spinners.

Pink salmon / good to excellent / 2-4 lbs., max. 6 lbs. / spoons and spinners.

Chum salmon / good / 6-12 lbs., max. 18 lbs. / spoons and spinners, attractor lures.

Silver salmon / good to excellent / 5-10 lbs., max. 15 lbs. / salmon egg clusters, spinners, attractor lures.

Rainbow trout / fair / 7-18 in., max. 5 lbs. / salmon egg clusters, single salmon eggs, spinners.

Grayling / fair / 7-14 in., max. 18 in. / single salmon eggs, spinners, flies.

60. RABIDEUX CREEK / SUSITNA RIVER CONFLUENCE

Access: From MP 104.4 of the Parks Highway. Turn west onto gravel road and follow 0.7 miles to confluence area. This road often is in poor condition during the summer months and caution is advised.

Regulations: Check the sport fishing regulations closely for open season and areas for king salmon. Only unbaited, artificial lures may be used from September 1 through December 31.

Time of Abundance:

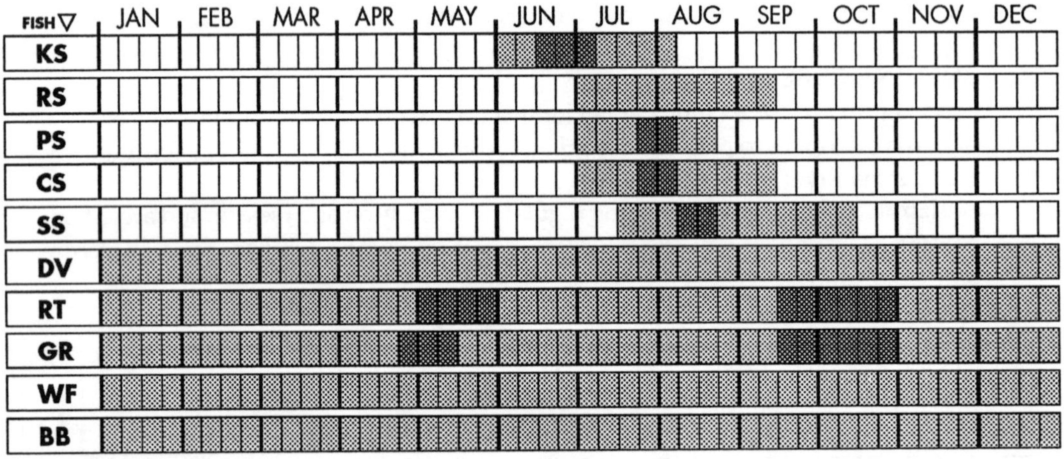

FISH▽	JAN	FEB	MAR	APR	MAY	JUN	JUL	AUG	SEP	OCT	NOV	DEC
KS												
RS												
PS												
CS												
SS												
DV												
RT												
GR												
WF												
BB												

Major Species:

King salmon / good / 15-45 lbs., max. 65 lbs. / attractor lures, salmon egg clusters, spoons, spinners.
Pink salmon / fair to good / 2-4 lbs., max. 6 lbs. / spoons and spinners, attractor lures.
Chum salmon / poor to fair / 6-12 lbs., max. 15 lbs. / spoons and spinners, attractor lures.
Silver salmon / good to excellent / 5-10 lbs. max. 15 lbs. / salmon egg clusters, attractor lures, spoons, spinners.
Rainbow trout / fair / 7-15 in., max. 5 lbs. / salmon egg clusters, attractor lures, spinners.
Grayling / fair / 7-14 in., max. 18 in. / salmon egg clusters, single salmon eggs, spinners.

61. RABIDEUX CREEK

Access: The Parks Highway crosses the stream at MP 105.8.
Regulations: King salmon fishing prohibited. Only unbaited artificial lures may be used from September 1 through December 31.
Major Species:

Pink salmon / poor to fair / late July, early August / 2-4 lbs.
Silver salmon / fair to good / early and mid-August / 5-10 lbs.
Rainbow trout / fair / June through September / 7-15 in.
Grayling / fair to good / May and September / 7-15 in.

62. TRAPPER CREEK

Access: The Parks Highway crosses the stream at MP 115.6. Also, turn east onto gravel road at MP 114.8 and drive 0.5 miles to the stream crossing.
Regulations: King salmon fishing prohibited. Only unbaited, artificial lures may be used from September 1 through December 31.
Major Species:

Silver salmon / fair / mid-August / 5-10 lbs.
Rainbow trout / poor to fair / August and September / 7-15 in.
Grayling / fair to good / May and September / 7-15 in.

AREA C: WEST SIDE SUSITNA RIVER DRAINAGE

Includes waters draining into the lower Susitna River.

63. MOOSE CREEK

Access: From MP 114.8 of the Parks Highway. Turn west onto the Petersville Road and drive 7.1 miles to the stream crossing. Also, drive 6.3 miles on Petersville Road and turn left on gravel road leading 6.0 miles to the stream.

Regulations: King salmon fishing prohibited. Catch-and release fishing only for rainbow trout. Only unbaited, single-hook, artificial lures may be used.

Major Species:

Silver salmon / fair / mid-August / 5-10 lbs.
Rainbow trout / poor to fair / mid-May through June / 8-22 in.
Grayling / fair to good / May and September / 7-15 in.

64. KROTO CREEK

Access: From MP 114.8 of the Parks Highway. Turn west onto the Petersville Road and drive 14.0 miles to the stream crossing.

Regulations: King salmon fishing prohibited. Catch-and release fishing only for rainbow trout. Only unbaited, artificial, single-hook lures may be used.

Major Species:

Silver salmon / fair / mid-August / 5-10 lbs.
Rainbow trout / poor to fair / mid-May through June / 8-22 in.
Grayling / fair to good / May and September / 7-15 in.

65. PETERS CREEK

Access: From MP 114.8 of the Parks Highway. Turn west onto the Petersville Road and drive 18.7 miles to a "Y." Take the left fork and drive 0.2 miles to parking area next to bridge over river. Also, continue on the right fork an additional 0.8 miles to pull-off on the left. Hike down hill towards the west to the river.

Regulations: King salmon fishing prohibited from July 14 through December 31. Only unbaited, artificial lures may be used from September 1 through December 31.

Time of Abundance:

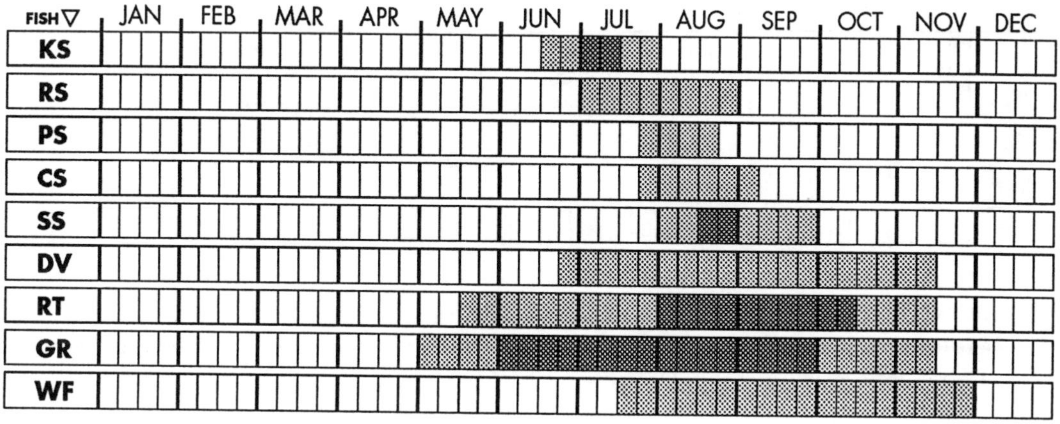

FISH▽	JAN	FEB	MAR	APR	MAY	JUN	JUL	AUG	SEP	OCT	NOV	DEC
KS												
RS												
PS												
CS												
SS												
DV												
RT												
GR												
WF												

Major Species:

King salmon / good / 15-40 lbs., max. 65 lbs. / attractor lures, spoons, spinners, streamer flies, salmon egg clusters.

Silver salmon / good to excellent / 5-12 lbs., max. 15 lbs. / salmon egg clusters, spinners, streamer flies.

Rainbow trout / good / 8-20 in., max. 12 lbs. / salmon egg clusters, single salmon eggs, flies, spinners.

Grayling / good / 7-14 in., max. 18 in. / spinners, flies, single salmon eggs.

66. MARTIN CREEK

Access: From MP 114.8 of the Parks Highway. Turn west onto Petersville Road and drive 18.7 miles to a "Y." Take the left fork and drive 0.2 miles to parking area and Peters Creek. Park and walk over bridge spanning the river and hike upstream about 0.25 miles to the mouth of Martin Creek.

Regulations: King salmon fishing prohibited from July 14 through December 31. Only unbaited, artificial lures may be used from September 1 through December 31.

Major Species:

King salmon / fair / early and mid-July / 15-35 lbs.

Silver salmon / fair / late August, early September / 5-10 lbs.

Rainbow trout / fair / August and September / 8-20 in.

Grayling / fair to good / July to mid-September / 7-15 in.

AREA D: CHULITNA RIVER DRAINAGE

Includes all waters draining into Chulitna River.

Time of Abundance:

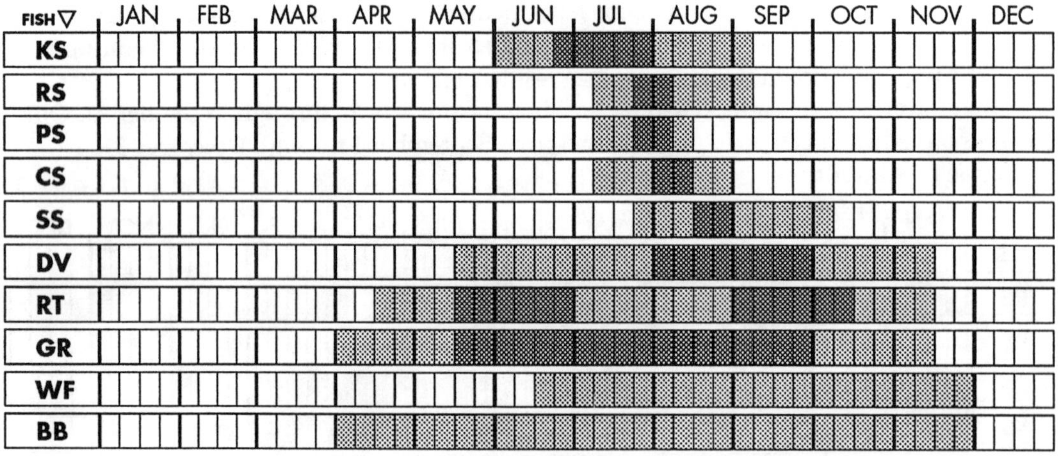

FISH▽	JAN	FEB	MAR	APR	MAY	JUN	JUL	AUG	SEP	OCT	NOV	DEC
KS												
RS												
PS												
CS												
SS												
DV												
RT												
GR												
WF												
BB												

67. SUNNY CREEK

Access: The Parks Highway crosses the stream at MP 128.5.

Regulations: King salmon fishing prohibited. Only unbaited, artificial lures may be used from September 1 through December 31.

Major Species:
Red salmon / poor to fair / early August / 4-8 lbs.
Silver salmon / fair / mid and late August / 5-10 lbs.
Dolly Varden / poor to fair / July through September / 8-15 in.
Rainbow trout / poor to fair / July through September / 7-15 in.
Grayling / fair to good / mid-May to mid-September / 7-14 in.

68. TROUBLESOME CREEK
Access: The Parks Highway crosses the stream at MP 137.4. The mouth of the creek and the confluence with Chulitna River can be reached by a trail along the south bank, about 0.3 miles.
Regulations: King salmon fishing prohibited. Only unbaited, artificial lures may be used from September 1 through December 31.
Major Species:
Red salmon / poor to fair / early August / 4-8 lbs.
Pink salmon / fair / early August / 2-4 lbs.
Chum salmon / poor to fair / early August / 6-12 lbs.
Silver salmon / fair to good / mid- and late August / 5-10 lbs.
Rainbow trout / fair / July through September / 7-16 lbs.
Grayling / good / mid-June to mid-September / 7-15 in.

69. BYERS CREEK
Access: The Parks Highway crosses the stream at MP 143.9.
Regulations: Salmon fishing prohibited upstream from the highway bridge. King salmon fishing is prohibited. Only unbaited, artificial lures may be used from September 1 through December 31.
Major Species:
Red salmon / fair to good / early and mid-August / 4-8 lbs.
Silver salmon / fair / late August / 5-10 lbs.
Rainbow trout / fair / June through September / 7-16 in.
Grayling / good / mid-June through mid-September / 7-15 in.

70. BYERS LAKE
Access: From MP 147.2 of the Parks Highway. Turn east onto gravel road and drive 0.3 miles to the lake and a campground.
Regulations: Salmon fishing prohibited.
Major Species:
Dolly Varden / poor to fair / August and September / 7-15 in.
Lake trout / fair to good / May, October, November / 2-8 lbs.
Grayling / fair to good / June through September / 7-15 in.
Burbot / fair / November through April / 2-5 lbs.

71. HORSESHOE CREEK
Access: The Parks Highway crosses the stream at MP 159.8.
Regulations: King salmon fishing is prohibited. Only unbaited, artificial lures may be used from September 1 through December 31.

Major Species:
Red salmon / poor to fair / mid-August / 4-8 lbs.
Silver salmon / fair / late August / 5-10 lbs.
Rainbow trout / fair / mid-June through September / 7-16 in.
Grayling / fair to good / mid-June to mid-September / 7-15 in.

72. COAL CREEK

Access: The Parks Highway crosses the stream at MP 161.3.
Regulations: King salmon fishing is prohibited. Only unbaited, artificial lures may be used from September 1 through December 31.
Major Species:
Silver salmon / poor to fair / late August / 5-10 lbs.
Rainbow trout / fair / June through September / 7-16 in.
Grayling / fair to good / mid-May to mid-September / 7-15 in.

73. HONOLULU CREEK

Access: The Parks Highway crosses the stream at MP 178.1.
Regulations: King salmon fishing is prohibited. Only unbaited, artificial lures may be used from September 1 through December 31.
Major Species:
Silver salmon / poor to fair / early September / 5-10 lbs.
Grayling / fair / June to mid-September / 7-15 in.

74. EAST FORK CHULITNA RIVER

Access: The Parks Highway crosses the river at MP 184.8.
Regulations: Check the sport fishing regulations closely for open season on king salmon. Only unbaited, artificial lures may be used from September 1 through December 31.
Major Species:
King salmon / fair / early July / 15-45 lbs.
Silver salmon / fair / early September / 5-10 lbs.
Rainbow trout / fair / June through September / 7-16 in.
Grayling / fair to good / June to mid-September / 7-15 in.
Whitefish / poor to fair / September, early October / 10-15 in.

75. MIDDLE FORK CHULITNA RIVER

Access: The Parks Highway crosses the river at MP 194.5.
Regulations: King salmon fishing is prohibited. Only unbaited, artificial lures may be used from September 1 through December 31.
Major Species:
Rainbow trout / fair / June through September / 7-16 in.
Grayling / fair to good / June to mid-September / 7-15 in.

AREA E: NENANA RIVER DRAINAGE

Includes all waters draining into and surrounding the Nenana River.

76. SUMMIT LAKE

Access: From 200.1 of the Parks Highway. Turn east onto gravel road leading a short distance to parking area. Hike 50 yards to the lake.

Major Species:

Grayling / fair to good / June through September / 7-15 in.
Lake trout / fair / June, September, October / 2-8 lbs.
Burbot / fair / October through April / 2-5 lbs.

77. MIRROR LAKE

Access: From MP 202.0 of the Parks Highway. Park and hike 0.25 miles through low brush to the lake.

Major Species:

Lake trout / fair / June, September, October / 2-5 lbs.
Grayling / fair to good / June through September / 7-15 in.
Burbot / fair / October through April / 2-4 lbs.

78. PASS CREEK

Access: The Parks Highway crosses the stream at MP 208.0.

Major Species:

Grayling / fair / June to mid-September / 7-12 in.

79. JACK RIVER

Access: The Parks Highway crosses the river at MP 209.6.

Major Species:

Grayling / fair / May and September / 7-15 in.

80. CARLO CREEK

Access: The Parks Highway crosses the stream at MP 223.9.

Major Species:

Grayling / poor to fair / June through August / 7-12 in.

81. EIGHTMILE LAKE

Access: From MP 251.2 of the Parks Highway. Turn southwest on Stampede Road and drive 8.2 miles to parking area. Hike 0.25 miles to the lake through open country, due northeast.

Major Species:

Grayling / fair to good / June through September / 7-15 in.

82. PANGUINGUE CREEK

Access: The Parks Highway crosses the stream at MP 252.4.

Major Species:

Grayling / fair / June to mid-September / 7-12 in.

83. SLATE CREEK

Access: The Parks Highway crosses the stream at MP 257.8.

Major Species:

Grayling / poor to fair / mid- and late May / 7-14 in.

84. BEAR CREEK
Access: The Parks Highway crosses the stream at MP 269.3.
Major Species:
Grayling / poor to fair / mid- and late May / 7-14 in.

85. BIRCH CREEK
Access: The Parks Highway crosses the stream at MP 272.5.
Major Species:
Grayling / poor to fair / mid- and late May / 7-14 in.

86. JULIUS CREEK
Access: The Parks Highway crosses the stream at MP 285.6.
Major Species:
Grayling / fair / mid-May to mid-September / 7-15 in.

87. JULIUS CREEK / CLEAR CREEK CONFLUENCE
Access: From MP 295.2 of the Parks Highway. Park and find trail leading 2.0 miles to confluence area, due west.
Major Species:
Silver salmon / fair / late September, early October / 5-12 lbs.
Grayling / fair to good / mid-May to mid-September / 7-15 in.

88. FISH CREEK
Access: The Parks Highway crosses the stream at MP 296.6.
Major Species:
Grayling / fair / mid-May to mid-September / 7-14 in.

89. NENANA POND
Access: From MP 303.4 of the Parks Highway. Turn west onto gravel road leading 0.7 miles to a campground and the lake.
Major Species:
Silver salmon / fair / March through December / 7-14 in.

CHAPTER 18

Steese Highway

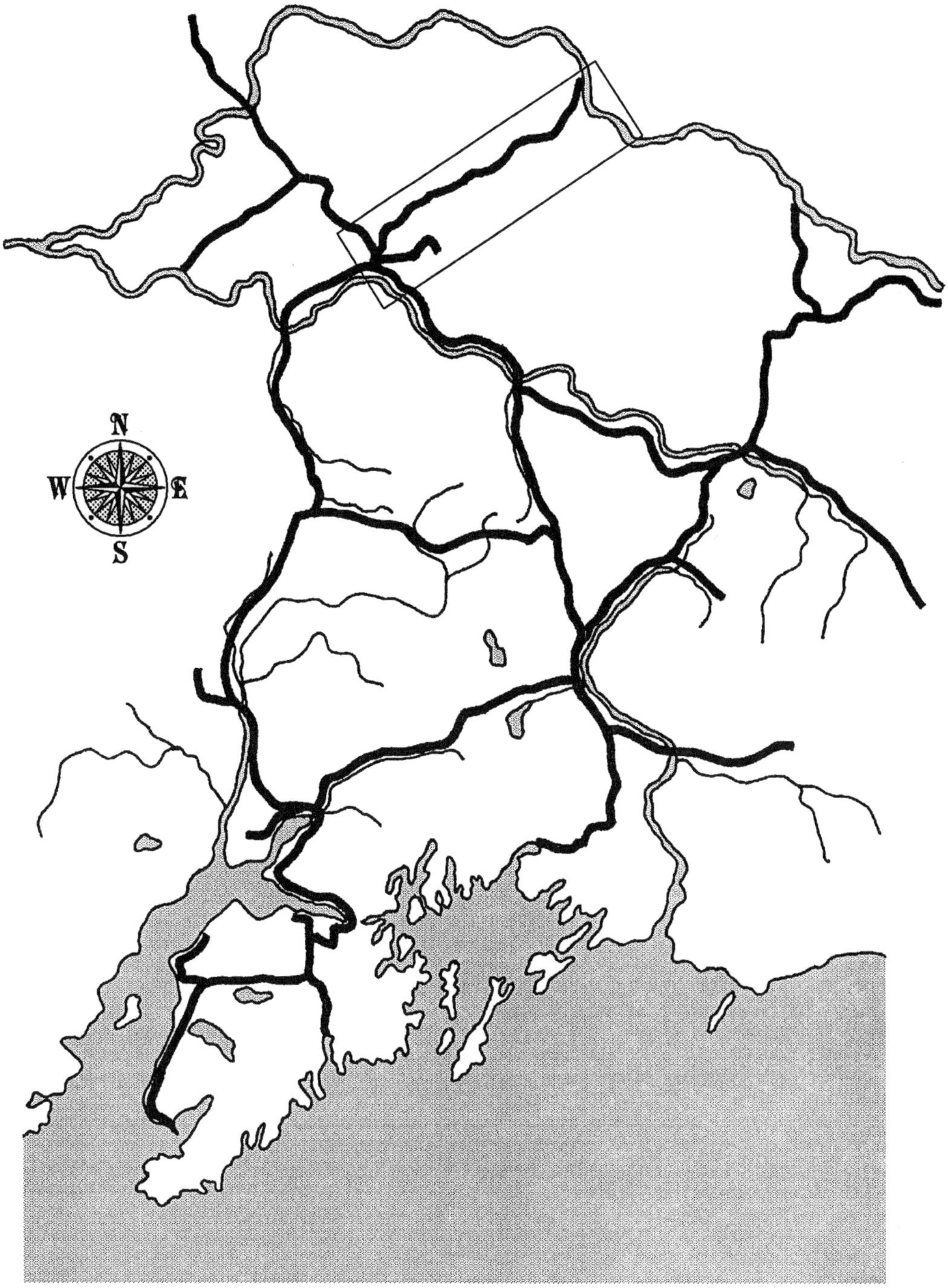

*T*he Steese Highway originates in Fairbanks as the Steese Expressway and heads off in a northeasterly direction to its end in Circle, on the Yukon River. Although most of the road is unpaved, the first section out of Fairbanks is paved.

CHAPTER 18

Steese Highway

It connects with Richardson and Parks highways in Fairbanks and with the Elliott Highway in Fox.

This chapter also includes the Chena Hot Springs Road, which joins with the Steese Highway.

Steese Highway provides good access to the Chena River drainage, the clearwater tributaries of the Tanana River, and a few streams draining into the middle Yukon River. Here, as throughout most of Interior Alaska, the grayling is the major sport fish species. But fairly good numbers of king and chum salmon, Arctic char, and rainbow trout are also present. In addition, a few silver salmon, sheefish, northern pike, whitefish, and burbot may be taken. Generally, the fishing season last from mid-May to mid-October.

Important: Please be aware of the current sport fishing rules and regulations for the area covered in this chapter, and abide by them. Remember, they have been applied to protect a fragile resource.

Following are the abbreviations used in this chapter for all the fish species and facility information:

KS - King Salmon
CS - Chum Salmon
SS - Silver Salmon
AC - Arctic Char
RT - Rainbow Trout
SF - Sheefish
GR - Grayling
WF - Whitefish
NP - Northern Pike
BB - Burbot

P - Parking
LP - Limited Parking
C - Camping
T - Toilet
BL - Boat Launch

Time of Abundance/Availability Charts

These charts are designed to show the reader during which time of the year the indicated species are present or available in the most popular fishing streams, lakes, or regions. The charts correlate to when the fish are in their prime for both angling sport and consumption, unless otherwise noted. Species which are closed to sport fishing are also included on the charts just for the purpose of interest but are shown in all stages of maturity.

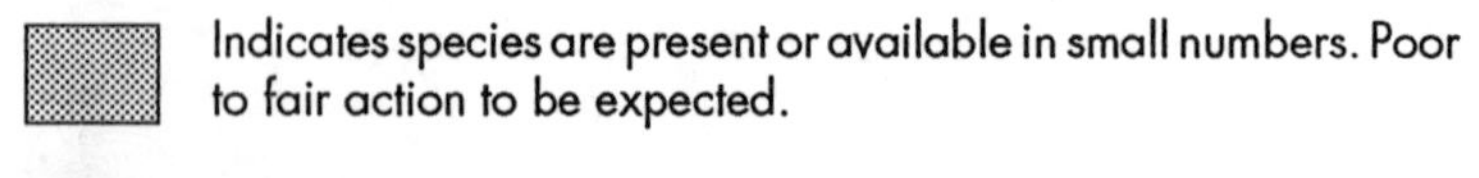
Indicates species are present or available in small numbers. Poor to fair action to be expected.

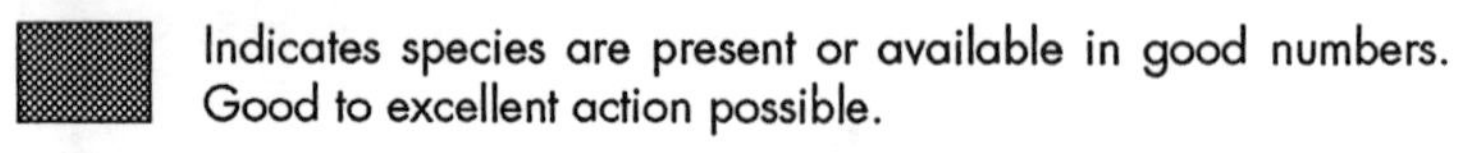
Indicates species are present or available in good numbers. Good to excellent action possible.

Note: The quality of fishing may vary due to certain fluctuations, such as weather conditions, angler experience, number of fish present, or other factors.

QUICK REFERENCE

This section of the chapter was designed to provide a quick overview of all the fishing spots in the region, their map locations and milepost numbers, species available, facility information, and the page number on which to find detailed access and fishing information for any one specific watershed.

Note: Species shown in parentheses may be present but are protected by law, and/or are only occasionally seen or hooked by anglers fishing that particular watershed.

STEESE HIGHWAY

Note: Mileposts shown in parentheses are for Chena Hot Springs Road.

	WATERSHED	MILE POST	SPECIES
1.	Little Chena River Facilities: LP	(11.9) Page: 207, 208	GR,(KS,CS,WF)
2.	Chena River Facilities: P/C/T	(27.0-32.8) Page: 208	GR,(KS,CS,SF,WF,BB,NP)
3.	Twin Bears Lake Facilities: P	(30.0) Page: 208	GR
4.	32.9-Mile Pond Facilities: P (trail)	(32.9) Page: 208	AC,GR
5.	N. Fork Chena River Facilities: P/T	(37.9-55.3) Page: 208	GR,(KS,CS,WF)
6.	43-Mile Pond Facilities: P/T	(42.8) Page: 208	GR
7.	45.5-Mile Pond Facilities: P	(45.5) Page: 208	GR,RT
8.	48-Mile Pond Facilities: P	(47.9) Page: 208, 209	GR
9.	29.5-Mile Pond Facilities: P	29.5 Page: 209	GR
10.	30.6-Mile Pond Facilities: P	0.6 Page: 209	AC,GR
11.	33-Mile Pond Facilities: P	33.0 Page: 209	GR
12.	33.5-Mile Pond Facilities: P	33.5 Page: 209	GR
13.	34.6-Mile Pond Facilities: P	34.6 Page: 209	GR
14.	35.8-Mile Pond Facilities: P	35.8 Page: 209	GR

CHAPTER 18

Steese Highway

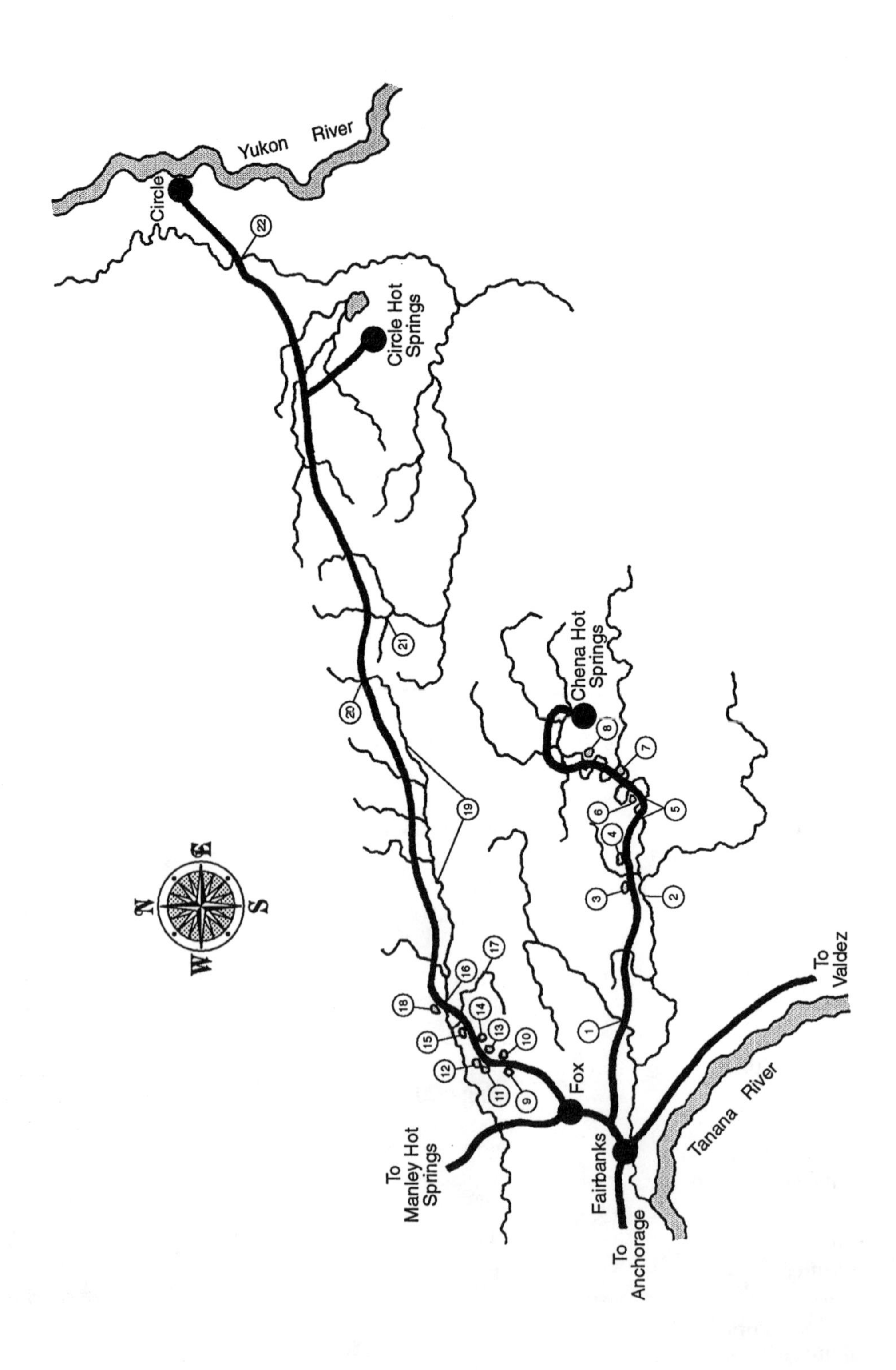

15. 36.6-Mile Pond Facilities: P	36.6 Page: 210	AC,GR
16. Chatanika River Facilities: P/C/T	35.6-39.0 Page: 210	CS,SS,SF,GR,WF,(KS,NP,BB)
17. Kokomo Creek Facilities: LP	37.3 Page: 210	GR
18. 39.9-Mile Pond Facilities: P	39.3 Page: 210	RT
19. Chatanika River Facilities: P/C/T	56.4-60.0 Page: 210, 211	GR,(KS,CS,SS,WF)
20. Faith Creek Facilities: P	69.0 Page: 211	GR
21. N. Fork Birch Creek Facilities: P	94.0 Page: 211	GR
22. Birch Creek Facilities: P	47.2/146.4 Page: 211	SF,NP,GR,(KS,CS,WF,BB)

AREA A: CHENA RIVER DRAINAGE

Includes Chena River and its branches and tributaries.

Time of Abundance:

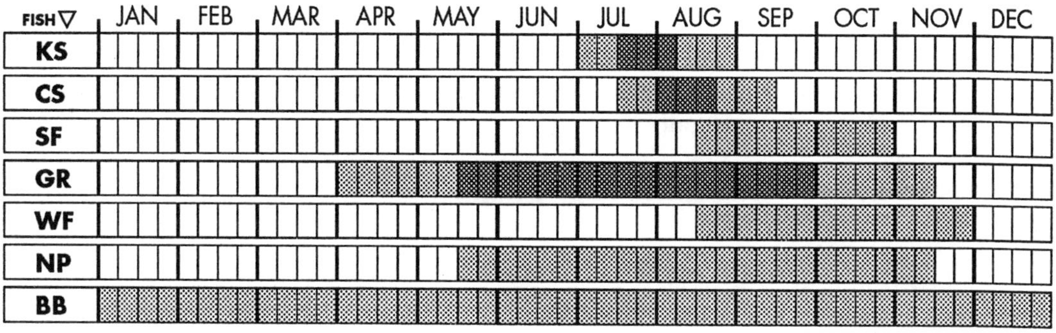

FISH▽	JAN	FEB	MAR	APR	MAY	JUN	JUL	AUG	SEP	OCT	NOV	DEC
KS												
CS												
SF												
GR												
WF												
NP												
BB												

Note: The Chena River and its tributaries along the Chena Hot Springs Road are closed to salmon fishing.

1. LITTLE CHENA RIVER

Access: Turn east on Chena Hot Springs Road on the outskirts of Fairbanks and drive to MP 11.9 and the river crossing.

Regulations: Salmon fishing prohibited. Catch-and-release only for grayling.

Major Species:
Grayling / fair to good / June to late September / 7-15 in.

2. **CHENA RIVER**
Access: Turn east on Chena Hot Springs Road on the outskirts of Fairbanks. Several access points between MP 27.0 and 32.8.
Regulations: Salmon fishing prohibited. Catch-and-release only for grayling.
Major Species:
Grayling / fair to good / June to late September / 7-15 in.

3. **TWIN BEARS LAKE**
Access: Turn east on Chena Hot Springs Road and drive to MP 30.0. Turn north onto gravel road leading short distance to lake.
Major Species:
Grayling / fair to good / late May to late September / 7-12 in.

4. **32.9 MILE POND**
Access: Turn east on Chena Hot Springs Road and drive to MP 32.9. Turn north onto gravel road leading short distance to state fence. Park here and walk around fence to pond, about 0.25 mile.
Major Species:
Arctic char / fair / June, September, and October / 7-16 in.
Grayling / fair to good / late May to early October / 7-12 in.

5. **NORTH FORK CHENA RIVER**
Access: Turn east on Chena Hot Springs Road on the outskirts of Fairbanks. Numerous access points with river crossing located at MP 37.9,39.5, 44.0, 49.0, 52.4, and 55.3.
Regulations: Salmon fishing prohibited. Catch-and-release only for grayling.
Major Species:
Grayling / fair to good / June to late September / 7-15 in.

6. **43 MILE POND**
Access: Turn east on Chena Hot Springs Road and drive to MP 42.8. Turn north on gravel road leading a short distance to pond.
Major Species:
Grayling / fair to good / late May to early October / 7-14 in.

7. **45.5 MILE POND**
Access: Turn east on Chena Hot Springs and drive to MP 45.5. Turn east and drive 0.2 miles to the pond.
Major Species:
Rainbow trout / fair / June, September, and October / 7-18 in.
Grayling / fair to good / late May to early October / 7-14 in.

8. **48 MILE POND**
Access: Turn east onto Chena Hot Springs Road and drive to MP 47.9. Turn east and drive

a short distance to pond. The pond on the right is stocked with fish; the one on the left is not.

Major Species:
Grayling / fair to good / late May to early October / 7-14 in.

AREA B: CHATANIKA - YUKON RIVER DRAINAGE

Includes the tributaries of Chatanika River and Yukon River, and all lakes and ponds within that region.

9. 29.5 MILE POND
Access: Pull off due west at MP 29.5 of the Steese Highway and drive a short distance to the pond.
Major Species:
Grayling / fair / late May to early October / 7-12 in.

10. 30.6 MILE POND
Access: Turn south on gravel road at MP 30.6 of the Steese Highway and drive a short distance to the pond.
Major Species:
Arctic char / fair / June, September, and October / 8-15 in.
Grayling / fair / late May to early October / 7-12 in.

11. 33 MILE POND
Access: Turn north on gravel road at MP 33.0 of the Steese Highway and drive a short distance to the pond.
Major Species:
Grayling / fair / late May to early October / 7-14 in.

12. 33.5 MILE POND
Access: Turn north on gravel road at MP 33.5 of the Steese Highway and drive a short distance to the pond.
Major Species:
Grayling / fair / late May to early October / 7-12 in.

13. 34.6 MILE POND
Access: Turn south on gravel road at MP 34.6 of the Steese Highway and drive a short distance to the pond.
Major Species:
Grayling / fair / late May to early October / 7-12 in.

14. 35.8 MILE POND
Access: Turn south on gravel road at MP 35.8 of the Steese Highway and drive a short distance to the pond.
Major Species:
Grayling / fair / late May to early October / 7-12 in.

15. 36.6 MILE POND

Access: Turn north on gravel road at MP 36.6 of the Steese Highway and drive a short distance to the pond.

Major Species:

Arctic char / fair / June, September, and October / 7-15 in.
Grayling / fair / late May to early October / 7-12 in.

16. CHATANIKA RIVER

Access: The Steese Highway parallels the river starting at MP 35.6 with numerous pull-offs alongside the road. The highway crosses the river at MP 39.0.

Regulations: King salmon fishing prohibited. Check the regulations.

Time of Abundance:

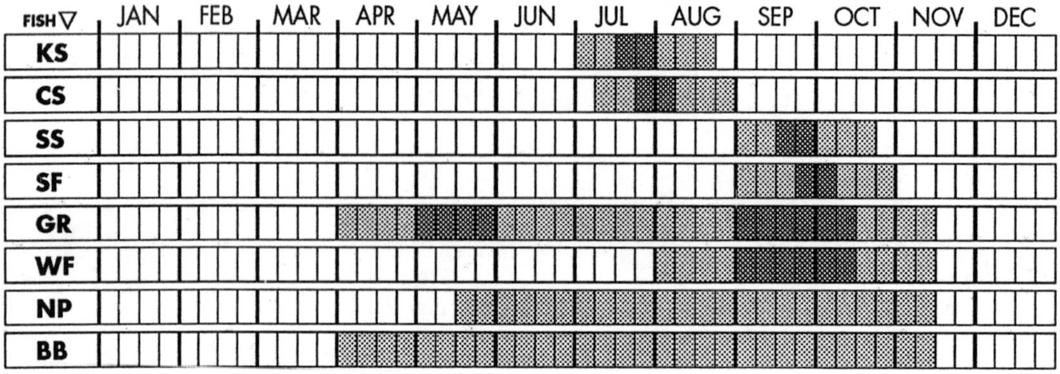

FISH▽	JAN	FEB	MAR	APR	MAY	JUN	JUL	AUG	SEP	OCT	NOV	DEC
KS												
CS												
SS												
SF												
GR												
WF												
NP												
BB												

Major Species:

Chum salmon / poor to fair / 5-10 lbs., max. 15 lbs. / spoons and spinners, streamer flies.
Silver salmon / poor to fair / 4-10 lbs., max. 12 lbs. / spoons, spinners, and streamer flies.
Sheefish / poor to fair / 4-8 lbs., max. 15 lbs. / spoons and spinners, streamer flies.
Grayling / fair to good / 7-12 in., max. 18 in. / spinners, dry and wet flies.
Whitefish / fair / 10-18 in., max. 6 lbs. / wet flies, salmon egg imitations.

17. KOKOMO CREEK

Access: The Steese Highway crosses the stream at MP 37.3.

Major Species:

Grayling / poor to fair / late May and June / 7-12 in.

18. 39.3 MILE POND

Access: Turn west on gravel road at MP 39.3 of the Steese Highway and drive a short distance to the pond.

Major Species:

Rainbow trout / fair / May and September, October / 7-15 in.

19. CHATANIKA RIVER

Access: The Steese Highway parallels the river from MP 56.4 to 60.0. There are numerous pull-offs east of the highway and gravel roads leading to the upper river.

Regulations: King salmon fishing prohibited. Check the regulations.

Major Species:
Grayling / good / June through September / 7-15 in.

20. FAITH CREEK
Access: The Steese Highway crosses the stream at MP 69.0.
Major Species:
Grayling / fair / June to mid-September / 7-12 in.

21. NORTH FORK BIRCH CREEK
Access: From MP 94.0 of the Steese Highway. Turn south onto small gravel road by sign and drive 0.2 miles to the stream.
Major Species:
Grayling / poor to fair / June to mid-September / 7-12 in.

22. BIRCH CREEK
Access: The Steese Highway crosses the stream at MP 147.2. Also, the road parallels the stream briefly at MP 146.4.
Major Species:
Sheefish / poor to fair / August through September / 4-8 lbs.
Northern pike / poor to fair / late May and June / 2-5 lbs.
Grayling / fair to good / late May to mid-September / 7-15 in.

CHAPTER 19

Elliott Highway

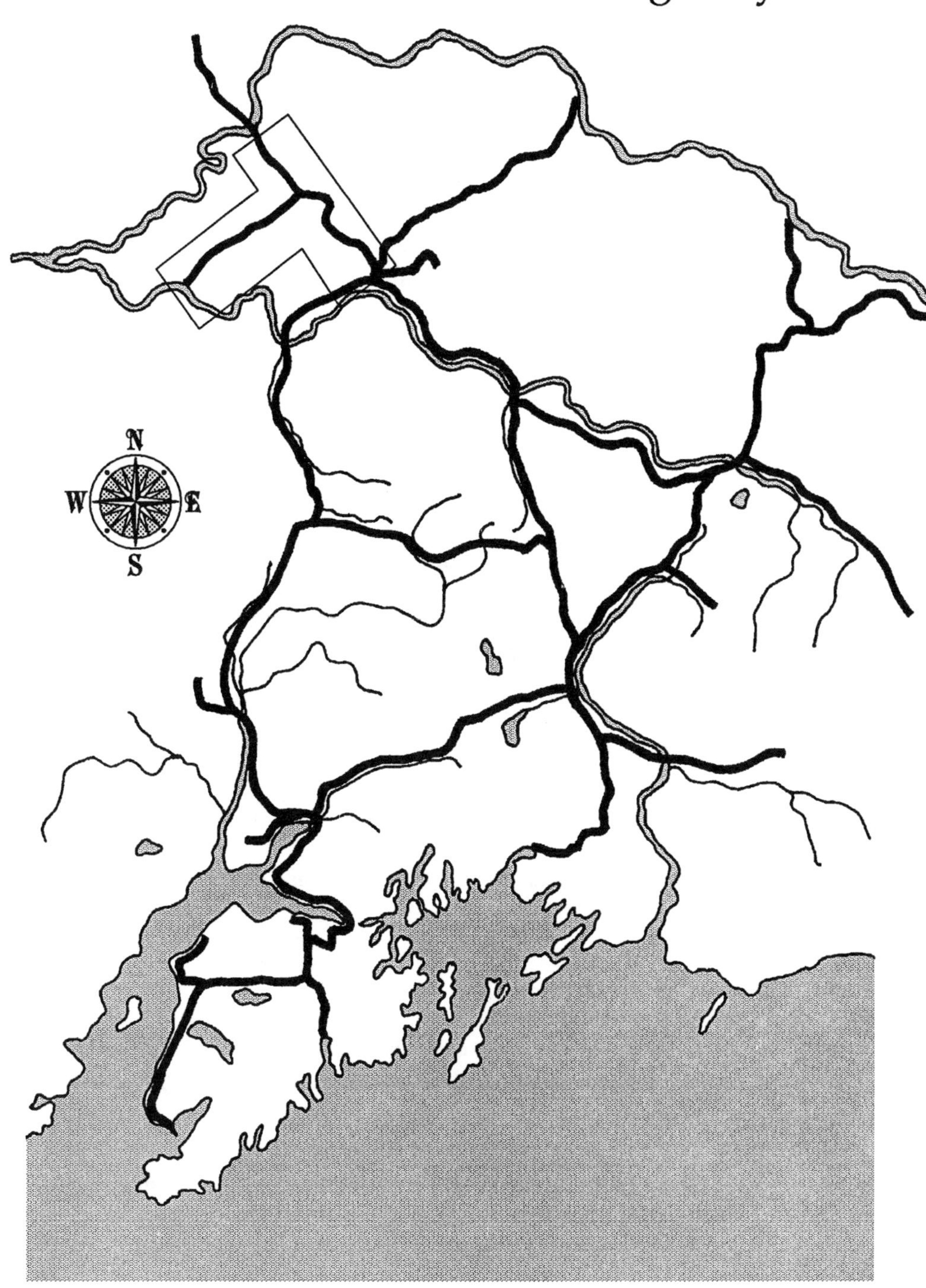

The Elliott Highway begins at Milepost 11.0 of the Steese Highway in Fox, and runs northwest to Manley Hot Springs. The first few miles of the road are paved, but eventually becomes unpaved. The highway also connects with the

Dalton Highway and serves as a route for long-haul trucks between Fairbanks and the North Slope.

The Elliott Highway provides extensive access to the Tolovana River drainage and a few clearwater tributaries of Tanana River. Grayling is the major sport fish species here, followed by whitefish, king and chum salmon, and fewer sheefish, Dolly Varden, northern pike, and burbot. A few silver salmon may also be present.

Most of the fishing activity in this region occurs between mid-May and mid-October, when open water is prevalent.

Important: Please be aware of the current sport fishing rules and regulations for the area covered in this chapter, and abide by them. Remember, they have been applied to protect a fragile resource.

Following are the abbreviations used in this chapter for all the fish species and facility information:

KS - King Salmon	DV - Dolly Varden	WF - Whitefish
CS - Chum Salmon	SF - Sheefish	NP - Northern Pike
SS - Silver Salmon	GR - Grayling	BB - Burbot
P - Parking	C - Camping	BL - Boat Launch
LP - Limited Parking	T - Toilet	

Time of Abundance/Availability Charts

These charts are designed to show the reader during which time of the year the indicated species are present or available in the most popular fishing streams, lakes, or regions. The charts correlate to when the fish are in their prime for both angling sport and consumption, unless otherwise noted. Species which are closed to sport fishing are also included on the charts just for the purpose of interest but are shown in all stages of maturity.

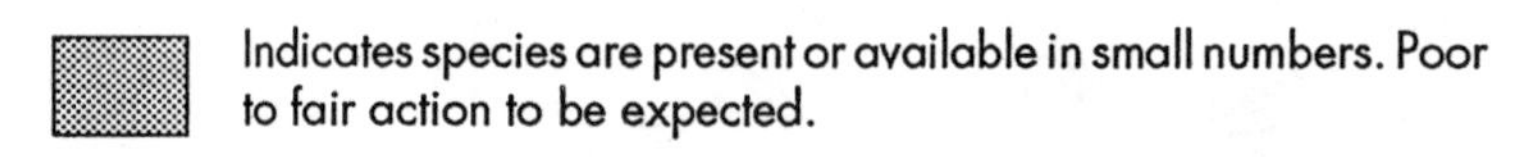
Indicates species are present or available in small numbers. Poor to fair action to be expected.

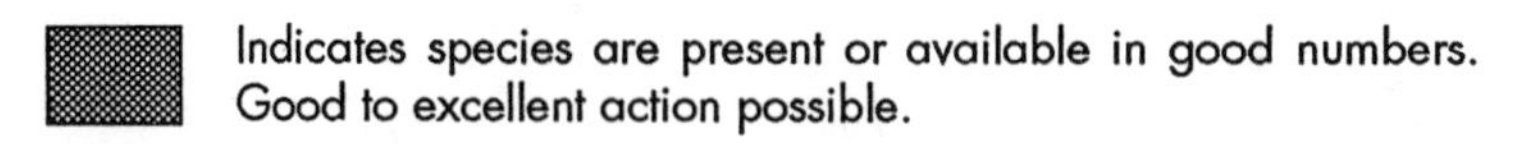
Indicates species are present or available in good numbers. Good to excellent action possible.

Note: The quality of fishing may vary due to certain fluctuations, such as weather conditions, angler experience, number of fish present, or other factors.

QUICK REFERENCE

This section was designed to provide a quick view of all the fishing spots in the region, their map location and mile post, species available, facility information, and the page number on which to find detailed access and fishing information for any one watershed.

Note: Species shown in parentheses may be present but are protected by law, and/or are only occasionally seen or hooked by anglers fishing that particular watershed.

ELLIOTT HIGHWAY

	WATERSHED	MILE POST	SPECIES
1.	Olnes Pond Facilities: P/T	10.6 Page: 217	GR,(WF,BB)
2.	Chatanika River Facilities: P/T	10.6/11.0 Page: 217, 218	KS,CS,SS,SF,GR,WF,NP,(BB)
3.	Washington Creek Facilities: P	18.3 Page: 218	GR,(WF,BB)
4.	Globe Creek Facilities: P	37.0 Page: 218	GR,(WF)
5.	Tatalina Creek Facilities: P	44.8 Page: 218	GR,(WF,BB)
6.	Tolovana River Facilities: P	57.0 Page: 218	GR,(WF,BB)
7.	Hess Creek Facilities: P	73.1 Page: 218	GR,WF,(NP,BB,SF)
8.	W. Fork Tolovana River Facilities: P	74.9 Page: 218	GR,WF
9.	Minto Flats Facilities: P/BL	109.8 Page: 218, 219	SF,GR,NP,BB,(KS,CS,SS,WF)
10.	Hutlinana Creek Facilities: LP	129.3 Page: 219	DV,GR,(CS,WF)
11.	Baker Creek Facilities: P	137.3 Page: 219	DV,GR,(CS,WF)
12.	Hot Springs Slough Facilities: P/T/BL	(Manley) Page: 219	SF,WF,NP,BB, (KS,CS,SS,GR)

Elliott Highway

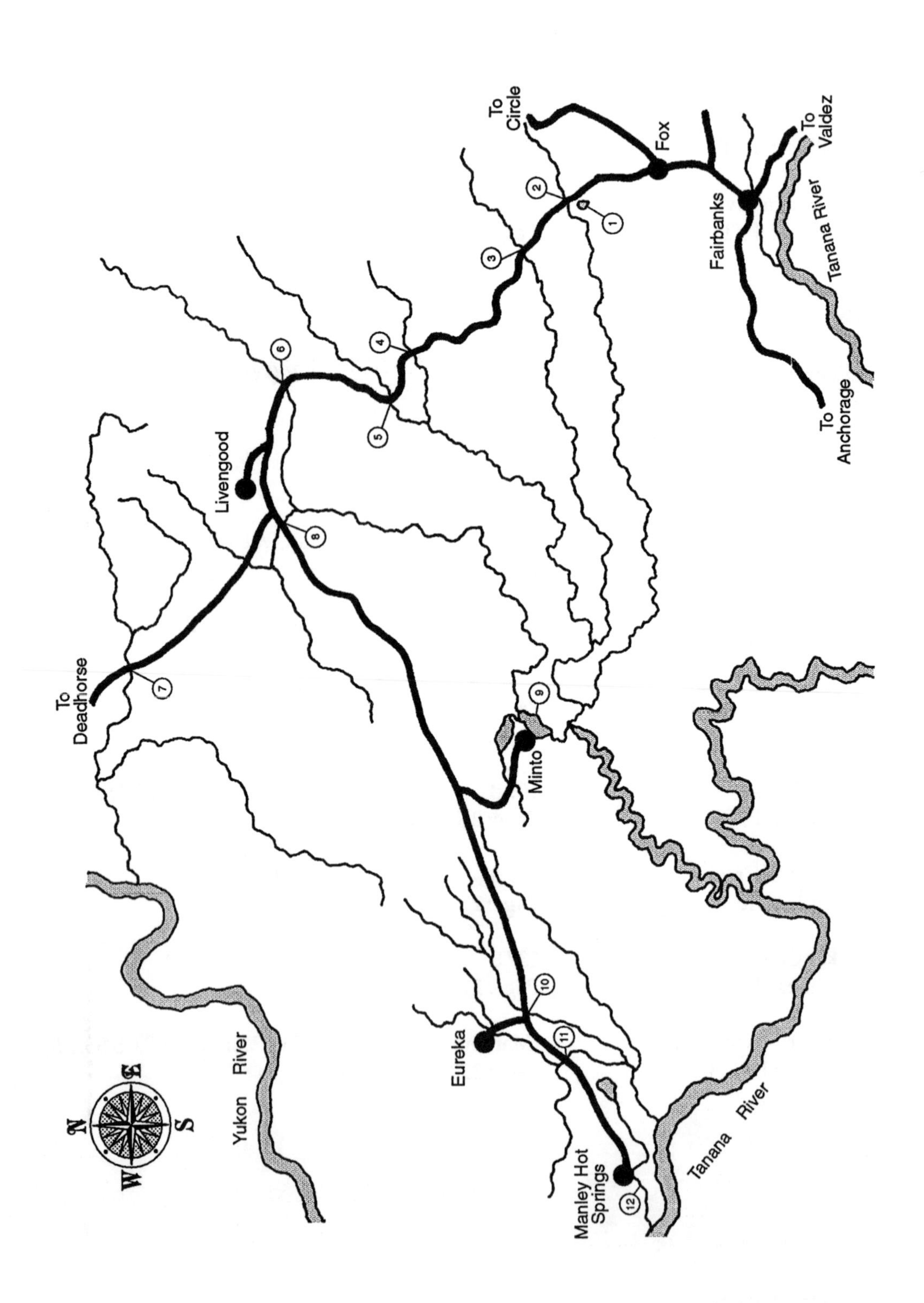

AREA: TOLOVANA - TANANA RIVER DRAINAGE

Includes all branches and tributaries to the Tolovana River and a few of Tanana River region.

Time of Abundance:

FISH▽	JAN	FEB	MAR	APR	MAY	JUN	JUL	AUG	SEP	OCT	NOV	DEC
KS												
CS												
SF												
DV												
GR												
WF												
NP												
BB												

Note: The salmon of this region, due to the distance they've travelled from the ocean, are mostly ripe and ready to spawn upon arrival. The "Time of Abundance" charts in this chapter reflect the presence of salmon in all stages of the spawning run, except for post-spawning.

1. **OLNES POND**

   Access: Turn west onto gravel road at MP 10.6 of the Elliott Highway and drive 1.0 mile to access road on right.

   Major Species:

   Grayling / fair to good / late May to mid-October / 7-14 in.

2. **CHATANIKA RIVER**

   Access: The Elliott Highway crosses the river at MP 11.0. Also, turn west onto a gravel road at MP 10.6 and drive 1.0 mile to an access road to Olnes Pond on right. Park by the pond and find one of two trails leading a short distance to the river.

   Regulations: Check regulations closely for this area.

   Time of Abundance:

FISH▽	JAN	FEB	MAR	APR	MAY	JUN	JUL	AUG	SEP	OCT	NOV	DEC
KS												
CS												
SS												
SF												
GR												
WF												
NP												
BB												

   Major Species:

   King salmon / fair to good / 8-20 lbs., max. 30 lbs. / spoons and spinners, attractor lures.

Chum salmon / poor to fair / 5-10 lbs., max. 15 lbs. / spoons and spinners, streamer flies.
Silver salmon / poor to fair / 4-10 lbs., max. 15 lbs. / spoons and spinners, streamer flies.
Sheefish / poor to fair / 4-8 lbs., max. 15 lbs. / spoons and spinners, streamer flies.
Grayling / fair to good / 7-12 in., max. 18 in. / spinners and wet and dry flies.
Whitefish / fair / 10-18 in., max. 6 lbs. / wet flies, salmon egg imitations.
Northern pike / poor to fair / 2-4 lbs., max. 6 lbs. / spoons and spinners, plugs.

3. **WASHINGTON CREEK**
Access: The Elliott Highway crosses the stream at MP 18.3.
Major Species:
Grayling / fair / mid-May through September / 7-14 in.

4. **GLOBE CREEK**
Access: The Elliott Highway crosses the stream at MP 37.0.
Major Species:
Grayling / fair / mid-May through September / 7-14 in.

5. **TATALINA CREEK**
Access: The Elliott Highway crosses the stream at MP 44.8.
Major Species:
Grayling / fair / mid-May through September / 7-14 in.

6. **TOLOVANA RIVER**
Access: The Elliott Highway crosses the stream at MP 57.0.
Major Species:
Grayling / fair / mid-May through September / 7-14 in.

7. **HESS CREEK**
Access: From MP 73.1 of the Elliott Highway. Turn north onto Dalton Highway and drive 23.8 miles to the stream crossing.
Major Species:
Grayling / fair to good / mid-May through September / 7-14 in.
Whitefish / poor to fair / September to mid-October / 10-18 in.

8. **WEST FORK TOLOVANA RIVER**
Access: The Elliott Highway crosses the river at MP 74.9.
Major Species:
Grayling / fair to good / mid-May through September / 7-14 in.
Whitefish / poor to fair / September to mid-October / 10-18 in.

9. **MINTO FLATS**
Access: From MP 109.8 of the Elliott Highway. Turn south on gravel road leading 10.8 miles through Minto Village to the flats.
Major Species:
Sheefish / fair / June through September / 4-8 lbs.
Grayling / fair / June through September / 7-15 in.

Northern pike / fair to good / late May and June / 3-8 lbs.
Burbot / fair / November through April / 2-6 lbs.

10. HUTLINANA CREEK
Access: The Elliott Highway crosses the stream at MP 129.3.
Major Species:
Dolly Varden / fair to good / mid-June to mid-October / 7-12 in.
Grayling / fair to good / mid-May to mid-June / 7-14 in.

11. BAKER CREEK
Access: The Elliott Highway crosses the stream at MP 137.3.
Major Species:
Dolly Varden / fair / mid-June to mid-October / 7-12 in.
Grayling / fair to good / mid-May through September / 7-14 in.

12. HOT SPRINGS SLOUGH
Access: The Slough is located in Manley at the end of the Elliott Highway.
Major Species:
Sheefish / poor to fair / July and August / 4-15 lbs.
Whitefish / poor to fair / mid-August to mid-October / 10-20 in.
Northern pike / fair / early June to mid-September / 2-10 lbs.
Burbot / fair / October through April / 2-8 lbs.

CHAPTER 20

Seward Highway

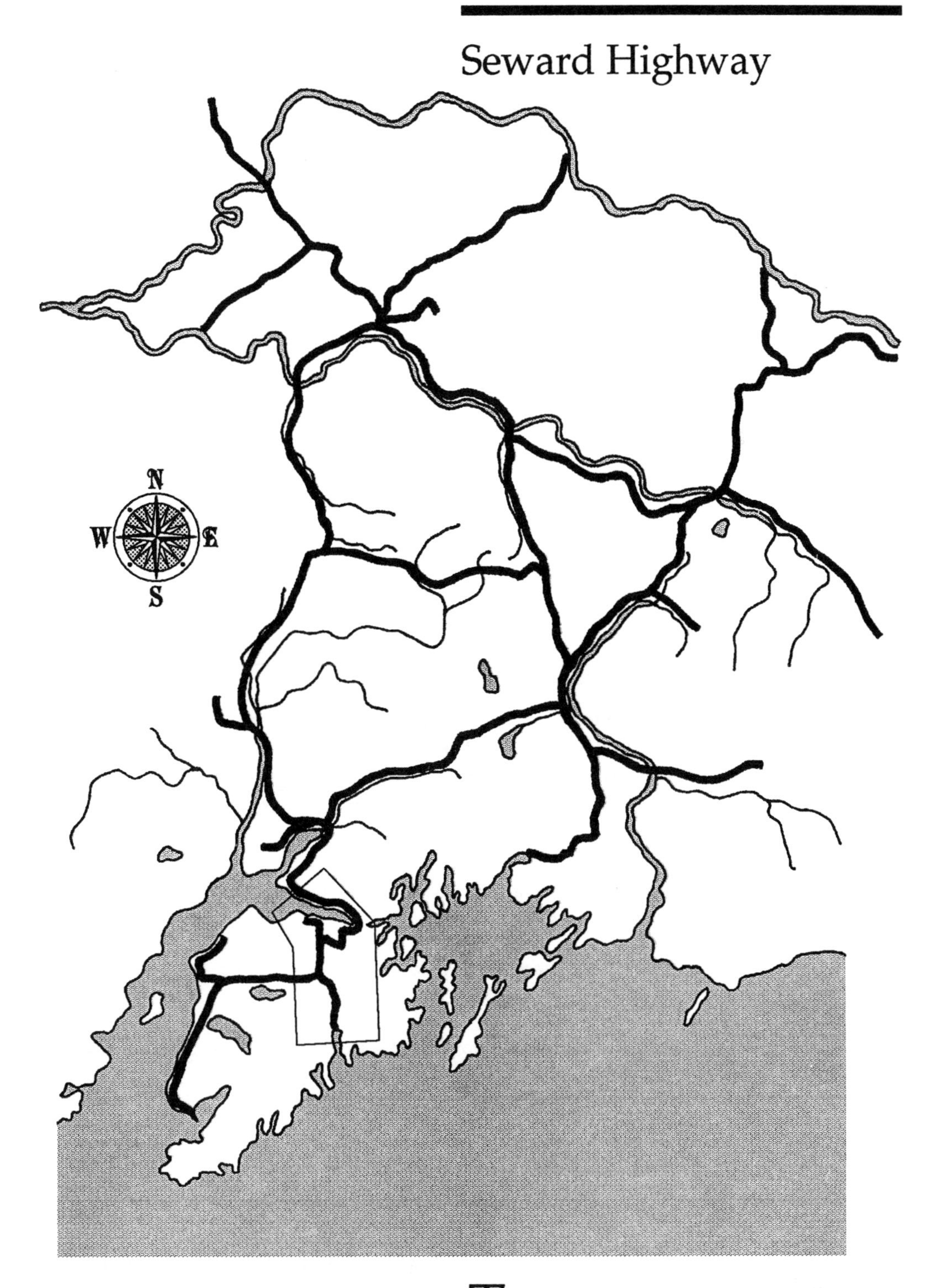

The Seward Highway originates in the coastal town of Seward at the head of Resurrection Bay, and runs northward to Anchorage. It joins up to the Sterling Highway at Tern Lake Junction. It also provides access to Portage Glacier through Portage Glacier Road, and parallels the Turnagain Arm for some 30 miles.

CHAPTER 20

Seward Highway

Seward Highway is the link between Anchorage and coastal fishing communities on the Kenai Peninsula. It parallels or crosses a multitude of fish-rich streams, rivers, and lakes with additional access to ocean fishing. Major sport fish species in this region includes king, pink, chum, and silver salmon, Dolly Varden, lake trout, and rainbow trout. Other species that frequent this area are red salmon, grayling, and whitefish. In salt water there is good fishing for halibut, ling cod, rockfish, and bottomfish available.

Important: Please be aware of the current sport fish rules and regulations for the area covered in this chapter, and abide by them. Remember, they have been applied to protect a fragile resource.

Following are the abbreviations used in this chapter for all the fish species and facility information:

KS - King Salmon	DV - Dolly Varden	HB - Halibut
RS - Red Salmon	LT - Lake Trout	LC - Ling Cod
PS - Pink Salmon	RT - Rainbow Trout	RF - Rockfish
CS - Chum Salmon	GR - Grayling	BF - Bottomfish
SS - Silver Salmon	WF - Whitefish	
P - Parking	C - Camping	BL - Boat Launch
LP - Pimited Parking	T - Toilet	

Time of Abundance/Availability Charts

These charts are designed to show the reader during which time of the year the indicated species are present or available in the most popular fishing streams, lakes, or regions. The charts correlate to when the fish are in their prime for both angling sport and consumption, unless otherwise noted. Species which are closed to sport fishing are also included on the charts just for the purpose of interest but are shown in all stages of maturity.

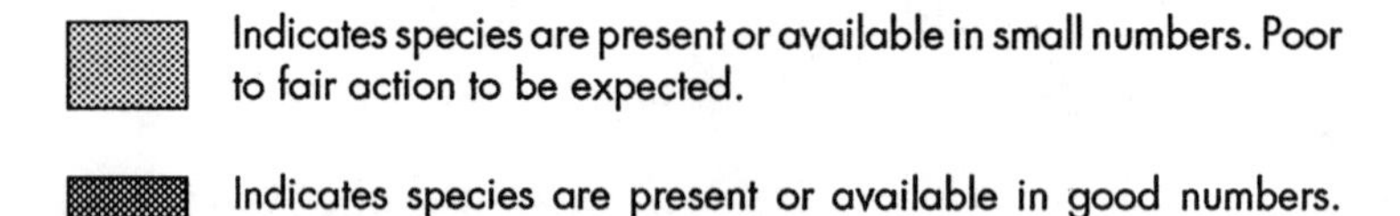
Indicates species are present or available in small numbers. Poor to fair action to be expected.
Indicates species are present or available in good numbers. Good to excellent action possible.

Note: The quality of fishing may vary due to certain fluctuations, such as weather conditions, angler experience, number of fish present, or other factors.

QUICK REFERENCE

This section of the chapter was designed to provide a quick overview of all the fishing spots in the region, their map locations and milepost numbers, species available, facility information, and the page number on which to find detailed access and fishing information for any one watershed.

Note: Species shown in parentheses may be present but are protected by law, and/or are only occasionally seen or hooked by anglers fishing that particular watershed.

SEWARD HIGHWAY

	WATERSHED	MILE POST	SPECIES
1.	Indian Creek Facilities: P/T	103.0 Page: 227	DV,(KS,PS,CS,SS,RT)
2.	Bird Creek Facilities: P/C/T	101.2 Page: 227, 228	PS,CS,SS,DV,(KS,RS,RT)
3.	California Creek Facilities: P	89.8 Page: 228	PS,CS,SS,DV,(KS,RS)
4.	Glacier Creek Facilities: P	89.8 Page: 228, 229	PS,SS,DV,(KS,RS,CS)
5.	Virgin Creek Facilities: LP	89.2 Page: 229	PS,SS,DV,(KS,RS,CS)
6.	Kern Creek Facilities: LP	86.3 Page: 229	PS,CS,SS,DV,(KS,RS)
7.	20-Mile River Facilities: P/BL	80.7 Page: 229, 230	RS,SS,DV,(KS,PS,CS)
8.	Portage Creek Facilities: P	79.4 Page: 230	PS,SS,DV,(KS,RS,CS)
9.	Portage Pond Facilities: P	79.2 Page: 230	RT
10.	Portage Creek Facilities: LP	79.2 Page: 230	SS,DV,(RS,CS)
11.	Placer River Facilities: P/BL	78.4/77.9 Page: 230	RS,SS,DV,(KS,PS,CS)
12.	Ingram Creek Facilities: P	75.3 Page: 231	PS,SS,DV,(KS,RS,CS)
13.	Granite Creek Facilities: P/C/T	63.3 Page: 231	SS,DV,(KS,RS,PS,CS,GR)
14.	East Fork Creek Facilities: P	61.6-56.7 Page: 231	SS,DV,(KS,RS,PS,CS,GR)

Seward Highway

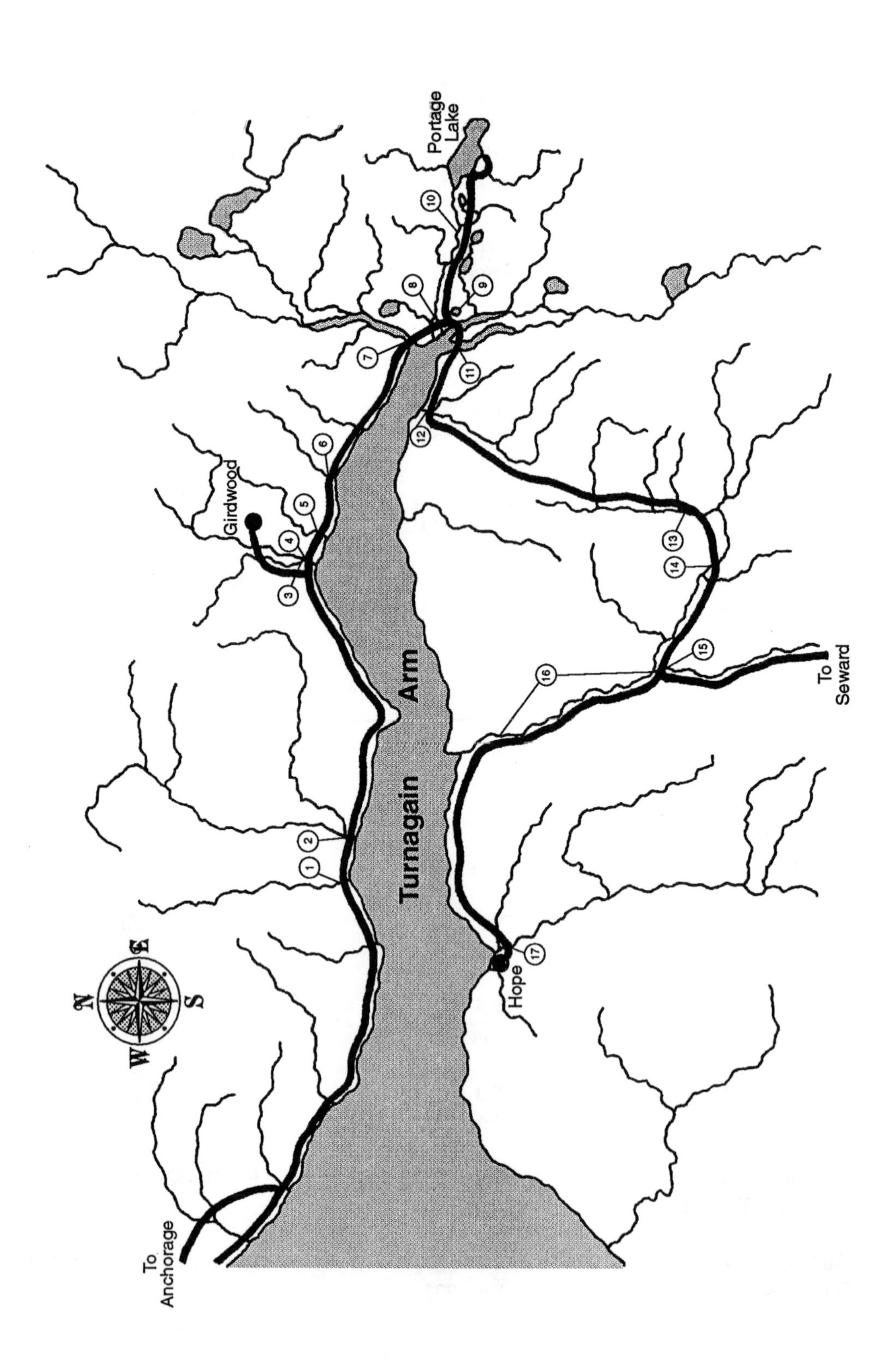

15. Canyon Creek Facilities: P/T	56.7 Page: 231	SS,DV,(KS,RS,PS,CS)
16. Sixmile Creek Facilities: P	56.1 Page: 231, 232	PS,CS,SS,DV,(KS,RS)
17. Resurrection Creek Facilities: P/T	56.1 Page: 232	PS,CS,SS,DV,(KS,RS)
18. Lower Summit Lake Facilities: P	47.3 Page: 232	DV,RT,(LT)
19. Canyon Creek Facilities: LP	47.3/46.0 Page: 233	DV,RT
20. Upper Summit Lake Facilities: P/C/T	45.8/46.0 Page: 233	DV,LT,RT
21. Summit Creek Facilities: LP	42.6 Page: 233	DV,(RS,SS,RT)
22. Quartz Creek Facilities: P	42.2-41.0 Page: 234	DV,(KS,RS,PS,SS,RT,GR,WF)
23. Jerome Lake Facilities: P	38.6 Page: 234	DV,RT
24. Moose Creek Facilities: P	32.9-32.2 Page: 234	DV,RT,(KS,RS,SS)
25. Upper Trail Lake Facilities: P/BL	32.2-30.3 Page: 234	DV,LT,RT,(KS,RS,SS,WF)
26. Lower Trail Lake Facilities: P	25.3 Page: 234	DV,LT,RT,(KS,RS,SS,WF)
27. Vagt Lake Facilities: P (trail)	25.3 Page: 234	RT
28. Trail River Facilities: P/C/T	25.3-24.1 Page: 234, 235	DV,RT,(KS,RS,PS,SS,LT,WF)
29. Ptarmigan Creek Facilities: P/C/T	23.2 Page: 235	DV,RT,(KS,RS,PS,CS,SS,WF)
30. Grayling Lake Facilities: P (trail)	13.3 Page: 235	GR

Seward Highway

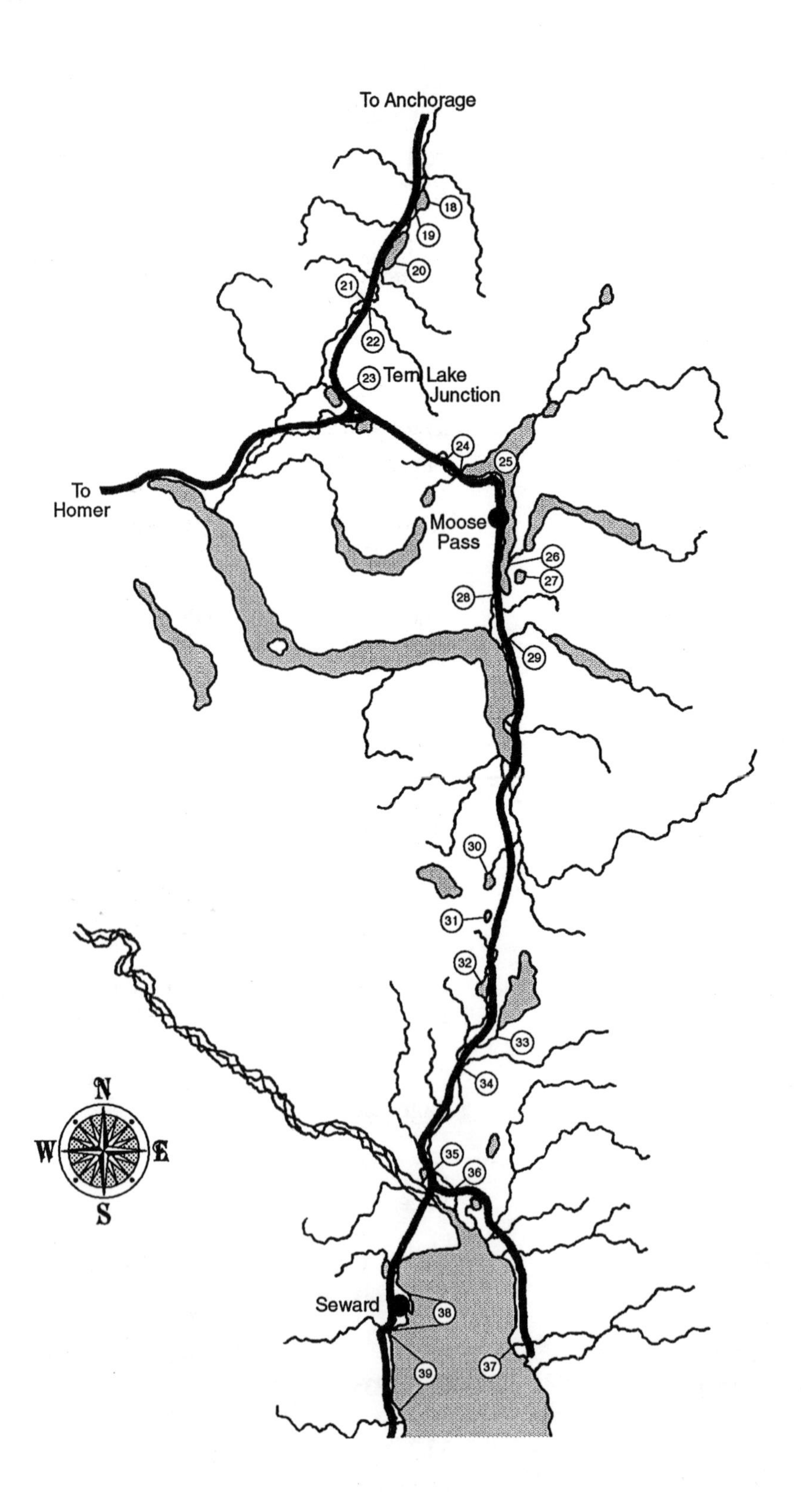

31. Goldenfin Lake Facilities: P (trail)	11.6 Page: 235	DV
32. Grouse Lake Facilities: P	7.4 Page: 236	DV,(KS,RS,PS,CS,SS,RT)
33. Bear Creek Facilities: LP	6.5 Page: 236	DV,(KS,RS,PS,CS,SS,RT)
34. Salmon Creek Facilities: LP	5.9 Page: 236	DV,(KS,RS,PS,CS,SS,RT)
35. Preacher Pond Facilities: P	3.4 Page: 236	DV,(KS,RS,PS,CS,SS,RT)
36. Salmon Creek Facilities: LP	3.3 Page: 236	DV,(KS,RS,PS,CS,SS)
37. Fourth of July Creek Facilities: P/T	3.3 Page: 236, 237	PS,CS,SS,DV,BF,(KS,RS)
38. Seward Harbor Facilities: P/T/BL	(Seward) Page: 237	KS,RS,PS,CS,SS,DV,BF,(HB,LC)
39. West Resurrection Bay Facilities: P	(Seward) Page: 237	KS,PS,CS,SS,DV,BF,(RS,LC,RF)

AREA A: TURNAGAIN ARM DRAINAGE

Includes all waters draining into the Turnagain Arm, except for the Portage region (Area B).

1. INDIAN CREEK

Access: The Seward Highway crosses the stream at MP 103.0.
Regulations: King salmon fishing prohibited. Closed to all fishing from July 1 through August 14.
Major Species:
Dolly Varden / fair to good / late May and June / 8-15 in.

2. BIRD CREEK

Access: The Seward Highway crosses the stream at MP 101.2.
Regulations: King salmon fishing prohibited.

Time of Abundance:

FISH ▽	JAN	FEB	MAR	APR	MAY	JUN	JUL	AUG	SEP	OCT	NOV	DEC
KS												
RS												
PS												
CS												
SS												
DV												
RT												

Major Species:

Pink salmon / good to excellent / 2-4 lbs., max. 7 lbs. / spoons and spinners, streamer flies.

Chum salmon / good / 6-12 lbs., max. 18 lbs. / spoons and spinners, streamer flies.

Silver salmon / good / 6-12 lbs., max. 18 lbs. / spinners, streamer flies, salmon egg clusters.

Dolly Varden / fair / 8-15 in., max. 5 lbs. / spoons and spinners, salmon egg clusters, single salmon eggs.

3. CALIFORNIA CREEK / GLACIER CREEK CONFLUENCE

Access: From MP 89.8 of the Seward Highway. Follow the north bank of Glacier Creek about 150 yards upstream to the railroad trestle bridge. The confluence is located just upstream from the bridge.

Regulations: King salmon fishing prohibited.

Time of Abundance:

FISH ▽	JAN	FEB	MAR	APR	MAY	JUN	JUL	AUG	SEP	OCT	NOV	DEC
KS												
RS												
PS												
CS												
SS												
DV												

Major Species:

Pink salmon / good / 2-4 lbs., max. 6 lbs. / spoons and spinners, streamer flies.

Chum salmon / fair / 6-10 lbs., max. 15 lbs. / spoons and spinners, salmon egg clusters.

Silver salmon / fair to good / 4-10 lbs., max. 15 lbs. / spinners, salmon egg clusters.

Dolly Varden / fair to good / 8-15 in., max. 4 lbs. / spinners, single salmon eggs or clusters.

4. GLACIER CREEK

Access: The Seward Highway crosses the stream at MP 89.8.

Regulations: King salmon fishing prohibited.

Major Species:
Pink salmon / fair / late July, early August / 2-5 lbs.
Silver salmon / fair / early to mid-August / 4-10 lbs.
Dolly Varden / fair / June and early July / 8-15 in.

5. **VIRGIN CREEK**
Access: The Seward Highway crosses the stream at MP 89.2.
Regulations: King salmon fishing prohibited.
Major Species:
Pink salmon / poor to fair / late July / 2-5 lbs.
Silver salmon / poor to fair / mid-August / 4-10 lbs.
Dolly Varden / fair / June and early July / 8-12 in.

6. **KERN CREEK**
Access: The Seward Highway crosses the stream at MP 86.3. The mouth of Kern Creek is visible at low tide only. Upstream reaches can be found on the other side of the railroad tracks.
Regulations: King salmon fishing prohibited.
Major Species:
Pink salmon / fair / mid- and late July / 2-5 lbs.
Chum salmon / poor to fair / late July, early August / 6-12 lbs.
Silver salmon / poor to fair / mid- and late August / 5-12 lbs.
Dolly Varden / fair / June and early July / 8-15 in.

AREA B: THE PORTAGE AREA OF TURNAGAIN ARM

Includes all waters draining into the 20-Mile and Placer River, and Portage Creek.
Time of Abundance:

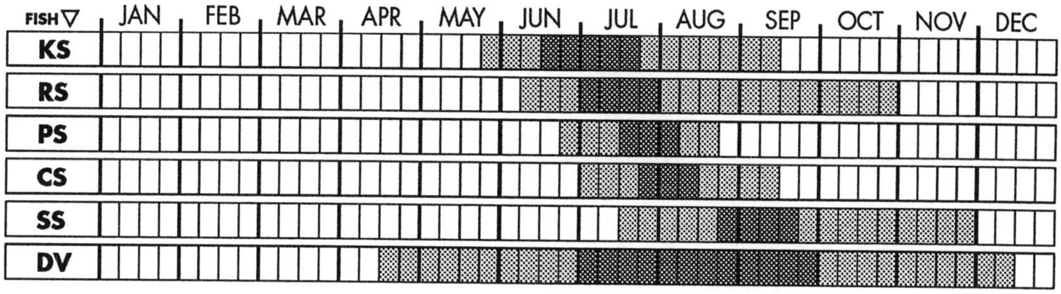

FISH ▽	JAN	FEB	MAR	APR	MAY	JUN	JUL	AUG	SEP	OCT	NOV	DEC
KS												
RS												
PS												
CS												
SS												
DV												

Note: All of the waters in this area are closed to king salmon fishing.

7. **20-MILE RIVER**
Access: The 20-Mile River crosses the Seward Highway at MP 80.7. Clearwater tributaries can be reached by power boat or canoe, or by a strenuous walk through brush along the banks of the river.
Regulations: King salmon fishing prohibited.

Fishing: The confluences of clearwater tributaries and the main river provide fair to excellent fishing for red and silver salmon and Dolly Varden. See the "Time of Abundance" chart for Area B on **page 229**. Also, for information on hooligan fishing, see **page 69**.

8. PORTAGE CREEK (NO. 2)

Access: The Seward Highway crosses the stream at MP 79.4. The upper parts of the drainage can be reached by car from Portage Glacier Road, but the best fishing can be found at the confluence of an unnamed tributary located on the north bank about one mile upstream from the highway bridge. Hike through brush along the creek or use a canoe.

Regulations: King salmon fishing prohibited.

Major Species:

Pink salmon / poor to fair / late July, early August / 2-5 lbs.
Silver salmon / fair / late August and September / 6-12 lbs.
Dolly Varden / fair / June and early July / 7-15 in.

Upstream Fishing:

The confluence of an unnamed tributary and Portage Creek offers fair to good fishing for red, pink, and silver salmon and Dolly Varden. See the "Time of Abundance" chart for Area B on **page 229**.

9. PORTAGE POND

Access: From MP 79.2 of the Seward Highway. Turn east on Portage Glacier Road and drive 1.5 miles to gravel road on the right. Follow the right fork of the "Y" a short distance to the pond.

Major Species:

Rainbow trout / good / August to mid-October / 7-12 in.

10. WILLIWAW CREEK / PORTAGE CREEK CONFLUENCE

Access: From MP 79.2 of the Seward Highway. Turn east on Portage Glacier Road and drive 3.6 miles to confluence area of left.

Regulations: King salmon fishing prohibited. The tributary stream, Williwaw Creek, is closed to salmon fishing, and is closed to all fishing from July 1 through September 15.

Major Species:

Silver salmon / poor to fair / late September / 6-12 lbs.
Dolly Varden / poor to fair / July and August / 7-12 in.

11. PLACER RIVER

Access: The Seward Highway crosses the river at MP 78.4 and 77.9. Clearwater tributaries can be reached by boat or canoe, or by a strenuous hike through brush along the river.

Regulations: King salmon fishing prohibited.

Fishing:

The confluence of clearwater tributaries and the main river offer fair to excellent fishing for red and silver salmon and Dolly Varden. One tributary can be reached by hiking the east bank of the river about 0.5 miles upstream from the bridge. See the "Time of Abundance" chart for Area B on **page 229**. Also, see **page 69** for hooligan fishing in the river.

AREA A: TURNAGAIN ARM DRAINAGE (CONT.)

Includes all waters draining into Turnagain Arm, except the Portage region, which is covered in Area B.

12. INGRAM CREEK

Access: The Seward Highway crosses the stream at MP 75.3.
Regulations: King salmon fishing prohibited.
Major Species:
Pink salmon / fair to good / late July, early August / 2-4 lbs.
Chum salmon / poor to fair / early August / 6-12 lbs.
Silver salmon / fair / mid- and late August / 5-12 lbs.
Dolly Varden / fair / June and early July / 8-18 in.

13. GRANITE CREEK

Access: The Seward Highway crosses the stream at MP 63.3. The lower section of Granite Creek and its confluence with East Fork Creek can be reached by turning south onto a gravel road at MP 62.5. Drive 0.5 miles to campground and confluence area.
Regulations: King salmon fishing prohibited.
Major Species:
Silver salmon / poor to fair / late August / 5-10 lbs.
Dolly Varden / poor to fair / July and August / 7-12 in.

14. EAST FORK CREEK

Note: Also known as East Fork Sixmile Creek
Access: The Seward Highway parallels the stream from the bridge crossing at MP 61.6 downstream to the confluence of Canyon Creek at MP 56.7.
Regulations: King salmon fishing prohibited.
Major Species:
Silver salmon / poor to fair / late August / 5-10 lbs.
Dolly Varden / poor to fair / July and August / 7-12 in.

15. CANYON CREEK

Access: The Seward Highway crosses the stream at MP 56.7. Hike down steep hill by bridge to stream. Also, to reach the confluence of Canyon Creek and East Fork Creek, turn onto dirt road located at the junction of Hope and Seward Highway's. Continue on this steep four-wheel-drive road about 0.4 miles to the confluence area.
Regulations: King salmon fishing prohibited.
Major Species:
Silver salmon / poor to fair / late August / 5-10 lbs.
Dolly Varden / poor to fair / July and August / 7-12 in.

16. SIXMILE CREEK

Access: From MP 56.1 of the Seward Highway. Turn north on Hope Highway. The road parallels the stream from near the confluence with Canyon Creek to about 7.3 miles north.

Regulations: King salmon fishing prohibited.
Time of Abundance:

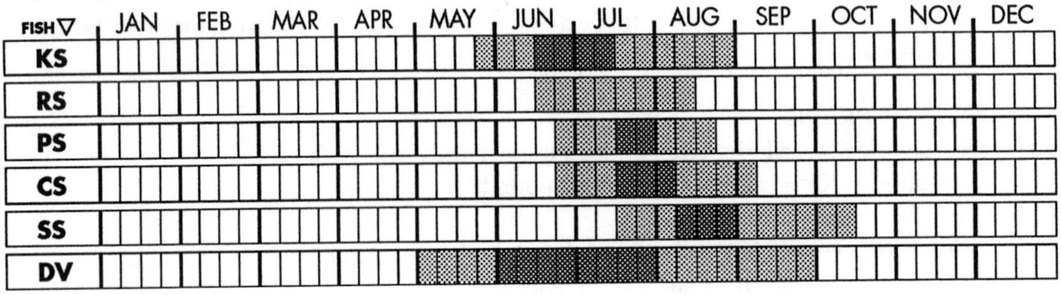

FISH ▽	JAN	FEB	MAR	APR	MAY	JUN	JUL	AUG	SEP	OCT	NOV	DEC
KS												
RS												
PS												
CS												
SS												
DV												

Major Species:
Pink salmon / fair to excellent / 2-4 lbs., max. 7 lbs. / spoons and spinners, streamer flies.
Chum salmon / fair to good / 6-12 lbs., max. 18 lbs. / spoons spinners, and streamer flies.
Silver salmon / fair to good / 6-12 lbs., max. 18 lbs. / salmon egg clusters, spinners.
Dolly Varden / fair / 7-15 in., max. 5 lbs. / single salmon egg or clusters, spoons.

17. RESURRECTION CREEK

Access: From MP 56.1 of the Seward Highway. Turn north on Hope Highway and drive 16.3 miles to the stream crossing in the community of Hope.
Regulations: King salmon fishing prohibited.
Time of Abundance:

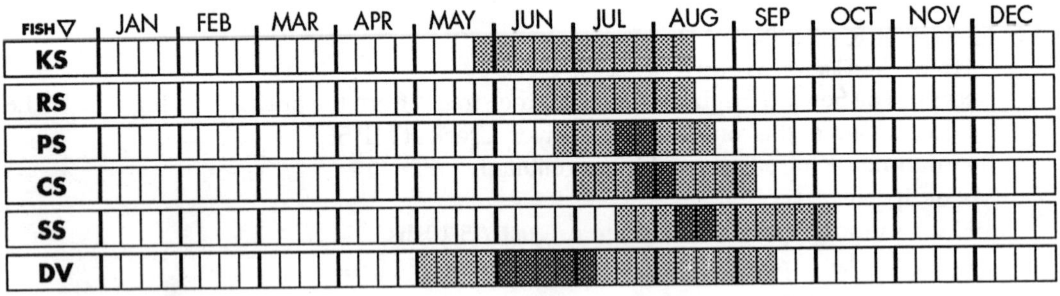

FISH ▽	JAN	FEB	MAR	APR	MAY	JUN	JUL	AUG	SEP	OCT	NOV	DEC
KS												
RS												
PS												
CS												
SS												
DV												

Major Species:
Pink salmon / fair to excellent / 2-4 lbs., max. 6 lbs. / spoons, spinners, streamer flies.
Chum salmon / poor to fair / 6-10 lbs., max. 15 lbs. / spoons, spinners, and streamer flies.
Silver salmon / fair to good / 6-12 lbs., max. 15 lbs. / salmon egg clusters, spinners, streamer flies.
Dolly Varden / fair / 7-15 in., max. 5 lbs. / single salmon eggs, salmon egg clusters, spoons.

18. LOWER SUMMIT LAKE

Access: The Seward Highway parallels the west shore of the lake at MP 47.3.
Major Species:
Dolly Varden / fair to good / June through September / 7-12 in.
Rainbow trout / fair / June and September / 8-20 in.

19. CANYON CREEK

Access: The Seward Highway parallels the stream from MP 47.3 to 46.0. Short hike due east through low brush.

Major Species:

Dolly Varden / fair / mid-June to mid-September / 7-12 in.
Rainbow trout / poor to fair / June through August / 7-15 in.

20. UPPER SUMMIT LAKE

Access: The Seward Highway parallels the west shore of the lake from MP 46.0. To reach the other side of the lake, turn east onto dirt road at MP 45.8 and drive 0.8 miles to lake and campground.

Major Species:

Dolly Varden / fair to good / June through September / 7-12 in.
Lake trout / fair / June, September, and October / 2-5 lbs.
Rainbow trout / fair to good / June and September / 8-20 in.

AREA C: CENTRAL KENAI PENINSULA

Includes all streams draining into Trail and Kenai Lakes.

Time of Abundance:

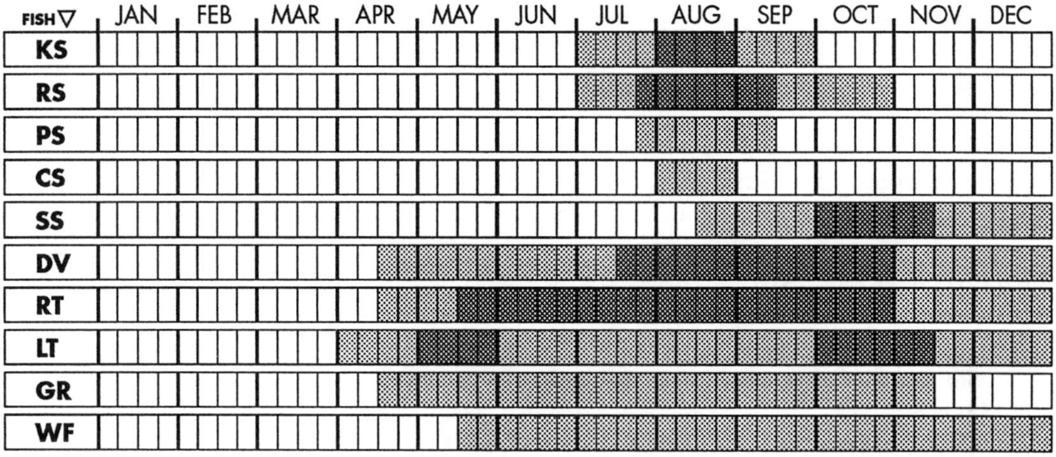

FISH ▽	JAN	FEB	MAR	APR	MAY	JUN	JUL	AUG	SEP	OCT	NOV	DEC
KS												
RS												
PS												
CS												
SS												
DV												
RT												
LT												
GR												
WF												

Note: All waters in Area C are closed to salmon fishing. The above chart correlates to all Trail Lake and Kenai Lake tributaries. Species are represented in all stages of maturity.

21. SUMMIT CREEK

Access: The Seward Highway crosses the stream at MP 42.6.

Regulations: Salmon fishing prohibited. Only unbaited artificial lures from September 16 through December 31.

Major Species:

Dolly Varden / fair / August and September / 10-20 in.

22. QUARTZ CREEK
Access: The Seward Highway parallels the stream from MP 42.2 to 41.0. At MP 39.5, turn west onto pull-off and hike along Devil's Pass Trailhead about 0.5 miles to stream.
Regulations: Salmon fishing prohibited. Only unbaited artificial lures from September 16 through December 31.
Major Species:
Dolly Varden / fair / August and September / 10-20 in.

23. JEROME LAKE
Access: The Seward Highway parallels the lake at MP 38.6.
Major Species:
Dolly Varden / fair to good / June through September / 7-15 in.
Rainbow trout / fair to good / June and September / 8-15 in.

24. MOOSE CREEK
Access: The Seward Highway crosses the stream at MP 32.9 and 32.3.
Regulations: Salmon fishing prohibited.
Major Species:
Dolly Varden / fair / late July through September / 7-15 in.
Rainbow trout / poor to fair / July and August / 7-15 in.

25. UPPER TRAIL LAKE
Access: The Seward Highway parallels the southwest of the lake. Main access points at MP 32.3 and 30.3.
Regulations: Salmon fishing prohibited.
Major Species:
Dolly Varden / fair / June through October / 7-15 in.
Lake trout / fair / June, September, and October / 2-5 lbs.
Rainbow trout / poor to fair / June, September, and October / 7-15 in.

26. LOWER TRAIL LAKE
Access: The Seward Highway parallels the west side of the lake with the main access point at MP 25.3 and the lake outlet.
Regulations: Salmon fishing prohibited.
Major Species:
Dolly Varden / fair / June through October / 7-15 in.
Lake trout / fair / June, September, October / 2-5 lbs.
Rainbow trout / fair / June, September, October / 8-15 in.

27. VAGT LAKE
Access: From MP 25.3 of the Seward Highway. Park by bridge and find trail leading 2 miles due east to lake.
Major Species:
Rainbow trout / fair to good / June and September / 8-15 in.

28. TRAIL RIVER
Access: The Seward Highway parallels the river beginning at the river crossing at MP 25.3

until MP 24.1. At MP 24.1, turn west on gravel road and drive 0.4 miles to river crossing; or continue 0.8 mile to campground and lower river.

Regulations: Salmon fishing prohibited. Only unbaited artificial lures from September 16 through December 31.

Major Species:

Dolly Varden / fair to good / July through September / 8-20 in.
Rainbow trout / fair / June through September / 8-15 in.

29. PTARMIGAN CREEK

Access: The Seward Highway crosses the stream at MP 23.2.

Regulations: Salmon fishing prohibited. Only unbaited artificial lures from September 16 through December 31.

Major Species:

Dolly Varden / fair to good / mid-July through mid-November / 10-20 in.
Rainbow trout / fair to good / July through October / 8-15 in.

30. GRAYLING LAKE

Access: From MP 13.3 of the Seward Highway. Park and hike 1.6 miles due west to the lake.

Major Species:

Grayling / fair to good / June through September / 7-15 in.

AREA D: RESURRECTION BAY DRAINAGE

Includes all water draining into Resurrection Bay along the Seward Highway.

Time of Abundance:

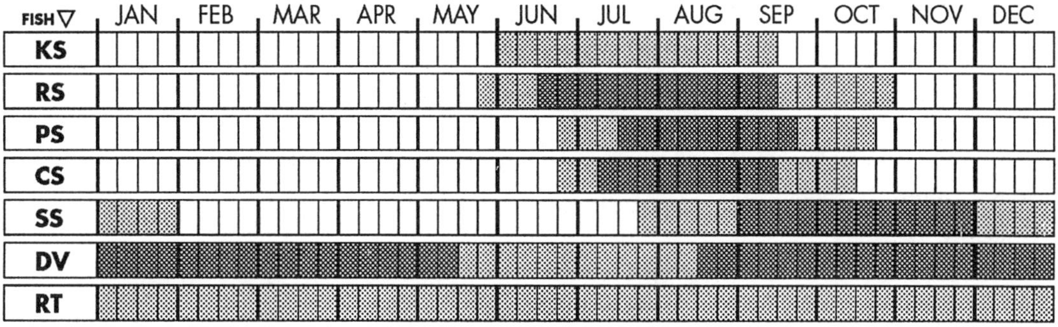

FISH▽	JAN	FEB	MAR	APR	MAY	JUN	JUL	AUG	SEP	OCT	NOV	DEC
KS												
RS												
PS												
CS												
SS												
DV												
RT												

Note: Salmon fishing is prohibited in all waters draining into Resurrection Bay. The above chart correlates to both lakes and flowing water. Species are represented in all stages of maturity.

31. GOLDENFIN LAKE

Access: From MP 11.6 of the Seward Highway. Park and hike 0.5 miles due east to the lake.

Major Species:

Dolly Varden / fair / June through October / 7-12 in.

32. GROUSE LAKE

Access: From MP 7.4 of the Seward Highway. Turn west on paved road and drive a short distance to the lake outlet.

Regulations: Salmon fishing prohibited.

Major Species:

Dolly Varden / fair to good / October through May / 8-22 in.

33. BEAR CREEK

Access: The Seward Highway crosses the stream at MP 6.5.

Regulations: Salmon fishing prohibited. Only unbaited artificial lures from September 16 through December 31.

Major Species:

Dolly Varden / fair / September and October / 8-20 in.

34. SALMON CREEK

Access: The Seward Highway crosses the stream at MP 5.9.

Regulations: Salmon fishing prohibited. Only unbaited artificial lures from September 16 through December 31.

Major Species:

Dolly Varden / fair to good / August and September / 8-22 in.

35. PREACHER POND

Access: From MP 3.4 of the Seward Highway. The pond is adjacent to the west side of the highway.

Regulations: Salmon fishing prohibited.

Major Species:

Dolly Varden / fair to good / October to mid-May / 8-22 in.

36. SALMON CREEK

Access: From MP 3.3 of the Seward Highway. Turn east on Nash Road and drive 0.5 miles to stream crossing.

Regulations: Salmon fishing prohibited. Only unbaited artificial lures from September 16 through December 31.

Major Species:

Dolly Varden / fair / late July through August / 8-22 in.

Note: Also, see page 69 for hooligan fishing.

37. FOURTH OF JULY CREEK MARINE

Access: From MP 3.3 of the Seward Highway. Turn east onto Nash Road and drive 5.1 miles. Turn right on gravel road just past Fourth of July Creek and drive a short distance to the mouth of the stream and Resurrection Bay.

Regulations: Salmon fishing is prohibited in Fourth of July Creek proper, but legal in the salt water at the mouth of the creek.

Time of Abundance:

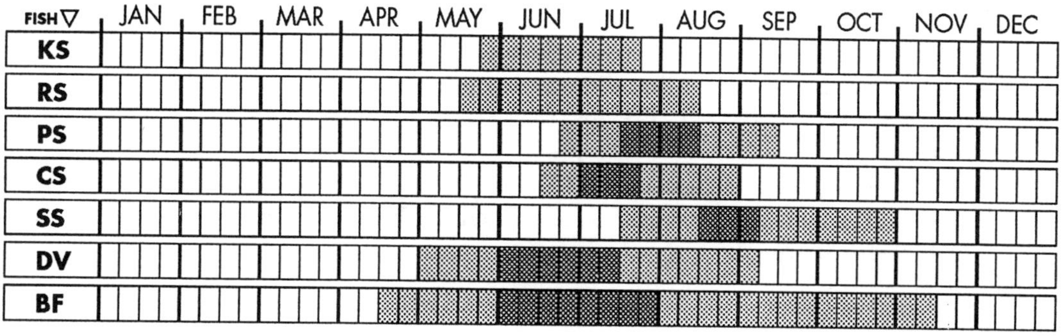

FISH▽	JAN	FEB	MAR	APR	MAY	JUN	JUL	AUG	SEP	OCT	NOV	DEC
KS												
RS												
PS												
CS												
SS												
DV												
BF												

Major Species:

Pink salmon / fair to excellent / 2-5 lbs., max. 7 lbs. / spoons and spinners, snag hooks.
Chum salmon / fair to excellent / 6-12 lbs., max. 18 lbs. / spoons and spinners, snag hooks.
Silver salmon / fair / 6-12 lbs., max. 20 lbs. / spoons and spinners, herring bait, snag hooks.
Dolly Varden / fair / 8-15 in., max. 10 lbs. / spoons, fishing imitation flies, herring bait.
Bottomfish / fair / species include flounder, sole, cod, greenling, and sablefish / herring bait and spoons.

38. SEWARD HARBOR

Access: The Seward Harbor is located at the northwest side of Resurrection Bay in front of the town of Seward, right at the start of the Seward Highway. This area includes the stretch of waterfront from the small boat harbor to the mouth of Lowell Creek. All city streets lead to the bay.

Regulations: Salmon fishing is prohibited in all fresh water areas of the bay. Seward Lagoon and the stream draining the lagoon are closed to all fishing. All fishing is legal at the mouth of all streams draining into the bay.

Time of Abundance:

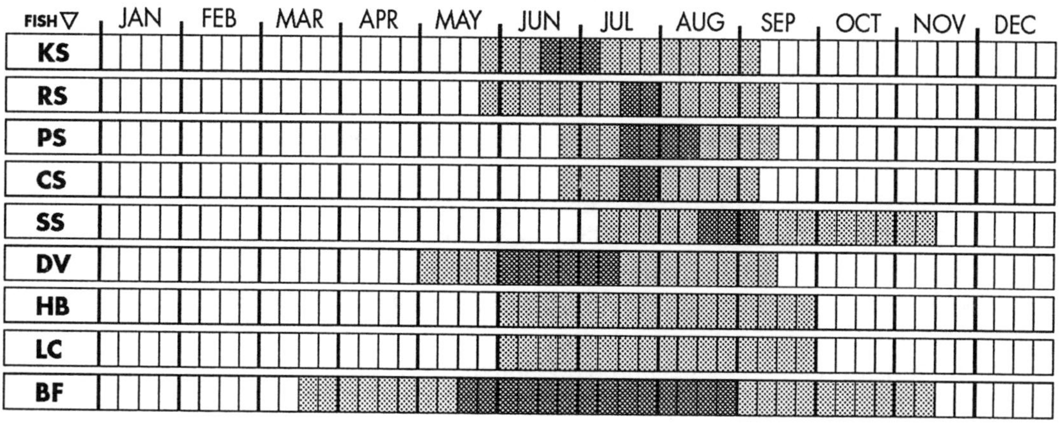

FISH▽	JAN	FEB	MAR	APR	MAY	JUN	JUL	AUG	SEP	OCT	NOV	DEC
KS												
RS												
PS												
CS												
SS												
DV												
HB												
LC												
BF												

Major Species:

King salmon / fair to good / 15-30 lbs., max. 50 lbs. / herring or clusters of salmon eggs, spinners, snag hooks.

Red salmon / poor to fair / 4-7 lbs., max. 12 lbs. / snag hooks, spinners.
Pink salmon / fair to excellent / 2-5 lbs., max. 7 lbs. / spoons and spinners, snag hooks, herring bait.
Chum salmon / fair / 6-12 lbs., max. 18 lbs. / spoons and spinners, snag hooks.
Silver salmon / fair to good / 6-12 lbs., max. 20 lbs. / spoons, spinners, herring bait, snag hooks.
Dolly Varden / fair / 8-15 in., max. 10 lbs. / herring bait, spoons, fish-imitation flies.
Bottomfish / fair to excellent / species include flounder, cod, sole, greenling, and sablefish / herring bait, spoons, jigs.

39. WEST RESURRECTION BAY

Access: From the downtown area of Seward. Find gravel road in the far north-west corner of the bay next to the state ferry dock and follow along the west side of the bay, about 2.5 mile stretch. This area includes the stretch of waterfront from Spruce Creek at Lowell Point to Lowell Creek Falls.
Regulations: Salmon fishing prohibited in Spruce Creek proper. Open to all species at creek mouth and in the bay.
Time for Abundance:

FISH▽	JAN	FEB	MAR	APR	MAY	JUN	JUL	AUG	SEP	OCT	NOV	DEC
KS												
RS												
PS												
CS												
SS												
DV												
LC												
RF												
BF												

Major Species:
King salmon / fair to good / 15-30 lbs., max. 50 lbs. / spoons, spinners, herring and salmon egg clusters, snag hooks.
Pink salmon / fair to excellent / 2-5 lbs., max. 7 lbs. / spoons and spinners, herring bait, snag hooks.
Chum salmon / poor to fair / 6-12 lbs., max. 18 lbs. / spoons and spinners, snag hooks.
Silver salmon / fair to good / 6-12 lbs., max. 20 lbs. / spoons and spinners, herring bait, snag hooks.
Dolly Varden / fair to good / 8-15 in., max. 10 lbs. / spoons, herring bait, fish-imitation flies.
Bottomfish / fair / species include cod, flounder, greenling / herring bait, spoons, and jigs.

CHAPTER 21

Sterling Highway

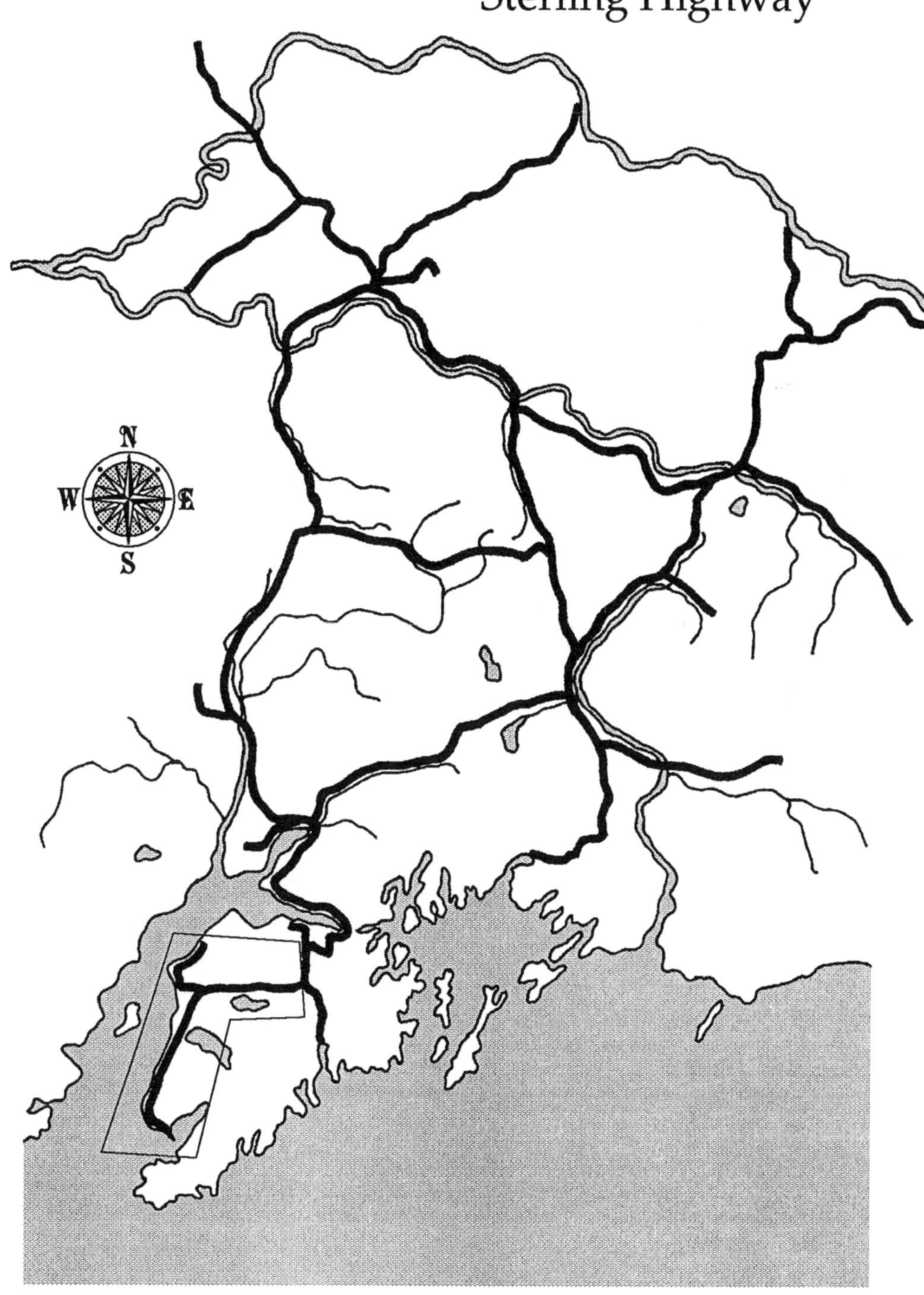

The Sterling Highway begins at MP 37.0 of the Seward Highway and runs westward to the coast of Kenai Peninsula and the town of Soldotna. Here it turns south along the coast to the town of Homer, on Kachemak Bay. Like the

Seward Highway, the Sterling Highway is a very important link between the coastal communities of the peninsula and Anchorage.

The Sterling Highway parallels the famed Kenai River for many miles, crossing several tributary streams along the way. It also provides excellent access to lakes on the Kenai Peninsula. Along the coast of the fish-rich Cook Inlet, the Sterling Highway intersects several productive rivers and streams.

Major sport fish species of this region include king, red, pink, and silver salmon, rainbow trout, Dolly Varden, lake trout, and land-locked salmon. Fair numbers of steelhead trout, grayling, and whitefish are also present in a few selected watersheds. In salt water, fishing is very productive for halibut and bottomfish. Although fishing can be good throughout most of the year, the main fishing season lasts from mid-May to mid-October.

Important: Please be aware of the current sport fishing rules and regulations for the area covered in this chapter, and abide by them. Remember, they have been applied to protect a fragile resource.

Following are the abbreviations used in this chapter for all the fish species and facility information:

KS - King Salmon
RS - Red Salmon
PS - Pink Salmon
CS - Chum Salmon
SS - Silver Salmon
LS - Land-locked Salmon
KO - Kokanee
SH - Steelhead Trout
DV - Dolly Varden
AC - Arctic Char
LT - Lake Trout
RT - Rainbow Trout
GR - Grayling
WF - Whitefish
HB - Halibut
RF - Rockfish
BF - Bottomfish

P - Parking
LP - Limited Parking
C - Camping
T - Toilet
BL - Boat Launch

Time of Abundance/Availability Charts

These charts are designed to show the reader during which time of the year the indicated species are present or available in the most popular fishing streams, lakes, or regions. The charts correlate to when the fish are in their prime for both angling sport and consumption, unless otherwise noted. Species which are closed to sport fishing are also included on the charts just for the purpose of interest but are shown in all stages of maturity.

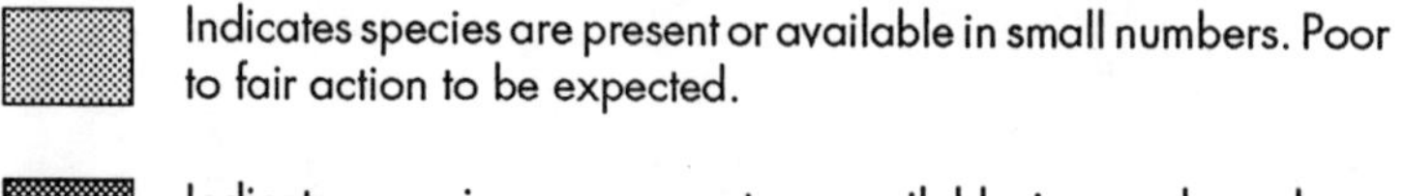

Indicates species are present or available in small numbers. Poor to fair action to be expected.

Indicates species are present or available in good numbers. Good to excellent action possible.

Note: The quality of fishing may vary due to certain fluctuations, such as weather conditions, angler experience, number of fish present, or other factors.

QUICK REFERENCE

This section was designed to provide a quick overview of all the fishing spots in the region, their map locations and milepost numbers, species available, facility information, and the page number on which to find detailed access and fishing information for any one specific watershed.

Note: Species shown in parentheses may be present but are protected by law, and/or are only occasionally seen or hooked by anglers fishing that particular watershed.

STERLING HIGHWAY

	WATERSHED	MILE POST	SPECIES
1.	Tern Lake Facilities: P/C/T	37.3 Page: 250	DV,RT,(KS,RS,PS,SS,GR,WF)
2.	Daves Creek Facilities: LP	37.3-40.0 Page: 250	DV,RT,GR,(KS,RS,PS,SS,WF)
3.	Quartz Creek Facilities: P/C/T	40.9-45.0 Page: 250, 251	DV,RT,GR,WF,(KS,RS,PS,SS)
4.	Crescent Creek Facilities: P	45.0 Page: 251	DV,GR,(RS,SS,RT)
5.	Kenai Lake Facilities: P	45.0-47.7 Page: 251	DV,LT,RT,(KS,RS,PS,CS,SS,GR,WF)
6.	Cleaver Lake Facilities: P (trail)	47.8 Page: 251	RT
7.	Rainbow Lake Facilities: P (trail)	47.8 Page: 251	RT
8.	Cooper Lake Facilities: P	47.8 Page: 251	DV,RT
9.	Kenai River Facilities: P/C/T/BL	47.7-55.0 Page: 252	RS,SS,DV,RT,WF,(KS,PS,CS,LT,GR)
10.	Russian River Facilities: P/C/T	52.7 Page: 252, 253	RS,SS,DV,RT,(KS,PS,GR,WF)
11.	Russian River Facilities: P/C/T	55.0 Page: 253	RS,PS,SS,DV,RT,(KS,CS,GR,WF)
12.	Kenai River Facilities: P/C/T/BL	55.0-58.0 Page: 254	RS,PS,SS,DV,RT,WF,(KS,CS,LT,GR)

13. Lower Fuller Lake Facilities: P (trail)	57.1 Page: 254	GR
14. Hidden Lake Facilities: P/C/T/BL	58.0 Page: 254, 255	KO,DV,LT,RT,(RS,SS,WF)
15. Kenai River Facilities: P (trail)	58.0 Page: 255, 256	RS,PS,SS,DV,LT,RT,WF,(KS,CS,GR)
16. Upper Ohmer Lake Facilities: LP	58.0 Page: 256	DV,RT
17. Skilak Lake Facilities: P/C/T	58.0 Page: 256	SS,DV,LT,RT,(KS,RS,PS,CS,GR,WF)
18. Lower Ohmer Lake Facilities: P/C/T	58.0 Page: 256	DV,RT
19. Engineer Lake Facilities: P/C/T	58.0 Page: 256	SS
20. Jean Lake Facilities: P/T	60.0 Page: 256	DV,RT,(RS,SS)
21. Upper Jean Lake Facilities: P (trail)	62.0 Page: 257	SS,RT
22. Kelly Lake Facilities: P/BL	68.4 Page: 257	RT,(RS,SS,DV)
23. Peterson Lake Facilities: P/BL	68.4 Page: 257	RT,(RS,SS,DV)
24. Egumen Lake Facilities: P (trail)	70.8 Page: 257	RT,(RS,SS,DV)
25. Watson Lake Facilities: P/C/T/BL	71.3 Page: 257	RT,(RS,SS,DV)
26. E. Fork Moose River Facilities: P	71.4 Page: 257	RT,(RS,SS,DV)
27. Skilak Lake Facilities: P/C/T/BL	75.3 Page: 257, 258	SS,DV,LT,RT,(KS,RS,PS,CS,GR,WF)
28. Kenai River Facilities: P/C/T/BL	80.2/84.9 Page: 258, 259	KS,RS,PS,SS,DV,RT,WF,(CS,LT)

Sterling Highway

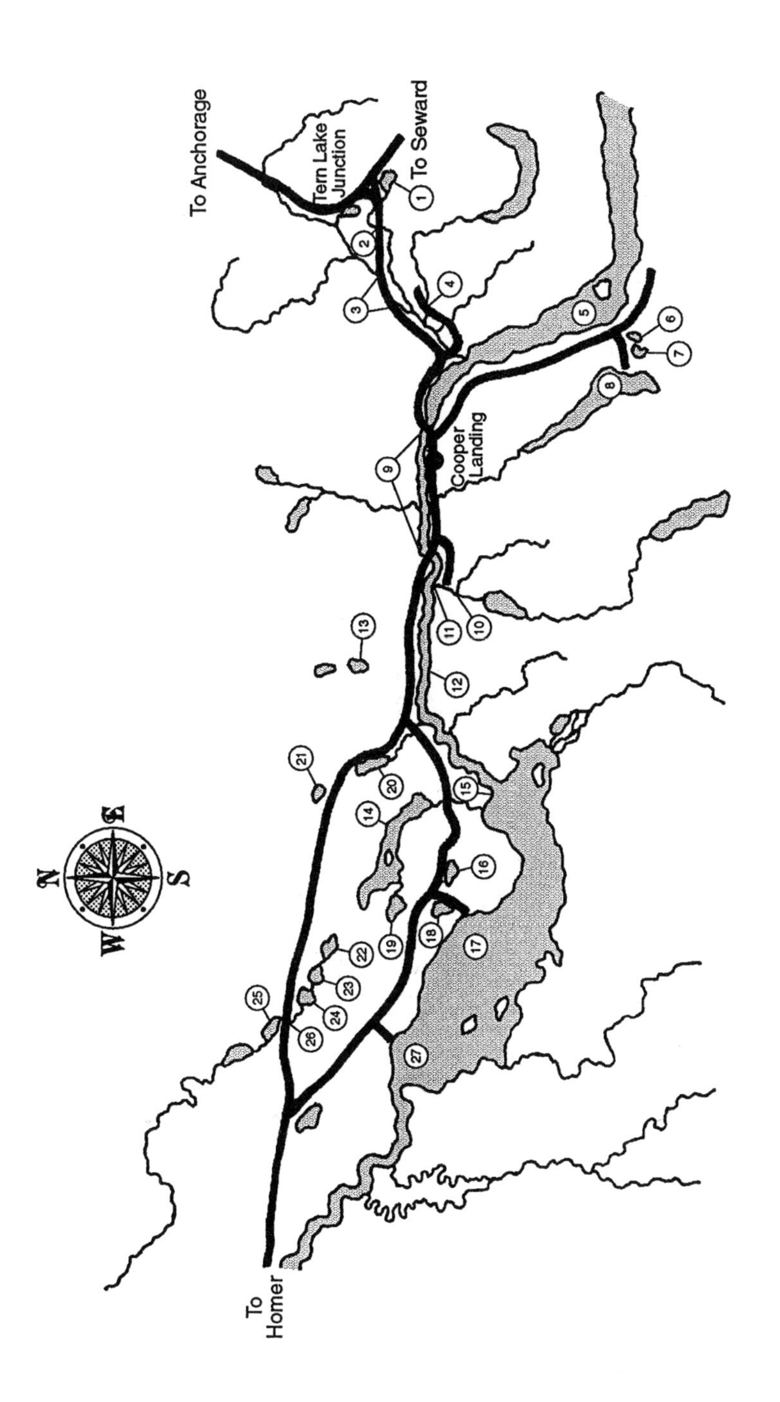

29. Moose River Facilities: P/C/T/BL	82.3 Page: 259	KS,RS,PS,SS,DV,RT,(CS,LT,WF)
30. Mosquito Lake Facilities: P (trail)	83.6 Page: 260	SS,RT
31. Forest Lake Facilities: P (trail)	83.6 Page: 260	RT
32. Weed Lake Facilities: P (trail)	83.6 Page: 260	RT
33. Breeze Lake Facilities: P (trail)	83.6 Page: 260	RT
34. Dolly Varden Lake Facilities: P/C/T	83.6 Page: 260	AC,RT
35. Rainbow Lake Facilities: P/C/T	83.6 Page: 260, 261	AC,RT,(RS)
36. Swanson River Facilities: P/C/T	83.6 Page: 261	SS,DV,RT,(RS)
37. Fish Lake Facilities: P	83.6 Page: 261	DV
38. Canoe Lake Facilities: P	83.6 Page: 261	DV,RT,(RS,SS)
39. Sucker Lake Facilities: P	83.6 Page: 261	RT,(RS,SS,DV)
40. Big Merganser Lake Facilities: P	83.6 Page: 261	RT
41. Little Merganser Lake Facilities: P/T	83.6 Page: 261, 262	RT,(RS,SS,DV)
42. Portage Lake Facilities: P	83.6 Page: 262	SS
43. Paddle Lake Facilities: P (trail)	83.6 Page: 262	DV,RT
44. Scout Lake Facilities: P/C/T	84.8 Page: 262	KS,SS

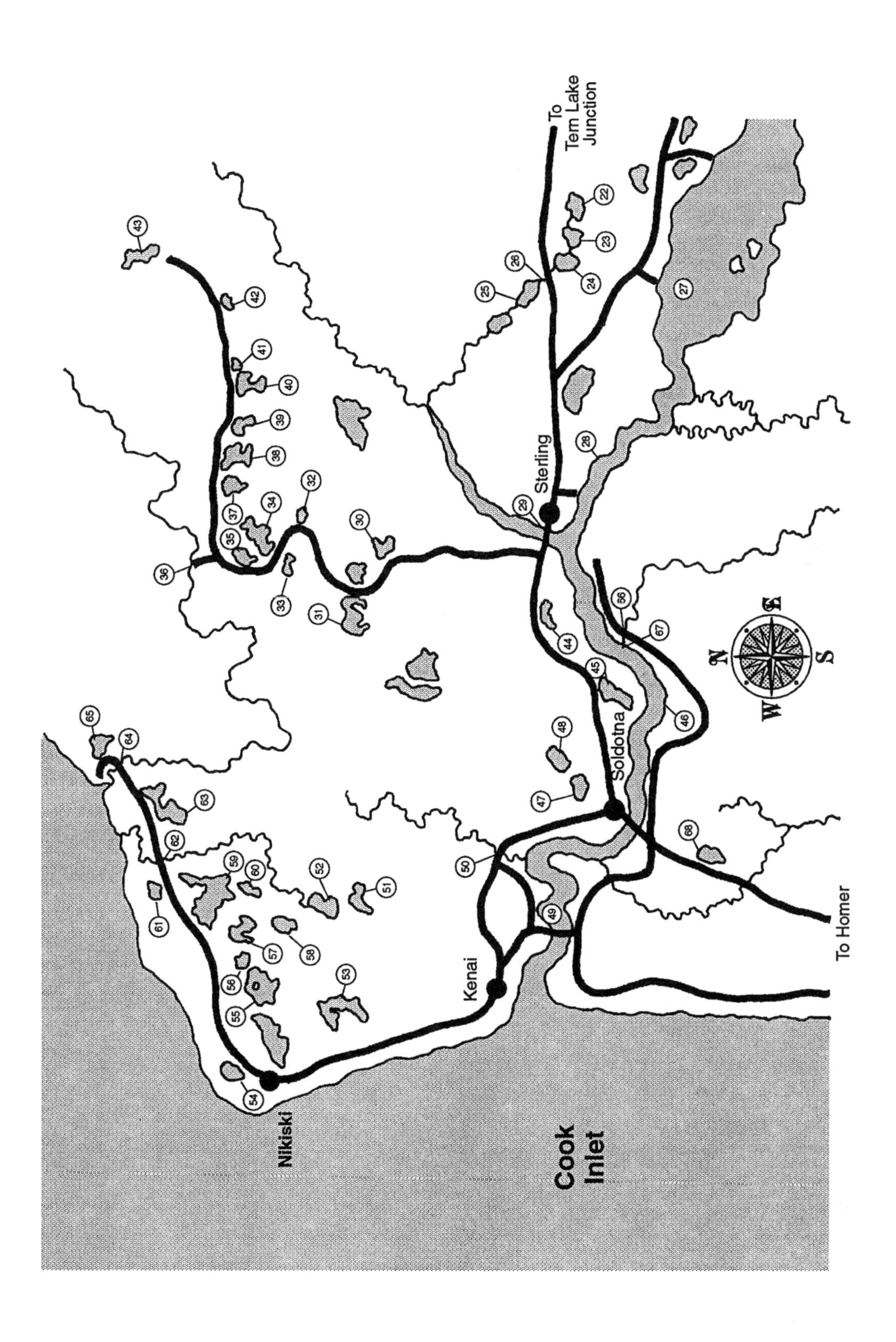
To
Tern Lake
Junction
Sterling
Soldotna
Kenai
Nikiski
Cook
Inlet
To Homer
N
E
S
W
22
23
24
25
26
27
28
29
30
31
32
33
34
35
36
37
38
39
40
41
42
43
44
45
46
47
48
49
50
51
52
53
54
55
56
57
58
59
60
61
62
63
64
65
66
67
68

45. Longmere Lake Facilities: P	88.2 Page: 262	RT
46. Kenai River Facilities: P/C/T/BL	(Soldotna) Page: 262, 263	KS,RS,PS,SS,DV,RT,WF,(CS,LT)
47. Sports Lake Facilities: P/BL	94.2 Page: 263, 264	RT
48. Union Lake Facilities: P	94.2 Page: 264	SS,RT
49. Kenai River Facilities: P/C/T/BL	(Kenai) Page: 264, 265	KS,RS,PS,SS,DV,RT,(CS,WF)
50. Beaver Creek Facilities: P	94.2 Page: 265	DV,RT,(KS,RS,PS,SS)
51. Douglas Lake Facilities: P	94.2 Page: 265	RT
52. Bishop Lake Facilities: LP	94.2 Page: 265	RT
53. Cabin Lake Facilities: P	94.2 Page: 265, 266	RT
54. Chugach Estates Lake Facilities: P	94.2 Page: 266	RT
55. Island Lake Facilities: P	94.2 Page: 266	SS
56. Thetis Lake Facilities: P	94.2 Page: 266	RT
57. Wik Lake Facilities: P	94.2 Page: 266	RT
58. Tirmore Lake Facilities: LP	94.2 Page: 266	RT
59. Daniels Lake Facilities: P	94.2 Page: 267	DV,RT
60. Barbara Lake Facilities: P	94.2 Page: 267	RT

61. Cecille Lake Facilities: P	94.2 Page: 267	RT
62. Bishop Creek Facilities: P	94.2 Page: 267	RT,(RS,PS,SS,DV)
63. Stormy Lake Facilities: P/T/BL	94.2 Page: 267	SS,DV,RT
64. Swanson River Facilities: P/C/T	94.2 Page: 267, 268	RS,PS,SS,DV,(KS,CS,RT)
65. Salmo Lake Facilities: P (trail)	94.2 Page: 268	RT
66. Funny River Facilities: P	96.4 Page: 268	PS,SS,DV,RT,(KS,RS,CS,WF)
67. Funny River Facilities: P/C/T	96.4 Page: 268, 269	KS,RS,PS,SS,DV,RT,WF,(CS,LT)
68. Arc Lake Facilities: P	98.3 Page: 269	SS
69. Kasilof River Facilities: P/BL	109.4 Page: 279	KS,RS,PS,SS,SH,DV,(RT,LT,WF)
70. Crooked Creek Facilities: P	110.9 Page: 270	RS,SS,SH,RT,DV,(KS,PS,CS,WF)
71. Johnson Lake Facilities: P/C/T	111.4 Page: 270	RT
72. Centennial Lake Facilities: P	111.4 Page: 271	SS
73. Kasilof River Facilities: P/T/BL	111.4 Page: 271	RS,PS,SS,DV,LT,RT,(KS,SH,WF)
74. Fish & Wildlife Lakes Facilities: P (trail)	111.4 Page: 271	DV
75. Quintin Lake Facilities: P	111.4 Page: 271	SS,RT
76. Crooked Creek Facilities: P/C/T	111.4 Page: 271, 272	KS,RS,PS,SS,SH,DV,(CS,LT,RT,WF)

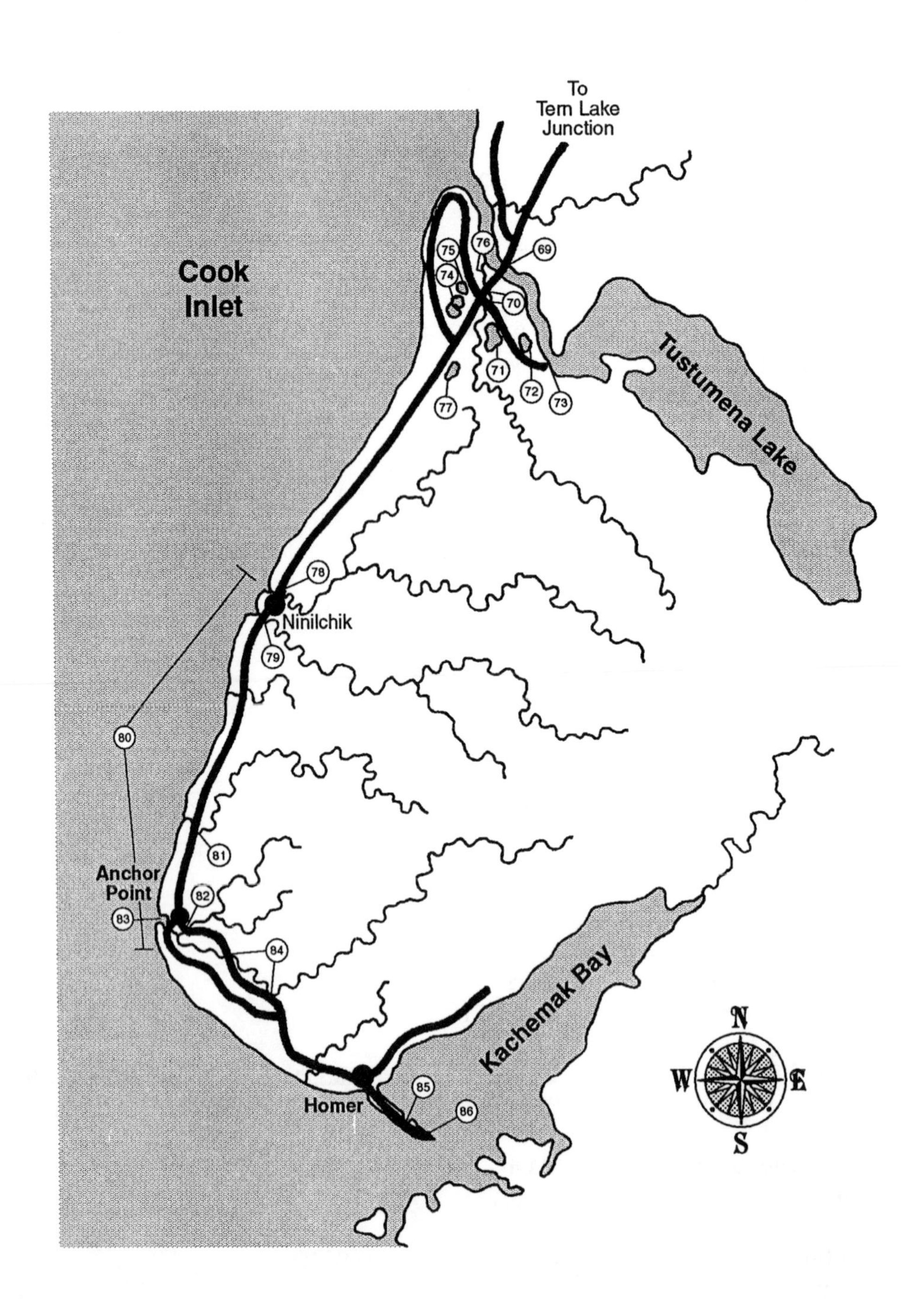
To
Tern Lake
Junction
Cook
Inlet
Tustumena Lake
Ninilchik
Anchor
Point
Homer
Kachemak Bay
N
S
W
E
69
70
71
72
73
74
75
76
77
78
79
80
81
82
83
84
85
86

77. Encelewski Lake Facilities: P	114.9 Page: 272	SS,RT
78. Ninilchik River Facilities: P/C/T/BL	135.0 Page: 272, 273	KS,RS,PS,SS,SH,DV,(CS,RT)
79. Deep Creek Facilities: P/C/T/BL	136.8/137.0 Page: 273, 274	KS,RS,PS,SS,SH,DV,(CS,RT)
80. Cook Inlet Marine Facilities: P/C/T/BL	135.1-156.7 Page: 274, 275	KS,RS,PS,SS,DV,HB,BF,(CS,SH)
81. Stariski Creek Facilities: P	150.8 Page: 275	PS,SS,DV,(KS,RS,CS,SH,RT)
82. N. Fork Anchor River Facilities: LP	156.9 Page: 275	DV,RT,(KS,PS,SS,SH)
83. Anchor River Facilities: P/C/T/BL	156.7 Page: 275, 276	KS,RS,PS,SS,SH,DV,(CS,RT)
84. Anchor River Facilities: P/T	159.9-163.9 Page: 276	SH,RT,DV,(KS,RS,PS,SS)
85. Homer Spit Lagoon Facilities: P/T	(Homer) Page: 276, 277	KS,PS,SS,(DV,BF)
86. Homer Spit Facilities: P/T	(Homer) Page: 277	KS,PS,SS,DV,BF,(RS,CS,HB)

AREA A: CENTRAL KENAI PENINSULA DRAINAGE

Includes all waters draining into and surrounding Kenai Lake and upper Kenai River.

Time of Abundance:

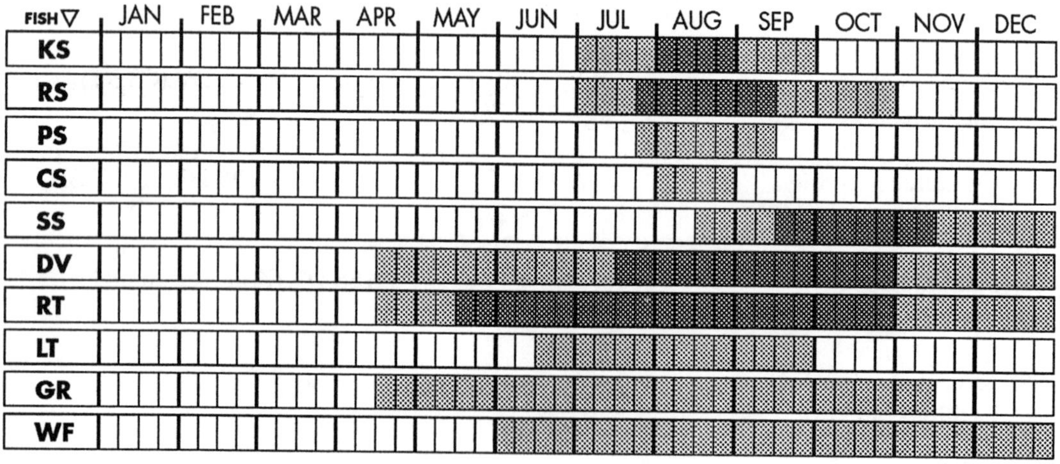

FISH▽	JAN	FEB	MAR	APR	MAY	JUN	JUL	AUG	SEP	OCT	NOV	DEC
KS												
RS												
PS												
CS												
SS												
DV												
RT												
LT												
GR												
WF												

Note: The above chart reflects the presence of salmon, char, and trout in all stages of maturity in the tributaries of Kenai Lake.

1. **TERN LAKE**

   Access: From MP 37.3 of the Sterling Highway. Turn south on a gravel road leading a short distance to the lake outlet.

   Regulations: Salmon fishing prohibited.

   Major Species:

   Dolly Varden / fair / September and October / 8-15 in.
   Rainbow trout / fair / May and September, October / 7-15 in.

2. **DAVES CREEK**

   Access: The Sterling Highway parallels the stream from MP 37.6 to 40.0. Also, turn onto a gravel road heading south at MP 37.3 and drive a short distance to stream crossing.

   Regulations: Salmon fishing prohibited. Only unbaited, artificial lures may be used from September 16 through December 31.

   Major Species:

   Dolly Varden / fair to good / September, October / 10-18 in.
   Rainbow trout / fair / July through September / 8-15 in.
   Grayling / poor to fair / June through September / 7-14 in.

3. **QUARTZ CREEK**

   Access: The Sterling Highway parallels the stream from MP 40.9 to 42.0. Or, turn southwest onto a gravel road at MP 45.0 and drive 0.7 miles to the stream crossing. There's a campground just before the bridge, with access to the stream mouth and Kenai Lake.

   Regulations: Salmon fishing prohibited. Only unbaited, artificial lures may be used from September 16 through December 31.

Major Species:
Dolly Varden / fair to good / August to mid-October / 10-20 in.
Rainbow trout / fair / July through September / 8-15 in.
Grayling / poor to fair / June through September / 7-15 in.
Whitefish / poor to fair / September and October / 10-15 in.

4. **CRESCENT CREEK**
Access: From MP 45.0 of the Sterling Highway. Turn southwest on a gravel road and drive 2.6 miles to the stream crossing.
Regulations: Salmon fishing prohibited. Only unbaited, artificial lures may be used from September 16 through December 31.
Major Species:
Dolly Varden / fair / August and September / 8-18 in.
Grayling / poor to fair / June through September / 7-15 in.

5. **KENAI LAKE**
Access: The Sterling Highway parallels the lake from MP 45.0 to 47.0; pull-offs present.
Regulations: Salmon fishing prohibited.
Major Species:
Dolly Varden / fair / July through December / 8-25 in.
Lake trout / fair / October and November / 2-5 lbs.
Rainbow trout / fair / mid-April to mid-October / 7-25 in.

6. **CLEAVER LAKE**
Access: From MP 47.8 of the Sterling Highway. Turn southeast on Snug Harbor Road, drive 8.7 miles to a "Y." Follow sign to the right and proceed 2.3 miles to parking area on the left. Find trail and hike 200 yards to the lake on the left.
Major Species:
Rainbow trout / fair / September and October / 7-15 in.

7. **RAINBOW LAKE**
Access: From MP 47.8 of the Sterling Highway. Turn southeast on Snug Harbor Road, drive 8.7 miles to a "Y." Follow sign to the right and proceed 2.3 miles to parking area on the left. Find trail and hike 0.25 miles to the lake.
Major Species:
Rainbow trout / fair / September and October / 7-15 in.

8. **COOPER LAKE**
Access: From MP 47.8 of the Sterling Highway. Turn southeast on Snug Harbor Road, drive 8.7 miles to a "Y," follow sign to the right and proceed 3.5 miles to dirt road on left leading to lake.
Major Species:
Dolly Varden / fair / August to mid-October / 7-15 in.
Rainbow trout / fair / September and October / 7-18 in.

9. KENAI RIVER (SECTION A)

Note: Includes that portion of the river from the outlet of Kenai Lake downstream to the confluence with the Russian River.

Access: The Sterling Highway parallels the river from MP 47.7 to 55.0; pull-offs present.

Regulations: King salmon fishing prohibited. The use of bait is illegal. Check the sport fishing regulations closely for this area.

Time of Abundance:

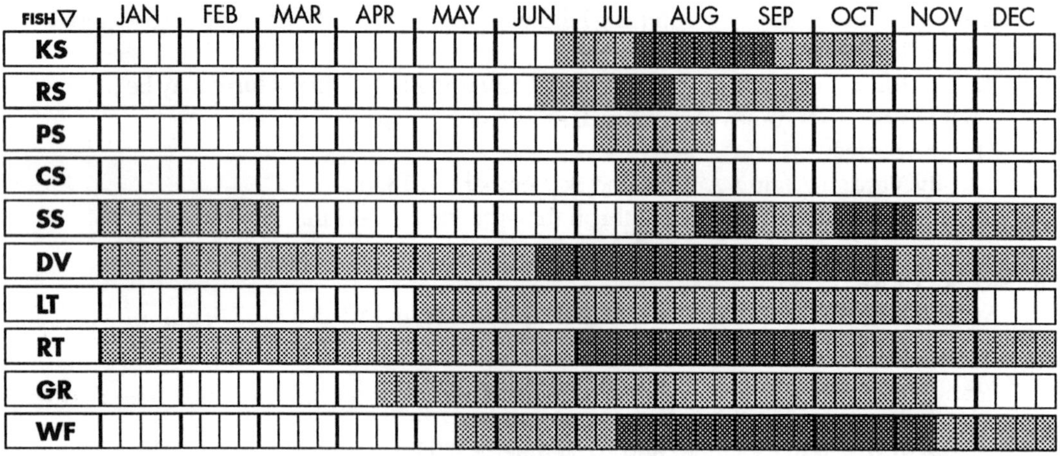

FISH▽	JAN	FEB	MAR	APR	MAY	JUN	JUL	AUG	SEP	OCT	NOV	DEC
KS												
RS												
PS												
CS												
SS												
DV												
LT												
RT												
GR												
WF												

Major Species:

Red salmon / fair to good / 4-10 lbs., max. 16 lbs. / egg imitation and streamer flies.

Silver salmon / fair to good / 6-15 lbs., max. 22 lbs. / spoons, spinners, and streamer flies, plugs.

Dolly Varden / good / 10-25 in., max. 15 lbs. / spoons and spinners, egg imitation flies and corkies.

Rainbow trout / fair to good / 8-25 in., max. 20 lbs. / egg imitation flies and corkies, and spinners.

Whitefish / poor to fair / 10-15 in., max. 17 in. / corkies and egg imitation flies.

10. RUSSIAN RIVER

Access: From MP 52.7 of the Sterling Highway. Turn onto paved road due south and drive 1.0 mile to parking and camping areas. Hike 50 yards by trail to the river.

Regulations: King salmon fishing prohibited. Catch-and-release fishing only for rainbow trout. Bait fishing is illegal. Fly-fishing-only from June 1 through August 20. Check the sport fishing regulations closely for this area.

Time of Abundance:

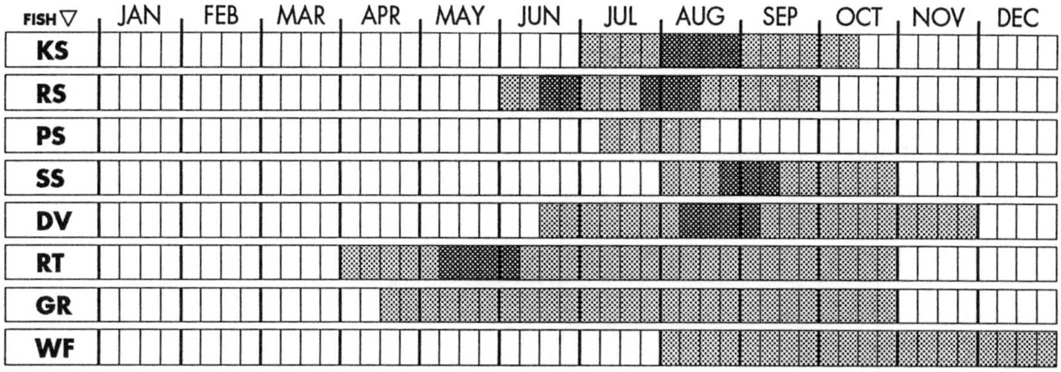

FISH ▽	JAN	FEB	MAR	APR	MAY	JUN	JUL	AUG	SEP	OCT	NOV	DEC
KS												
RS												
PS												
SS												
DV												
RT												
GR												
WF												

Major Species:

Red salmon / good to excellent / 4-10 lbs., max. 15 lbs. / egg imitation and streamer flies.
Silver salmon / fair to good / 6-12 lbs., max. 15 lbs. / egg imitation and streamer flies.
Dolly Varden / fair to good / 10-25 in., max. 7 lbs. / egg imitation and streamer flies, corkies.
Rainbow trout / fair / 8-20 in., max. 18 lbs. / streamer and egg imitation flies, corkies.

11. RUSSIAN RIVER / KENAI RIVER CONFLUENCE

Access: From MP 55.0 of the Sterling Highway. Turn south onto gravel road by sign and drive short distance to parking area. Take ferry across the Kenai River to the other side and to the confluence of the two rivers.

Regulations: King salmon fishing prohibited. Bait fishing is not permitted. Check the sport fishing regulations closely for this area.

Time of Abundance:

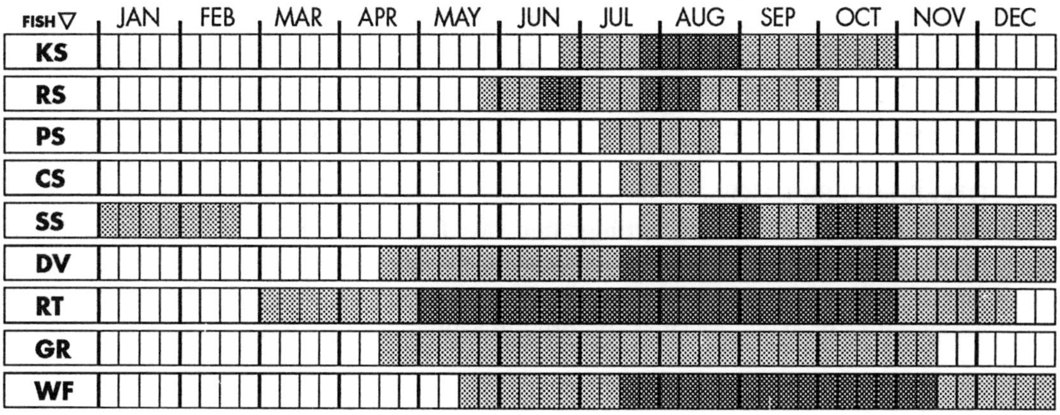

FISH ▽	JAN	FEB	MAR	APR	MAY	JUN	JUL	AUG	SEP	OCT	NOV	DEC
KS												
RS												
PS												
CS												
SS												
DV												
RT												
GR												
WF												

Major Species:

Red salmon / good to excellent / 4-10 lbs., max. 16 lbs. / egg imitation and streamer flies.
Pink salmon / poor to fair / 2-5 lbs., max. 8 lbs. / spoons, spinners, streamer flies.
Silver salmon / good / 6-12 lbs., max. 22 lbs. / streamer and egg imitation flies.
Dolly Varden / good / 10-25 in., max. 15 lbs. / egg imitation and streamer flies, corkies.
Rainbow trout / fair to good / 8-25 in., max. 20 lbs. / egg imitation and streamer flies, corkies.

12. KENAI RIVER (SECTION B)

Note: Includes that portion of the river from the confluence with Russian River downstream to the inlet of Skilak Lake.

Access: The Sterling Highway parallels the river from MP 55.0 to 58.0; several pull-offs and trails are present. Also, turn south on Skilak Lake Road and drive a short distance to the gravel road on left. Continue a short distance to campground and the river.

Regulations: King salmon fishing prohibited. Bait fishing is not permitted. Check the sport fishing regulations closely for this area.

Time of Abundance:

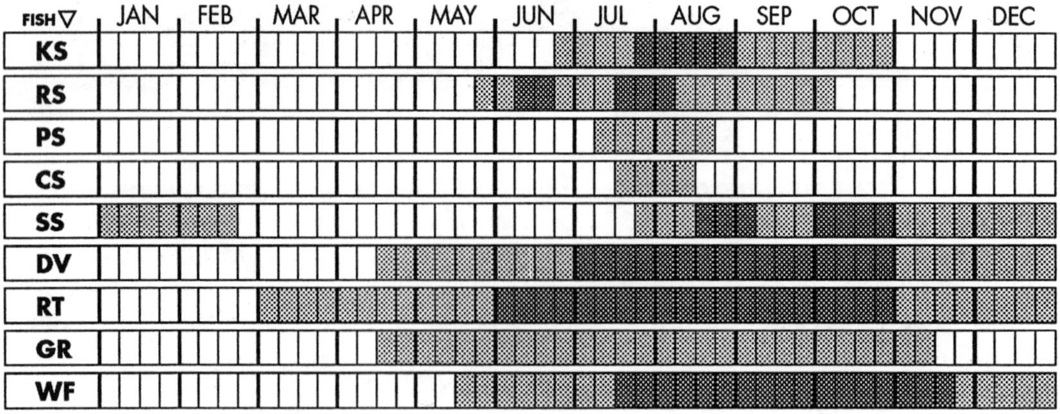

FISH▽	JAN	FEB	MAR	APR	MAY	JUN	JUL	AUG	SEP	OCT	NOV	DEC
KS												
RS												
PS												
CS												
SS												
DV												
RT												
GR												
WF												

Major Species:

Red salmon / good to excellent / 4-10 lbs., max. 16 lbs. / egg imitation and streamer flies.
Pink salmon / poor to fair / 2-5 lbs., max. 10 lbs. / spoons and spinners, streamer flies.
Silver salmon / fair to good / 6-15 lbs. max. 22 lbs. / spinners, egg imitation and streamer flies.
Dolly Varden / good / 10-25 in., max. 15 lbs. / egg imitation flies, corkies, spinners, plugs.
Rainbow trout / fair to good / 10-25 in., max. 20 lbs. / egg imitation flies, spinners, plugs, corkies.
Whitefish / poor to fair / 10-15 in., max. 17 in. / corkies, egg imitation flies.

13. LOWER FULLER LAKE

Access: From MP 57.1 of the Sterling Highway. Turn north into a pull-off and find trail leading 1.5 miles to the lake.

Major Species:

Grayling / fair to good / late May through September / 7-14 in.

14. HIDDEN LAKE

Access: From MP 58.0 of the Sterling Highway. Turn southwest on Skilak Lake Road, drive 3.6 miles to access road on right, proceed 0.7 miles to a campground and the lake.

Regulations: King salmon fishing prohibited.

Time of Abundance:

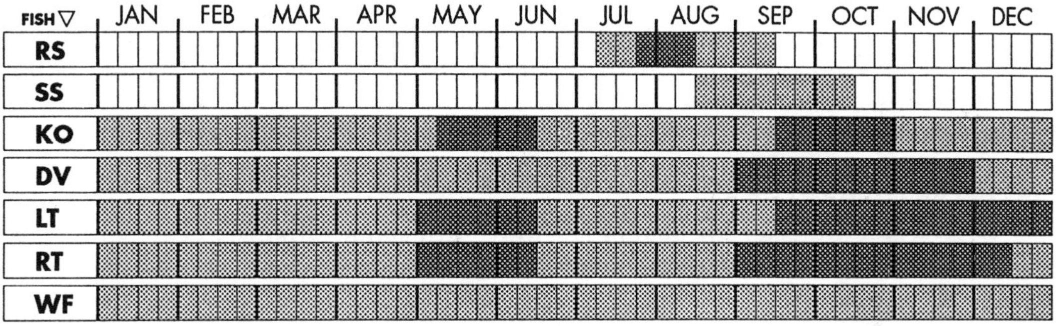

FISH ▽	JAN	FEB	MAR	APR	MAY	JUN	JUL	AUG	SEP	OCT	NOV	DEC
RS												
SS												
KO												
DV												
LT												
RT												
WF												

Major Species:

Kokanee / good / 8-14 in., max. 18 in./ spoons, spinners, wet flies, single salmon eggs.
Dolly Varden / fair / 8-15 in., max. 4 lbs. / spoons and spinners, salmon egg clusters, single salmon eggs.
Lake trout / good / 2-6 lbs., max. 25 lbs. / spoons, plugs, herring and smelt bait.
Rainbow trout / fair / 8-15 in., max. 5 lbs. / spoons and spinners, plugs, salmon egg clusters, and flies.

15. KENAI RIVER / SKILAK LAKE INLET

Access: From MP 58.0 of the Sterling Highway. Turn southwest on Skilak Lake Road and drive 4.7 miles to trailhead on left. Park and take Hidden Creek Trail 1.5 miles to 2.0 miles to mouth of Hidden Creek, Kenai River, and the inlet of Skilak Lake.

Regulations: King salmon fishing prohibited. Check the sport fishing regulations closely for this area.

Time of Abundance:

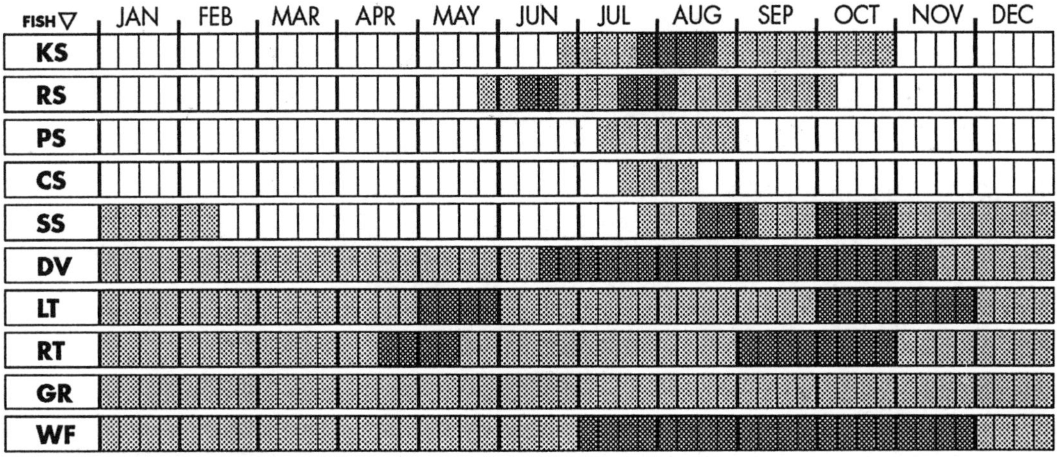

FISH ▽	JAN	FEB	MAR	APR	MAY	JUN	JUL	AUG	SEP	OCT	NOV	DEC
KS												
RS												
PS												
CS												
SS												
DV												
LT												
RT												
GR												
WF												

Major Species:

Red salmon / good to excellent / 4-10 lbs., max. 16 lbs. / streamer and egg imitation flies, spinners.
Pink salmon / fair / 2-6 lbs., max. 10 lbs. / spoons and spinners, streamer flies.
Silver salmon / good to excellent / 6-15 lbs., max. 22 lbs. / spoons, spinners, plugs, streamer flies.

Dolly Varden / good to excellent / 10-25 in., max. 15 lbs. / egg imitation flies, corkies, spoons, and plugs.
Lake trout / fair / 2-5 lbs., max. 15 lbs. / spoons, spinners, plugs, and streamer flies.
Rainbow trout / good / 8-25 in., max. 20 lbs. / spinners, egg imitation and streamer flies, plugs.
Whitefish / poor to fair / 10-15 in., max. 17 in. / corkies and egg imitation flies.

16. UPPER OHMER LAKE

Access: From MP 58.0 of the Sterling Highway. Turn southwest on Skilak Lake Road, drive 7.7 miles to access road on left, proceed 0.2 miles to the lake.

Major Species:
Dolly Varden / fair / September and October / 8-15 in.
Rainbow trout / good / May and September, October / 8-15 in.

17. SKILAK LAKE

Access: From MP 58.0 of the Sterling Highway. Turn southwest on Skilak Lake Road, drive 8.5 miles and turn left at sign. Proceed 1.9 miles to a campground and the lake.

Regulations: King salmon fishing prohibited. Check the sport fishing regulations closely for this area.

Major Species:
Silver salmon / fair / mid-August, early October / 6-15 lbs.
Dolly Varden / fair / June through October / 8-25 in.
Lake trout / fair / May and October, November / 2-5 lbs.
Rainbow trout / fair / May through October / 8-25 in.

18. LOWER OHMER LAKE

Access: From MP 58.0 of the Sterling Highway. Turn southwest on Skilak Lake Road, drive 8.6 miles to access road on left by sign. Proceed a short distance to a campground and the lake.

Major Species:
Dolly Varden / fair / September and October / 8-15 in.
Rainbow trout / good / May and September, October / 8-15 in.

19. ENGINEER LAKE

Access: From MP 58.0 of the Sterling Highway. Turn southwest on Skilak Lake Road, drive 9.5 miles to access road on right by sign. Proceed 0.3 miles to the lake.

Major Species:
Silver salmon / excellent / March through December / 7-15 in.

20. JEAN LAKE

Access: From MP 60.0 of the Sterling Highway. Turn west on dirt road leading short distance to the lake. Also, the highway parallels the east shore of the lake from MP 59.9 to 60.5.

Regulations: King salmon fishing prohibited.

Major Species:
Dolly Varden / fair / August to mid-October / 8-15 in.
Rainbow trout / good / May and September, October / 8-20 in.

21. UPPER JEAN LAKE
Access: From MP 62.0 of the Sterling Highway. Turn north on dirt road and park. Hike 200 yards to the lake due north.
Major Species:
Silver salmon / good / March through December / 7-15 in.
Rainbow trout / fair / May and September, October / 7-15 in.

22. KELLY LAKE
Access: From MP 68.4 of the Sterling Highway. Turn south on gravel road and drive 0.3 miles to a "Y." Bear to the left and drive 0.3 miles to the lake.
Major Species:
Rainbow trout / good / May and September, October / 8-18 in.

23. PETERSON LAKE
Access: From MP 68.4 of the Sterling Highway. Turn south on gravel road and drive 0.3 miles to a "Y." Bear to the right and drive 0.2 miles to the lake.
Major Species:
Rainbow trout / good / May and September, October / 8-18 in.

24. EGUMEN LAKE
Access: From MP 70.8 of the Sterling Highway. Turn south into pull-off and park. Hike 0.25 miles due south on trail to lake.
Major Species:
Rainbow trout / good / May and September, October / 8-18 in.

25. WATSON LAKE
Access: From MP 71.3 of the Sterling Highway. Turn north onto a gravel road leading 0.7 miles to the lake.
Major Species:
Rainbow trout / good / May and September, October / 8-18 in.

26. EAST FORK MOOSE RIVER
Access: The Sterling Highway crosses the stream at MP 71.4.
Regulations: Salmon fishing prohibited. Closed to all fishing from April 15 through June 14.
Major Species:
Rainbow trout / fair / August to mid-October / 7-18 in.

27. SKILAK LAKE
Access: From MP 75.3 of the Sterling Highway. Turn southeast on Skilak Lake Road and drive 5.2 miles to access road on right by sign, proceed 0.9 miles to a campground and the lake.
Regulations: King salmon fishing prohibited. Check the sport fishing regulations closely for this area.
Major Species:
Silver salmon / fair / mid-August, early October / 6-15 lbs.
Dolly Varden / fair / June through October / 8-25 in.

Lake trout / fair / May and October, November / 2-5 lbs.
Rainbow trout / fair / May through October / 8-25 in.

AREA B: LOWER KENAI RIVER DRAINAGE

Includes all waters draining into and surrounding the lower Kenai River from the outlet of Skilak Lake to Cook Inlet.

28. KENAI RIVER (SECTION C)

Note: This description includes the portion of Kenai River from the outlet of Skilak Lake downstream to its confluence with Funny River.

Access Point A: Bing's Landing
From MP 80.2 of the Sterling Highway. Turn south on Bing's Landing Road by sign and drive 0.8 miles to the river.

Access Point B: Morgan's Landing
From MP 84.9 of the Sterling Highway. Turn south on Scout Lake Loop Road, drive 1.6 miles to a "T" and turn right on Lou Morgan Road, continue 2.4 miles and turn right on gravel road leading 1.5 miles to a campground and the river.

Regulations: King salmon fishing prohibited from August 1 through December 31. Check the sport fishing regulations closely for this area.

Time of Abundance:

FISH▽	JAN	FEB	MAR	APR	MAY	JUN	JUL	AUG	SEP	OCT	NOV	DEC
KS												
RS												
PS												
CS												
SS												
DV												
LT												
RT												
GR												
WF												

Major Species:

King salmon / fair to good / 25-60 lbs., max. 100 lbs. / attractor lures, salmon egg clusters, spoons, plugs.
Red salmon / good to excellent / 4-10 lbs., max. 16 lbs. / egg imitation and streamer flies.
Pink salmon / good to excellent / 2-6 lbs., max. 12 lbs. / spoons and spinners, plugs, streamer flies.
Silver salmon / good to excellent / 6-15 lbs., max. 22 lbs. salmon egg clusters, spinners, attractor lures, plugs.
Dolly Varden / good to excellent / 10-25 in., max. 15 lbs. / salmon egg clusters, spoons, spinner, plugs, corkies.

Rainbow trout / good to excellent / 8-25 in., max. 20 lbs. / egg imitation flies, corkies, spinners, plugs.
Whitefish / poor to fair / 10-15 in., max. 17 in. / single salmon eggs, egg imitation flies, corkies.

29. MOOSE RIVER / KENAI RIVER CONFLUENCE

Access: The Sterling Highway crosses the river at MP 82.3. Turn south onto a gravel road just east of the bridge, and drive a short distance to a campground and the rivers' confluence.

Regulations: King salmon fishing prohibited from August 1 through December 31. Check the sport fishing regulations closely for this area. Flyfishing-only from May 15 through August 15.

Time of Abundance:

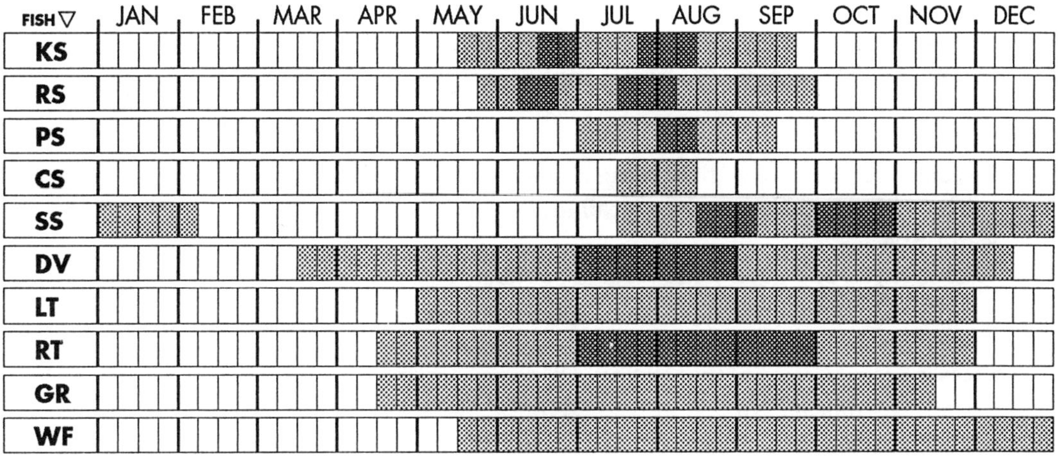

FISH ▽	JAN	FEB	MAR	APR	MAY	JUN	JUL	AUG	SEP	OCT	NOV	DEC
KS												
RS												
PS												
CS												
SS												
DV												
LT												
RT												
GR												
WF												

Major Species:

King salmon / poor to fair / 25-60 lbs., max. 100 lbs. / egg imitation and streamer flies.
Red salmon / good to excellent / 4-10 lbs., max. 16 lbs. / egg imitation and streamer flies.
Pink salmon / good to excellent / 2-6 lbs., max. 12 lbs. / spoons and spinners, streamer flies.
Silver salmon / good / 6-15 lbs., max. 22 lbs. / salmon egg clusters, spoons, spinners, attractor lures.
Dolly Varden / fair to good / 10-25 in., max. 15 lbs. / egg imitation flies, spoons, plugs, salmon egg clusters.
Rainbow trout / fair / 8-25 in., max. 20 lbs. / salmon egg clusters, spinners, corkies, egg imitation flies.

AREA C: NORTH KENAI PENINSULA DRAINAGE

Includes all waters draining into and surrounding the Swanson and Moose rivers along Swanson River Road and North Kenai Road, off of the Sterling Highway.

Time of Availability:

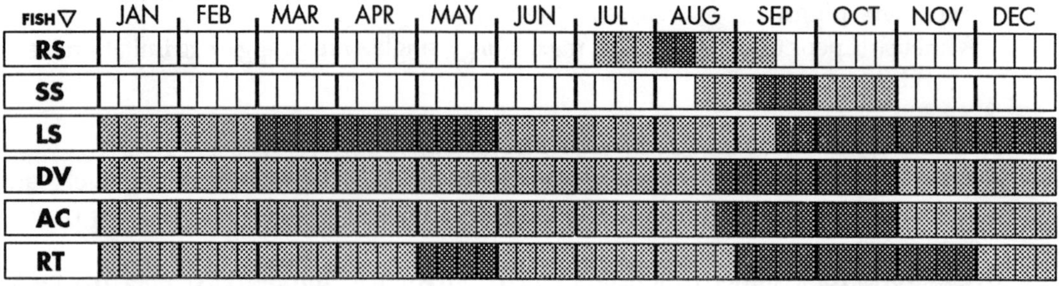

FISH ▽	JAN	FEB	MAR	APR	MAY	JUN	JUL	AUG	SEP	OCT	NOV	DEC
RS												
SS												
LS												
DV												
AC												
RT												

30. MOSQUITO LAKE

Access: From MP 83.6 of the Sterling Highway. Turn north onto Swanson River Road and drive 7.8 miles. Park and find trail heading due east 200 yards to the lake.

Major Species:

Silver salmon / good / March through December / 7-15 in.
Rainbow trout / good / May and September, October / 8-18 in.

31. FOREST LAKE

Access: From MP 83.6 of the Sterling Highway. Turn north onto Swanson River Road and drive 10.5 miles. Park and find trail heading northwest; it's 200 yards to the lake.

Major Species:

Rainbow trout / good / May and September, October / 8-18 in.

32. WEED LAKE

Access: From MP 83.6 of the Sterling Highway. Turn north onto Swanson River Road and drive 12.9 miles to trail on the right. Hike some 200 yards due east to lake.

Major Species:

Rainbow trout / fair / May and September, October / 7-15 in.

33. BREEZE LAKE

Access: From MP 83.6 of the Sterling Highway. Turn north onto Swanson River Road and drive 13.9 miles to trail on the left. Hike 200 yards southwest to the lake.

Major Species:

Rainbow trout / fair / May and September, October / 7-15 in.

34. DOLLY VARDEN LAKE

Access: From MP 83.6 of the Sterling Highway. Turn north onto Swanson River Road and drive 14.1 miles to campground site on the right next to lake.

Major Species:

Arctic char / good / late August to mid-October / 8-18 in.
Rainbow trout / excellent / September and October / 8-20 in.

35. RAINBOW LAKE

Access: From MP 83.6 of the Sterling Highway. Turn north onto Swanson River Road and drive 15.5 miles to campground site on the right next to the lake.

Major Species:
Arctic char / fair / late August to mid-October / 8-18 in.
Rainbow trout / good / May and September, October / 8-18 in.

36. SWANSON RIVER

Access: From MP 83.6 of the Sterling Highway. Turn north onto Swanson River Road and drive 17.1 miles to a "Y" and turn left. Continue 0.5 miles to the river.

Regulations: King salmon fishing prohibited. Closed to all fishing from April 15 through June 14.

Major Species:
Silver salmon / fair to good / early September / 5-12 lbs.
Dolly Varden / fair / July through September / 8-15 in.
Rainbow trout / good / July through September / 8-18 in.

37. FISH LAKE

Access: From MP 83.6 of the Sterling Highway. Turn north onto Swanson River Road and drive 17.1 miles to a "Y." Take right fork and Swan Lake Road and drive 3.0 miles to pull-off on the right.

Major Species:
Dolly Varden / fair / late August to mid-October / 7-15 in.

38. CANOE LAKE

Access: From MP 83.6 of the Sterling Highway. Turn north onto Swanson River Road and drive 17.1 miles to a "Y." Take right fork, called Swan Lake Road, and drive 3.9 miles to access site on the right.

Major Species:
Dolly Varden / fair / late August to mid-October / 7-15 in.
Rainbow trout / fair / May and September, October / 7-18 in.

39. SUCKER LAKE

Access: From MP 83.6 of the Sterling Highway. Turn north onto Swanson River Road and drive 17.1 miles to a "Y." Take right fork, called Swan Lake Road, and drive 3.9 miles to access site on the right.

Major Species:
Rainbow trout / fair / May and September, October / 7-15 in.

40. BIG MERGANSER LAKE

Access: From MP 83.6 of the Sterling Highway. Turn north onto Swanson River Road and drive 17.1 miles to a "Y." Take right fork, called Swan Lake Road, and drive 3.9 miles to access site on the right.

Major Species:
Rainbow trout / fair / May and September, October / 7-18 in.

41. LITTLE MERGANSER LAKE

Access: From MP 83.6 of the Sterling Highway. Turn north onto Swanson River Road and drive 17.1 miles to a "Y." Take right fork, called Swan Lake Road, and drive 3.9 miles to access site on the right.

Major Species:
Rainbow trout / fair / May and September, October / 7-18 in.

42. **PORTAGE LAKE**
Access: From MP 83.6 of the Sterling Highway. Turn north onto Swanson River Road and drive 17.1 miles to a "Y." Take right fork, called Swan Lake Road, and drive 3.9 miles to access site on the right.
Major Species:
Silver salmon / good / March through December / 7-15 in.

43. **PADDLE LAKE**
Access: From MP 83.6 of the Sterling Highway. Turn north onto Swanson River Road and drive 17.1 miles to a "Y." Take right fork, called Swan Lake Road, and drive 3.9 miles to access site on the right. Park and find trail leading 0.25 miles due north to the lake.
Major Species:
Dolly Varden / fair / late August to mid-October / 8-18 in.
Rainbow trout / good / May and September, October / 8-20 in.

AREA B: LOWER KENAI RIVER DRAINAGE (CONT.)

Back to the Sterling Highway, this section includes the area from Scout Lake to Beaver Creek.

44. **SCOUT LAKE**
Access: From MP 84.8 of the Sterling Highway. Turn south on Scout Lake Road, drive a short distance to first road on the right, and proceed to the lake.
Major Species:
King salmon / good / March through December 7-15 in.
Silver salmon / excellent / March through December / 7-15 in.

45. **LONGMERE LAKE**
Access: From MP 88.2 of the Sterling Highway. Turn south on Longmere Lake Road, drive a short distance to a "Y" and turn right. Drive 0.2 miles to access road on left.
Major Species:
Rainbow trout / good / May and September, October / 8-22 in.

46. **KENAI RIVER (SECTION D)**
Note: Includes that portion of the river from the mouth of Funny River downstream to the upper edge of tidal influence and Eagle Rock.
Access Point A: Swiftwater Campground
From MP 94.1 of the Sterling Highway. Turn east onto East Redoubt Avenue, drive 0.6 miles and turn right on Griffin Avenue. Proceed 0.8 miles and turn right on gravel road leading to the river.
Access Point B: Soldotna Creek Park
From the town of Soldotna. Turn southeast on a gravel road next to the State of Alaska

Maintenance Station and proceed to the left. Drive 0.2 miles to parking area and hike 200 yards by trail to the river.

Access Point C: Kenai Bridge

The Sterling Highway crosses the river at MP 95.6 in the town of Soldotna.

Access Point D: Centennial Campground

Turn onto Kalifornsky Beach Road heading west at intersection just south of the river bridge in Soldotna. Proceed a short distance and turn right on Centennial Park Drive. Continue 0.8 miles to the campground and the river.

Access Point E: Slikok Creek State Recreation Site

Turn west onto Kalifornsky Beach Road at intersection just south of the river bridge in Soldotna. Drive to MP 20.5 and turn right on College Loop Road, proceed 1.4 miles to a "T" and turn right on East Poppy Lane. Continue to the community college parking area. It's a short hike from here to the confluence of Slikok Creek and river.

Regulations: King salmon fishing prohibited from August 1 through December 31. Check the sport fishing regulations closely for this area on various restrictions.

Time of Abundance:

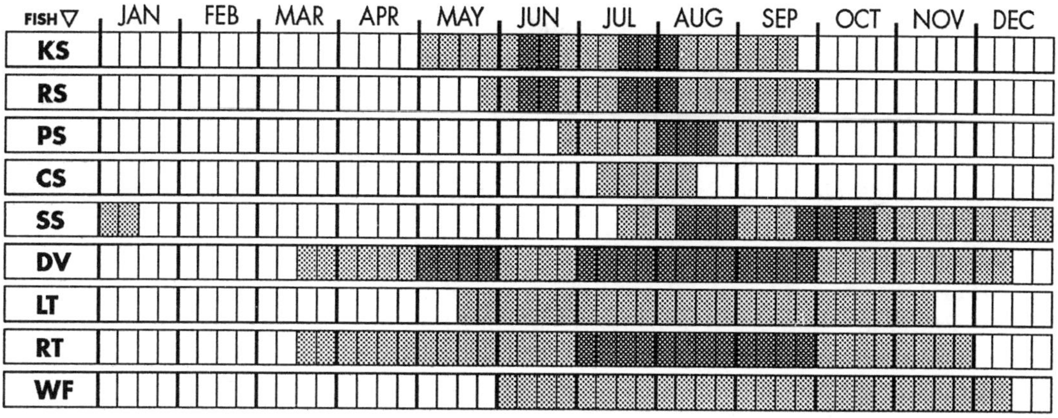

FISH▽	JAN	FEB	MAR	APR	MAY	JUN	JUL	AUG	SEP	OCT	NOV	DEC
KS												
RS												
PS												
CS												
SS												
DV												
LT												
RT												
WF												

Major Species:

King salmon / fair from shore, good from boat / 25-60 lbs., max. 100 lbs. / plugs, attractor lures, salmon egg clusters.

Red salmon / good to excellent / 4-10 lbs., max. 16 lbs. / egg imitation and streamer flies.

Pink salmon / good to excellent / 2-6 lbs., max. 12 lbs. / spoons and spinners, plugs, streamer flies.

Silver salmon / good to excellent / 6-15 lbs., max. 22 lbs. / salmon egg clusters, spinners, plugs, attractor lures.

Dolly Varden / good to excellent / 10-25 in., max. 15 lbs. / salmon egg clusters, spoons, spinners, plugs, corkies.

Rainbow trout / good to excellent / 8-25 in., max. 20 lbs. / egg imitation flies, corkies, spinners, plugs.

Whitefish / poor to fair / 10-15 in., max. 17 in. / single salmon eggs, egg imitation flies, corkies.

47. SPORT LAKE

Access: From the "Y" in Soldotna, MP 94.2 of the Sterling Highway. Turn west on Kenai

Spur Highway, drive 2.5 miles and turn right on Sports Lake Road. Proceed 1.0 mile to a "Y," turn right, and continue 0.2 miles to lake turn-off on the left.

Major Species:

Rainbow trout / good / May and September, October / 8-20 in.

48. UNION LAKE

Access: From the "Y" in Soldotna, MP 94.2 of the Sterling Highway. Turn west on Kenai Spur Highway, drive 2.5 miles and turn right on Sport Lake Road. Proceed 1.0 mile to a "Y," continue straight a short distance to Conner Road, and turn left. Drive 1.3 miles to gate and turn right on gravel road,. Proceed a short distance to access road on right.

Major Species:

Silver salmon / good / March through December / 7-15 in.
Rainbow trout / fair / May and September, October / 8-18 in.

49. KENAI RIVER (SECTION E)

Note: Includes that portion of the river from the upper limits of tidal activity at Eagle Rock downstream to the mouth of the river.

Access Point A: Eagle Rock Campground

From the "Y" in Soldotna. Turn west on Kenai Spur Highway and drive 5.1 miles. Turn left on Eagle Rock Drive and follow road 0.4 miles to the river.

Access Point B: Cunningham Park

From the "Y" in Soldotna. Turn west on Kenai Spur Highway and drive 6.4 miles, turn left on Beaver Loop Road and drive 2.7 miles to access road on the left leading to parking area and river.

Access Point C: Warren Ames Bridge

Turn west on Kalifornsky Beach Road at the intersection just south of the Kenai River Bridge in Soldotna. Drive to MP 16.1 and turn right on Bridge Access Road leading 0.5 miles to the river bridge.

Regulations: King salmon fishing prohibited from August 1 through December 31. Check the sport fishing regulations closely for this area and other restrictions.

Time of Abundance:

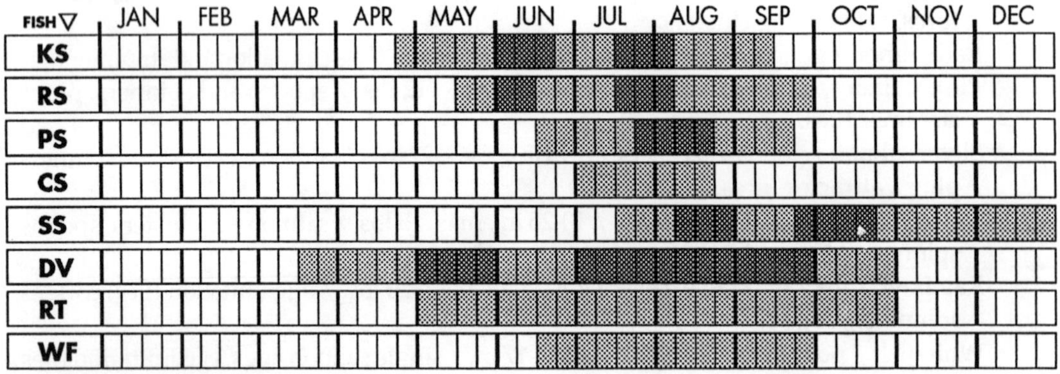

FISH ▽	JAN	FEB	MAR	APR	MAY	JUN	JUL	AUG	SEP	OCT	NOV	DEC
KS												
RS												
PS												
CS												
SS												
DV												
RT												
WF												

Major Species:

King salmon / fair to good / 25-60 lbs., max. 100 lbs. / plugs, salmon egg clusters, attractor lures.

Red salmon / good / 4-10 lbs., max. 16 lbs. / egg imitation and steamer flies, salmon egg clusters.
Pink salmon / good to excellent / 2-6 lbs., max. 12 lbs. / spoons and spinners, plugs, attractor lures.
Silver salmon / good to excellent / 6-15 lbs., max. 22 lbs. / salmon egg clusters, spinners, attractor lures, plugs.
Dolly Varden / good / 10-25 in., max. 12 lbs. / salmon egg clusters, spoons, plugs.
Rainbow trout / fair / 8-25 in., max. 15 lbs. / salmon egg clusters, egg imitation flies, corkies.

50. BEAVER CREEK

Access: From the "Y" in Soldotna. Turn west on Kenai Spur Highway and drive 6.3 miles to the stream crossing.
Regulations: King salmon fishing prohibited. Only unbaited, artificial lures may be used from September 16 through December 31.
Major Species:
Dolly Varden / fair / August to mid-October / 7-15 in.
Rainbow trout / fair / mid-May through June / 7-22 in.

AREA C: N. KENAI PENINSULA DRAINAGE (CONT.)

This section covers watersheds accessible via the Kenai Spur Highway, off the Sterling Highway.

51. DOUGLAS LAKE

Access: From the "Y" in Soldotna, MP 94.2 of the Sterling Highway. Turn west on Kenai Spur Highway and continue through the town of Kenai to MP 19.3. Turn right on Miller Road and proceed 2.1 miles to Holt Road. Turn right and drive 2.9 miles to Douglas Lane, then turn right and drive 0.8 miles to Drew Street. Turn right again and continue 75 yards to the lake.
Major Species:
Rainbow trout / good / May and September, October / 8-16 in.

52. BISHOP LAKE

Access: From the "Y" in Soldotna, MP 94.2 of the Sterling Highway. Turn west on Kenai Spur Highway and continue through the town of Kenai to MP 19.3, turn right on Miller Road and proceed 2.1 miles to Holt Road. Turn right and drive 4.5 miles to lake on right; park and hike short distance to lake.
Major Species:
Rainbow trout / fair / May and September, October / 8-20 in.

53. CABIN LAKE

Access: From the "Y" in Soldotna, MP 94.2 of the Sterling Highway. Turn west on Kenai Spur Highway and continue through the town of Kenai to MP 21.4. Turn right on Miller Road and drive 1.2 miles. Turn right on Cabin Lake Drive and proceed 0.4 miles, then turn left on Interlake Drive. Continue 0.3 miles to access road on right.

Major Species:
Rainbow trout / excellent / May and September, October / 8-16 in.

54. CHUGACH ESTATES LAKE

Access: From the "Y" in Soldotna, MP 94.2 of the Sterling Highway. Turn west on Kenai Spur Highway and continue through the town of Kenai to MP 23.9. Turn left on Tustumena Street, drive 0.2 miles and turn left on McKinley Avenue. Proceed 0.2 miles and turn right on Shumya Way. Drive a short distance, then turn left on Tyonek Circle and follow through to lake.

Major Species:
Rainbow trout / good / May and September, October / 8-16 in.

55. ISLAND LAKE

Access: From the "Y" in Soldotna, MP 94.2 of the Sterling Highway. Turn west on Kenai Spur Highway and continue through the town of Kenai to MP 25.7. Turn right on Island Lake Road, drive 2.4 miles to Pipeline Road and turn left, and proceed 0.7 miles to Moose Run Road. Turn left, continue 0.8 miles and turn left on access road leading a short distance to the lake.

Major Species:
Silver salmon / good / March through December / 7-14 in.

56. THETIS LAKE

Access: From the "Y" in Soldotna, MP 94.2 of the Sterling Highway. Turn west on Kenai Spur Highway and continue through the town of Kenai to MP 25.7. Turn right on Island Lake Road, drive 2.4 miles to Pipeline Road and turn left. Proceed 0.7 miles to Moose Run Road and turn left. Continue 0.8 miles and turn right. Then cross the north end of airstrip and continue a short distance to access road on left.

Major Species:
Rainbow trout / fair / May and September, October / 8-20 in.

57. WIK LAKE

Access: From the "Y" in Soldotna, MP 94.2 of the Sterling Highway. Turn west on Kenai Spur Highway and continue through the town of Kenai to MP 28.7. Turn right on Lamplight Road, drive 1.4 miles, and turn right on dirt road leading a short distance to the lake.

Major Species:
Rainbow trout / good / May and September, October / 8-20 in.

58. TIRMORE LAKE

Access: From the "Y" in Soldotna, MP 94.2 of the Sterling Highway. Turn west on Kenai Spur Highway and continue through the town of Kenai to MP 28.7. Turn right on Lamplight Road and drive 2.5 miles to lake on right. Public easement located where the lake is closest to the road.

Major Species:
Rainbow trout / fair / May and September, October / 8-20 in.

59. DANIELS LAKE

Access: From the "Y" in Soldotna, MP 94.2 of the Sterling Highway. Turn west on Kenai Spur Highway and continue through the town of Kenai to MP 29.6. Turn right on Halibouty Road, drive 0.3 miles to Rappe Road on left, then proceed 0.2 miles to lake area.

Major Species:
Dolly Varden / fair / August to mid-October / 8-15 in.
Rainbow trout / good / May and September, October / 8-20 in.

60. BARBARA LAKE

Access: From the "Y" in Soldotna, MP 94.2 of the Sterling Highway. Turn west on Kenai Spur Highway and continue through the town of Kenai to MP 29.6. Turn right on Halibouty Road, drive 2.3 miles to Ramona Road and turn right. Proceed 0.4 miles to Pipeline Road and turn right, continuing 0.4 miles to public access road on right.

Major Species:
Rainbow trout / good / May and September, October / 8-20 in.

61. CECILLE LAKE

Access: From the "Y" in Soldotna, MP 94.2 of the Sterling Highway. Turn west on Kenai Spur Highway and continue through the town of Kenai to MP 33.2. Turn left on Seascape Road and drive 0.3 miles to lake on left.

Major Species:
Rainbow trout / good / May and September, October / 7-15 in.

62. BISHOP CREEK

Access: From the "Y" in Soldotna, MP 94.2 of the Sterling Highway. Turn west on Kenai Spur Highway and continue through the town of Kenai to MP 35.1 and the stream crossing. Also, drive to MP 35.9 and turn left into a parking area. Stream is close by.

Regulations: Salmon fishing prohibited. Closed to all fishing from April 15 through June 14. Only unbaited artificial lures from September 16 through December 31.

Major Species:
Rainbow trout / fair / mid-June through September / 7-18 in.

63. STORMY LAKE

Access: From the "Y" in Soldotna, MP 94.2 of the Sterling Highway. Turn west on Kenai Spur Highway and continue through the town of Kenai to MP 36.9. Turn right on access road leading to parking area. Find trails to lake. Or, turn right on gravel road at MP 37.8 leading to the lake.

Major Species:
Silver salmon / good / March through December / 7-15 in.
Dolly Varden / good / August to mid-October / 8-20 in.
Rainbow trout / good / May and September, October / 8-20 in.

64. SWANSON RIVER

Access: From the "Y" in Soldotna, MP 94.2 of the Sterling Highway. Turn west on Kenai Spur Highway and continue through the town of Kenai to river crossing at MP 38.7. To reach the mouth of the river, continue to MP 39.0 and turn left at the "Y." Proceed 0.4

miles to access road on left leading to a campground with trails to the lower river.

Regulations: King salmon fishing prohibited. Closed to all fishing from April 15 through June 14.

Time of Abundance:

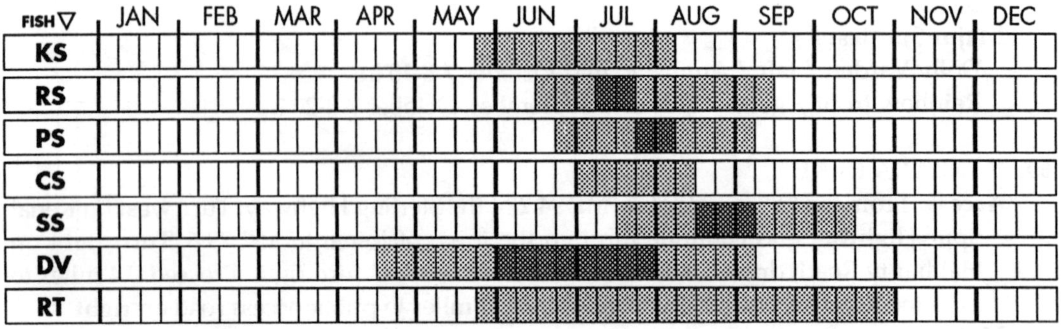

FISH▽	JAN	FEB	MAR	APR	MAY	JUN	JUL	AUG	SEP	OCT	NOV	DEC
KS												
RS												
PS												
CS												
SS												
DV												
RT												

Major Species:

Red salmon / poor to fair / 4-8 lbs., max. 12 lbs. / egg imitation and streamer flies.
Pink salmon / poor to fair / 2-4 lbs., max. 6 lbs. / spoons and spinners, streamer flies.
Silver salmon / good / 6-12 lbs., max. 18 lbs. / salmon egg clusters, spinners, spoons.
Dolly Varden / fair / 7-15 in., max. 5 lbs. / salmon egg clusters, spoons, attractor lures.

65. SALMO LAKE

Access: From the "Y" in Soldotna, MP 94.2 of the Sterling Highway. Turn west on Kenai Spur Highway and continue through the town of Kenai to MP 39.0 and a "Y." Take right fork and drive to parking area. Find trail leading 0.3 miles to the lake.

Major Species:

Rainbow trout / fair / May and September, October / 8-20 in.

AREA B: LOWER KENAI RIVER DRAINAGE (CONT.)

This section covers the Kenai River's confluence with the Funny River, and Arc Lake.

66. FUNNY RIVER

Access: From MP 96.4 of the Sterling Highway. Turn onto Funny River Road heading east at the intersection just south of the Kenai River bridge. Drive 11.3 miles to the river crossing.

Regulations: King salmon fishing prohibited. Only unbaited, artificial lures may be used from September 16 through December 31.

Major Species:

Pink salmon / fair / late July, early August / 2-4 lbs.
Silver salmon / fair / late August / 5-10 lbs.
Dolly Varden / fair / August and September / 7-18 in.
Rainbow trout / fair / mid-May through June / 7-20 in.

67. FUNNY RIVER / KENAI RIVER CONFLUENCE

Access: From MP 96.4 of the Sterling Highway. Turn onto Funny River Road heading east at the intersection just south of the Kenai River bridge. Drive 11.5 miles to access road left heading to a campground with trails to the confluence area.

Regulations: King salmon fishing prohibited from August 1 through December 31. Check the sport fishing regulations closely for this area on various restrictions.

Time of Abundance:

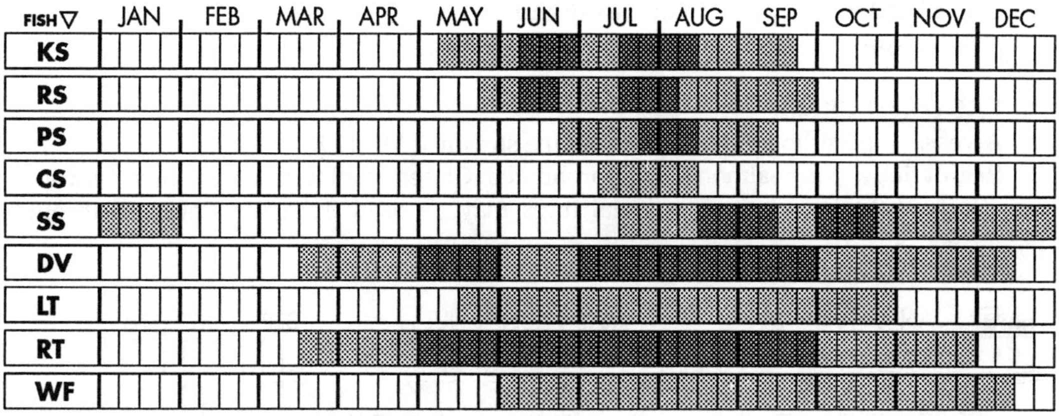

FISH ▽	JAN	FEB	MAR	APR	MAY	JUN	JUL	AUG	SEP	OCT	NOV	DEC
KS												
RS												
PS												
CS												
SS												
DV												
LT												
RT												
WF												

Major Species:

King salmon / fair to good / 25-60 lbs., max. 100 lbs. / salmon egg clusters, attractor lures, spoons.

Red salmon / good to excellent / 4-10 lbs., max. 16 lbs. / egg imitation and streamer flies.

Pink salmon / good to excellent / 2-6 lbs., max. 12 lbs. / spoons and spinners, attractor lures.

Silver salmon / good to excellent / 6-15 lbs., max. 22 lbs. / salmon egg clusters, spinners, attractor lures.

Dolly Varden / good / 7-25 in., max. 15 lbs. / salmon egg clusters, spoons, attractor lures, plugs.

Rainbow trout / good / 7-25 in., max. 20 lbs. / salmon egg clusters, corkies, spinners.

Whitefish / poor to fair / 10-15 in., max. 17 in. / salmon egg clusters, single salmon eggs.

68. ARC LAKE

Access: From MP 98.3 of the Sterling Highway. Turn east on gravel road and follow a short distance to the lake.

Major Species:

Silver salmon / good / March through December / 7-15 in.

AREA D: SOUTH KENAI PENINSULA DRAINAGE

Includes all waters of and around the southern portion of the Kenai Peninsula.

69. KASILOF RIVER

Access: The Sterling Highway crosses the river at MP 109.4.

Regulations: King salmon fishing prohibited from August 1 through December 31. Only unbaited, artificial lures may be used from September 16 through December 31. Check the sport fishing regulations for this area.

Major Species:
King salmon / fair / mid-June and late July / 15-45 lbs.
Red salmon / fair to good / mid-July / 4-10 lbs.
Pink salmon / poor to fair / late July, early August / 2-4 lbs.
Silver salmon / fair to good / mid- and late August / 6-10 lbs.
Steelhead trout / poor to fair / early and mid-May / 5-12 lbs.
Dolly Varden / fair to good / June through August / 8-20 in.

70. CROOKED CREEK
Access: The Sterling Highway crosses the stream at MP 110.9.
Regulations: King salmon fishing prohibited. Closed to all fishing from June 1 through July 31. Only unbaited, artificial lures may be used from September 16 through December 31.
Time of Abundance:

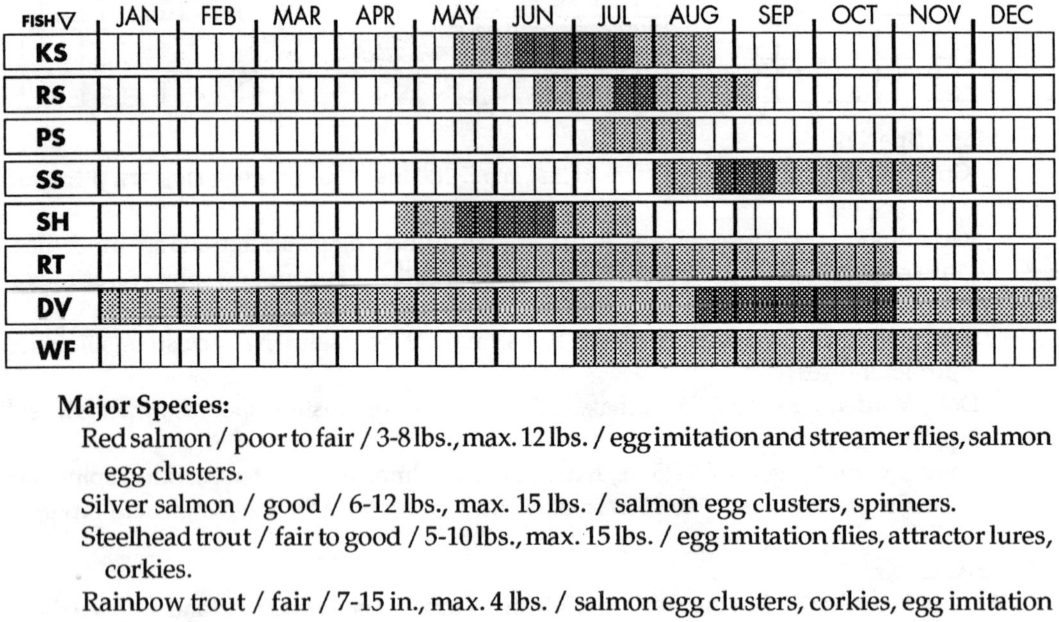

FISH▽	JAN	FEB	MAR	APR	MAY	JUN	JUL	AUG	SEP	OCT	NOV	DEC
KS												
RS												
PS												
SS												
SH												
RT												
DV												
WF												

Major Species:
Red salmon / poor to fair / 3-8 lbs., max. 12 lbs. / egg imitation and streamer flies, salmon egg clusters.
Silver salmon / good / 6-12 lbs., max. 15 lbs. / salmon egg clusters, spinners.
Steelhead trout / fair to good / 5-10 lbs., max. 15 lbs. / egg imitation flies, attractor lures, corkies.
Rainbow trout / fair / 7-15 in., max. 4 lbs. / salmon egg clusters, corkies, egg imitation flies, spinners.
Dolly Varden / good to excellent / 7-15 in., max. 5 lbs. / salmon egg clusters, corkies, attractor lures, spinners.

71. JOHNSON LAKE
Access: From MP 111.4 of the Sterling Highway. Turn east onto Johnson Lake Road, drive 0.2 miles to Tustumena Lake Road and turn right. Proceed 0.1 miles and turn right, following road a short distance to a campground and the lake.
Major Species:
Rainbow trout / good / September and October / 7-16 in.

72. **CENTENNIAL LAKE**

Access: From MP 111.4 of the Sterling Highway. Turn east onto Johnson Lake Road, drive 0.2 miles to Tustumena Lake Road and turn right. Proceed 3.9 miles to access road on left and continue a short distance to the lake.

Major Species:

Silver salmon / good / March through December / 7-15 in.

73. **KASILOF RIVER/TUSTUMENA LAKE OUTLET**

Access: From MP 111.4 of the Sterling Highway. Turn east onto Johnson Lake Road, drive 0.2 miles to Tustumena Lake Road and turn right, proceed 5.9 miles to the end of the road and the river. Tustumena Lake is located about 1.5 miles up the Kasilof River.

Regulations: King salmon fishing prohibited from July 1 through December 31. Check the sport fishing regulations closely for details on upper Kasilof River and Tustumena Lake.

Major Species:

Red salmon / poor to fair / late July / 4-8 lbs.
Pink salmon / fair / late July, early August / 2-4 lb.
Silver salmon / fair to good / late August / 6-12 lbs.
Dolly Varden / good / mid-May to mid-October / 8-20 in.
Lake trout / fair / May and October, November / 2-6 lbs.
Rainbow trout / fair / May and September, October / 7-15 in.

74. **FISH & WILDLIFE LAKES**

Access: From MP 111.4 of the Sterling Highway. Turn west on Cohoe Loop Road, drive 0.6 miles and turn left on Thalia Drive. Proceed 0.4 miles and turn left on Naiad Drive. Continue a short distance to public access site and park. Find trail leading 1.0 mile to the lake.

Major Species:

Dolly Varden / good / September and October / 8-15 in.

75. **QUINTIN LAKE**

Access: From 111.4 of the Sterling Highway. Turn west on Cohoe Loop Road, drive 0.6 miles and turn left on Thalia Drive. Proceed 0.4 miles and turn left on Naiad Drive. Follow the road a short distance to access road on right to the lake.

Major Species:

Silver salmon / good / March through December / 7-15 in.
Rainbow trout / good / May and September, October / 7-15 in.

76. **CROOKED CREEK / KASILOF RIVER CONFLUENCE**

Access: From MP 111.4 of the Sterling Highway. Turn west on Cohoe Loop Road, drive 1.7 miles and turn right on Relinda Road. Proceed 1.5 miles to a parking area. Hike 0.25 miles to the confluence.

Regulations: King salmon fishing prohibited from August 1 through December 31. Only unbaited, artificial lures from September 16 through December 31. Check the sport fishing regulations closely for area open to king salmon fishing.

Time of Abundance:

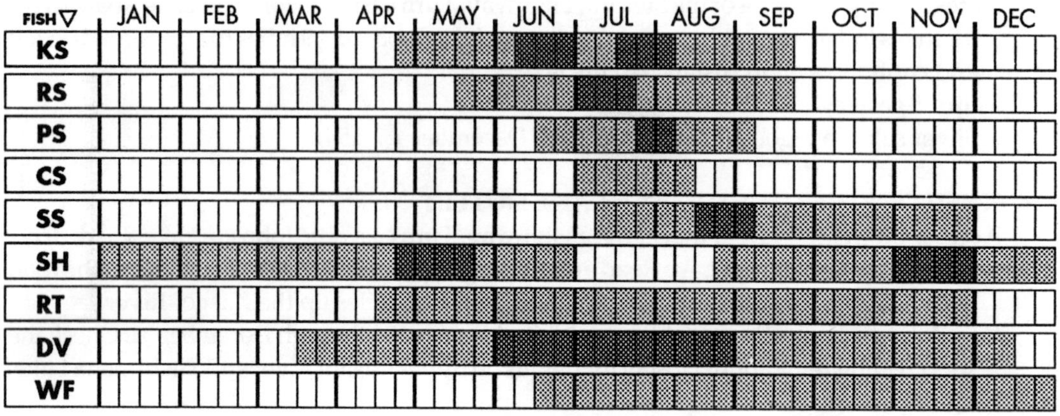

FISH ▽	JAN	FEB	MAR	APR	MAY	JUN	JUL	AUG	SEP	OCT	NOV	DEC
KS												
RS												
PS												
CS												
SS												
SH												
RT												
DV												
WF												

Major Species:

King salmon / good to excellent / 15-35 lbs., max. 75 lbs. / attractor lures, salmon egg clusters, spoons, plugs.

Red salmon / fair to good / 4-10 lbs., max. 14 lbs. / egg imitation and streamer flies.

Pink salmon / poor to fair / 2-4 lbs., max. 7 lbs. / spoons and spinners, attractor lures.

Silver salmon / good to excellent / 6-12 lbs., max. 18 lbs. / salmon egg clusters, attractor lures, spoons, spinners.

Steelhead trout / fair to good / 5-10 lbs., max. 20 lbs. / attractor lures, salmon egg clusters, corkies, plugs.

Dolly Varden / fair to good / 8-20 in., max. 7 lbs. / salmon egg clusters, spoons, attractor lures, corkies.

77. ENCELEWSKI LAKE

Access: From MP 114.9 of the Sterling Highway. Turn west on Tolum Road, drive 0.4 miles to Lake View Court and turn left. Proceed 0.9 miles to access road on the right. Continue straight a short distance to cul-de-sac and the lake.

Major Species:

Silver salmon / good / March through December / 7-15 in.

Rainbow trout / good / May and September, October / 7-16 in.

78. NINILCHIK RIVER

Access: The Sterling Highway crosses the river at MP 135.0. To reach the mouth of the river, turn west on gravel road just south of the highway bridge and drive 1.2 miles to the end of the road and the mouth.

Regulations: Check the sport fishing regulations closely for open season and area for king salmon. Steelhead/Rainbow trout fishing is catch-and-release only. Only unbaited, artificial lures may be used from September 1 through December 31.

Time of Abundance:

FISH ▽	JAN	FEB	MAR	APR	MAY	JUN	JUL	AUG	SEP	OCT	NOV	DEC
KS												
RS												
PS												
CS												
SS												
SH												
RT												
DV												

Major Species:

King salmon / good to excellent / 15-30 lbs., max. 55 lbs. / salmon egg clusters, attractor lures, spinners.

Red salmon / fair to good / 4-8 lbs., max. 15 lbs. / egg imitation and streamer flies.

Pink salmon / good to excellent / 2-4 lbs., max. 7 lbs. / spoons and spinners, attractor lures.

Silver salmon / fair to good / 6-12 lbs., max. 18 lbs. / salmon egg cluster, attractor lures, spinners.

Steelhead trout / fair / 5-10 lb., max. 18 lbs. / corkies and egg imitation flies.

Dolly Varden / good / 7-20 in., max. 7 lbs. / salmon egg clusters, corkies, egg imitation flies, spinners.

79. DEEP CREEK

Access: The Sterling Highway crosses the river at MP 136.8. To reach the mouth of the river, turn west onto a gravel road at MP 137.0 and drive 1.0 mile.

Regulations: Fishing prohibited from January 1 through June 30, except during the king salmon season. Check the sport fishing regulations for details. Catch-and-release only for steelhead/rainbow trout. Only unbaited, artificial lures may be used from September 1 through December 31.

Time of Abundance:

FISH ▽	JAN	FEB	MAR	APR	MAY	JUN	JUL	AUG	SEP	OCT	NOV	DEC
KS												
RS												
PS												
CS												
SS												
SH												
RT												
DV												

CHAPTER 21

Sterling Highway

Major Species:

King salmon / good to excellent / 15-30 lbs., max. 55 lbs. / salmon egg clusters, attractor lures, streamer flies.

Red salmon / poor to fair / 4-8 lbs., max. 15 lbs. / streamer and egg imitation flies.

Pink salmon / good to excellent / 2-4 lbs., max. 7 lbs. / spoons and spinners, attractor lures.

Silver salmon / fair to good / 6-12 lbs., max. 18 lbs. / salmon egg clusters, attractor lures, spinners, streamer flies.

Steelhead trout / fair / 5-10 lbs., max. 18 lbs. / corkies, egg imitation flies.

Dolly Varden / good / 7-20 in., max. 7 lbs. / salmon egg cluster, corkies, spinners, egg imitation flies.

80. COOK INLET MARINE

Access Point A: Ninilchik River

Turn west on gravel road at MP 135.1 of the Sterling Highway and drive 1.2 miles to Ninilchik Harbor and the mouth of the Ninilchik River.

Access Point B: Deep Creek

Turn west on gravel road at MP 137.0 of the Sterling Highway and drive 1.0 mile to the mouth of Deep Creek and Cook Inlet.

Access Point C: Whiskey Gulch

Turn west on gravel road at MP 152.7 of the Sterling Highway and drive 0.4 miles to beach area and Cook Inlet.

Access Point D: Anchor River

Turn west on gravel road at MP 156.7 of the Sterling Highway in the community of Anchor Point. Follow road 0.4 miles to access road just after bridge over Anchor River and turn right, proceed 1.5 miles to the mouth of Anchor River and Cook Inlet.

Regulations: Halibut fishing prohibited from January 1 through 31. King salmon fishing is prohibited within a 1-mile radius of the mouths of Ninilchik and Anchor river, and Deep and Stariski creeks, from January 1 through June 30. Catch-and-release fishing only for steelhead trout.

Time of Abundance:

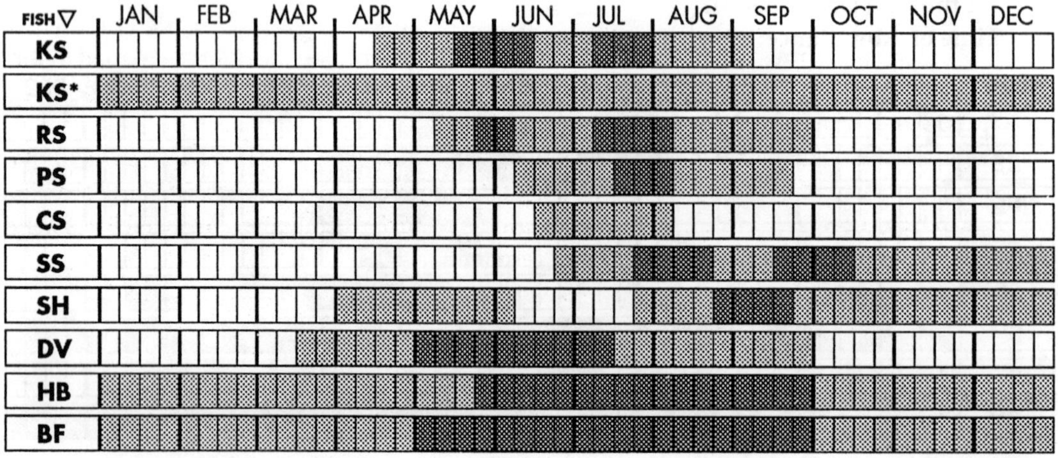

FISH▽	JAN	FEB	MAR	APR	MAY	JUN	JUL	AUG	SEP	OCT	NOV	DEC
KS												
KS*												
RS												
PS												
CS												
SS												
SH												
DV												
HB												
BF												

* Feeder King Salmon

Major Species:
King salmon / good to excellent / 15-60 lbs., max. 100 lbs. / herring bait, spoons, and spinners.
Red salmon / poor to fair / 4-10 lbs., max. 16 lbs. / spoons and spinners.
Pink salmon / good / 2-6 lbs., max. 12 lbs. / herring bait, spoons and spinners.
Silver salmon / good / 6-15 lbs., max. 22 lbs. / herring bait, spoons and spinners.
Dolly Varden / fair to good / 8-25 in., max. 12 lbs. / spoons, spinners, and herring bait.
Halibut / good to excellent / 10-50 lbs., max. 450 lbs. / herring and squid bait, jigs.
Bottomfish / fair to excellent / species include flounder, sole, and grey cod / herring and squid bait, jigs.

81. STARISKI CREEK
Access: The Sterling Highway crosses the stream at MP 150.8.
Regulations: King salmon fishing prohibited. Closed to all fishing from January 1 through June 30. Catch-and-release fishing only for steelhead/rainbow trout. Only unbaited artificial lures may be used from September 1 through December 31.
Major Species:
Pink salmon / fair / late July , early August / 2-4 lbs.
Silver salmon / poor to fair / early September / 6-10 lbs.
Dolly Varden / fair / August and September / 7-15 in.

82. NORTH FORK ANCHOR RIVER
Access: The Sterling Highway crosses the stream at MP 156.9. Also, turn east onto North Fork Road in the community of Anchor Point and drive 0.7 miles to the stream crossing.
Regulations: Salmon fishing prohibited. Closed to all fishing from January 1 through June 30. Catch-and-release fishing only for steelhead / rainbow trout. Only unbaited, artificial lures may be used from September 1 through December 31.
Major Species:
Dolly Varden / good / August and September / 7-18 in.
Rainbow trout / poor to fair / July and August / 7-15 in.

83. ANCHOR RIVER
Access: From MP 156.7 of the Sterling Highway in the community of Anchor Point. Turn southwest on gravel road leading 0.4 miles to bridge crossing the river. Take road to the right just after the bridge; it will parallel the river for 1.5 miles to the mouth of the river and Cook Inlet.
Regulations: Check the sport fishing regulations for open season and areas for king salmon. Fishing prohibited from January 1 through June 30, except during king season. Catch-and-release only for steelhead / rainbow trout. Only unbaited, artificial lures may be used from September 1 through December 31.

Time of Abundance:

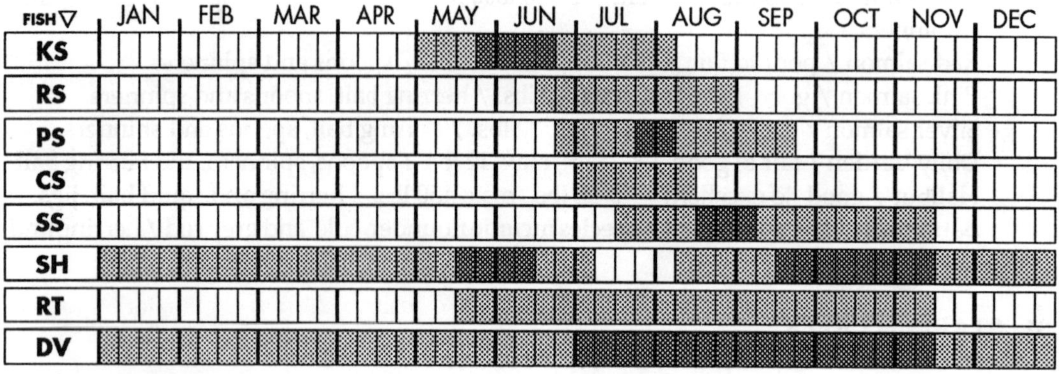

FISH ▽	JAN	FEB	MAR	APR	MAY	JUN	JUL	AUG	SEP	OCT	NOV	DEC
KS												
RS												
PS												
CS												
SS												
SH												
RT												
DV												

Major Species:

King salmon / good to excellent / 15-30 lbs., max. 60 lbs. / salmon egg clusters, attractor lures, spinners, streamer flies.

Red salmon / poor to fair / 4-8 lbs., max. 15 lbs. / egg imitation and streamer flies.

Pink salmon / good to excellent / 2-4 lbs., max. 7 lbs. / spoons and spinners, streamer flies.

Silver salmon / good / 6-12 lbs., max. 18 lbs. / salmon egg clusters, attractor lures, spinners, streamer flies.

Steelhead trout / fair to good / 5-10 lbs., max. 20 lbs. / egg imitation and streamer flies, corkies.

Dolly Varden / good to excellent / 7-20 in., max. 7 lbs. / salmon egg clusters, spinners, corkies, egg imitation flies.

84. ANCHOR RIVER

Access: The Sterling Highway parallels the river from MP 159.9 to 163.9, crossing the river at MP 161.0.

Regulations: Salmon fishing prohibited. Closed to all fishing from January 1 through June 30. Catch-and-release only for steelhead/rainbow trout. Only unbaited, artificial lures may be used from September 1 through December 31.

Major Species:

Steelhead trout / poor to fair / October, November / 5-12 lbs.

Rainbow trout / fair / July through October / 7-18 in.

Dolly Varden / good / August through October / 7-20 in.

85. HOMER SPIT LAGOON

Access: From the town of Homer, the end of Sterling Highway. Turn right on Spit Road at the "Y" and drive 4.3 miles out onto the Homer Spit. The lagoon is located on the left side of the road.

Regulations: Snagging is permitted by emergency order. Look for posted information.

Time of Abundance:

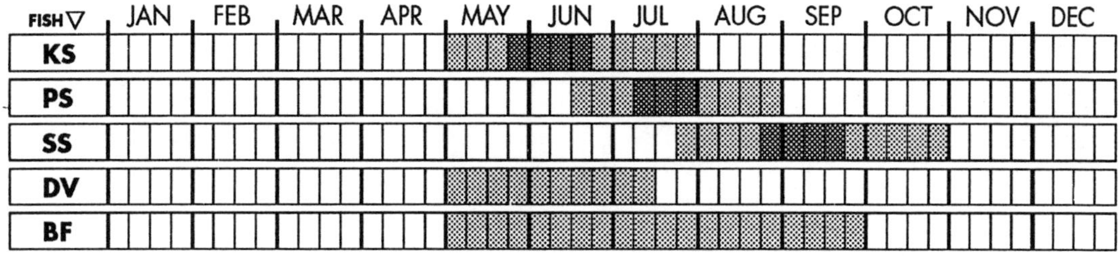

FISH▽	JAN	FEB	MAR	APR	MAY	JUN	JUL	AUG	SEP	OCT	NOV	DEC
KS												
PS												
SS												
DV												
BF												

Major Species:

King salmon / good to excellent / 15-30 lbs., max. 50 lbs. / salmon egg clusters, spoons, spinners, herring bait.
Pink salmon / fair to good / 2-4 lbs., max. 6 lbs. / spoons and spinners, herring bait.
Silver salmon / good to excellent / 6-12 lbs., max. 15 lbs. / salmon egg clusters, spinners, herring bait.

86. HOMER SPIT

Access: From the town of Homer, the end of the Sterling Highway. Turn right on Spit Road at the "Y" and drive 5.5 miles to the end of the road and the spit.
Regulations: Halibut fishing is prohibited from January 1 through 31.
Time of Abundance:

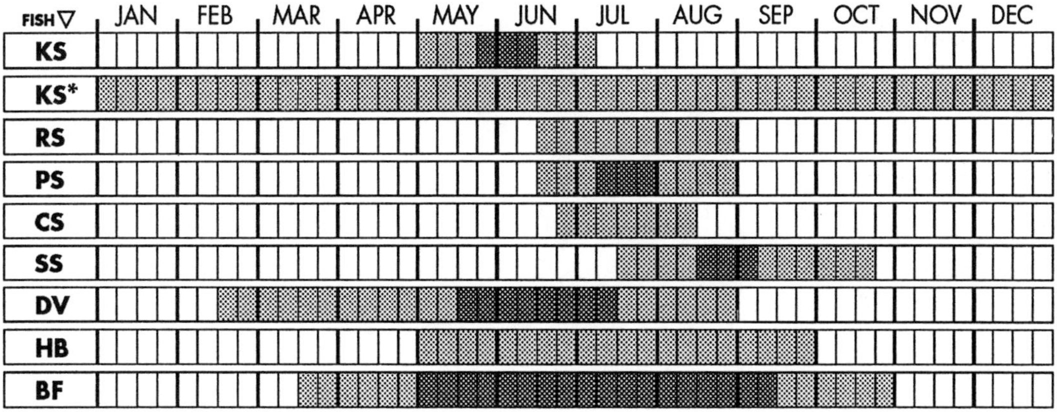

FISH▽	JAN	FEB	MAR	APR	MAY	JUN	JUL	AUG	SEP	OCT	NOV	DEC
KS												
KS*												
RS												
PS												
CS												
SS												
DV												
HB												
BF												

* Feeder King Salmon.

Major Species:

King salmon / fair to good / 15-35 lbs., max. 50 lbs. / spoons, spinners, herring bait.
Pink salmon / good / 2-4 lbs., max. 6 lbs. / spoons and spinners, herring bait.
Silver salmon / fair to good / 6-12 lbs., max. 15 lbs. / spoons, spinners, herring bait.
Dolly Varden / good / 8-20 in., max. 7 lbs. / spoons, smolt imitation flies, herring bait.
Bottomfish / good / species include sole, flounder, and grey cod / spoons, herring bait, jigs.

CHAPTER 22

Trophy And Record Sport Fish Of Alaska

As is true anywhere, trophy or record sport fish are not found in every lake or stream, but are concentrated in a few selected waters. The reason is somewhat of a mystery, but the secret of trophy-sized fish probably lies with a number of crucial factors: abundance and availability of important food sources, above average rearing environment, ideal water temperature, size of watershed, or several other biological factors, including genetic composition. This is not to say that trophy or record fish can only be caught in certain waters, but rather that the chances of finding abnormally large specimens are vastly enhanced if all the above factors are working in your favor.

What constitutes a trophy fish reflects the angler's personal taste more than any textbook rule. One angler may regard a 15-inch rainbow trout caught on a dry fly from an undisturbed mountain lake as the ultimate trophy. Another would definitely root for a 20-pound chum salmon in brilliant calico spawning colors, or an ocean-fresh 60-pound king salmon taken on 15-pound test line. But in most cases, a trophy specimen is one of unusually large dimensions.

The Alaska Department of Fish & Game has established, for the purpose of anglers' interest, an official list of record and trophy sport fish. Larger specimens than the ones listed here have doubtless been caught, but for some reason or another were never reported or recorded officially. But larger fish are known to exist, because commercial fishermen catch larger specimens than these now and then.

CHAPTER 22

Trophy And Record Sport Fish Of Alaska

The list below shows the current record game fish specimens taken on sport gear for each species, including location and area caught, and the minimum trophy weight required to qualify as a state trophy.

THE ADF&G OFFICIAL STATE RECORD AND TROPHY LIST:

SPECIES	LBS.-OZ.	LOCATION/REGION	TROPHY WEIGHT
Arctic Char / Dolly Varden	19-12	Noatak River (NW)	10 Lbs.
Burbot	24-12	Lake Louise (SC)	8 Lbs.
Chum Salmon	32-0	Caamano Point (SE)	15 Lbs.
Cutthroat Trout	8-6	Wilson Lake (SE)	3 Lbs.
Grayling	4-13	Ugashik Narrows (SW)	3 Lbs.
Halibut	450-0	Tutka Bay (SC)	250 Lbs.
King Salmon	97-4	Kenai River (SC)	75/50 Lbs.*
Lake Trout	47-0	Clarence Lake (SW)	20 Lbs.
Ling Cod	66-0	Resurrection Bay (SC)	45 Lbs.
Northern Pike	38-8	Innoko Lake (IN)	15 Lbs.
Pink Salmon	12-9	Moose River (SC)	8 Lbs.
Rainbow / Steelhead Trout	42-3	Bell Island (SE)	15 Lbs.
Red Salmon	16-0	Kenai River (SC)	12 Lbs.
Rockfish	26-0	Kachemak Bay (SC)	18 Lbs.
Sheefish	53-0	Pah River (NW)	30 Lbs.
Silver Salmon	26-0	Icy Strait (SE)	20 Lbs.
Whitefish	9-0	Tozitna River (IN)	4 Lbs.

*Trophy weight for king salmon in the Kenai River is 75 lbs., and the rest of the state 50 lbs.

Abbreviations: SC = Southcentral; IN = Interior; NW = Northwest; SW = Southwest; SE = Southeast.

Anyone who has caught a fish equal to or greater than the specified trophy weight may earn a trophy fish certificate from the ADF&G. Contact one of the department's offices for information on how to participate.

CHAPTER 23

Where To View Spawning Salmon

Some of the waterways along Alaska's roads and highways provide excellent opportunities for watching salmon spawn in the shallows of their own environment. A few of these clearwater streams even have viewing platforms set up to make it easier to observe this spectacular annual event. Although salmon can be seen in the final stage of their life cycle in a great many rivers, creeks, lakes, and ponds, there are some spots that provide exceptional viewing. These are places where the water is often crystal clear, easy to reach, and offers viewers a good number of fish to observe.

The following section lists some of the more well-known locations to witness this dramatic scene of salmon death, birth, and survival.

Following are the abbreviations used in this chapter for all the fish species.

KS - King Salmon	PS - Pink Salmon	SS - Silver Salmon
RS - Red Salmon	CS - Chum Salmon	SH - Steelhead Trout

Time of Abundance Charts

These charts are designed to show the reader during which time of the year the indicated species are present and the best viewing time in the particular watershed. Species on the charts are shown in all stages of maturity.

CHAPTER 23

Where To View Spawning Salmon

Indicates species are present in small numbers.

Indicates best viewing time. Species are present in good numbers.

TOK CUTOFF HIGHWAY

FISH CREEK

Access: From MP 81.0 of the Tok Cutoff Highway. Turn northwest onto a paved road and drive 0.2 miles. Turn left on gravel road leading 7.1 miles to and through Mentasta Village, ending at the bridge over Fish Creek and the inlet to Mentasta Lake.

Species / Time of Abundance:

FISH▽	APR	MAY	JUN	JUL	AUG	SEP	OCT	NOV
RS								

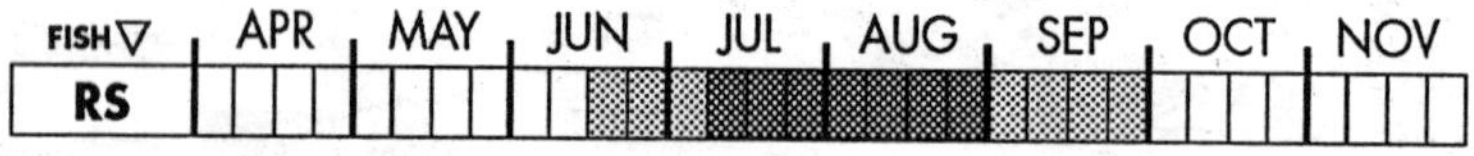

RICHARDSON HIGHWAY

CROOKED CREEK

Access: This small clearwater stream is located in the town of Valdez and has a viewing platform available. Pull into the parking area next to the highway.

Species / Time of Abundance:

FISH▽	MAY	JUN	JUL	AUG	SEP	OCT	NOV	DEC
RS								
PS								
CS								

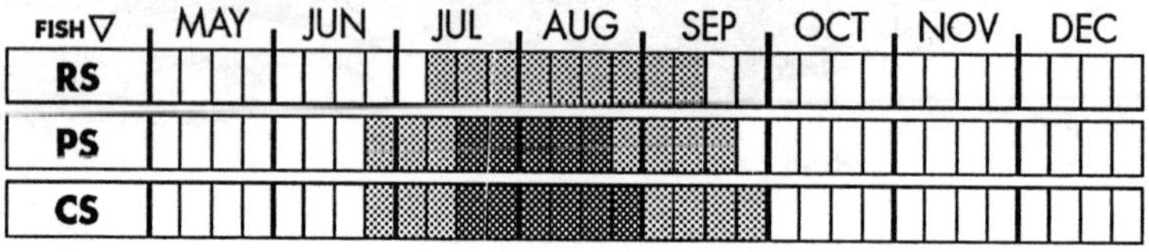

PORT VALDEZ DRAINAGE

Access: In addition to Crooked Creek, above, there are several other clearwater streams and ponds in and around the town of Valdez that offer good viewing of spawning salmon.

Species / Time of Abundance: Red, pink, and chum salmon are primarily present during July and August, along with an occasional king salmon. Silver salmon are more commonly spotted in October and November.

GULKANA RIVER

Access: The Richardson Highway parallels the upper portion of the Gulkana River from the outlet of Summit Lake at MP 191.0 downstream to MP 186.5. Park next to the road or at the designated paved parking area.

Species / Time of Abundance:

FISH▽	MAY	JUN	JUL	AUG	SEP	OCT	NOV	DEC
RS								

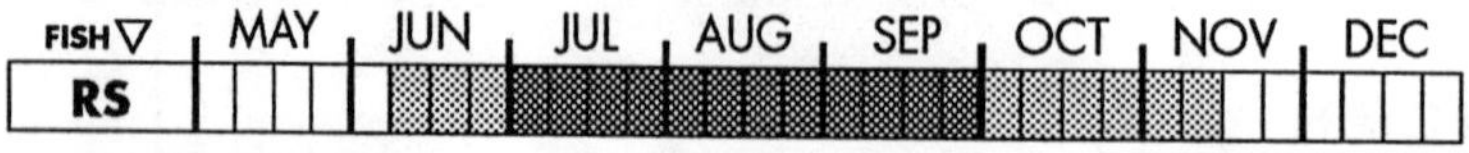

GLENN HIGHWAY

BODENBURG CREEK

Access: The stream is located at MP 12.9 of the Old Glenn Highway, from MP 29.5 or Arctic Ave. in Palmer. Pull into gravel parking area next to the creek.

Species / Time of Abundance:

FISH▽	MAY	JUN	JUL	AUG	SEP	OCT	NOV	DEC
RS								
CS								

MATANUSKA CLEARWATER CREEK

Access: The Glenn Highway parallels the stream at MP 68.9. Park by the road.

Species / Time of Abundance:

FISH▽	MAY	JUN	JUL	AUG	SEP	OCT	NOV	DEC
KS								
RS								
CS								
SS								

PARKS HIGHWAY

BIG LAKE OUTLET / FISH CREEK

Access: From MP 52.3 of the Parks Highway. Turn southwest onto Big Lake Road and drive 5.0 miles to stream crossing and lake outlet. Park by the road. A viewing platform is available by the lake shore.

Species / Time of Abundance:

FISH▽	MAY	JUN	JUL	AUG	SEP	OCT	NOV	DEC
KS								
RS								
PS								
CS								
SS								

MEADOW CREEK

Access: From 52.3 of the Parks Highway. Turn southwest onto Big Lake Road and drive 3.4 miles to Beaver Loop Road on right. Proceed 0.8 miles to stream crossing. Pull into parking area. A viewing platform is available.

Species / Time of Abundance:

FISH▽	MAY	JUN	JUL	AUG	SEP	OCT	NOV	DEC
KS								
RS								
PS								
CS								
SS								

SEWARD HIGHWAY

RABBIT CREEK

Access: From MP 117.8 of the Seward Highway. Turn east onto a paved road leading to large parking area. Take boardwalk to the viewing area.

Species / Time of Abundance:

FISH▽ MAY JUN JUL AUG SEP OCT NOV DEC
KS
RS
PS
CS
SS

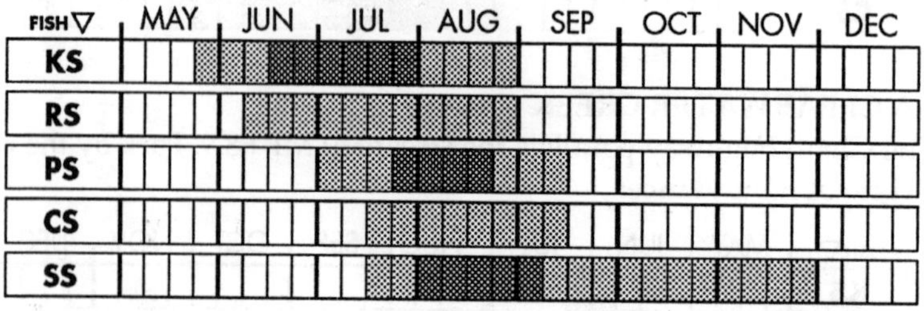

WILLIWAW CREEK

Access: From MP 79.2 of the Seward Highway. Turn east on Portage Glacier Road and drive 4.1 miles to stream crossing. Pull into the parking area on right. A viewing platform is available.

Species / Time of Abundance:

FISH▽ JUN JUL AUG SEP OCT NOV DEC JAN
RS
CS
SS

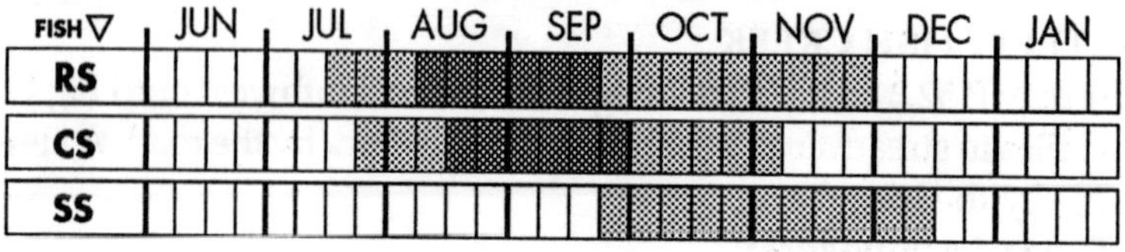

MOOSE CREEK

Access: The Seward Highway crosses the stream at MP 32.9 and 32.3. Parking area is present next to fish hatchery by lake.

Species / Time of Abundance:

FISH▽ APR MAY JUN JUL AUG SEP OCT NOV
RS

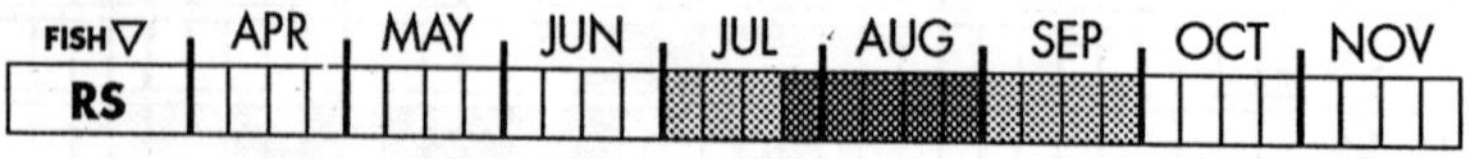

PTARMIGAN CREEK

Access: The Seward Highway crosses the stream at MP 32.2. Park at the campground and hike a short distance to stream.

Species / Time of Abundance:

FISH▽ MAY JUN JUL AUG SEP OCT NOV DEC
KS
RS
PS
SS

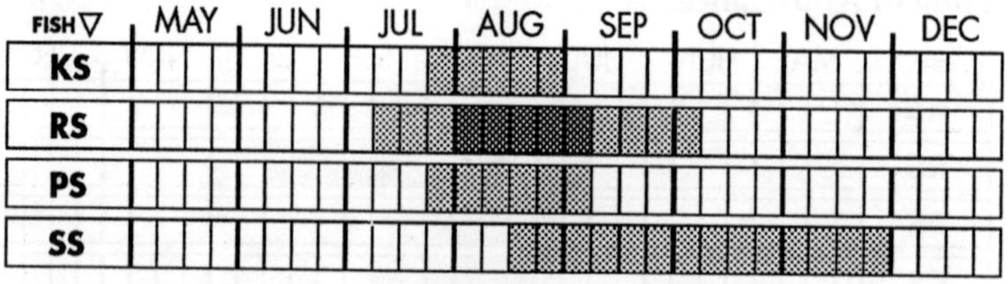

GROUSE CREEK

Access: The Seward Highway parallels the stream from MP 10.5 to 8.1. Park by the road.

Species / Time of Abundance:

FISH▽	MAY	JUN	JUL	AUG	SEP	OCT	NOV	DEC
RS								
PS								
CS								
SS								

SEWARD LAGOON CREEK

Access: This small stream drains out of Seward Lagoon in the town of Seward. Park by the road.

Species / Time of Abundance:

FISH▽	JUN	JUL	AUG	SEP	OCT	NOV	DEC	JAN
KS								
RS								
PS								
CS								
SS								

RESURRECTION BAY DRAINAGE

Access: Several clearwater streams and ponds emptying into the bay area in and around the town of Seward provide opportunities to view spawning salmon. Some of the larger waters include Salmon, Spruce, and Fourth of July creeks, and Preacher Pond among others.

Species / Time of Abundance: Red salmon are present anytime between June and September along with an occasional king salmon in June and July. Pink and chum salmon are chiefly present in July, August, and September, while silver salmon are more common during September, October, and November.

STERLING HIGHWAY

DAVES CREEK

Access: From MP 37.3 of the Sterling Highway. Turn south onto a gravel road leading a short distance to the stream crossing and the outlet of Tern Lake. Pull into designated parking area.

Species / Time of Abundance:

FISH▽	JUN	JUL	AUG	SEP	OCT	NOV	DEC	JAN
KS								
RS								
PS								
SS								

CROOKED CREEK

Access: From MP 111.4 of the Sterling Highway. Turn east onto Johnson Lake Road and drive short distance to stream crossing and a pond. Park by the hatchery on right.

Species / Time of Abundance:

FISH▽	APR	MAY	JUN	JUL	AUG	SEP	OCT	NOV
KS								
RS								
PS								
SS								
SH								

Index

Numbers

A

B

C

D

E

F

G

M

N

O

P

Q

R

S

T